THE
LABOR WARS

THE LABOR WARS

From the Molly Maguires to the Sitdowns

SIDNEY LENS

Haymarket Books
Chicago, IL

Jon Kelley Wright
Workers' Memorial Book Series

On September 22, 2007, the Chrysler Corporation murdered Jon Kelley Wright. After working over twenty years at their Kokomo, Indiana, die-casting plant, the machine he operated crushed him to death because faulty safety equipment had been disabled instead of replaced. Kelley was an outspoken critic of management's dangerous practices and an advocate for safety on the job. Months before his death, he helped organize meetings where management said that replacing the safety equipment "wouldn't be cost effective."

As the beneficiary on one of my uncle's modest life insurance policies, I endowed the Jon Kelley Wright Workers' Memorial Fund through the Center for Economic Research and Social Change. This fund allows Haymarket Books to publish a series of books about the labor movement and struggles of working people to change the world.

Thousands of people are killed on the job each year just in the United States. We invite anyone who has lost someone due to an unsafe workplace to memorialize their loved one through this book series. To read the memorials and find out more, please visit: http://WorkersMemorialFund.org.

I hope that the Jon Kelley Wright Workers' Memorial Book Series will inspire others to dedicate their lives to the struggle for a world where safety on the job is more important than profits, and that it will help keep the memory of my beloved uncle alive.

In solidarity,
Derek Wright

To contribute to this project, please send tax-deductible donations to the fund payable to "CERSC" (with "Workers' Memorial Fund" in the memo) to:

CERSC
P.O. Box 258082
Chicago, IL 60625

Originally published in 1973 by Doubleday & Company, Inc., Garden City, New York
© 1973 Sidney Lens

This edition published in 2008 by Haymarket Books
P.O. Box 180165
Chicago, IL, 60618
773-583-7884
www.haymarketbooks.org
ISBN: 978-1931859-70-7

Trade distribution:
In the U.S. through Consortium Book Sales and Distribution, www.cbsd.com
In the UK through Turnaround Publisher Services, www.turnaround-psl.com
In Australia through Palgrave MacMillan, www.palgravemacmillan.com.au
In all other countries though Publishers Group Worldwide
www.pgw.com/home/worldwide.aspx

Cover design by Ragina Johnson. The cover photo shows the "little children" of
Lawrence holding one of the solidarity pickets they held in support of strike in cities
across the country. Additional photo credit information for photos published within
the book is available on page viii.

Published with the generous support of the Wallace Global Fund.

The 1973 edition of this book is catalogued by the Library of Congress under card
number 72–84926.

To my mother, Sophie,
whose life was spent in a sweatshop

PHOTO CREDITS

Contents

Preface

The protest movement of the last twenty years differs in one major respect from those of the past: it has no feeling of kinship for its predecessors.

Movements of the past usually considered themselves new links in a chain that went back many decades. The ninety-three delegates who came together in Utica, New York, in September 1836 to form the Equal Rights Party—the so-called "locofocos"—drafted a "Declaration of Independence." A union paper which supported their cause spoke of "a second Revolution," comparable to the first American Revolution. "The Revolution of 1776," it said, "was against the monarchy and aristocracy, this of 1836 is against charters and monopolies."

George Henry Evans, who promoted the imaginative "vote yourself a farm" movement of the 1840s, which eventually led to passage of the Homestead Act, traced his political lineage to the agrarian theories of Tom Paine, the great pamphleteer of the Revolution.

The same sense of history was evident among the leftists of the 1930s. They were all the children of Karl Marx. Most of them also considered themselves part of the same tradition as the Paris Commune, the Russian revolutions of 1905 and 1917, Lenin, the socialist leader Eugene V. Debs, the bruising Wobbly "Big Bill" Haywood.

By contrast the young radicals who have surfaced in the 1950s and 1960s seem to float in midair. They have no strong attachment to the leftist movements or leftist leaders of yesteryear. Few have heard of William Z. Foster or James P. Cannon, Elizabeth Gurley Flynn or Vincent St. John, Norman Thomas or A. J. Muste. The May Day anti-war demonstrators of 1971, 13,000 of whom were arrested, did not recognize that they were fighting the same fight or expounding a radical philosophy similar to that of the socialists and Wobblies of 1917–18. Indeed they knew painfully little about their forebears and their struggles.

Late in 1969 I took a plane to Washington to help prepare for the massive anti-war demonstration sponsored by the New Mobilization Committee to End the War in Vietnam. A twenty-year old student from the University of Wisconsin, sitting next to me, was reading *Liberation* magazine. *Liberation* was founded by the late A. J. Muste, the octogenarian who was also the leading figure in the emergence of the present anti-war movement. I was surprised to learn that the student had never heard of Muste—though Muste was less than two years dead. I'm sure this is also true of at least 90 or 95 per cent of those who today consider themselves part of the anti-war movement.

The tragedy in this is not that today's youth refuse to elevate mortal men and women to the status of radical sainthood. They indeed have their own heroes—Huey Newton, Bobby Seale, the Conspiracy Eight, the Berrigan brothers—but their span of interest even in these "heroes" is ephemeral. They seem to have no roots in the past, no set of principles that are derived from generations of past experience. This may be explained, perhaps, by the revulsion of humanistic young radicals against the non- and anti-humanism of so many radical forebears. But it does not explain why they refuse to sift through history to find common denominators with their own positions or study the principles propounded by radical humanists of other periods.

The point was driven home to me most forcefully during a strike of television station employees in Chicago a few years ago. One of the most active anti-war protesters in the city was scheduled to appear on a talk show. I tried with might and main to convince her that she should not walk through the picket line. She refused. The union leaders, she said, were "finks." She did not recognize the legitimacy of their struggle. She felt light years removed from labor's past—from the 1877 railroad strikes, the Pullman boycott of 1894, the labor wars at Coeur d'Alene and Cripple Creek, the 1919 steel strike, the sitdowns of 1937, most of which she had never heard of. This was simply not her tradition—nor that of hundreds of thousands of other radicals of this generation.

Yet the labor wars were a much longer protest than the present protests against war, racism, and sexism. They were also far more militant and bloody. The 13,000 May Day protesters of 1971 were treated like aristocrats compared to the treatment meted out by General Sherman Bell to strikers at Cripple Creek or Telluride. The confrontation between anti-war demonstrators and troops at the Pentagon in late 1967 was mild compared to the confrontation between railroad strikers and militia in Pittsburgh in 1877 or between steel workers and soldiers along the Monongahela River in Pennsylvania in 1919.

I have written this book on the labor wars in an effort to restore some of the lost sense of kinship between the protesters of today and those of yesterday. There are many excellent books on labor history, including the multi-volume works of Philip S. Foner and those of John R. Commons and his associates. There are also many fine studies of individual movements and individual strikes—Melvyn Dubofsky on the Industrial Workers of the World (Wobblies), Joyce Kornbluh on the same subject, Charles Rumford Walker on the 1934 Minneapolis trucker strikes, Henry Kraus on the 1937 auto sitdowns, McAlister Coleman on the coal miners. Samuel Yellen's book on American Labor Struggles, published in 1936, is a classic, and covers many of the struggles which I have dealt with here.

What I have tried to do is to pull all these facts and the significance of these facts together in a new, single, updated book that I hope portrays the idealism, dedication, and almost unbelievable sacrifices of three generations of working people who fought the good fight for human freedom. What I have attempted is to put the labor wars in the context of the past and the future. It is my belief that unless and until the new protesters incorporate the story of the labor wars into their own tradition and values, their present protest will lack direction.

SIDNEY LENS

THE
LABOR WARS

1

A Tale of
Six Decades

For ten weeks in 1970 the largest industrial corporation in the United States, General Motors, confronted the largest industrial union in the United States, the United Auto Workers. The firm, with resources larger than the gross national product of many countries, was shut tight as 400,000 card-carrying members of the UAW "hit the bricks."

In an earlier day, four or five decades ago, a strike of this sort would have provoked a burst of corporate energy. The company would have prepared itself with a small army of "guards" and Pinkerton spies; would have stockpiled guns and tear gas; and organized a "citizens' committee" to prepare a "back-to-work" movement. Its personnel department would have combed the hinterlands for strikebreakers, professional and amateur; its lawyers would have drafted injunctions to be presented by pliable district attorneys to equally pliable judges. The tenor at the GM offices would have been one of war and accelerated activity. In the union offices throughout the country the pulse would have been equally rapid. Flying squadrons would have been formed to guard against an influx of strikebreakers at railroad stations or highways. Visiting committees would have been delegated to talk with scabs. Plans would have been formulated for mass picketing. Calls would have been made to other unions in other shops to alert them to the possible need for help on the picket lines. And as the lines formed on the first day of the walkout—September 14—there would be an air of tension. Would Johnny So-and-So of the tool and die shop go through? Were the men on the assembly line solid? Would the police attack this morning? A judge issue an injunction?

Among those outside the plant gates in September 1970 were some who had participated in the sitdown strikes against GM back in 1936–37. Many still remembered the Battle of Bulls Run outside Fisher Body No. 2 in Flint on January 11, 1937. While the strikers sat inside the plant that cold, wintry afternoon, hoping for Governor Frank Murphy to get talks started with the great corporation, the company shut off the heat, and police prevented food from being sent in. Soon the battle lines formed. Strikers on the outside crashed through the small wall of police to carry bread and coffee to their beleaguered comrades within, and when the cops reformed their ranks two hours later a three-hour battle ensued in which the men in blue used tear gas, clubs, and guns; the unionists metal pipes, nuts, bolts, sticks, bottles, coffee mugs, and two-pound auto-door hinges. "We wanted peace," said strike leaders over the microphone in their sound truck, "General Motors chose war. Give it to them." Within minutes the sedan of Sheriff Thomas Wolcott was toppled over, and before hostilities ended, three other police vehicles were similarly treated. At midnight, as the sitdown strikers turned a powerful water hose on the officers, the fighting came to a halt. Fourteen strikers had been taken to the hospital with bullet wounds that day. Across the country thousands of unionists faced the police and National Guardsmen in front of GM plants, and not a few were injured in the ensuing melees.

Now in 1970 the strike situation evoked very different responses. The company did not try to keep its plants open, except for those that the union agreed were needed to feed parts to other manufacturers. There were no strikebreakers, scabs, back-to-work movements, or citizens' committees. There were no shootings, tear-gassings, clubbings, nothing even remotely resembling the Battle of Bulls Run—and, no arrests. The union organized no flying squadrons, sent no urgent alerts to anyone, and its members picketed perfunctorily in order to qualify for strike benefits. There was no fear of attack by the police or National Guard and small likelihood that management would seek injunctions in the courts. The most lethal weapon used by the UAW this time was a strike fund, upward of a hundred million dollars, collected from dues and assessments, out of which weekly benefits were paid to those on the picket line.

By and large this kind of non-violent confrontation was now the pattern in all the strikes between so-called big labor and big business—in auto, steel, trucking, aircraft, railroads—and in most of the 3,000 to 6,000 work stoppages each year of lesser import. During the 1956 national steel strike, U. S. Steel at its South Works mill in Chicago furnished the picket captain with a desk just inside the gate and ran a power line and water to the union's six trailers. One night it supplied the pickets with beer. In another mill, management provided portable toilets for the men who had walked off the job. Republic Steel, which a generation before had relentlessly opposed the right of its men to be represented by a union of their choice, told its workers to take their vacations during the strike so that they would lose little or no pay, and would be ready and fit when the mills stoked up again. Not everyone, of course, conformed to the new "rules." The Kohler Company near Sheboygan, Wisconsin, precipitated a strike in 1954 that lasted eight long years. General Electric usually gave the two electrical unions it dealt with much more trouble than GM gave UAW. Yet picket line fights and arrests were comparatively rare, and bloodshed even more so.

The labor wars seemed to be over. If the adversaries had not exactly found a *modus vivendi* whereby all disputes could be adjusted automatically, nevertheless their quarrels usually were as bland as those of two corporate lawyers negotiating a contract for real estate. And the strikes were simply waiting games to see which side would feel the economic pinch first, rather than wars of extermination. A truce of sorts existed between labor and capital in which neither side exactly learned to love the other but did not go to former extremes either.

A generation of young zealots today has deduced from such circumstances either that labor has always been a quiescent adjunct to the American establishment, or that its struggles in the long past have been somehow irrelevant. Oriented as the younger generation is to the quest for peace, and racial and sexual equality, it has downgraded the battles of another epoch, though they were far bloodier, far more militant and most certainly "relevant" to today's struggles. It has closed its eyes so tightly to the earlier efforts, that it seldom bothers to study strikers' tactics or strategies, though they bear great resemblance to those of the present. For all practical purposes the labor wars—that was the term applied by the New York *Tribune* to the 1877 railroad strikes and used frequently thereafter—are now all but forgotten. It is as if they have been drawn into and covered by historical quicksand, with no one to mourn their martyrs and no one to remember their import and legacy.

The labor wars were a specific response to a specific set of in-
justices at a time when industrial and financial capitalism was
establishing its predominance over American society. In a sense the
battles were no different from the hundreds of other violent clashes
against social injustice, as normal as the proverbial apple pie in the
nation's annals.

Colonial America witnessed armed uprisings of small farmers and
backwoodsmen against authoritarian governments, or tenants against
landlords, and at least forty conspiracies and revolts by black slaves
and white "indentured" servants. The colonial equivalents of Eugene
V. Debs, Big Bill Haywood, and Harry Bridges were Nathaniel
Bacon, Jacob Leisler, the North Carolina Regulators, and a dozen
blacks whose names have slipped into the recesses of history. In
post-revolutionary America, from 1783 to the Civil War, social opposition took a dozen forms, varying from Shays' Rebellion and the
bloody collisions between Jéffersonians and Hamiltonians in the 1790s,
to the hesitant efforts of unions to establish themselves in the face
of "conspiracy" prosecutions, to the workingmen's parties of the
1820s, to the utopian communities of Robert Owen and the
Fourierists, and to George Henry Evans' "new agrarianism" which
in much-diluted form became the Homestead Act.

In this tempestuous period, when the nation threatened to burst
asunder on more than one occasion, the United States was still an
agricultural and rural nation. In 1840 only one out of twelve people
lived in cities of more than 8,000, and in 1860 the ratio was still a
mere one out of six. But industry was flexing its muscles and would
soon burst the shackles of technological backwardness and political
restraint. From 1840 to 1860 the value of industrial products quadrupled, from a half-billion dollars a year to 2 billion, and from
1860 to 1889 quadrupled again to 9 billion. As of 1909 factory production had jumped to $21 billion and as of 1919 to $62 billion.
The railroads, a barometer of industrial advance, boasted 2,800 miles
of track in 1840; 30,600 miles in 1860; and approximately 200,000
miles at the end of the century. In this development heavy industry,
such as steel, relentlessly and inexorably replaced light industry, such
as shoemaking, as the core of the economy. And as industries mush-
roomed and the railroads crisscrossed the land, some men made
fabulous fortunes, grew fat and arrogant. The merchant-capitalist of
the first half of the century was considered rich if his wealth
spiraled to a few hundred thousand dollars. The industrial capitalist
of the last half of the century measured his wealth in millions, some-

times tens of millions. "Commodore" Cornelius Vanderbilt, the railroad magnate who died in 1877, left an estate of $105 million and a heritage of contempt for the populace that was epitomized in his famous statement: "Law? What do I care about law? Hain't I got the power?"

Growth was accompanied by an orgy of corruption and thievery such as the nation had never seen before. Men like Vanderbilt, J. P. Morgan, E. H. Harriman, and Jay Cooke flouted all the rules in an unmatched display of materialism. Typical was the transaction of J. P. Morgan during the Civil War, by which he bought defective rifles, already condemned, *from* the government, for $17,500 one day, and resold them *to* the government the next day for $110,000. Philip Armour, just twenty-six years old, bought pork at $18 a barrel and sold it in quick turnover for $40.

A symbol of the time was the rail tycoon Jay Gould, about whom it may be said that nothing illegal or immoral was alien to his character. He got his start by cheating two partners in a leather business. He printed and sold counterfeit share certificates in the Erie Railroad, and, when the fraud was discovered, slipped away to New Jersey with his partner, Jim Fisk, and a tidy $6 million in cash, plus the Erie's financial records. Later he bribed New York legislators to pass a law making his act legal. Ironically, with the haul from the Erie brigandage Gould set out to corner the $15 million in gold then in circulation.

It would be false to say that all entrepreneurs were as bereft of conscience as Gould or Vanderbilt. But for the acquisitive classes money became a religion and "Social Darwinism" a salient dogma. "Under the natural order of things," wrote the oracle of Social Darwinism, Herbert Spencer, "society is constantly excreting its unhealthy, imbecile, slow, vacillating, faithless members" in order to leave room for the competent ones entitled to reward. As in the animal world the fit survived; the unfit were rightly ground under. Gould and Vanderbilt became buccaneers before Spencer arrived on the scene, but they and their contemporaries operated on the simple thesis that the capitalists, by their proven superiority, were entitled to rule; the workers, by their proven ineptness, obligated to accept their judgments. And when workers strayed from the prescribed path—to form unions and go on strike, for instance—it was only just and proper that they be spanked with strikebreakers, Pinkerton spies, and blacklisting. They had trespassed the area of decision-making allotted to their "betters," and their due was the stick—not the carrot. Thus it was that for six decades, from the panic of 1873 to the end of the New Deal, an autocratic capitalist class fought one war after another against a working class made desperate by the hard-nosed abuse it had absorbed.

III

Properly speaking, the labor wars were wars of capital—and its unswerving ally, government—*against* labor. The owners of capital justified their attacks on the lofty theory that they were defending society from rabble, scum, and outsiders, intent on desecrating law and order and uprooting the great free enterprise system which allegedly was responsible for America's high living standards. They were upholding, they said, the inalienable democratic right of a man to work wherever he pleased, even as a strikebreaker. The record shows, however, that the corporations' true objective was to limit wages or reduce them, to retain or lengthen the work week, and to wring as much work for each dollar of pay as human energy could deliver. The rest of what was said was persiflage to allay possible public criticism. The government too justified its dispatch of troops and its requests for injunctions on the theory that it was defending society against lawlessness. In reality, however, the lawlessness was usually created by the troops and by the government's own denial of civil liberties. The real purpose, thinly disguised in phrases of "impartiality," was to aid management in emasculating the unions.

The labor wars, then, played a pivotal role in American history. They were the antidote to an insolent philosophy, expressed best in robber baron Jay Gould's classic remark: "I can hire one-half of the working class to kill the other half." The labor wars were indispensable to achieving the present levels of consumption. They helped win a measure of industrial and political freedom for the underclasses. They placed limits on the power of the robber barons and financial goliaths. And toward the end, in the 1930s, they were part of a social upheaval that transformed *laissez-faire* capitalism to controlled capitalism.

Along with the Revolution and certain farm and slave uprisings during colonial days, the labor wars were among the most heroic events in the American epic. They typified the ageless conflict between the privileged and underprivileged, the oppressor and oppressed. In an era of unbridled *laissez-faire*, the prevailing thesis was every man for himself, devil take the hindmost. A worker was deemed to have no other right—if he were dissatisfied, as he was all too often—but to leave his job and seek another. If there were no jobs to be had, he could move in with relatives, join the soup line, or starve. Even some "socialists" questioned whether the proletariat was justified in taking concerted action. Thus, *The American Socialist,* published by John Humphrey Noyes' communitarian group at Oneida, New York, wrote during the 1877 railroad riots: "The laborers . . . have no legal or moral right to insist that certain men who have been employing them shall pay them whatever wages they demand. They have a right to quit work and seek better pay elsewhere, but have no right to make war or destroy property, or prevent others from taking their places at the reduced wages."

The labor wars, after torturous decades and innumerable picket line murders, secured for the workingman a right which he had been previously denied, totally or partially: the right to collective action. Without that right much of what we consider progressive today in the American way of life would have been impossible—the abolition of child labor, workmen's compensation for accidents, safety standards, protection of women and immigrants, unemployment compensation, social security, low-cost housing (inadequate as it is), Medicare, and many other reforms. Tens of millions of proletarians would be chained to their machines without benefit of shorter hours, seniority rights, grievance machinery, paid vacations and holidays, sick pay, supplemental unemployment compensation, and health insurance.

All of these benefits had to be won through bitter contention. The battles were related to that ceaseless struggle for power between the radical and reactionary strains of American life, between Jeffersonians and Hamiltonians in early America, between something vaguely called the New Left and the military-industrial complex today. The struggle always has been unequal, but in the last third of the nineteenth century the gap widened to a chasm. Tenuous labor unions fell more and more on the defensive against the escalating might of the new transport and mass-production industries that were fast replacing the old small-producer economy. In the beginning, labor made no headway at all, suffering one defeat and bloodbath after another. Then, in the last decade and a half of the century, it was able to sink stable roots in one corner of the economy, the decentralized industries—such as construction. The bastions where the giant corporations prevailed, however, still eluded working-class penetration. Indeed it took six stinging decades before the underclasses achieved sufficient countervailing power against the impersonal industrial and financial duchies that even today still tower over society. Along the way the road was strewn with the martyrs of the Pennsylvania coal fields of the 1870s, the so-called Molly Maguires; of the railroad workers of 1877 and 1894; the Homestead strikers; the metal miners in the West and the coal miners in the East; the garment workers; the steel workers of 1919 and 1937; and of the auto, rubber, and other mass production laborers of 1933–38. During those three or four generations the American proletariat was preyed upon by industrial spies, company police, sheriffs' deputies, National Guardsmen, federal troops, unsympathetic judges, and a hostile press. The end result was not a final victory by any means, but a victory nonetheless. The labor movement made a quantum jump in numbers and influence; its struggles in the 1940s and 1950s were no longer primarily for union recognition or against wage cuts, but for positive benefits such as wages, seniority rights, supplementary unemployment compensation. And, above all, they no longer met the persistent violent reaction of employers and government so characteristic of an earlier day.

In this grand scenario three distinct features are evident:

1. The labor wars were conducted outside the pall of narrow legality. Had the workers abided by court injunctions against picketing and had they shown the expected respect for the organs of law and order—police, militia, federal troops—unions today would have been dwarfs in size and impotent in influence.

2. The ultimate enemy was almost always the city, state, and federal governments. Had government been truly impartial, let alone oriented toward the exploited classes, unions would have attained decisive power before the end of the nineteenth century.

3. The labor wars, at first two-sided encounters between labor and capital, became triangular as a progressively entrenched AFL hierarchy gave both witting and unwitting aid to the scions of business. Certainly the mass production industries would have yielded to unionism decades before it did if it had not been for the Tory attitudes of AFL leadership; and the unions would unquestionably have been more dynamic if their own reactionary officials had not signed backdoor contracts in the 1930s to prevent militant unions from organizing.

When great events pass into history they are given the cosmetic treatment. Violence, bitterness, deception, illegality, immorality, conflict, are scraped away to give the appearance of friendly, orderly progress. But it didn't happen that way between labor and capital in America, and it is well to remember that what was won was won by flouting both institutionalized conformity and one-sided legality.

2

The Molly Maguires

June 21, 1877 has been memorialized as "Pennsylvania's Day with the Rope." At the hills around the jail yard at Pottsville, center of the anthracite-coal industry, stood an emotional crowd of wives and children, relatives and friends, crying to the last that the men about to be hung were innocent. First to mount the double gallows were James Boyle and Hugh McGeehan, the former an American-born miner who worked for five years at the No. 5 Colliery in the Panther Creek Valley; the latter, a young Irishman who had been blacklisted by the operators for his role in the Long Strike of 1875. As two thousand people watched from a distance Boyle turned to McGeehan and said "Good-by, old fellow, we'll die like men!" In McGeehan's buttonhole were two roses, pink and white, and in one hand a brass crucifix, in the other a porcelain statuette of the Blessed Virgin. Boyle carried a huge, red rose in his hand, which fell to the ground as the trap was sprung. Both men, convicted on the charge of killing Benjamin Yost, one of the two policemen in the town of Tamaqua, had been members of the Ancient Order of Hibernians in Summit Hill, and, like the others to be executed that day, were accused of affiliation with the dreaded Molly Maguires.

Next to be brought to the scaffold were James Carroll, a tavern owner about forty, father of four children, secretary of the Tamaqua AOH; and James Roarity, a recent arrival from Ireland (1869) who worked in the mines of the Lehigh and Wilkes-Barre Coal Company, and was an AOH bodymaster (leader) in Coaldale. In Roarity's belongings was a letter received fifteen days before, from his father in the old country: "Dear Loving Son, don't be afraid, God is merciful and good. And before you die, declare to your Judge and to the world whether you are guilty or innocent, and we are not sorry, for well I believe your letter saying you are innocent. But we are not sorry for your death, when you are going to die so." From the gallows now, Roarity and Carroll repeated their declarations of innocence.

Finally, Thomas Munley, a Gilberton AOH member and miner who had arrived from Ireland in 1864 at the age of nineteen, and Thomas Duffy, a young engineer at the Buckville Colliery of the Philadelphia and Reading Coal and Iron Company, were also sent to their doom. Father Daniel McDermott, implacable enemy of the AOH, had pleaded with the authorities: "I know, beyond all reasonable doubt that Duffy was not a party to the murder of Policeman Yost, and I think the same remark will apply with almost equal force to Carroll." The intercession, however, was in vain.

Meanwhile a similar drama was being enacted in the town of Mauch Chunk, Pennsylvania, where Edward Kelly, Alexander Campbell, Michael J. Doyle, and John (Yellow Jack) Donahue, all "Hibernians" and all presumably Molly Maguires, were hung on a specially built gallows which accommodated all four simultaneously. Donahue was accused of having killed mine boss Morgan Powell way back in 1871, and the others of doing away with mine boss John P. Jones. The widowed Mrs. Jones had asked for the privilege of pulling the trap lever, as had her son, but both requests had been denied. Rumors that other Mollies might make an effort to rescue their brothers had caused Governor John F. Hartranft to emplace a squad of "Eastern Grays with 26 muskets" at the site of the hangings. There were no attempts at rescue, however; ten men died that day, seven more during the rest of the year, and two on January 14, 1879. With them died that shadowy movement called the Molly Maguires.

JUSTICE AT LAST, blared the Philadelphia *Times* June 22, 1877, to be echoed by the Chicago *Tribune's* headline: A TRIUMPH OF LAW AND JUSTICE. A coal owners' sheet, the *Miners' Journal*, asked, midst a blare of invective against the Mollies: "What did they do?" and answered, as if it were a crime: "Whenever prices of labor did not suit them they organized and proclaimed a strike."

At the opposite pole of opinion, New York workers held a protest meeting under the auspices of the Working Men's Party, and adopted a resolution charging that the testimony against the Mollies was almost totally from the lips of a corporation "stool pigeon," and that the whole thing was a plot by the operators to divert "attention

from their own cruel and outrageous robbery of the workmen."
Demonstrators in Philadelphia denounced "the hasty and inhuman
manner in which the so-called 'Molly Maguires' have been sentenced
to death."

The view from the Left was probably best articulated by Eugene
V. Debs thirty years later. He hailed the hanged men as martyrs
who had "protested their innocence and all died game. Not one of
them betrayed the slightest evidence of fear or weakening. Not one
of them was a murderer at heart. All were ignorant, rough and
uncouth, born of poverty and buffeted by the merciless tides of fate
and chance. To resist the wrongs of which they and their fellow
workers were victims and to protect themselves against the brutality
of their bosses, according to their own crude notions, was the prime
object of the organization of the 'Mollie Maguires' . . ."

II

Who were the Mollies? Did they in fact exist? *Irish World*, a nation-
alist sheet published in New York, wrote nine days after the first
hangings: "A deal of wild talk was said, and a deal of random
writing found its way into print, about the 'terrible organization of
the Molly Maguires. . . . [But] how many of the editors . . . asked
themselves the question: 'Does there in reality exist such a body of
men, as an organization, or is it all a myth?' . . . Not six! They took
all for granted. Their readers, in turn, took it for granted." *Irish
World* charged flatly that it was the "coal ring" which invented the
term Molly Maguires because they "found it necessary . . . to frighten
the country with a bugbear." In fact, however, it went on to say,
Molly Maguireism had no more reality than "fairies or hobgoblins."

Irish World, of course, was sympathetic to its miner kin in eastern
Pennsylvania and hostile to the "coal ring—which has striven and
which still endeavors to reduce the miners to a condition actually
worse than serfdom." But its remarks hit very close to the truth.
Despite numerous investigations no one has ever uncovered membership lists or correspondence files of the Mollies. The *Daily Miners'
Journal* of Pottsville, an employers' publication, gave as its expert
opinion that the Mollies "commenced in Boston and now extend all
over the country, controlling all the nominations of the Democratic
Party in our cities and in some parts of the country . . ." That a
movement so strong and active for three decades, according to the
Journal, should have left no records behind, no leaders to share
their reminiscences with the public, is inconceivable. The primary
source for the Molly Maguire legend was the famous detective, Allan
Pinkerton, and his spy, James McParlan, who infiltrated the move-

ment and was the main witness in the trials. But spies and detectives, pursuing their own dark motives, are not famous for their historical accuracy.

Competent labor historians, writing long afterward, endorsed the theory that there never was such an organization as the Molly Maguires. Joseph G. Rayback wrote that the Mollies were a figment of Pinkerton's and coal operators' imagination "with the express purpose of destroying all vestiges of unionism in the area after the Long Strike of 1875." Herbert Harris argued that the name was simply a popular synonym for the secret fraternal organization of Irishmen, the Ancient Order of Hibernians. If this view is disputed by some, there is enough that is suspect to leave the matter of the Mollies' existence under a cloud.

It is certainly within the realm of reason that when the anthracite industry sought a name for its detractors, carrying a terrorist stigma, it adopted one from Irish legend.

According to one folklore, Molly Maguire was a widowed Irish lady who was evicted from her little farm near Ballymena, County Antrim, in June 1839. As the bailiffs and constabulary carried out her meager belongings, crowds from nearby parishes tried vainly to prevent the eviction. In this account Molly is depicted as a "feeble and helpless" woman abused by a landlord's agent, trying mightily to keep her little clan together. Another version has it that Molly was a strapping woman who carried a pistol on each thigh and led bands of young Irishmen, disguised in women's clothing and armed with staves, on night raids against landlord agents and government officials. In the condition of Eire those days injustice inspired innumerable secret bands bent on righting their wrongs—Whiteboys, Defenders, Threshers, Carders, Ribbonmen, and finally Molly Maguires.

All that is certain is that the men referred to as Molly Maguires were Irish, were members of the Ancient Order of Hibernians, were miners or miner sympathizers, and were participants in the strikes that brought turmoil to eastern Pennsylvania for a long time. Doubtless they engaged in violence, but they were as frequently the victims as the victimizers, and their violence was usually linked to grievances in the coal pits. In any event, the roots of this labor war lie in the fascinating evolution of the hard coal industry.

III

Anthracite coal had been used by local blacksmiths before 1776 and by the gunlock factory at Carlisle Armory during the Revolution, but it was generally considered unsatisfactory for heating homes or smelting pig iron. Farmers preferred wood in their fireplaces, and the iron plantations used charcoal. In 1808, however, Jesse Fall of Wilkes-Barre illustrated the hidden combustible qualities of hard coal by burning it in an open grate without bellows; and in 1833 Frederick W. Geisenheimer took out a patent for smelting iron with anthracite in blast furnaces. Stimulated by these discoveries and by advances in transportation "black gold" grew into a major industry. Two canals, completed in the 1820s, made it possible to ship the coal cheaply to New York and Philadelphia, and then came the railroads to make matters even easier.

From 1808 to 1820 only 12,000 tons of the black stones were mined, mostly by local farmers. Soon, however, an area 120 miles by 50 miles (at its widest point) was bustling with activity. In the two southern fields, running through Pottsville and slightly to the north, and the two northern fields, around Hazleton, Wilkes-Barre, and Scranton, production of the precious fuel increased to a million tons a year by 1840 and to eight and a half million just before the Civil War. By 1855 hard coal had replaced charcoal as the fuel for pig-iron production, and in the same year the Philadelphia & Reading Railroad (usually called the Reading) was already shipping twice as much black gold to Philadelphia as the Schuylkill Canal. It was a typical American Cinderella story, complete with technological innovation, the settling of a sparsely inhabited region, immigrants flocking to a new haven, and a few men making fortunes.

In step with this expansion Welsh, English, German, and Irish settlers flocked to the five anthracite counties. Of these the Irish were the most numerous and the most downtrodden. Victims of potato famines and wholesale evictions by landlords back in Eire, they were part of a larger contingent of approximately two million who fled to the promised land during the first half of the nineteenth century. From 1846 to 1854, when 1.2 million Irish came over, they were the largest single group of immigrants arriving in the United States—fully 44 per cent of the total.

For a long time the Irish—apart from native Indians, black slaves, and Orientals—were the most maltreated ethnic minority in the United States. Being Roman Catholics, they were abused and assaulted by bigots such as the Native American Party (the so-called "Know-Nothings"), and not infrequently subject to organized attacks—the worst one being in Philadelphia in 1844—that took the form of mob raids, lootings, fire-bombings, and personal beatings. Being unskilled, the men of the Shamrock had little choice but to take menial jobs, sometimes a long distance from home—such as on turnpikes and canals—for wages as meager as 62, 75, and 87 cents a day, and under

conditions so grueling many died of sickness or accident. According
to Matthew Carey, a liberal businessman writing in 1830: "They
labour frequently in marshy grounds which destroys their health,
often irrevocably. They return to their poor families—with ruined
constitutions, with a sorry pittance, most laboriously earned, and take
to their beds sick and unable to work. Hundreds are swept off
annually . . ."

The tens of thousands that alighted in Schuylkill and its neighboring counties once hard coal became an established industry, fared
no better. Their poverty, like that of the poor at all times, was
transformed into a culture. At the epicenter of their lives was "the
company," not merely their employer but the monarch of virtually
everything in the gloomy coal patch. The company owned the mine,
the land, the streets, and usually workers' little makeshift houses.
Diggers were forced to rent cheap three-room apartments from the
operators, made of clapboard, tin or tar-papered roofs, and lacking
plumbing or other necessary home facilities. Any miner classed as a
"trouble-maker" could be, and sometimes was, evicted. The streets
were patrolled by company police; the children were brought into
the world by a company doctor; the schools and churches were run
by men beholden to the squires of the coal patch. Even the local
store was a monopoly of the employer, and those who sought to
evade its high prices by trading elsewhere were often threatened
with dismissal. Not atypically, one notice by a mineowner advised
employees that in the layoffs "near at hand . . . such men as have
no account at the store will be dropped, and those who have shown
the sense to deal justly will be retained at work so long as it is in our
power to keep them . . ."

Mining itself was torturously unpleasant. Working stooped in the
bowels of the earth in damp and fetid atmosphere, the miner was
subject to all kinds of health hazards—noxious fumes such as "stink
damp" and "rotten gas," carbon monoxide, and coal dust which caused
bronchial catarrh. The rate of accidents from explosions, falling rock,
fire, suffocation, and other mishaps was far higher than in industry
over-all, and the number of miners who were killed or injured,
astronomical compared to workers in other crafts. In one seven-year
period 566 miners were killed; 1,655 injured in Schuylkill County
alone. Tens of thousands of men worked in semi-darkness, knee-deep
in water, always in fear of cave-ins and explosions that entombed
hundreds each year. Their lot, as one mining clerk put it, was "little
better than semi-slavery." Hours were long, from dawn to dusk, sani-
tary conditions impossibly bad.

One quarter of the workers were children, seven to sixteen, paid one to three dollars a week for separating coal from slate as it came down the chutes. Pay for adults was computed by the cubic yard of coal mined, or by the ton or car. Opportunities for cheating the wage earner were endless—for instance by claiming more slate in the coal than there actually was, or by "short-weighing." Under the contract system the miner bought his own powder and supplies, and paid his own helper. Though most men netted $11 or $12 a week, what was left over sometimes was negligible. Thus a miner's pay stub for the month of July, 1877, reproduced by J. Walter Coleman, gave the following figures on earnings:

mined 65½ cars at 66¢ a car	$43.33
less powder, oil, soap and rent for house	12.30
leaving	31.03
⅓ gross to laborer	14.61
net wage	16.42

Note that, apart from "rent for house," the skilled miner received six cents a day more than his unskilled assistant.

In this oppressive atmosphere the Irish behaved much like other immigrant groups clawing their way upward. They joined mutual-aid societies, a common feature of nineteenth- and early-twentieth-century America, when millions of foreign-born sought help in getting settled, finding a home, securing a job, preparing for citizenship. The Ancient Order of Hibernians, to which the Irish flocked, was actually the largest mutual-aid group in the nation at the time. An amalgam of many societies in Ireland, with branches on both sides of the ocean, its stated purpose was to "promote friendship, unity, and true Christian charity among the members." As such it raised a "fund of money for aiding the aged, sick, blind, and infirm members," and acted as a center for social comraderie, and sundry other activities. In union towns it was also the focal point for Irish workers to mobilize support and plan strategy.

If there were anything unique about AOH it was that it practiced secret rituals and passwords (such as two fingers downward on the throat) that lent it an aura of mystery. This too, however, was not unusual in the nineteenth century. Labor organizations, such as the Knights of St. Crispin, or, in its early years, the Knights of Labor, operated with a paraphernalia of secrecy to protect members from discharge and blacklisting. It was not strange, then, that the Irish who had lived through seven centuries of English repression should adopt passwords and signs to guard against unwanted infiltrators.

A second vehicle for achieving what today would be called "Irish power" was politics. The Irish pitmen in eastern Pennsylvania nominated and elected a sizable number of local officials, such as county commissioners, tax collectors, school directors. In one borough an Irishman was chief of police; in another, Mahanoy Township, Jack Kehoe, a so-called Molly Maguire, who was executed in 1879 for an 1862 murder, was high constable. Finally, there were the trade unions, which Irish diggers joined in droves whenever the opportunity presented itself. So militant, indeed, were the men of Eire that employers sometimes appended to help-wanted advertisements the now well-known phrase "no Irish need apply." Employers justified this ethnic exclusion on the grounds that the sons of Eire were "the first to insist on higher wages" and the first to strike.

IV

Unionism came to the coal fields early, before the boom, when production was still low and before the takeover by large corporations. The first recorded anthracite strike took place on July 8, 1842—a spontaneous upheaval by 1,500 diggers who "were joined," so it was said in the *History of Schuylkill County, Pa.*, "by many idle and vicious men . . ." In 1849, an ephemeral organization founded by John Bates and called the Bates Union conducted a strike of 2,000 men. The central demand was for payment in cash rather than company scrip, which was redeemable only at the company store. But the Bates Union disappeared after a year, to be followed by a host of benevolent societies and local unions, none of which was particularly effective for the workers. A national union, the American Miners' Association, born in West Belleville, Illinois, early in the Civil War, sank deeper roots among the workers and held the torch for six or seven years, but failed to sweep eastern Pennsylvania.

Meanwhile the pitmen of Schuylkill and nearby counties took off on the tangent of anti-draft riots, often involving clandestine terror. The Irish, who decried abolitionism as "an import from England," and the second American Revolution as "a rich man's war and a poor man's fight," were convinced that "abolitionist capitalists" would import "Negroes into the northern cities to replace workers who were striking for higher wages." On a number of occasions Irish miners stopped trains with draftees aboard, or pulled workers out of the collieries to help dissuade conscripts from entraining for Harrisburg or Pottsville.

By the grace of federal forbearance none of this activity flamed into the kind of anti-draft riots which resulted in 400 to 2,000 deaths in New York. Nonetheless the anthracite fields had its share of killings. From January 1, 1860, to April 1, 1867, there were, by the tally of the

Miners' Journal, at least 63 murders in the eastern Pennsylvania area—
every one of them marked "unsolved" on police blotters. While some of
these may have been unconnected to labor problems, most of them
were acts of vengeance against abhorrent supervisors. F. W. Langdon,
a mine foreman notorious for "short-weighing," for instance, was isolated from friends at the 1862 July Fourth celebration in Carbon
County (just northeast of Schuylkill) and beaten and stoned so
badly he died the next day. Mineowner George K. Smith, equally
hated for similar maliciousness was attacked by a group of men with
blackened faces and shot through the head in sight of his family. Without a union to absorb their pain and relieve their fury, a few zealots
took to terror. The murders were carefully co-ordinated, frequently
committed by a friendly spirit from another county, and planned in
AOH meeting places. Moreover, for every murder there were dozens
of threats, aimed at driving hated bosses from the scene. Typical was
a penciled note with a rough picture of a coffin and a pistol, which
read: "Mr. John Tylor—We will give you one week to go but if you are
alive on next Saturday you will die."

It must have been obvious even to the perpetrators of such threats,
however, that terror was an act of retribution without constructive reward. Toward the end of the decade the miners rekindled the union
flame, under the leadership of another talented immigrant, John
Siney.

Siney, described by McAlister Coleman in his *Men and Coal* as a
"brilliant, courageous, and at the end, tragic figure," was born in Ireland. Like so many distinguished labor leaders (the three Reuther
brothers in our day, for instance) he came from radical forebears.
Patrick Siney, the family's breadwinner, a tenant farmer on the old
sod, was a rebel whose tirades against landlords and the English won
him eviction from the land in 1835. Unable to make his way in Eire
any more, he transplanted his brood to Lancashire, England, where
young John at the age of seven went to work in the textile mills—and
his older brothers in the mines. Little that was noteworthy occurred to
Siney while he was in England, except that in later years, while working in a brickyard, he formed a small union and became its president.
He had no schooling and no particular industrial skills, only an unusual talent for organizing fellow workers, which he would soon put to
use in the New World.

After losing his brickyard job in England, the young Irishman
migrated in 1862 to St. Clair, Pennsylvania, north of Pottsville, where
he wielded pick and shovel in a local mine. Five years later he was
leading a small strike of 400 diggers for the Eagle Colliery, which in
the face of a glutted market had imposed a 10 per cent wage cut on

its workers. A stroke of good fortune—or employer disunity—brought quick victory. When Eagle Colliery found its competitors intended to sell coal while it was *hors de combat,* it rescinded the wage cut, and with this sudden success Siney was able to amalgamate a number of local unions in the area into the Workingmen's Benevolent Association —with himself as president. By the end of the decade he had extended the scope of unionism to thirty locals and 30,000 members—four fifths of the laborers in Pennsylvania anthracite.

From 1868 to 1875 it was a race between a union—and Siney—trying to heal divisions between miners in the southern and the northern fields which tended to cancel out each other's efforts, and the industry, increasingly being taken over by the railroads. Strikes wracked the collieries almost every year—the one in 1870 lasting six months, the Long Strike of 1875 five months—but Siney never quite forged the unity he needed to assure total victory or optimum strength. During the 1868 walkout squads of diggers from the south prowled northern collieries to induce hesitant brethren there to join them. The latter, mindful of a similar situation in 1865 when the southerners stayed on the job, refused, and the strike was broken. For the same reason the 1869 strike was only a partial success.

Nonetheless Siney did achieve some results for his men, the most notable being that the operators agreed to bargain collectively. In 1869 the union leader prevailed on the owners in the Schuylkill and Lehigh regions to accept a "sliding scale of wages" pegged to the price of coal. Rates of pay at Lehigh were determined by what a ton sold for in Elizabethport, New Jersey. At $5 a ton the miner's share was 57½ cents, and if ton price rose the digger's rate increased 15 per cent for each dollar. If the price fell below $5 the miner continued receiving 57½ cents per ton, the minimum. For Schuylkill the minimum was pegged at a selling price of $3 a ton at Port Carbon, with an increase of 5 per cent for every jump of 25 cents in coal prices.

On another front Siney secured a number of legislative improvements. Three quarters into the nineteenth century there were still no laws on the books recognizing labor unions as legal entities—such as corporations, for instance—and union leaders and unions were still subject to prosecution under the doctrine of "conspiracy." (Siney himself was indicted for this "crime" in 1875.) But as a result of lobbying and effective threats by the Workingmen's Benevolent Association not to vote for legislators unfriendly to labor, a law passed by Pennsylvania's legislature in 1869 granted legal sanction for working people "to form societies, and associations for their mutual aid, benefit, and protection . . ." The same year a mine inspection bill was enacted for the first time, providing for the "better regulation and ventilation of mines"

and empowering the governor to appoint an inspector. Though limited
at first to a single county, safety protection was extended to the rest of
the anthracite area after a disastrous accident at the Avondale mine
in Luzerne County, which took the lives of 109 men.

None of these gains, either in the economic or political spheres were
sensational, but they were substantial enough to offer the miners hope.
The operators recognized the union, dealt with it, and thus gave the
men a channel for resolving differences within the established order
of business.

v

The man who put the miners in a vise and eventually demolished
both the union and the so-called Molly Maguires, was a young clean-
shaven, second-generation Irish-American, with thin lips, even features
and a benign expression, Franklin Benjamin Gowen. Fifth son of an
Irish Episcopalian who had emigrated to Philadelphia penniless and
made a fortune selling groceries and liquor, Franklin was educated at
the elite John Beck's Academy which catered to patrician youth. After
a stint in a retail coal business and in a coal mine at Mount Laffee,
north of Pottsville, which went bankrupt in 1859, Gowen at twenty-
three decided to read law in the office of a Pottsville lawyer and, like
so many up-and-coming men of the nineteenth century, became a bar-
rister after a short time. His natural enthusiasm and flair for the florid
phrase made him popular in literary and debating circles. At twenty-
six he was nominated for district attorney on the Democratic Party
slate in Schuylkill County and won a resounding victory, outpolling
all members on the slate but one. Nothing eventful happened during
his two years in office, but Gowen made enough of an impression to
graduate into the legal department of the Reading Railroad. At thirty
he won an impressive court victory for his company against the
Pennsylvania Railroad system, and at thirty-three, when another man
quit, was offered and accepted the president's chair.

Other rail companies in the anthracite area had used their leverage
as transporters as a means of buying or otherwise gaining control over
the major mining firms. The Reading, however, had not yet reached
this stage. It was, to be sure, the main transporter of coal from the two
southern fields to Philadelphia, having made a pooling agreement with
the Schuylkill canal and purchased or leased feeder railroads. But it
was not yet involved in the production of coal as were the railroads
and canal companies of the northern regions. The Delaware & Hudson
Canal and the Delaware, Lackawanna & Western Railroad, which
controlled transport to the lucrative market of New York not only
held pit owners in the Wyoming field under their thumb, but had long

since bought their way into the coal industry itself. So had the Lehigh Valley Railroad and the Lehigh Coal and Navigation Company in the Lehigh field around Hazleton. But the Reading had not kept pace, and it remained for Gowen to rectify this situation. And he did: from 1871 to 1874 he purchased 100,000 acres of coal lands.

Gowen, who was to commit suicide twenty years later after being ousted from his job, exercised his power with imaginative ruthlessness. Typical was the way he undercut the strike of 1871. In January of that year miners in the northern regions downed tools for what was becoming a monotonously common reason—wages had been cut by one third. This time all of the anthracite workers were united, the men from the southern region joining their brethren in common cause. Since this was the third strike in three years, by February both the men and the companies were hurting badly. "Men, women and children are suffering from lack of clothing and food," reported the *Miners' Journal*. Many children, it said, were dying. On the other side of the industrial equation not a few independent operators were near bankruptcy, and several agreed to reopen their shafts on WBA terms.

Gowen, however, was determined not to permit any break in the ranks of management. Those operators that attempted it suddenly found that it was impossible to ship their black diamonds—the Reading raised freight rates from $2 a ton to a prohibitive $4. And after a secret conference in New York the railroads that serviced the northern region followed suit. It was not for nothing that reformers of that day cried out that "he who owns the rails, owns all." Such manipulation of the anthracite economy terrified even the organs of respectability. "If a railroad company," said the Harrisburg *State Journal,* "can advance and lower its charges for transportation at will, there is not an industrial operation that may not be destroyed in a month." The state legislature was so alarmed that a Senate committee decided to investigate the affair. Gowen, however, turned away its attack and succeeded in deflecting its interest from freight rates to the Molly Maguires. There was within WBA, he charged, "an association which votes in secret, at night, that men's lives shall be taken, and that they shall be shot before their wives, murdered in cold blood, for daring to work against the order." Listing two instances of shooting and dynamiting, he left the impression that such activities against strikebreakers had the sanction of WBA. By the time Siney had finished denying the charge, the issue of freight rates was all but forgotten. The strike was ended by referring differences to arbitration, and in the process the diggers had to swallow bile on two major issues. The arbitrator ruled that they could no longer refuse to work with non-union men, and he cut minimum wages from a $3 basis to $2.50.

Gowen's technique of shifting attention from the social problems of workers to lawlessness incidental to a strike was to be a common employer technique, influencing public and press reaction in all the labor wars. Under the American system of jurisprudence property owners are considered to have a vested interest in their property, and strikers deemed criminals if they try to prevent its use. But jobholders do not enjoy any vested interest in their jobs and if management replaces them with strikebreakers—protected by the coal and iron police or by the army—legality is on the side of management and the "black-legs." Thus men who see their jobs and livelihoods in jeopardy and who have no legal recourse frequently have used force against their replacements and the police. Characteristically, the employers have pointed to this "lawlessness" as if it were the true issue of the strike, rather than wage cuts, company store prices, safety, or long hours. The effect has been paraded as the cause.

In 1873 Gowen consolidated the management front. On his initiative the railroad tycoons in anthracite held a secret meeting in New York where they agreed on a fixed price for coal at $5 a ton. They also divided the market among themselves, with the Reading receiving 27.85 per cent of the total; the Hudson, 18.37; Jersey Central, 16.15; Lehigh, 15.98; Lackawanna, 13.80; and the Pennsylvania Coal Company 9.85. There were as yet no anti-trust laws on the books directed at this sort of collusion, but it is obviously ironic that the corporations felt impelled to take concerted action, whereas they looked askance at similar action by their employees.

VI

Siney was promoted to president of the newly founded Miners' National Association in October 1873, embracing both anthracite and bituminous miners, but, of course, kept a hand on developments in eastern Pennsylvania. Testifying to a desire for harmony, MNA expressed the hope that arbitration, rather than strikes, would soon govern relationships with employers. It would quickly find this, unfortunately, a vain aspiration. For at almost the same time, Gowen was holding a conference in Philadelphia with a detective who had done some work for him in the past, Allan Pinkerton, for exactly the opposite purpose.

Pinkerton, an immigrant from Scotland who had once been a radical firebrand, had fled his native land in 1842 rather than face arrest for his activities during the 1842 Chartist Disorders. In Dundee, Illinois, he went to work as a cooper, and after some impressive amateur detective work he did on the side, was rewarded with the post of deputy sheriff of Kane County. Four years later, in 1850, he struck out on his own, opening one of the first detective agencies in the country, and enjoyed considerable personal and financial glory until 1873 when business was so bad he feared the agency might go under. Gowen's summons was like manna from heaven for him.

The assignment that Gowen had for Pinkerton, according to the detective, was to plant an operative in the "Molly Maguires" to expose and destroy the terrorist society which "wields with deadly effect . . . two powerful levers, secrecy and combination." According to an official history of the Ancient Order of Hibernians, on the other hand, which swears it is quoting Gowen's exact words, the task was more devilish. Gowen, AOH said, wanted an informer who would simultaneously insinuate himself into the Mollies "and become its leader." As its new head, he would be expected to provoke strikes; have his men kill mine bosses; murder English, Welsh, and German miners; and generally cause so much trouble that "the collieries will be unable to run for want of competent men." In the ensuing chaos, independent operators would have to sell their holdings to the Reading at depreciated prices. Such knavery sounds bizarre, but it evidently was not unusual. Wayne G. Broehl, Jr., a historian who, incidentally, believes that the Molly Maguires did exist as a separate, murderous agency, writes that: "Anti-unionism in the 1870's included such devices. Gowen's private motives were such that, given certain circumstances, he could well have countenanced violence."

That year, 1873, was a turbulent one for the nation at large, as well as for Gowen. The best-known banking firm in the country, Jay Cooke & Company, had gone bankrupt earlier in the year, plunging the United States into a terrible depression that would last five years. The Reading, however, was not in financial trouble, and as a robber baron in good standing, it was not above Gowen to use the adversity of smaller firms to try and absorb them into his empire. At the very least he had a keen appreciation of the fact that curtailed mine production would sustain, or even boost, prices. Added to this was his swelling hatred of unions. Their leaders, he said, were foreigners, "advocates of the [Paris] Commune and emissaries of the [First] International." They imposed their tyranny on the "poor laboring man [who] had to crouch like a whipped spaniel before their lash." Whether Gowen intended to force a strike, as the New York *Times* charged, in order to cut production and raise prices, or, as the *Commercial Advertiser* claimed, to "corner" the market, it is certain that he wanted to smash the miners' union beyond resurrection.

Pinkerton, at the time, was just the man for such a job. Paid $100,000 by Gowen and others, to start, he insinuated dozens of spies into the union ranks. One of them, P. M. Cummings, became an official of the WBA and a close associate of Siney's. There were so many operatives around that an industry organ, the *Miners' Weekly Journal,* noted with satisfaction that the diggers "do not know how many like him [McParlan] there are . . . There may be a McParlan in every group of a half a dozen that assembles in the backroom of somebody's liquor store to plot the murder of a man."

The most effective Pinkerton, it transpired, was James McParlan, a twenty-nine-year-old native of Ireland, who assumed the name James McKenna. McParlan or McKenna was a charming extrovert, with red hair and a fine tenor voice, who danced a tolerable jig, told a smutty story, drank with the best of them, and used his fists handily. His work record was anything but stable: he had been employed in a chemical factory and a linen warehouse in Belfast, and after coming to America in 1867 had worked as a teamster, wood chopper, coachman, policeman, and at assorted other jobs before turning to industrial espionage for $12 a week. Posing now as a counterfeiter and a murderer "on the lam," and an AOH member from other parts, he was able after some months to have himself initiated into the Shenandoah Lodge of AOH, which claimed a membership of 200. He traveled widely, seeking evidence of "murder plots" for his employer, always flashing ample funds and buying drinks for all and sundry.

Meanwhile the center of the stage was pre-empted by the five-month-long labor war of 1875. Gowen prepared for it meticulously, not only with an enlarged staff of spies, but by coalescing independent producers into the Schuylkill Coal Exchange and accelerating production beforehand so that there would be enough coal above ground to meet public and industrial demand for a long time. In December miners' fears that management was deliberately precipitating a strike were confirmed when the owners unilaterally reduced wages by 20 per cent for contract miners and 10 per cent for laborers and abolished the minimum wage so that earning could drop below the established floor by one per cent for every three cents' fall in coal prices below $2.50. Wages, however, were not really the issue in this situation. "It is well known," observed a correspondent for the *Miners' Journal,* "that the coal market can afford to pay last year's prices, but it seems that the wages question is not the trouble, but the disbanding of the Miners' and Laborers' Benevolent Association," formerly called the Workingmen's Benevolent Association (WBA).

In a report to his stockholders subsequently, Gowen admitted that he had spent $4 million to break the strike, but that it was worth every penny to save the company "from the arbitrary control of an irresponsible trades union." During the strike, two squadrons of agents had been organized, one headed by a Pinkerton named Robert J. Linden, and another by Captain W. J. Heisler, whose purpose was to attack strikers and hold open the door for strikebreakers. The private coal and iron police were augmented, and a "vigilance committee" organized, which in Pinkerton's words was "to take fearful revenge on the Molly Maguires." "Gowen," writes Broehl, "appeared to realize that violence connected with the strike could be meshed with the violence long attributed to the Molly Maguires, and the two tied up into a neat package for clubbing all union activity under the guise of preserving law and order."

Gowen got what he bargained for, especially as the months ticked by and the men of the mines grew more desperate. "Hundreds of families," reported a contemporary, Andrew Roy, "rose in the morning to breakfast on a crust of bread and a glass of water, who did not know where a bite of dinner was to come from. Day after day, men, women, and children went to the adjoining woods to dig roots and pick up herbs to keep body and soul together." Meanwhile they watched grimly as the operators recruited strikebreakers to take their jobs, and unleashed the coal and iron police to maim and kill striker activists.

In March, Edward Coyle, a union leader and AOH chief, was murdered at the Plank Colliery, which belonged to the Philadelphia and Reading Coal and Iron Company. Another active figure of the Hibernians was killed by a mine engineer at Mine Hill Gap. Patrick Vary, a mine boss, shot indiscriminately into an assemblage of 300 strikers, and as Gowen subsequently boasted, the fleeing miners "left a long trail of blood behind them." Vary was never brought to trial. Vigilantes and a mine boss fired their guns in a meeting of 100 miners in Tuscarora, killing one digger and wounding others. The assailant was arrested and tried but found not guilty on the ground he had "protected himself from the mob of assassins." Colliery foremen were given guns to brandish at strikers, as were "blacklegs," and before long state troops were patrolling the coal patches, and hoodlum groups such as the Modocs and Sheet Iron Gang—subsidized by the operators—were raining terror on strikers far and wide.

On the other side, the coal diggers, as might have been anticipated, replied in kind. Strikebreakers were frequently found dead in ditches. Any worker who entertained notions of going back to work was warned in stern language that if he did so he would soon meet his maker. Hungry and desperate, the strikers chased "blacklegs," damning them as "a disgrace to their race," "traitors to their fellow miners," and beating them wherever they could find them. The diggers were determined to hold out, as reflected in this song they composed early in the "war":

Now two long months are nearly over—that no one can deny,
And for to stand another we are willing for to try,
Our wages shall not be reduced, tho' poverty do reign,
We'll have seventy-four basis, boys, before we work again.

The miners were just as determined in the sixth month of the walk-out. On June 3, a crowd gathered at Glover's hill, opposite a West Shenandoah Colliery still in production, bent on pulling the "scabs" out. They were met by Gowen's agents Linden and Heisler and a force of twenty-four men armed with Winchesters. In the strikers' group, reported Linden, were 613 men, with the Pinkerton spy, McParlan (McKenna), in the vanguard, shouting and screaming, two pistols in his belt and his bulldog by his side. The rest of the miners evidently had no weapons more lethal than hickory clubs, for they backed away from the Winchesters and moved from Shenandoah to Mahanoy City, where they put three collieries out of production. Then, joined by strikers from Hazleton, who had also closed down five or six pits, they moved toward the Little Drift Colliery. Here the two forces came eye to ball to eyeball with the state militia that Governor John F. Hartranft had stationed nearby since mid-April. In the face of this overwhelming force the miners decided to disperse.

Provocation on the one hand and bitterness on the other elicited violence on a wide scale. Gowen listed ninety-two separate instances of worker assault, arson, murder, riots, and destruction of property in a seven-month period. J. Walter Coleman, in his book *The Molly Maguire Riots*, printed thirteen pages of the acts of violence, which ranged from the burning of a telegraph office at a railroad station, to the derailing of trains, dumping of coal cars, beatings, threats, and to a few actual murders and attempted murders. But many if not most, of the illegal acts were instigated by the operators and perpetrated by their agents. Marvin W. Schlegel, an assistant state historian of Pennsylvania, even asserts in his *favorable* biography of Gowen, that "the facts show that there was much more terror waged against the Mollies than those illiterate Irishmen ever aroused." McParlan himself reported that arson at a Reading colliery in East Norwegian, allegedly committed by the Mollies, was believed by the strikers to have been set by the railroad itself to gain sympathy from the state legislature, which was preparing to investigate the railroads' monopoly of the coal mining industry.

The almost universal hostility to the miners' cause was joined even by the Church, the press, the courts, and other respectable institutions. Their attitude was manifest in a dozen ways before and after the upheavals. During one of the Molly Maguire trials, for instance, a judge defended industrial spying in these words: "We employ spies in wars

between nations; is it any worse to employ them in wars in society?"
During a strike of bituminous miners in Clearfield County, in central
Pennsylvania, which occurred simultaneously with the anthracite stoppage, John Siney, Xeno Parks, an official of the Miners' National Association, and twenty-six others were arrested for "conspiracy and
riot." Their crime consisted of picketing the mines in an effort to
persuade a trainload of strikebreakers to leave the region. Parks and
twenty-six others were found guilty and sentenced to a year in jail.
Only Siney was acquitted. In sentencing two of the men, the judge
indicated revealingly what the Establishment saw as the real issue: "I
find you, Joyce," he said, "to be president of the union, and you, Ma-
loney, to be secretary, and therefore I sentence you to one year's imprisonment."

Siney's summary of the miners' lament, made on another occasion,
was an eloquent defense of all workers who engaged in the labor
wars, then and thereafter. "We have been called agitators," he said,
"we have been called demagogues, because we have counseled . . .
our members to try and secure" better wages and harmonious settlements. "Is it wrong to teach men to seek a higher moral standard? . . .
Is it wrong to advance our financial interests? If so, let those who operate our mines and mills and all others abandon the various enterprises
in which they are engaged in the pursuit of wealth. It appears to me
. . . that that which, if advised by the church, by the press or by the
wealthy would be applauded to the heavens, when advised by workingmen consigns them to perdition, or ranks them in the catologue of
. . . mischief makers."

After five months the strikers were at last forced to give up. Short of
funds and food, incapable of matching the power of money, police,
militia, and goon squads, drained by strikes in previous years, they
could no longer hold out. "Since I last saw you," a striker wrote in a
letter to a friend, "I have buried my youngest child, and on the day
before its death there was not one bit of victuals in the house with six
children." Toward the end of May the corporations began reopening
their pits, offering police protection to those willing to cross picket
lines. On June 8 the union's executive board made a last plea to
Gowen to arrange a compromise, but the rail baron turned a deaf
ear. On the fourteenth the union conceded—"we can continue the
fight no longer." "We are beaten," cried John Walsh, their local leader,
"forced by the unrelenting necessities of our wives and little ones to
accept terms which . . . we could never under any other circumstances have been forced to accept." Those men who were not blacklisted returned to work on Gowen's terms, in non-union mines and
with a 20 per cent wage cut.

A miner's ballad, "After a Long Strike," indicated the pathos of defeat:

> Well, we've been beaten, beaten all to smash
> And now, sir, we've begun to feel the lash,
> As wielded by a gigantic corporation,
> Which ran the commonwealth and ruins the nation.

VII

Like a flood after the dam breaks, the bitter animosities engendered by a defeated strike brought further outbursts when it was over. On the one side, Irish miners, now without a union, fought rear guard, guerrilla battles—organized within the Hibernians—to rebuild their organization. They were hardly effete, and were no doubt responsible for many of the killings, threats, burnings, and other acts that harried the area in the latter half of 1875. On the other side, as Peter Roberts notes in his *Anthracite Coal Communities*, "many operators . . . then furnished arms to their foremen. . . . When labor in many instances sought relief, it was answered with an oath supplemented with the pointing of a revolver." A few of the more radical miners disappeared, their bodies later found in unused shafts. On December 1, 1875, at Wiggan's Patch, near Mahanoy City, disguised terrorists invaded the home of a militant miner, Charles O'Donnell, while the family was sleeping. Though O'Donnell and one of his boarders, Charles McAllister, were able to flee the house, they were captured and killed. O'Donnell had fourteen bullets in his body.

Management was clearly continuing on the offensive. With the union disbanded, Gowen craftily pursued those rebels who might reestablish it, by stigmatizing them as "Molly Maguires." The Mollies, hailed and bloated in scores of newspaper stories, were a made-to-order scapegoat—"it was sufficient to hang a man," the railroad president himself admitted, "to declare him a Molly Maguire."

It was now that James McParlan's two years of espionage activities were put to use. After secret meetings with the Reading's General Superintendent, George H. Bangs, McParlan compiled a "List of Members of the AOH" in Luzerne, Northumberland, Columbia, Carbon, and Schuylkill Counties, with addresses, occupations, and posts in the society. The list, surprisingly, had only 347 names. At about the same time a handbill, marked "Strictly Confidential," was distributed "for the consideration of the Vigilance Committee of the Anthracite Coal Region." Compiled from McParlan's reports, the circular gave details of the murder of seven men from June 28 to September 3—after the Long Strike, in other words—as well as the names and addresses of fourteen members of the Molly Maguires who were described as "murderers and accessories." Some of these accused turned fugitive; one—Charles O'Donnell—was himself assassinated in a gruesome murder at Wiggan's Patch; one turned state's evidence.

The first trial of the Mollies began in Mauch Chunk on January 18, 1876. But it was the Yost proceedings in May that were the more pivotal. Five so-called Mollies were accused of killing policeman Benjamin F. Yost on July 5 the year before, while he was putting out a gas lamp near his home at Tamaqua. As the trial opened, Franklin B. Gowen, the most powerful man in the Reading Valley, appeared in the courtroom as special prosecutor, and henceforth dominated the event just as he did the area's coal and rail industries. His beautiful baritone voice rose and fell in measured cadence as militia with bayonets patrolled the courts, and wives and friends of the Irish defendants filled every seat. A few of the defense witnesses were arrested, on Gowen's command, as they left the stand, charged with perjury.

McParlan naturally was the key prosecution witness—indeed making almost the whole case—claiming that the five men on trial had personally confessed to him. On the second day of his testimony the district attorney, George Kaercher, introduced a statement—over the vehement objections of the defense—which laid bare the hidden motives of the trial. "The detective," it said, "came to Schuylkill County to become familiar with the workings of a secret association known generally in this locality as 'Mollie Maguires' but the real name of which is the Ancient Order of Hibernians." The trial, in other words, was not merely of individuals accused of crime but of an organization whose members, said Kaercher, "aid and assist each other in the commission of crimes, and in defeating detection and punishment." The only other witness of importance for the state was James Kerrigan who had decided to appear in order to save his own neck. His testimony was rebutted by his wife who stated he had confessed to her that he had been the actual murderer. The trial ended when a juror took sick on May 18 and died a few days later, but the case came to court again and ended in a total victory for the prosecution. It set the pattern for all the other sensational Molly Maguire cases.

Much of the corroborating evidence in these cases was obviously faulty—for instance, the claim of one witness, Richard Andrews, that he had seen Thomas Munley, a union leader, kill a mine foreman named Thomas Sanger. When Munley was asked to stand, Andrews said: "That is not the man I can recognize at all." Munley's lawyer cried out to the jury: "For God's sake give labor an equal chance. Do not crush it. Let it not perish under the imperial mandates of capital in a free country." Munley, nonetheless, was convicted and hung. In the embittered climate of the day, the defense could make no case stand on behalf of the workers. One after another, nineteen men were found guilty and executed, others sentenced to prison terms.

"The Molly Maguires," commented the Pittsburgh *Gazette* on May 9, 1876, "represented the spirit of French Communism and enforced their views by secret murders. The principle involved was simply that of permitting them to dictate the operations of labor. Their men were to be employed, their prices admitted and their directions obeyed . . ."

Stripped of venom and bias, it was a fitting epitaph. Plainly and simply, the miners were guilty of wanting a union.

3

Two Weeks
of Insurrection

Less than a month after the first Molly Maguires were hanged, there were reports of "trouble" at Martinsburg, West Virginia, a railroad center 100 miles south of Baltimore, not far from Harpers Ferry where old John Brown had led his famous raid in 1859. According to the New York *Times*, the trouble that hot and humid Monday, July 16, 1877, was a strike on the Baltimore & Ohio Railroad which seemed to be "assuming alarming proportions." The headline over the story read like a war dispatch: "Firemen and brakemen obstructing freight trains. A volunteer company put to flight. 1,000 cars blockaded at Martinsburg. The Governor of West Virginia on his way to the Front." On page 5, readers learned that the strike was aimed at restoring a 10 per cent wage cut that had gone into effect that Monday. "All the employees acceded to the reduction," wrote the correspondent, except firemen who "commenced a rebellion . . ." and were joined by brakemen the following day.

The report was not entirely accurate, since no one had "acceded" to the wage cut—no one in fact had been asked. The decision had been announced by John W. Garrett, president of the B&O, to a directors' meeting on July 11, and like another ten per cent reduction instituted eight months before, the new one too had been put into effect unilaterally. If the employees "acceded," it was only in the same sense that a prisoner "accedes" to his jail cell. Since many of the men were only working three or four days a week they would be taking home a pay check of five or six dollars. And, having to pay their own expenses while on overnight layovers away from home, such as one dollar for the company hotel, would be usually taking home much less. What was accurate in the *Times* story was the role of the firemen who stalked from their jobs that day in cold fury, leaving their trains both at Camden Junction, a couple of miles outside Baltimore, and in the city itself. It was, to management, a small matter, for which B&O's vice-president, John King, Jr., Garrett's son-in-law, was adequately prepared. He had assembled strikebreakers in anticipation of the strike, and when the "trouble" broke out, had his supervisors and forty Baltimore policemen escort the blacklegs to the yards. Before the day was over the trains were running again and King assured newsmen that the malcontents having been fired, there would be no more problems. President Garrett remained at the Brevoort House in New York, similarly confident all was well, and set out for home that night only because he received a telegram that his eighty-five-year-old mother was dying.

Garrett and King, it turned out, were more optimistic than the situation warranted. The "rebellion," brought under control in Baltimore, leapfrogged to Martinsburg, a city of 8,000 with a small police force, and a population entirely sympathetic to the rail workers. Having learned of events in Baltimore earlier in the day, crew members of a cattle train in Martinsburg abandoned it, and try as it would, the company could find no one to take their places. Led by Richard M. Zepp, a young brakeman in his twenties, the locomotives were uncoupled from the cars and run into the roundhouse, while men, women, and children stood on the tracks and cheered lustily. When Mayor A. P. Shutt, horrified by the events, ordered police to arrest the ringleaders, the men in blue let the order go unheeded; and when the mayor himself appeared before the crowd to plead for law and order, it hooted him down. The authorities and the company were helpless. By midnight all the railroad's facilities in Martinsburg were deserted—except for pickets.

Next morning, the seventeenth, the strike passed its first test and suffered its first martyr. Governor Henry M. Matthews, reached after midnight by B&O's vice-president, immediately dispatched the Berkeley Light Guards to "prevent the obstruction of the trains." The indecent haste with which he acted that day and the following, when he asked for federal troops, prompted a New York *World* reporter to comment that "if the rights of the strikers had been infringed" rather than those of the company, "it is probable that Governor Matthews would have hesitated a long while" before acting. By the time the militia arrived at 9 A.M., the strikers had already thwarted one effort—by a supervisor—to move the cattle train. Now the company tried it with two strikebreakers in the engine cab and armed soldiers aboard for protection.

As the train pulled out, one of the soldiers, John Poisal, noticed that the switch had been adjusted to derail the locomotive. With rifle in hand, he jumped from the cowcatcher to turn the switch, only to be met by a twenty-eight-year-old striker, William P. Vandergriff, holding a pistol. In the ensuing shoot-out Poisal was slightly wounded, but Vandergriff hurt so badly he had to have his arm amputated, and died nine days later. The unexpected development sobered everyone; militiamen and scabs fled the train, the colonel in charge of the Light Guards sent his men home. "The great trouble . . . ," wrote the New York *Times* reporter, "is that the people along the line of the road are thoroughly in sympathy with the strikers, and the military cannot be depended on to act against them in an emergency." The strikers were in "absolute control" of Martinsburg, he wrote, and the walkout had spread to Wheeling, Keyser, and along the Parkersburg branch.

Thus began the first nationwide strike in American history, and the first (except for a minor one in 1834) in which federal troops were used. Within six days, ten states mobilized 60,000 militia. The staid *Times* called it "The Railroad Men's War," accurately predicting that "bloodshed impends." In the next two weeks as the strike spread from coast to coast, through fourteen states, at least a hundred people were killed by state and federal troops, and hundreds more wounded. Property set afire or otherwise destroyed ran into the millions—five million in Pittsburgh alone. In Chicago, in one fiery orgy from July 26 to July 28, thirty to fifty people died and a hundred were maimed, while 10,000 special deputies, soldiers, police and others patrolled the streets.

How and why did it all start?

Not only the *Times*, but many journals, as well as clergymen, businessmen, and government officials called the walkout an "insurrection," a "revolution" initiated by "communists." The Philadelphia *Inquirer* charged that the malcontents "have practically raised the standard of the [Paris] Commune in free America." What began as a "riot," wrote Thomas A. Scott, president of Pennsylvania Railroad, in a long letter to the *North American Review*, "rapidly grew . . . to an insurrection." Allan Pinkerton called it a conspiracy hatched by Karl Marx's International. The strikes, he wrote, "were the direct result of the communist spirit spread through the ranks of railroad employees by communistic leaders and their teachings. When they were fairly begun, the communists commenced to grow bold and fairly defiant, and showed their hands; and when the strikes were well under way, every act of lawlessness that was done was committed by them."

In actual fact, though the "communists" did win some influence among strikers—especially in Chicago, St. Louis and Cincinnati—after the work suspension had been under way for some time, they were no more responsible for the "railroad men's war" than they had been for the "Long Strike" of 1875 in anthracite. Indeed, Karl Marx's First International had been quietly dissolved by a remnant of eleven delegates, meeting in Philadelphia exactly a year before; and the Workingmen's Party of the United States, formed in the same city at approximately the same time, comprised a mere 3,000 members at birth (mostly foreign born) and only 4,500 in 1877. The communists might have grown substantially in number had the strike lasted longer or been victorious, but they certainly showed that they lacked the means to foment anything approaching a nationwide strike, let alone an insurrection.

The fact is that even the existing labor movement, such as it was, had neither the resources or vitality at that time to undertake so grand a venture. The long depression, beginning with the 1873 panic, had enervated the movement, siphoning off its membership until it had fallen from 300,000 to a slim 50,000. More than two thirds of the thirty national unions had disappeared entirely, including the Knights of St. Crispin, which had claimed 50,000 adherents in 1872. So many unionists had been fired and blacklisted, writes Robert V. Bruce, that "labor organizations . . . turned to secret rituals, handgrips and passwords, met in secret, concealed their membership, their purposes, even their names." The "insurrection" of 1877 was certainly not their handiwork.

More realistic was a later report by a Pennsylvania legislative committee, investigating the violence in its state, which found not a shred of evidence that the riots were "a rising against civil or political authority." It ascribed them, instead, to "the general depression of business . . . by means of which many men were thrown out of work and the wages of those who could get work were reduced." Viewed thus, the "Railroad Men's War" was an unplanned upsurge by tens of thousands who had suffered the lash of economic slump in silence, until blind fury drove them into battle against what was then America's richest and most important industry.

II

The railroads were the pampered brats of the American economy. Not that their promoters were effete; on the contrary, they were bold, ruthless, piratical. Old "Commodore" Cornelius Vanderbilt built an empire out of $100 he borrowed from his mother to buy a barge in 1801. When he moved from shipping to railroads late in life, he drove the New York Central Railroad to its knees by the simple device of refusing to run his own Hudson Railroad, which connected to the Central, into Albany. By forcing the Central's passengers to slosh through two miles of snow and mud to make connections with a New York City-bound train at East Albany he forced down Central's stock to the point where he could purchase controlling interest for $18 million. Thereupon he passed around a few dollars to legislators at Albany to permit merger of the Central and Hudson, and recapitalized—"watered"—the stock of the company by $44 million, to almost double its value. His personal profit was $6 million in cash and $20 million in stock, an impressive dividend for a single operation.

Like his contemporaries in the railroads, Vanderbilt had nothing to do with the inventions that sired the industry. Back in 1804 a versatile inventor, Oliver Evans, put the steam engine on wheels and drove it on hard ground through Philadelphia's streets. Fourteen years later, another innovator, John Stevens, drove the "steamboat on wheels" over a narrow-gauge track on his estate in Hoboken, New Jersey, and in 1829 George Stephenson's locomotive, *Rocket,* dragged a thirteen-ton train over the tracks of the Liverpool and Manchester Railroad at the phenomenal speed of fifteen miles an hour.

Though there had been doubts originally that the rail lines could ever compete with canals, it became obvious after a while that locomotives were superior to steamboats. They were much quicker. They were not limited to the low terrain where canals or rivers flowed. They could reach almost anywhere, including the rear entrance of a grain mill or a factory, obviously making delivery easier than a steamboat could.

The first modern road, the Baltimore & Ohio, was completed in 1830, a mere span of thirteen miles from Baltimore to Ellicott's Mills. Almost simultaneously charters were granted for what was to become the New York Central and the Pennsylvania systems, and while most of these early ventures were feeder lines—to canals or rivers—they evolved in due course into trunk lines, transporting freight and passengers independent of the steamboats. By 1860, 30,625 miles of track had been laid, and from 1867 to 1873 another 33,000 miles, including the first continental line. By 1890 there were 167,191 miles of track in the country, and by 1900, there were 200,000. In economic terms the railroad was the single most important factor in the development of the nation during the last half of the nineteenth century. It made possible the settling of the West, the mass-production industries, the spurt in agriculture.

Americans generally and farmers in particular originally hailed the railroad with great joy. Innumerable yeomen invested in rail stocks, often mortgaging their farms to do so, and local communities offered bounties to have the lines run through their territories. No industry has ever been plied with such generosity by federal and local authorities—monopolistic charters, loans, subsidies for laying track, and enormous amounts of free land. From 1850 to 1871 the railroads received two hundred million acres of free land (later pared down to 137 million because some of the corporations failed to carry out their share of the bargain), a gratuity equivalent to the size of France or five times the size of New York State. The one grant to Northern Pacific alone in 1864 was equal in area to that of the six New England states. Two hundred and ninety-four towns, cities, and counties in New York gave the carriers $30 million to run tracks through their domain, keenly aware that access to transportation added value to their property. According to the governor of Kansas, four fifths of the municipal debt in his state in 1888 was committed to spur-railroad construction. Mitchell County offered $180,000 to the Santa Fe to run its line through its territory. Jewel County paid a bounty of $95,000 to the Rock Island for the same arrangement.

Harold U. Faulkner estimates that the land benefactions to the railroads "included one-fourth of the states of Minnesota and Washington; one-fifth of Wisconsin, Iowa, Kansas, North Dakota, and Montana; one-seventh of Nebraska; one-eighth of California; and one-ninth of Louisiana." The corporations were showered with three or four times as much acreage as was given to 377,000 families up to 1890 under the Homestead Act. It was in the public interest, Americans felt, to make these gifts, among other reasons because the rail lines eliminated dangerous and laborious trips in covered wagons, and made it possible for farmers to send their crops to Chicago or the eastern seaboard with a speed unknown before. It says something for the early popularity of the railroads that Ignatius Donnelly of Minnesota, a leader of the agrarian revolt for decades, felt no pangs of conscience, as a young congressman, for accepting a $10,000 "gift" from the Lake Superior and Mississippi Railroad Company. Encouraging the railroads was a means of settling the state.

It soon became apparent, however, that the railroad promoters were manipulating their way to unmatched riches, not only oblivious of public interest, but in opposition to it. They inflated construction charges, bribed legislators, watered stocks, arranged fraudulent bankruptcies, and passed on these costs to the public, in particular the farmers, in the form of higher freight rates.

Though there were some railmen such as James J. Hill of the Great Northern who performed valuable services for the farmer such as finding foreign markets for his products, a majority equated social consciousness with the weight of their own wallets. The Erie Railroad boosted its outstanding shares from $17 million to $78 million, with no appreciable new assets to show for it. In Kansas, $300 million of stock certificates were issued for 8,000 miles of rail, laid at a cost of $100 million. The *Commercial and Financial Chronicle* of May 15, 1869, noted that twenty-eight corporations had increased their capital value in less than two years by 40 per cent. It was not for naught that the rail tycoons won the title "robber barons." Typically, the La Crosse and Milwaukee Railroad, according to a Wisconsin investigating committee, had passed around a million dollars in bonds and cash to thirteen senators, thirty assemblymen, the governor ($50,000) and various newsmen to assure a land grant valued at $17 million.

The 1872 Crédit Mobilier scandal was an extreme example of railroad brigandage, but differed only in size and details from many others. Ten years previously, Congress had entrusted to the Union Pacific, in which Congressman Oakes Ames of Massachusetts was the key figure, the right to complete the trans-continental system from Omaha to California. The federal legislature was more than lavish in its endowment. It allotted the road two hundred feet right of way for hundreds of miles; the privilege of using whatever wood, stone, and other materials it found nearby; gifts of alternate sections of land running twenty miles on either side of the tracks; and credits of $16,000 to $48,000 for each mile of track laid. That Congress should be so considerate of a firm that could barely raise a half million dollars on its own is perhaps best explained by the fact that Ames spread around $436,000 where it would "do the most good," and promised instant wealth to a host of insiders, such as the future presidential candidate Senator James G. Blaine, and a future President, James A. Garfield.

Not content with this beneficence, however, the promoters assigned construction of the line to a company with a fancy French name, Crédit Mobilier, which they themselves controlled. Crédit Mobilier then charged Union Pacific $94 million for a road that cost $50 million to build, leaving a handsome profit of $44 million for Ames and his friends, which in the final analysis came from the federal government and the public. Ames was not wrong when he told envious friends he had hit "a diamond mine."

Nor was he alone in such machinations. Major stockholders of
Central Pacific formed a company which did $58 million construction
work for Central Pacific and charged it $120 million—a neat profit
for themselves of $62 million. All this and much more was possible
because the carriers bribed their way to wealth and held in their
vest pocket governors, senators, and many officials at the local and
state levels. Historians are in agreement that, until the agrarian
revolt changed matters, the railroad barons owned the political systems
of every western state. Union Pacific and Burlington, for instance,
were joint sovereigns of Nebraska; Santa Fe ran Kansas.

As supplementary acts in their quest for the fast buck, the carriers
squeezed little people and small business mercilessly. They gave
handsome rebates to John D. Rockefeller and his Standard Oil, for
instance, that made it possible for the oil tycoon to drive his competitors to the wall. They formed "pooling" arrangements which
boosted rates sky-high. Typically, President Garrett of the Baltimore
& Ohio reported to Junius Morgan, his London banker in March
1877, that as a result of a pooling deal with William H. Vanderbilt
of New York Central and others, he had raised freight charges by
50 per cent at one fell swoop. "The great principle upon which we
all joined," he wrote, "was to earn more and spend less."

Farmers and workers paid heavily for this "great principle." For
example, it cost 52½ cents in 1869 to ship a bushel of corn from the
Mississippi Valley to the seaboard where eventually it sold for 70 cents.
In the words of one wag, the farmer farmed corn, while the railroads
"farmed the farmers." The worker paid for corporate greed in low
wages and loss of limb through accidents. Brakemen in 1877 averaged
$1.75 for a twelve-hour day, for work so dangerous—coupling cars—
that according to Robert V. Bruce, "a brakeman with both hands
and all his fingers was either remarkably skillful, incredibly lucky, or
new on the job." In Massachusetts alone forty-two railroad workers a
year were killed through accidents, and since there were as yet no
workmen's compensation laws, the companies disclaimed liability, for
such accidents. A widow, unless she was prepared to settle for a vapid
condolence message, had to sue management in the courts to prove
it was the railroad's negligence, rather than her husband's, that
caused the accident.

The industry was so injury-prone that the early rail unions were
much less concerned with collective bargaining than with insurance
against mishap. The twelve locomotive engineers who met secretly in
Detroit in 1863 to form the Brotherhood of the Footboard (later
changed to the Grand International Brotherhood of Locomotive Engineers), called "post-mortem security" their main problem. The hand-

ful of conductors of the Illinois Central who formed a union later known as the Order of Railway Conductors in 1868 proclaimed as their object "material aid . . . from a fund attained upon the assessment plan, to disabled members . . . and their widows, children, and heirs." The Brotherhood of Firemen originated in 1873 when eleven men met to take a collection for an associate killed in a boiler explosion on the Erie the day before.

The railroads were the cornerstone of industrial feudalism in the last half of the nineteenth century, recognizing and receiving no checks on their power, either from government or the workers. They refused to accept state regulation, challenging the matter in the courts for decades. And they refused to recognize any right of their chattels to join unions. Michigan Central's president in 1864 instructed his superintendent to "find out who the [union] leaders are or were and be sure to let them go one at a time." Garrett of B&O fired a committee of firemen who tried (unsuccessfully) to make an appointment with him. Franklin Gowen of the Reading, fresh from his victories against the Molly Maguires, ordered his locomotive engineers either to quit their brotherhood or quit their jobs; when half of them went on strike he gave raises to the "loyal" men and fired the others. The Burlington—and others—required applicants for jobs to sign a pledge "in case of strikes or combinations [to] work faithfully for the company's interest, and . . . run my engine to the best of my ability . . ." "Capital," wrote the Scranton *Republican,* "cannot consistently advocate combination among the employers, and at the same time denounce it among the employed." But railroad management felt no qualms about its double standard.

III

In March 1877, the heads of four trunk lines, Vanderbilt of New York Central, Thomas A. Scott of the Pennsylvania, Hugh J. Jewett of the Erie, and Garrett of the B&O, met in New York to formalize the pooling arrangement referred to above. In addition they adopted a concerted plan to cut wages, and agreed to insure each other against possible strikes. One of the four would take the lead and if its employees walked out, the other three would subsidize it for its loss of profits. There was no urgent reason for this joint planning. Seventy-six of the weaker carriers had been placed in receivership the previous year, but over-all industry earnings generally were a bit higher than in 1873. What with wage cuts and other economies, operation expenses per mile of freight were one-fifth lower than before the economic slump, and most carriers either paid normal dividends or higher. New York Central declared its usual 8 per cent throughout the depression (10 per cent in 1875) and retained enough cash surplus so that real earnings were almost double the 8 per cent. Pennsylvania too paid its regular 8 per cent. There was no financial need to trim pay, except that it was accepted practice when there was a large labor surplus.

On May 24, the biggest corporation in America, the Pennsylvania Railroad, with a capitalization of $398 million and thousands of miles of track directly and indirectly under its control, announced a second 10 per cent wage reduction, to go into effect June 1. As the news spread, engineers, conductors, and firemen in their respective brotherhoods elected delegates to make a direct appeal to Tom Scott, Pennsylvania's president. Filing into his office in Philadelphia, three dozen workers confronted one of the truly powerful figures in the nation.

At fifty-three, handsome, bewhiskered, erect, and quiet-spoken, Scott looked more like a school principal than a rail tycoon. Yet, as Wendell Philipps, the great abolitionist leader, once said of him, he could make all thirty-eight state legislatures dance to his tune with the wink of an eye. It was in Scott's specially outfitted railroad car that Rutherford B. Hayes rode to Washington after receiving word that he had been confirmed in the disputed presidential election of 1876. Orphaned at twelve and a self-made man, he had begun his career with the Pennsylvania Railroad as a lowly station agent and climbed to its presidency in 1874.

The awe-struck delegation, meeting the great man for the first time, tried to explain the four points in their program: the rescinding of the wage reduction, regular runs, abolition of the "classification" system under which the company graded men's efficiency unilaterally, and free passes to take them home when there was a long layover. Scott, suave and persuasive, listened attentively, then rebutted each argument with spell-binding counterpoints. In the end he persuaded the men to accept their lot until times improved. Only one hundred longshoremen on the Pennsylvania's docks in New York broke ranks and downed tools after learning of the meeting's outcome. Their pay had been twenty cents an hour in 1873; fifteen cents in 1877, and was now to be reduced to 13½ cents. When Scott replaced the stevedores with clerks (whose own pay had dropped from $80 to $45 a month), and raised the ante to 14 cents, the strike collapsed. It appeared now that management's gambit had worked: the men would accept their lot, if not placidly, at least passively.

After all, there were at least a million workers jobless—some said 3 million—in a national population of 45 million. Hundreds of thousands of "tramps," for whom the Chicago *Tribune* prescribed "a little strychnine or arsenic," and other journals "a stout rope thrown over the limb of a tree," were roaming the land, seeking work and a place to alight. In New York alone one fourth the labor force was without work, and 30,000 homeless men sought shelter in New York's police stations each night. (They were called "revolvers" because city rules refused them a cell in any station for more than one night running.) "Never," wrote the Washington *Inter-Ocean,* "was a time . . . when a greater amount of misery, poverty and wretchedness existed than at the present time. . . . There are hundreds of well-born, well-bred, and well-informed men walking the streets without a cent, and without knowledge of where to get a dinner or bed." There were ten "tramps" ready to take a man's job in a nonce. Clearly, this was no time to be organizing unions or planning strikes—as the coal miners of eastern Pennsylvania, 3,000 textile workers in Fall River, Massachusetts, cigar makers, weavers, and many others had learned.

Yet, on a lonely Saturday evening, a day after the pay slash went into effect, a group of railroaders on the Pittsburgh, Fort Wayne & Chicago—a Pennsylvania subsidiary—met at Dietrich's Hall in Allegheny City, near Pittsburgh, and formed what they called the "Trainmen's Union." Disgusted with the feeble efforts of the brotherhoods and the discord between crafts, they decided on an industrywide organization, to embrace all the trades—engineers, conductors, firemen, switchmen, brakemen, etc.—and planned a quick organizing drive. The new union's leader was a tall, powerfully built young man, not yet twenty-five, named Robert A. Ammon. Son of an affluent insurance man, college-educated, Ammon had done a stint in the cavalry and kicked around in many places, here and abroad, before reaching voting age. In 1876 he finally settled down in the smoky Pennsylvania city, with his wife and child, and took a job as a brakeman. With a small private income to supplement his wages, he lived comfortably and peaceably for the next year, until the pay slice compelled him to call the Allegheny City meeting. Now he became a whirlwind. After enrolling a few hundred members in the new organization in the Pittsburgh area, all sub rosa, he set out on a three-week tour along the B&O line, the Pennsylvania, the Lake Shore, and other lines to recruit other railroaders. Thousands joined with little urging—the field was fertile, ready for an idea whose time had come.

The carriers were simultaneously and equally active. Informed by a host of paid spies of the workers' new organizing efforts, they began to fire the malcontents. Before a week had gone by B&O issued orders for discharge of all union members. Ammon himself, and others, were given the pink slip by Pennsylvania. Had the Trainmen's Union been more firmly rooted it might have survived these blows. Even so, Ammon and forty associates made a last try, issuing a call for a general strike to begin June 27. No one knows what might have happened had the men remained united, but some wanted a longer period to prepare a strike; others, fearful of the prospects, spread the word that the strike had been called off. To allay those rumors Ammon composed a telegram to the various lodges, only to find himself stymied when the railroads refused to send it over their telegraph lines. Amid all this confusion, the strike fizzled. Only two hundred men showed up for it in Pittsburgh. A handful of men tried to flag down a freight on the Pennsylvania line but were driven from the yards by police.

The Trainmen's Union was dead. Young Ammon went looking for a job in the Pennsylvania oil fields.

IV

Unionists claim that "no strike is ever fully lost." It softens employers for the next round and prepares a cadre of union leaders who will be heard from again. Among the impromptu commanders of the strike at Martinsburg on July 16, 1877, were men who had joined the Trainmen's Union in its brief flurry and were saddened by its abortive stoppage. It was they who now lit the fuse for the 1877 "insurrection." Having held out the night of the sixteenth and the next full day, their strike was spreading, as if carried by an undetectable virus, to Grafton, Keyser, and Wheeling, involving, all told, "600 belligerents." "They are more pugnacious than ever in their talk," reported the New York *Times*, "and declare themselves willing to fight any power for the sake of maintaining what they call their rights." At Grafton, railroad firemen slipped bolts and cut pump hoses between tenders and locomotives. A few strikebreakers were removed from their perches at pistol point. Seventy trains with 1,200 freight cars remained blockaded at Martinsburg. Reports persisted that four hundred to five hundred men were marching from Williamsport, Maryland, to join pickets in West Virginia.

The Berkeley Light Guards having fled in disarray the day before, West Virginia's Governor Matthews sent another militia force to the scene on Wednesday, but as everyone suspected beforehand, they were too sympathetic to the workers to be reliable, not to mention being slightly inebriated. Matthews and Garrett thereupon wired President Hayes for federal troops, and though none had ever been used in labor disturbances before—except for a small incident in Andrew Jackson's day—the Republican President immediately called up two companies of artillery and promised three more. Ironically, four months earlier Hayes had inscribed in his diary the credo: "My policy is trust, peace, and to put aside the bayonet." But that had applied apparently only to the defeated Confederate states which he had pledged to relieve of occupying troops, not to railroad strikers.

Three hundred riflemen, assembled in Washington and Baltimore, arrived in Martinsburg early on the nineteenth, reinforced with two pieces of artillery and Gatling guns. To test the strikers once more, two trains, heavily loaded with troops, were dispatched east and west, one to Baltimore, the other to Cumberland. Riding as fireman on freight 423, going west, was George Zepp, brother of the strike's "ringleader," who was arrested that day on charges of "rioting." So one brother went to jail, while the other, disregarding his own mother's pleas, brandished a pistol at the strikers as he boarded the cab. Both trains reached their destinations—though not without incident. At Sir John's Run, canal men pelted the train with stones, one of which hit George Zepp in the head; and at Cumberland, a sizable crowd, including school youngsters, jeered the crew and clambered aboard the cars. Up and down the road, rail workers tried to persuade blackleg engineers to leave their locomotives, only to be driven off at the point of bayonets.

Having succeeded with two freights on the nineteenth, the B&O tried its luck with sixteen on the twentieth. Again they left Martinsburg safely, headed for Cumberland, Maryland, and Keyser, West Virginia. At Cumberland, however, they ran into real trouble. A canal, rail, and rolling mill center, the town seethed with the discontent of the jobless, many of whom were literally starving. Gathering before the Queen City Hotel, disorderly crowds made up of the unemployed from the rolling mill, a few dozen "tramps," many boys fourteen to eighteen years old, as well as railroaders, began stopping the trains. Only one of the sixteen freights made it through the city, and that one was harried with pistol shots, one of which went through a strikebreaker's pants. When two strike leaders were arrested, swarms of people converged around the mayor's house and forced their release. Soon thousands of cars were immobilized.

With each crisis the B&O demanded more troops, and governors and the federal administration complied automatically. No one in authority seemed to have a better prescription for the trouble than "bayonets." Governor John Lee Carroll of Maryland, learning from the experience of West Virginia, avoided the error of assigning nearby local militia to the "insurrection." Instead Brigadier General James R. Herbert of the Maryland National Guard was instructed to call out the 5th Regiment and units of the 6th at Baltimore to re-establish order in Cumberland. They were to entrain at the Camden Station late in the afternoon.

The guard regiments, for some reason, were late congregating at their armories and a special alarm signal—"151"—rang at City Hall early in the evening reminding the men of their task. The alarm had the effect not only of mobilizing the militia but a distraught citizenry as well, suspecting something amiss. Baltimore then had about 125,000 wage earners, one third of them in the factories, as well as a large number of unemployed. Thousands soon gathered at Camden Station and as some of the troops came out of the armory on Garden Street they were greeted first with cheers, then with a barrage of stones. A dozen were injured. At Camden Station the guardsmen were confronted by a great mass which refused to stand aside. Their commander ordered the Guard to go through, and again a few dozen people were hurt—on both sides this time—but no one killed as yet.

At the 6th Regiment's armory the situation was even more ominous. The crowd on Front Street began breaking windows and harassing the guardsmen as they straggled into the armory, tossing one man into Jones Falls. At 8:15 P.M., after the train at Camden Station had been waiting more than three hours, the men of the 6th, blocked from leaving their headquarters, began firing in panic, indiscriminately into the crowd. "Give them hell, boys," someone outside shouted, "they're only using blanks." But there was live ammunition in the rifles and Thomas Byrne, a forty-year old register of voters in the Fifth Ward, fell with a bullet in his head. Successive companies moved out of the building in much the same way, with the crowd alternately retreating and reassembling, but intent on preventing the troops from boarding the train. Before long there was fighting along Baltimore Street, blood flowing freely. An adolescent boy, shot in the groin, lay screaming on the sidewalk. An Irish tinner, with no interest in the strike, was shot in the stomach and died within two hours. A fifteen-year old newsboy was killed, as was a shoemaker, a sixteen-year old who wanted to become a photographer, and a man identified by the New York *Times* as an "Arab." Of the soldiers only one man suffered a flesh wound.

By this time 15,000 strike sympathizers had gathered around the Camden Station, and someone set fire to the depot. Rumor spread that the whole city would be burned down before long. But the fire was put out quickly at the station, and nothing more happened that night except that the soldiers' train and all freights were immobile.

The next day more multitudes gathered on Baltimore Street. The saloons closed. Storekeepers boarded up their panes. President Hayes sent detachments to the scene from as far away as New York—again on the theory that troops from the immediate vicinity would inevitably side with the demonstrators—and he called up one hundred Marines from the Navy Yard at Washington. As night fell there was another engagement with police and militiamen at the station, scores of people being wounded; many hundreds arrested. In the aftermath, a lumberyard was set afire, a foundry attacked, and a train of oil cars put to the torch. By Sunday, with five hundred federal forces on land, a tenuous peace reigned. Thirteen people had been killed, dozens wounded.

v

There was by this time an unexpected continuity to the strike, from line to line, from city to city, as if a common, subconscious will moved tens of thousands of workers in the same direction. On July 18, the day before federal troops had arrived in Martinsburg, firemen in Newark, Ohio, stopped B&O freights, and after the usual plea from the carrier, Governor Thomas Young ordered four companies of militia to the scene. At Hornellsville, New York, an Erie Railroad center, Barney Donahue, who had been discharged earlier for protesting the wage cut, led fellow brakemen and firemen off the job, and added a new wrinkle to events by detaining passenger trains—usually unmolested—as well as freights. The governor of New York, an Erie director, needed little prodding to send six hundred militiamen to the junction town; he was disappointed, however, when the troops fraternized with the strikers.

Simultaneously unrest spilled over to the nation's largest line, the Pennsylvania. On July 16, the superintendent of Pennsylvania's Pittsburgh division had announced that certain eastward-bound trains would be "doubleheaders"—two locomotives pulling twice as many cars as one did previously. The number of firemen and engineers employed would remain the same as before but conductors and brakemen faced the prospect of a 50 per cent layoff. On Thursday, the nineteenth, when the doubleheaders were to start running, no one anticipated any trouble. The engineers had docilely accepted the 10 per cent wage cut and were not expected to raise a protest. Even the president of what was left of the local Trainmen's Union had no idea that any plans were in the wind, for he slept through the morning and didn't hear of the strike until he woke up at noon.

In the yards that morning, however, while the crews read of the "Railroad War" one hundred miles away in Martinsburg, a flagman named August Harris reported to his friends that he would not work the doubleheader scheduled to leave at 8:40 A.M. It was his own individual decision, taken without consulting anyone, but the rest of Harris' crew joined the plan immediately. Twenty-five other men were asked by the company to take their place, but they refused to budge and were fired on the spot. When management finally found three yard men to volunteer for the job, they were roughed up by two dozen of their fellow workers and forced to flee. Now, as each train came in, its crew joined the walkout and a small crowd of perhaps a hundred people gathered around the switch that controlled the main track near the Twenty-eighth Street crossing. A flagman who seemed to be leading the crowd shouted at a company official, who told him he had no right to stop others from working, that "it's a question of bread or blood, and we're going to resist."

In the next few hours the assemblage at Twenty-eighth Street grew to a couple of hundred, most of them workers from nearby iron factories and, of course, including the inevitable group of young boys who not only were bent on adventure, but reflected the attitude of their parents. What might be called a saturation process was evidently at work in the city of Pittsburgh that day. Men in all industries had absorbed one humiliation after another. Back in 1875 puddlers in the mills had struck for four long months against a 25 per cent wage decrease, and considered it a victory when it was whittled down to 10 per cent. Almost everyone in town hated the Pennsylvania Railroad, including businessmen who felt the company's freight rates were outlandishly high. When the mayor, William ("Billy") McCarthy was asked by the Pennsylvania's Chief Clerk, David Watt, for police protection, he responded lackadaisically—in part because his police force had been cut in half as a depression economy measure, and in part because he had been elected with a large labor vote and had little sympathy for the carrier. Sheriff Robert H. Fife, a mild-mannered middle-aged man, acted with more vigor with his forces, but his efforts to disperse the crowd were fruitless. At the urging of railroad officials, Fife appealed to the governor's office—Governor Hartranft himself was on vacation in the West—for troops, and a whole division of militia was ordered out. On the other side, strikers and millmen met at Phoenix Hall in the evening to proclaim their solidarity, pledging to fight on until wages were restored to pre-June levels, doubleheaders eliminated, and strikers re-employed.

No trains ran that Thursday or Friday—or for the next few days for that matter. The militia had been slow to mobilize, and were obviously so sympathetic to the railroaders as to be virtually useless. Late Friday not a single member of the 14th Regiment had arrived for duty and the other regiments were clearly short-handed and unenthusiastic about their assignment. Both at Twenty-eighth Street and at another center, Torrens Station, they did little to help move the two thousand idled freight cars. The Pittsburgh *Leader* reported that a "representative workingman" had told the assemblage at Twenty-eighth Street that "This may be the beginning of a great civil war in this country, between labor and capital." He was certain, said the newspaper, that the strikers could "easily" rout the troops if necessary, since "the laboring people, who mostly constitute the militia, will not take up arms to put down their brethren."

But if the militia in Pittsburgh was untrustworthy, there were soldiers available in Philadelphia with fewer inhibitions. Again, at the behest of the Pennsylvania, the 1st Division of the State's National Guard was called in from the City of Brotherly Love, and put aboard special cars provided by the railroad at 2 A.M. Saturday morning. Pennsylvania's president, Scott, was confident he would terminate "this business with Philadelphia troops."

The thousand Philadelphians, both workers and unemployed, who arrived at midday, after being stoned in Harrisburg, Johnstown and Altoona, began marching in fours along the tracks, with seventeen deputy sheriffs in front of them, holding warrants for the arrest of eleven dissidents. At the crossing they found a crowd variously estimated between five thousand and twenty thousand, tense and ready. A few boys threw stones, coal, shoes, sticks; demonstrators sitting on four loaded coal cars joined in with a hail of black gold. Once or twice a soldier pushed a bayonet into someone's back. So far the only injury in the Pittsburgh strike had been a black eye administered to Chief Clerk David Watt when he had tried to turn a switch. Most of the crowd had been convinced that the guardsmen would refuse to shoot, would in fact retreat. "Shoot, you sons of bitches," shouted one man, "why don't you shoot!"

The Philadelphia guardsmen, however, had boasted that they were going to teach the Pittsburghers a lesson. And they now did. Without formal order the muskets began firing two, three, four times a second. In less than five minutes it was all over; twenty people lay dead (none of them soldiers), and between thirty and seventy were badly injured, including fifteen militiamen, three children, and one woman. The actual numbers of casualties was never known because the crowd dragged with it many of its martyrs. As it fled in disorder, General Brinton gave the belated order to stop shooting.

Shooting, however, was no longer the problem. News of the carnage, passed by word of mouth, inflamed the people of Pittsburgh as never before. Many thousands of all classes, including doctors, businessmen, and members of the Pittsburgh militia were welded into a single force determined "to fight the Pennsylvania Railroad" and to send "every damned Philadelphia soldier . . . home in a box." Bands of young people invaded gunshops and the armory on Market Street for arms, and but for a bit of bad luck would have carried off 36,000 weapons from the Allegheny Arsenal, belonging to the U. S. Army.

Meanwhile the Philadelphians had retreated to the roundhouse at Twenty-sixth and Liberty, beleaguered on all sides. Men marched behind fife and drums as in real war, and sporadic shots rang out on both sides. Finally the crowd settled on a new weapon: fire. At 10:45 P.M. the first freight was set afire a couple of blocks beyond Twenty-eighth Street, and shoved down the grade. Coal, then oil cars were fed into the blaze, and firemen were prevented from dousing it literally at pistol and cannon point. By midnight the great fire could be seen a dozen miles away.

Clusters of incendiaries set the torch to whatever they could, and mounted a small cannon taken from the Pittsburgh militia which they aimed at the railroad's machine shop. General Robert M. Brinton, seeing the cannon poised at 2 A.M. that Sunday, ordered his troops to fire. Eleven more people on the strikers' side were killed or wounded; the cannon never got off its first shot. Still the war continued. In the morning the rioters set fire to freights filled with whiskey and pushed them toward the buildings held by the Philadelphians. By 8 A.M. the roundhouse and machine shop, as well as the surrounding block, were consumed in a massive blaze.

That day and the next looting and arson replaced law and order in Pittsburgh—and only the Pennsylvania Railroad seemed unhappy about it. Hundreds of miners from nearby towns came to witness the excitement; women brought sandwiches and coffee to the be-grimed men. A grain elevator went up in smoke as well as twelve tenement houses, stables, a cooper shop and small private homes. There was no safety valve, only a mob driven in fury. An effort by prominent citizens to effect a compromise with the Railroad went for naught; the company was in no mood for reconciliation. As of Monday morning the twenty-third, one hundred and four of its locomotives and 2,152 of its railroad cars of all kinds lay in ashes, not to mention the many buildings—a toll of more than $5 million, according to Tom Scott. An official coroner's report—undoubtedly low—claimed twenty-four people dead, five of them Philadelphia soldiers.

VI

Seven or eight days after the walkout in Martinsburg, the United States had the appearance of a nation near revolution. The Paris

Commune of 1871 was still fresh in many minds, and comparison with that historic event came easily. On July 22 the New York *World* asserted that the Smoky City was "in the hands of men dominated by the devilish spirit of communism," and on the twenty-fifth the New York *Times*, reporting on events in Chicago, headlined its story: "The City in Possession of Communists." "We look upon the importation of the communistic and like European notions," said the Reverend Henry Ward Beecher on the twenty-ninth, "as abominations."

Normalcy was certainly not the mood of the moment. In Pittsburgh it was the strikers themselves, plus volunteers from among those who had made common cause with them, who patrolled the streets to restore order. Governor Hartranft, returning from his vacation, mobilized 10,000 guardsmen, and President Hayes sent in three thousand federal troops to deal with the chaos following the massacre. It was like the chain reaction of nuclear fission, strikes breaking out on the railroads in two dozen more cities and a dozen other major lines, strikes of miners, mill men and many others. At Reading, Franklin Gowen's bailiwick, six strikers were killed Monday night, July 23, and the next morning there would have been much more bloodshed if the members of the 16th Regiment had not threatened to shoot the Easton Grays of the 4th Regiment if they molested the strikers any further. For the next two weeks the Governor traveled with troops from place to place—sometimes on wagons because no trains were available—to suppress the mass strike, and arrest its leaders.

In Washington, after July 20, President Hayes met with his cabinet every day to map military strategy. Soldiers and warships were deployed at the capital to guard its ramparts, while General Winfield S. Hancock tried to break the strike in Pennsylvania, and General John M. Schofield in West Virginia and Maryland. On July 25th, when almost all the lines in the central and western states were enveloped in the freight blockade, Hayes threatened to impose martial law throughout the country. The President like other "respectable" men, subscribed fully to the thesis propounded by *The Nation* magazine that "The right to seize other people's property and to prevent other men from selling their labor on terms satisfactory to themselves is denied by the law of every civilized country. Common sense does not allow any parleying over that fallacy, but insists that it be refuted with gunpowder . . ." Shades of Louis XVI in 1789 and a foreshadowing of the Czar in 1917.

The "mania" that hit the B&O at Martinsburg engulfed the Pennsylvania, the Erie, William H. Vanderbilt's New York Central and was moving westward with incredible swiftness, finally reaching the Central Pacific on the West Coast. This was a remarkable outcome for an unorganized affair—a labor strike where no labor union existed. The four existing railroad brotherhoods might have provided guidance, but the brotherhoods were essentially fraternal organizations more concerned with insurance than with collective bargaining. The Brotherhood of Locomotive Engineers had called a strike against the Boston & Maine in February 1877. But it ended in a debacle when the company put strikebreakers at the throttles. It also had been involved in the strike against the Reading, some months later, but had been checkmated in that situation by Franklin Gowen. With its treasury limping, the Locomotive Engineers—strongest of the four brotherhoods—was all but emasculated, and played no further role in the events of that year.

The one group that did try to give the Railroad Men's War a central focus was the Workingmen's Party. Though it had played no role in the original outbreak it tried both to consolidate support for the strikers and spread the stoppage. While the rioting was going on in Baltimore and Pittsburgh, the party held two meetings in Cincinnati —a few thousand people attending each—urging solidarity with "the downtrodden, outraged railroad employees," and as a result of the party's efforts, rail men of that city joined the walkout. In Boston, Philadelphia, New York, San Francisco, Paterson, Brooklyn, and Newark, the Marxist party organized protest meetings and proclaimed demands for the eight-hour day, abolition of conspiracy laws against unions, and nationalization of the railroads and telegraph lines. As a spinoff of the meetings, small detachments of leftists visited the rail yards to induce those still working to "down tools."

It was in Chicago and St. Louis that the Marxist influence made its greatest impact. Only six years before, the Windy City had been sent reeling by the Great Fire, but it was rebuilding rapidly. Its half-million population was heavily weighted with foreign-born, including 15 per cent German-Americans, large numbers of whom were confirmed Marxists. Along with the Bohemians, they formed the hard core of the Workingmen's Party, possessing a strength and solidarity that prompted the party to establish its national office in Chicago.

Among the handful of native-born in the leadership of the communist movement was Albert R. Parsons, destined to become world-famous nine years later when he was convicted for inciting the "riot" at Haymarket Square. Parsons' oratorical eloquence made him an idol of the many Germans who usually distrusted the native-born, even native-born communists. As news of the Great Strike filled the front pages of Chicago's press, including an upstart penny sheet, the

Daily News, sympathetic to labor, Parsons and his comrades held one meeting and conference after another to denounce capital and encourage support for the railroad men. "If the proprietor has a right to fix the rates and say what labor is worth," Parsons told one crowd, "then we are bound hand and foot, slaves, and we should be perfectly happy; content with a bowl of rice and a rat a week . . ."

The agitation by the Workingmen's Party helped in spreading and expanding the railroad strike. On Monday, July 23, forty switchmen of the Michigan Central walked off the job. The following morning they ran through shops and freight houses calling on others to join them, and were soon assisted by what the Chicago *Tribune* called "an uncombed, unwashed mob of gutter-snipes and loafers." Before sundown the "unwashed" were appealing not only to rail workers, but those in stockyards, factories, stores, docks, construction projects, transport—in all of commerce to join them. Wherever the mobs went they were chased by police, clubbed and arrested, but the wave was becoming a typhoon; a general strike was in the making, stretching from the railroads, Chicago's pride and joy, into all the industrial spheres. It could not be stopped.

With the strike enlarging hourly, Mayor Monroe Heath and the chief of police called Albert Parsons to City Hall for a heart-to-heart talk that proved to be prophetic. The socialist leader had been fired from his job earlier in the day after addressing a meeting of strikers and had been castigated by one of the papers as the "leader of the American Commune." Interrogated now by the authorities, in front of a group of businessmen, Parsons was told in flat language to go back where he came from. "Your life is in danger," he was told by the chief of police. "Those men in there belong to the Board of Trade and they would as leave hang you to a lamp-post as not. You'd better get out of town and get out quick." Parsons, of course, returned to his agitation. The Board of Trade meanwhile enlisted five thousand of the "better citizens," including Civil War veterans, as special deputies; federal soldiers nearby were put on the alert.

Parsons and his comrades in the party tried to hold matters in rein, repeatedly admonishing members against violence, but the violence was already under way in the form of police clubbings, dispersal of meetings and the shooting of blank cartridges at strikers and sympathizers. Wednesday and Thursday, the twenty-fifth and twenty-sixth, the strike flared into warfare and Chicago lapsed into anarchy. Lumbermen, tailors and factory workers left their normal posts to take to the streets. Sailors and longshoremen walked out at the ports; streetcars stopped running on the South Side; saloons were shut down. Merchants loaned their dray horses to police, thousands of men were given muskets by the authorities to defend the city from "communists." The Secretary of War in Washington dispatched an urgent telegram to General Philip H. Sheridan, who was fighting Indians in Sioux country, to return to Chicago at once. On the other side, all day Wednesday, fifty groups chased militiamen and the volunteer "specials." A thousand "radicals" hooted "scabs" and fought police on the "Black Road" along Blue Island Avenue leading to the McCormick Reaper Works. Locomotives were destroyed at the Burlington roundhouse on West Sixteenth Street.

By now the city was being patrolled by at least ten thousand regular officers, "specials," and troops. Scores of prominent citizens had left the city in fright. On Thursday morning a seesaw battle took place between police and soldiers on the one hand and ten thousand strike sympathizers on the other at the Halsted Street Viaduct. When it was over a dozen men and women on the labor side lay dead and another one hundred were arrested. A meeting at the Vorwarts Turner Hall on Twelfth Street was invaded by police, wildly wielding clubs in every direction. Scuffles, small and large, were under way in scores of places. The mob's anger, however, had burnt itself out after two days of battle, and with the steady arrival of more fresh troops. In the two days of fighting between thirty and fifty men and women had been killed, and many more wounded. The workers were unable to take any more bloodletting. On Saturday the first freight train left the yards, under military escort.

After Baltimore, Pittsburgh, and Chicago, what transpired in St. Louis was anticlimactic. It was noteworthy, however, because the Workingmen's Party briefly took control of the city. The party in St. Louis numbered about one thousand members, almost two-thirds German-speaking. On July 22 it issued a circular for a mass meeting calling on "the public to condemn the government for its action in sending troops to protect capitalists and their property against the just demands of railway men." That afternoon the leftists sent a mass of five hundred people across the Mississippi into East St. Louis, Illinois, where they were greeted by one thousand railroaders and friends with thunderous cheers. "All you have to do . . ." one speaker told them, "is to unite on one idea—that the workingmen shall rule the country." Within hours a strike engulfed East St. Louis, and the city was for all practical purposes in the hands of the strikers.

Back on the other side of the river in the next few days, the party was able to close down one business after another, in addition to the Missouri Pacific and other rails. Mississippi steamers tied up to the docks, factories, mills and shops were called out. Alarmed by events, the Laclede Gas Works canceled a 25 per cent wage cut that had gone into effect July 1 and the Missouri Pacific offered to reinstate the wage rates of May 15. By July 29 the city was paralyzed and, as Philip Foner notes, "the city authorities practically left the Executive Committee [of the strikers] in charge . . ." In St. Louis, as elsewhere, however, the establishment quickly recovered its poise to put down the malcontents. President Hayes sent in troops and merchants raised $15,000 to arm one thousand "specials." The Workingmen's Party could not withstand such pressures. To add to its woes, police raided its headquarters and arrested seventy-three of its leaders. Four were eventually sentenced to five years in jail and $2,000 fines.

After St. Louis the strike sputtered for a day or two, but the two-week "insurrection" had now spent itself. A simple stoppage to restore a wage cut had escalated to a political confrontation that took on some of the character of a civil war. But labor was too weak, and the combined forces of capital and the government too strong for the workers to prevail in the end.

4

The Bomb at Haymarket

The Long Strike of 1875 and the Railroad War of 1877 were defensive actions to avert wage cuts at a time when the advance of organized labor generally was sliding backward. The national strike for the eight-hour day that began on May 1, 1886, marked a change in proletarian direction. The movement had expanded since the setbacks of the 1870s and was poised for a major leap forward, the accomplishment of a dream held for generations.

The *National Laborer* had expressed the belief back in 1836, when the work day was still twelve hours long and often more, that "eight hours daily labor is more than enough for any man to perform." The demand was heard more fervently in the 1850s through the efforts of a few special groups launched specifically to win that objective and proclaimed at many labor meetings. Then in 1863 the Machinists and Blacksmiths Union and the Boston Trades Assembly jointly appropriated $800 to lobby for eight hours, entrusting the task to a relatively young machinist in his early thirties, Ira Steward. For Steward, who devoted his life to this one goal, the shorter workday was more than a means of gaining leisure; it would give the workingman an opportunity to study politics and formulate plans to check the "corruptions of capital." It was the only means, said Steward, to preserve democracy and emancipate workers "from slavery and ignorance and the vices and poverty." Steward's wife, Mary, composed a couplet, soon to be heard on thousands of lips:

> Whether you work by the piece or work by the day,
> Decreasing the hours, increases the pay.

On Steward's initiative hundreds of Eight-Hour Leagues were formed from 1865 to 1868, fifty in California alone, and together with the National Labor Union—founded by one of the noblest of labor leaders, William H. Sylvis—the agitation was accelerated. Responding to *vox populi* six states and a number of cities legislated eight-hour labor laws in 1868, and Congress passed a bill covering its own employees. Most of the laws, however, were full of glaring loopholes, some requiring, for instance, that both the worker and the employer concur before the shorter workday could become operative. In other instances wages were cut proportionate to the cut in hours, thus making the law meaningless. In the end the entire effort turned out to be a pyrrhic victory.

But the idea of the eight-hour day, which was latent during the bleak 1870s, became overt in the 1880s—as a combination of prosperity and interunion rivalry gave it momentum. The 1880s, despite the 1883–85 slump, witnessed fabulous economic expansion. Capital invested in manufacture zoomed from $2.8 billion to $6.5 billion, the number of factory hands doubled and five and a quarter million immigrants came to these shores seeking surcease from Europe's sorrow. Though labor shared minutely, if at all, in the materialist glories of the decade—President Grover Cleveland in 1888 spoke of the poor being "trampled to death beneath an iron heel"—no nation on earth was doing nearly so well over-all as the United States. There was a feeling in proletarian circles that capital could afford the shorter day (at the old pay) without too much strain, and that now was the time to get it.

The union rivalry referred to above was more subtle. It was between two organizations with unwieldy names—the Federation of Organized Trades and Labor Unions of the United States and Canada, formed in 1881 under the guiding hand of a Dutch-Jewish cigarmaker born in London, Samuel Gompers; and the Noble Order of the Knights of Labor, secretly established in 1869 by nine garment workers in Philadelphia. Neither was particularly massive in membership at the beginning of the decade, but by 1886 the Knights had spurted to 700,000 members, probably more than all the previous labor federations combined. A strike in 1885 against the three rail lines controlled by Jay Gould—the Wabash, the Missouri Pacific, and the Missouri, Kansas and Texas—had gained for the Knights a quick victory, restoration of a 15 per cent wage cut, and such acclaim that its national membership increased thirteenfold from what it had been in 1883.

Ironically, the Knights were opposed to strikes in principle. Terence V. Powderly, the vain but able former mayor of Scranton, who headed the organization in its most productive years, considered the strike "a relic of barbarism." It might be, he conceded, necessary on occasion, but was to be avoided as much as possible since it offered only "temporary relief." This thesis flowed inexorably from Powderly's doctrine that while there was friction between workers and capitalists, especially the greedier ones among the latter, there was no *fundamental* conflict between the two. And the strength of this attitude was reinforced by a long list of disasters: defeat of the telegraphers in 1883; of 4,000 coal miners in Hocking Valley after two years on the picket line; of 5,000 textile operatives in Fall River whose ranks were sundered by the import of Swedish strikebreakers; of building tradesmen in Buffalo; of molders and cigarmakers in Cincinnati; and so on.

Instead of strikes, then, the Knights of Labor concentrated on "uplift." It created two hundred producer and consumer co-operatives, agitated on the legislative front for such reforms as free land, the eight-hour day, abolition of child labor, the income tax, public ownership of railroads. And when it took action against rapacious capitalists, it was in the form of boycotts far more than strikes. In its day the Knights conducted the most successful labor boycotts in history—against newspapers, manufacturers and retailers of beer, flour, cigars, stoves, shoes, clothing, carpets, pianos, etc.

Naïve as this program of co-operation, reform, and boycotts seems today, it excited workingpeople passionately in the 1880s. The slogan of the Knights, "an injury to one is the concern of all," welded men and women into a religious solidarity that neither the AFL nor the CIO have ever been able to match. Many a socialist who believed in revolution rather than "uplift" joined the Knights because of its "beautiful watchword"—as one socialist put it.

In 1884 Powderly's organization was on the ascendancy, the Federation of Organized Trades and Labor Unions, though only three years old, in decline. Eschewing both "uplift" and revolution, the Federation, formed by representatives of about one hundred local and national organizations, promoted what became known as "simple" unionism. Its basic philosophy—and that of the AFL later on—was contained in a statement made to the Senate Committee on Education and Welfare in 1883: "We have no ultimate ends. . . . We are fighting only for immediate objects, objects that can be realized in a few

years. We are opposed to theorists. . . . We are practical men." Not
that these men were hostile to radicalism. To the contrary. Sam Gompers, as a young cigarmaker in New York, used to read socialist tracts
to his fellow workers as they rolled the noxious weed, and boasted he
was a socialist sympathizer. Peter J. McGuire, secretary of the carpenters' union, was a card-carrying member in the socialist movement.
But they believed that there was a time and place for revolutionary
propaganda, a time and place for trade-union activity, and that the
two were mutually exclusive. Being practical, they also rejected "uplift" as pie in the sky. They argued that the goals of labor ought to be
mundane—higher wages, shorter hours—and the primary instrument for
achieving them, when negotiations failed, the strike.

Much to the chagrin of the simple unionists, the American worker
was not yet buying their notion of practicality. Succeeding federation
conventions attracted a maximum of twenty-six and as few as nineteen
delegates. In an effort, therefore, to save itself from extinction the federation inaugurated an eight-hour campaign in 1884. Next year the
federation renewed its proposal and set May 1, 1886 as the date for a
general strike, nationwide, to attain the shorter workday. The federation, of course, was in no position to undertake such a venture on its
own—its membership at most was 25,000—and the leadership of the
Knights of Labor, while advocating an eight-hour day, intended to win
it on the legislative front, not through "relics of barbarism" such as the
strike. Nonetheless the call had electrifying impact, and if Powderly
shunned it, the "general assemblies" of the Knights, at the grass roots,
embraced it jubilantly. So did another force, the anarcho-syndicalists
of Chicago, whose role in the impending walkout was to prove more
important than that of any other.

The slogan "Eight Hours to Constitute a Day's Work" was so
popular thousands of laborers bought and wore "Eight-Hour Shoes,"
smoked "Eight-Hour Tobacco," and sang an "Eight-Hour Song."

> We mean to make things over;
>   we're tired of toil for naught
> But bare enough to live on: never
>   an hour for thought.
> We want to feel the sunshine; we
>   want to smell the flowers;
> We're sure that God has willed it,
>   and we mean to have eight hours.
> We're summoning our forces from
>   shipyard, shop and mill:
> Eight hours for work, eight hours
>   for rest, eight hours for what we will!

As the appointed day for the strike approached excitement ran high everywhere and particularly in the metropolis of Chicago where the anarcho-syndicalists were in the vanguard of events.

II

May 1, 1886, was a beautiful Saturday in Chicago, clear, with a bright sun beaming on the quiet panorama below. On Michigan Avenue, near the lake, thousands of men, women, and children exchanged pleasantries, joshed with each other, as they waited for the parade to begin. Elation was in the air: employers had aready granted the shorter workday to 45,000 workers in the city, incuding 35,000 in the packinghouses. All told, in the next couple of days, 340,000 men and women would down tools in 12,000 establishments nationally, almost a quarter of them in Chicago.

Waiting with the multitude was Albert Parsons, the young man who in 1877 had been warned by Chicago's police chief to leave town or be hung "to a lamp-post." Parsons was now thirty-eight years old, a national figure in the labor and radical movement, idol of both the native and foreign-born workers in his city. On the Sunday before, April 25, he and his close friend August Spies had addressed a massive rally of 25,000 in preparation for this parade and the accompanying strike. On the morning of May 1, the Chicago *Mail* gave the city an editorial warning that "There are two dangerous ruffians at large in this city; two skulking cowards who are trying to create trouble. One of them is named Parsons; the other is named Spies. . . . Mark them for today. . . . Make an example of them if trouble does occur."

With Parsons on Michigan Avenue were his lovely wife, the former Lucy Eldine Gonzales, and their two children, Lulu, seven, Albert, eight. Parsons, a trim, high-spirited man, logical in thought, poetic in expression—he often ended a speech with a recitation of poetry—was as much fitted, by his early background, to be a reactionary as a blazing radical. Youngest of three children in a solid middle-class Yankee family that traced its American heritage back to 1632, he was born in 1848 in Montgomery, Alabama, to which his parents emigrated immediately after their wedding in New England. Orphaned at five, he was sent to live on the ranch of his oldest brother in Texas, and was brought up by a black slave, Aunt Esther, who, he later recalled, was "my constant companion and had always given me a mother's love." At eleven Albert was apprenticed as a printer in Galveston and at thirteen, though short in stature, went to fight with the Confederate cavalry in the Civil War. A good horseman and an excellent shot, he remained with the southern forces until the end of hostilities.

Returning after four years of war, Parsons had second thoughts about having fought to uphold slavery; he could not face his Aunt Esther, now freed from bondage. Ultimately he had a talk with the black woman who had virtually been his mother; it was, he said later, the turning point in his life. He started publishing a small weekly in Waco, Texas, the *Spectator*, espousing the rights of liberated blacks. For a long time none of his white friends would talk to him; he received repeated threats of lynching. Nonetheless he continued publishing the paper until his money was gone, and often stumped for the Republican Reconstructionists—"scalawags"—who had similar views. By the simple process of extending his humanism from the race issue to social problems generally, Parsons became an ardent socialist.

In 1873 he married a comely girl of Mexican-Indian extraction, who lived with an uncle on a large ranch at Buffalo Creek. Lucy Gonzales was not only to be his wife but political comrade, and an important leftist figure in her own right many years after Albert Parsons had been hung from the gallows. The two newlyweds departed from Texas for Philadelphia in 1873, then Chicago. Here, as they were getting settled and Parsons took a job as typesetter for the Chicago *Times*, they observed the effects of the depression on the underclasses: the misery, the hunger, the demonstrations and police clubbings, the denial of free speech. They pored over the works of Karl Marx and Lewis Morgan to find an explanation for such tragedies, and in 1876 joined the Workingmen's Party. A year later, as already noted, Parsons was embroiled in the 1877 riots. He emerged with a national reputation and was called upon to address working-class meetings as far west as Nebraska and as far east as New York.

Meanwhile the socialist movement was in another of its interesting upheavals, enmeshed in a dispute between those who held that the party (now rechristened the Socialist Labor Party) could seize state power through elections, and those who claimed that elections or no, the bourgeoisie would never yield its position, unless compelled to do so by "armed resistance." Though Parsons had run for alderman in Chicago in 1877 and had put a local ticket on the ballot in 1880, he was one of the key figures that seceded from the SLP in 1881 to launch the Revolutionary Socialist Party. It was not a large group —5,000 or 6,000 members at its peak, one third of them in Chicago— and it was seriously divided from the outset. An eastern wing, under Johann Most, advocated "propaganda of the deed" and shunned existing unions; a western wing, under Parsons and Spies, considered

unions the embryo of the future society and work within them indispensable for creation of the "workers' commonwealth." Both subscribed to the theory that the state per se was the enemy of social
progress and that tomorrow's society would be run by some kind of
loose federation of producers' groups. But Parsons believed that
the Revolutionary Socialists had to work to alleviate the lot of the
worker immediately as well as for tomorrow; and it was this concept
which propelled his Chicago anarcho-syndicalists into national prom-
inence.

Taking to their task with vigor the revolutionists founded five
journals in 1884 and thereafter: the semi-monthly *Alarm* in English
(2,000 circulation, Parsons as editor), the daily *Arbeiter-Zeitung*
(3,600 circulation, edited by Spies, assisted by Michael Schwab),
two other German sheets, and one in Bohemian, the *Budoucnost*.
Within a year the anarcho-syndicalists doubled their influence, and
what was more, weaned away enough unions from the conservative
Amalgamated Trades and Labor Assembly, and unionized enough in
their own organization to become the dominant force in the labor
movement. Their Central Labor Council boasted twenty-two affiliates,
including the eleven largest locals in Chicago. They provided, in
addition to ideology and militancy, men of unquestioned talents
for leadership—Parsons, August Spies, Michael Schwab, Samuel
Fielden, a preacher, Adolph Fischer, a printer. It was such men as
these who gave the eight-hour movement its primary impetus in
1886. Had it not been for the Haymarket affair on May 4, this effort
might have become the rallying point for the national labor movement. The American Federation of Labor, organized that year, had
but 138,000 adherents, and the Knights of Labor was already beginning its decline into oblivion. What happened at Haymarket, however,
put an end to anarcho-syndicalist aspirations.

III

Parsons could not have suspected this on that warm Saturday,
May 1, as he, Lucy, and the two children marched in the front lines
of the procession to the lake front. There was an onimous atmosphere surrounding the parade: on the rooftops along the route,
police, Pinkertons, and militiamen were deployed with rifles poised,
and in the city's armories 1,350 National Guardsmen were waiting
nervously for a call to action. But no one paid much attention to the
sinister gunmen, and the parade took place without incident. At the
meeting site speakers vented their feelings on the eight-hour day in a
potpourri of languages, German, English, Bohemian, Polish. Spies,
thirty-one years old, with blue eyes and exceptionally white skin,

made a loud, dramatic speech that won the greatest applause. Parsons spoke eloquently discoursing with his usual logic about the need for proletarian unity if labor were to become invincible. The crowd went home encouraged and enlivened.

With the parade over, Chicago tightened to meet the bigger crisis —the strike for the eight-hour day. Once again the city was in a state of semi-paralysis. The building industry and metal foundries were silent. Lumber-laden ships had tied up at the docks and three hundred more were expected to follow suit. Some of the rail yards had already been shut down by a strike over another issue. Within a day or two 65,000 to 80,000 workers were walking picket lines. Employers, in small and large groups, were meeting frantically, at the Hotel Sherman and elsewhere to plan retaliatory strategy. Except for police clubbings to break up meetings, however, there was as yet no serious violence.

Trouble came on the afternoon of May 3—from another quarter. At the McCormick Harvester Works on the south side, 1,400 workers had been locked out since mid-February and were partly replaced by three hundred strikebreakers. Unrelated to that event, 6,000 lumber-shovers, on strike for eight hours, were meeting near Black Road, a few hundred yards away to select a committee for talks with the employers. While August Spies addressed them, the work shift changed at McCormicks, and some of the lumber-shovers drifted toward the harvester plant to help the locked-out workers heckle and attack the scabs. In a few minutes two hundred police arrived, and what had been a minor skirmish now became serious. Hearing gunfire and watching patrol wagons rush by, Spies and many others in his audience hastened to the scene—to be greeted with clubs and a hail of bullets. As the crowd scattered, at least four workmen lay dead, and more were wounded.

Blazing with anger, Spies headed for the *Arbeiter-Zeitung*'s print shop where he issued a fiery circular in English and German: Headed, "Revenge! Workingmen, to Arms!!!" The text read: "The masters sent out their bloodhounds—the police; they killed six of your brothers at McCormicks this afternoon. They killed the poor wretches because they, like you, had the courage to disobey the supreme will of your bosses. . . . They killed them to show you, 'Free American Citizens' that you must be satisfied with whatever your bosses condescend to allow you, or you will get killed. . . . If you are men, if you are the sons of your grand sires, who have shed their blood to free you, then you will rise in your might, Hercules, and destroy the hideous monster that seeks to destroy you. To arms we call you, to arms." It was signed "Your Brothers." A second leaflet called for a mass protest the next day at Haymarket Square on Randolph Street.

On the fourth, police continued their attacks on strikers—at Eighteenth Street and Morgan, at Thirty-fifth Street and elsewhere. In the evening 3,000 people showed up at Haymarket. Parsons, just back from a trip to Cincinnati, took Lucy and the two children to the event, expecting no trouble. When he arrived, Spies was speaking, and the crowd, on seeing Parsons, burst into applause. He mounted the wagon which served as a platform and told the audience: "I am not here for the purpose of inciting anybody," he said, "but to speak out and tell the facts as they exist." He finished at 10 P.M., and left for a nearby saloon with Spies. Mayor Harrison, who attended part of the meeting to see how things were going, left at about the same time, and advised police at the Desplaines Street Station, a half-block away, that everything was in order. The meeting's attendance was by now about a third of its original size, partly because it was late in the day and partly because a raw wind was blowing and rain beginning to fall. Just as Fielden was concluding a rambling speech the crowd suddenly noticed Captain John Bonfield coming at them with 180 policemen. The Captain, not known for his subtlety and dubbed "clubber" by working people, gruffly commanded the assemblage to disperse "immediately and peaceably." "But Captain," said Fielden, "we are peaceable." In that moment, without warning, there was an earsplitting explosion. Someone had thrown a bomb, probably from an alley, into police ranks. One policeman was killed on the spot, seven died later, sixty-seven were wounded. In the maddening confusion that followed, police fired wildly and clubbed everyone in sight. A number of citizens were killed—how many is unknown—and two hundred were injured.

To this day it has never been determined who threw the bomb. Police of course attributed it to an anarchist; Parsons claimed it was the work of an *agent provocateur*. "The possibility of an agent provocateur," comments Samuel Yellen in his chronicle of labor struggles, "must not be dismissed offhand. The police officials in Chicago were at this time quite equal to such a scheme." Another hypothesis was that the bomb had been produced by Louis Lingg, a carpenter and an anarchist leader, and thrown by Rudolph Schnaubelt, Michael Schwab's brother-in-law. But Schnaubelt was twice arrested and twice released. Governor John P. Altgeld, when he pardoned three of the convicted men in 1893—destroying his career in the process—postulated that "the bomb was, in all probability, thrown by someone seeking personal revenge," rather than as a political manifestation. Altgeld gave as justification "that for a number of years prior to the

Haymarket affair there had been labor troubles, and in several cases a number of laboring people, guilty of no offense, had been shot down in cold blood by Pinkerton men, and none of the murderers were brought to justice."

It did not much matter who actually threw the bomb, however, since the ten men indicted for the crime (one fled to Europe, another was released) were not charged with the actual murder, but with conspiracy to commit murder. What was on trial, it developed, was inflammatory speeches, writings, a political philosophy that called for liberation through violence. Only Fielden had been on the scene at the time of the explosion, but under the wide-ranging doctrine of "conspiracy" the other seven anarcho-syndicalist leaders could be tried for inciting the act. "Convict these men," cried State's Attorney Julius S. Grinnell, "make examples of them, hang them, and you save our institutions."

In the days that followed Haymarket, the newspapers, both in Chicago and throughout the nation, opened the floodgates of hysteria about unionism. "These serpents . . . ," shouted the Chicago *Tribune*, "have been emboldened to strike at society, law, order, and government." From the epithets hurled at the anarchists—"Dynamarchists," "Red Flagsters," "Bomb Slingers"—the general impression was that Parsons and his friends had themselves tossed the explosive, and so it was believed by a considerable segment of the population. The Chicago police immediately initiated a reign of terror. They arrested twenty-five printers at *Arbeiter-Zeitung*, wrecked presses, took subscription lists—used for further arrests—invaded radical offices, meeting halls, private homes and beat and tortured conspiracy suspects while in jail. "Make the raids first and look up the law afterwards," Grinnell instructed minions of the law. Everywhere the police announced they had found pistols, swords, rifles, ammunition, anarchist literature, dynamite, red flags. Nor was repression confined to Chicago: in Milwaukee the whole executive board of the local Knights of Labor was incarcerated, as were four officials of the Knights in Pittsburgh. Leaders of District Assembly 75 in New York were held on charges of "conspiracy" for conducting a strike against the Third Avenue Elevated.

Parsons, expecting the worst, went into hiding at once and only surfaced six weeks later when he calmly walked into court to stand trial with his comrades. Meanwhile Spies, Schwab, Fielden, Lingg, Adolph Fischer, a printer, Oscar Neebe, a beer-wagon driver, George Engel, a toymaker, had been picked up and in quick order indicted for conspiracy to kill patrolman Mathias J. Degan. The trial in Judge Joseph E. Gary's courtroom was a travesty. Candidates for the jury had been chosen by a special bailiff, instead of being selected at random. One of those picked, after the defense had exhausted its peremptory challenges, was a relative of a police victim. Others frankly conceded their prejudice against the accused but were permitted to serve anyway. Altgeld, in his later pardon message, asserted that "much of the evidence given at the trial was a pure fabrication . . ." Witnesses contradicted each other, some obviously lied. The jury was inundated with anarchist writings and documents, indicating that what was really on trial was a philosophy, not men charged with specific crimes. And, as expected, the jury found all eight guilty. Seven were sentenced to be hung. Neebe was given a fifteen-year prison sentence.

On November 11, 1887, after all appeals had been exhausted, Spies, Engels, Fischer and Parsons, mounted the gallows. Lingg had already cheated the hangmen by exploding a dynamite cap in his mouth. Schwab and Fielden had asked for executive clemency and had had their sentences commuted to life imprisonment by Governor Richard Oglesby. The other four were executed. With nooses around their heads, waiting for the traps to be sprung, Fischer cried out: "Hurrah for Anarchy—this is the happiest moment of my life." Parsons said: "Will I be allowed to speak, O men of America? Let me speak, Sheriff Matson! Let the voice of the people be heard! O—" From inside his hood, Spies made a short statement which would be heard for decades in working-class circles: "There will be a time when our silence will be more powerful than the voices you strangle today."

IV

On the heels of Haymarket the strike over the eight-hour day virtually disintegrated. Scores of thousands drifted back to work before the end of May, without gaining their objectives, and many who had secured the shorter work day in advance, such as the 35,000 packing-house workers in Chicago, saw the policy change rescinded. "It may be fairly assumed . . . ," reported *Bradstreet's*, a businessman's organ, in January 1887, "that so far as the payment of former wages for a shorter day's work is concerned the grand total of those retaining the concession will not exceed, if it equals, 15,000."

5

Naval War
at Homestead

The aftereffects of the Haymarket crisis on the labor movement
were distressing. Aided by the press, the view gained prevalence
that the explosion of May 4 simply climaxed a decade of labor criminality that had begun with the Molly Maguires and the 1877 "insurrection." Cartoons and news stories portrayed union leaders as arson-
ists and murderers. Quick to take advantage of the public mood,
legislatures passed a host of anti-labor bills, courts convicted a considerable number of strikers on the charge of "conspiracy." Employers
fired union leaders wholesale, and blacklisted them so that they could
not find similar work anywhere. Spies were insinuated into the labor
movement by the hundreds; worker committees that sought to discuss
grievances were as often as not discharged on the spot and driven off
company property.

Haymarket, of course, obliterated the anarcho-syndicalists as a force
in the labor movement. For different reasons, the Knights of Labor
also began to disintegrate after Haymarket. Apart from the fact that
the press linked it with the bomb-throwers as the object of poisonous
attack, its own members became disillusioned about Terence Powderly's lukewarm approach to strikes. He not only had opposed the eight-
hour stoppage, but had an unfortunate habit of leaving workers in the
lurch during their greatest travail. Samuel Gompers accused him of
letting down laundry workers in Cohoes, clothing cutters in New

York, railroaders in the Southwest and butchers in Chicago by acceding "to the demands of the employers" when there was no need to give in. In 1887 and 1888 the Grand Master workman, Powderly, turned a cold shoulder to appeals for strike funds by 7,000 shoeworkers locked out in Massachusetts, thousands of men on the Reading Railroad, steelworkers at Andrew Carnegie's mill in Braddock, Pennsylvania—though all were affiliated with the Noble Order. Not for naught did steelmaker Carnegie hail Powderly as "one of the wisest counsellors that labor ever had." The Knights slipped from 700,000 members in 1886 to 510,000 in 1887, to 222,000 the following year.

The vacuum in the movement created by the demise of the anarcho-syndicalists and the decline of the Knights was filled primarily by the American Federation of Labor. And with this occurrence, simple, "practical" unionism found its day in the sun. Inaugurated in December 1886 through an amalgamation of the remnants of the Federation of Organized Trades and Labor Unions and of dissident Knights of Labor assemblies, the AFL was not an instant success. But it survived and it forged slowly ahead. Its president, Samuel Gompers, was a small whirlwind. He consolidated hundreds of local unions into national organizations of their respective crafts, and made them the epicenter of the movement—replacing the city central bodies which had done most of the organizing, fund-raising, and strike guidance until then.

Immensely intelligent, as well as imaginative, Gompers avoided conflict in situations where the odds were adverse. At the 1888 AFL convention, for instance, a resolution passed calling for another general strike for the eight-hour day. A realistic assessment of forces convinced Gompers, however, that he did not have the troops for so grand an effort. Instead it was decided to take on one industry at a time, beginning with construction where the AFL had its strongest contingent of members. In accord with this plan, Peter J. McGuire's Brotherhood of Carpenters and Joiners, then the largest AFL affiliate, with 28,000 members, took the lead. In a spate of stoppages, in May 1890, the Brotherhood won eight-hour days in thirty-six cities and nine-hour days in 234 other localities, covering altogether 55,000 carpenters. It was, writes Robert A. Christie, historian of the union, "the most enormous victory which had ever been won by trade unions in America" up to that time. In the reflected glory of this success—and others—the AFL slowly enlarged its ranks, doubling its original 138,000 membership by 1898. Of greater significance, the union survived the depression of 1893—the first national federation of labor in U.S. history to outlive an economic slump.

II

For all of Gompers' competence and the AFL's durability, the organization suffered from an inherent weakness which became strikingly apparent in the labor war at Homestead, Pennsylvania, in 1892. The Federation had catered primarily to skilled workers, leaving the unskilled to the winds of fate—and their bosses. Gompers, it is true, wooed and won over a few industrial unions to the AFL cause, such as the coal miners, but in accord with the precepts of practicality, he concentrated on the skilled, those with a "trade." This might have been a valid approach in 1860 or 1870, when small-scale enterprise predominated American commerce and the quotient of craftsmen in industry was high. It was a position increasingly less viable, however, as technology opened the door to massive factories, and financial manipulation to pools, trusts and monopolies. With yeoman's effort the AFL might thrive in decentralized industries where aggregates of capital were relatively small and competition brutally fierce. But when it confronted one of the new titans it ran the same gamut as the anarcho-syndicalists or the Molly Maguires. It was poorly prepared for the kinds of things that happened at Homestead.

This town of 12,000, seven miles east of Pittsburgh, was dominated by one of Andrew Carnegie's steel mills, which employed 3,800 workers. Back in 1889, as a result of a short stoppage in which strikers routed one hundred deputies, the Amalgamated Association of Iron and Steel Workers had been able to establish six lodges, with eight hundred skilled members, and negotiate a sliding scale of wages, much like that in the anthracite fields during Molly Maguire days. Wages were pegged to the price of 4×4 Bessemer steel billets, going up or down with the market, but in no case lower than the wage that corresponded to a billet price of $25 a ton. Under this pact, set to expire June 20, 1892, the eight hundred craftsmen earned $180 a month, a very respectable wage in 1889. The Amalgamated, one of the oldest unions in the country and the second-largest AFL affiliate, with 24,000 adherents, seemed to be headed toward labor glory, with the cornerstone of the American factory system, steel, on the verge of domestication.

But the fact that Carnegie had yielded once did not mean he would do so again. The canny Scotsman was an industrial giant, one of the three men—along with John D. Rockefeller and J. P. Morgan—who dominated U.S. business in the last quarter of the nineteenth century. When he sold his empire to the Morgans in 1900 it was producing three million tons of steel and earning an annual profit of $40 million. The empire was powerful beyond anything that the AFL had ever challenged before. And Carnegie himself was a rags-to-riches potentate who had seized the opportunity, as technology hurtled steel into the forefront of American industry.

When Carnegie, born in Dunfermline, Scotland, landed in Allegheny City, Pennsylvania, in 1848, at the age of thirteen, pig iron was the chief metal used in industry, steel a rare commodity reserved mostly for fine cutlery. In 1856 two Englishmen, Henry Bessemer and Robert Mushet developed the Bessemer process, which revolutionized steel production and relegated iron to secondary industrial status and use. The process was introduced in America at Wyandotte, Michigan, just at the time that Andrew Carnegie, twenty-nine years old, was making his first fortune. Virtually uneducated, he had advanced from bobbin boy in an Allegheny City cotton mill to messenger and telegraph clerk for the Pennsylvania Railroad in Pittsburgh (where he hitched his star to that of Thomas A. Scott), and finally had become a part-time speculator in various businesses, which were netting him $50,000 a year or thereabouts by 1863.

Bright, incredibly ambitious, a super-salesman—his outstanding characteristic—Carnegie left the Pennsylvania, opened an office for dealing in rail securities, and attended to his own ventures, one of which was a Pittsburgh mill. The average capitalization for a rolling mill in the Pittsburgh area before the war had been a mere $156,000; the largest one, the Cambria Iron Works, was then assessed at a million. In 1874, when Carnegie became senior partner in the Edgar Thomson Steel Works—the first plant to use the Bessemer process in the U.S.—the size of investments had grown massively. Steel mills cost millions, then tens of millions, and somehow Carnegie always assembled the right partners and raised the required monies to be able to buy and build new facilities, while remaining financially independent of the clutches of J. P. Morgan on Wall Street. Beginning with Edgar Thomson he expanded his empire to include two other plants, at Homestead and Duquesne, then a bridge company, additional blast furnaces, coke properties, iron works and a couple of railroads. Carnegie himself knew little or nothing about operating steel mills—or most of his other investments for that matter. His forte, as mentioned above, was salesmanship. He left the mundane matter of day-to-day supervision to such geniuses as Billy Jones or Henry Clay Frick, while he traveled abroad, consorted with celebrities like Herbert Spencer, collected art works, and cabled business directives only on major decisions.

Carnegie, for all his wealth, was no troglodyte like some of his peers—Commodore Vanderbilt, for instance. He believed with other Social Darwinists that only the "fit," those picked by nature, could or should grow rich. But he had a unique attitude toward wealth. A man's life, he said, should be divided into two phases, one in which he made his fortune and the other in which he gave it away. No man, he told an English friend, ought to die rich. Carnegie himself still had a few dollars when he passed on in 1919, but befitting his own preachings, publicized in articles and books, did give away $10 million for libraries from 1881 to 1900, and $50 million more for a host of projects in the next two decades.

His views on labor, at least abstractly, were also enlightened compared, for example, to those of Jay Gould or Franklin Gowen. "The right of the workingmen to combine and to form trades-unions," he wrote in the *Forum* of April 1886, "is no less sacred than the right of the manufacturer to enter into associations and conferences with his fellows, and it must be sooner or later conceded." While deploring violence, he understood, he said, "the terrible temptation to which the working-man on strike is sometimes subjected. To expect that one dependent upon his daily wage for the necessaries of life will stand by peaceably and see a new man employed in his stead is to expect too much."

Yet in practice Carnegie's behavior differed not one whit from that of his contemporaries. Emperors, even benevolent ones, are invariably tempted to wield their power, especially when they are in contention with midgets. By 1892 the "Star-Spangled Scotchman" decided to destroy the Amalgamated Association of Iron and Steel Workers. He did not do it himself; he left the sordid task to his major domo, Henry Clay Frick. Frick, owner of large coke properties later absorbed by Carnegie, was remorselessly anti-union. He had already gained notoriety by using the Coal and Iron Police, the Pinkertons, and the state militia to suppress strikes in the coke regions. He now put his talents to work at Homestead.

The Frick campaign against the Amalgamated Association proceeded at two levels. In negotiations for a new agreement, the company demanded that the skilled men accept a wage cut—and did not budge from that position through four months of haggling. According to management's Superintendent J. A. Potter the reduction would amount to 18 per cent, and affect only 302 men. According to the union committee, the proposal would ultimately slash everyone's pay, including that of the unskilled, by 26 per cent. Either way, the figures did not really matter, for on a second level Frick was preparing for war. He had already received a private message from Carnegie, on April 4, defining the company's labor policy for the future: "As the vast majority of our employees are Non-Union, the Firm has decided that the minority must give place to the majority.

These works, therefore, will be necessarily non-union after the ex-
piration of the present agreement." To convert a union shop to non-
union status requires either that the union surrender or be defeated
in battle. Frick, on May 30, laid down the terms of surrender: if the
Amalgamated refused to accept the Carnegie company proposal—"the
most liberal that can be offered"—management would put it into
effect on its own and would bargain with the men henceforth only
individually. He urged the union committee to adopt the non-union
"system in vogue at Edgar Thomson and Duquesne."

No self-respecting union, of course, could accept such an ultimatum
—especially in a period of prosperity when the industry, like others,
was booming. Frick doubtless understood that, because concurrently
he prepared for the inevitable smashing of the union. He built a
three-mile, fifteen-foot-high fence on three sides of the property (the
other side faced the Monongahela River), topped with barbed wire
and equipped with searchlights. At regular intervals slits were cut
into the fence, obviously for rifles, though the company later insisted
before a congressional committee that they were solely for "observa-
tion." A would-be poet, quoted by Philip S. Foner, described "The
Fort That Frick Built" thus:

> Twixt Homestead and Munhall
> If you'll believe my word at all
> Where once a steel works noisy roar
> A thousand blessings did pour
> There stands today with great pretense
> Enclosed within a whitewashed fence
> A wondrous change of great import
> The mills transformed into a fort.

Frick's plan was elaborated with military precision. The fence would
hold off strikers while Pinkertons escorted strikebreakers into the
plant by boat and barge from the Monongahela River side. Twenty
foremen were sent to major cities to beat the bushes for 260 skilled
workers—a minimum needed to begin operations—and an arrangement
was made with Robert A. Pinkerton to supply three hundred detectives. In a letter of instructions, Frick outlined the strategy for the
forthcoming sorties: the three hundred Pinkertons were to be assembled at Ashtabula, Ohio, on July 5, brought by rail to Youngstown,
where they would be placed on barges at night, and then towed
by steamboats along the river to Homestead. The barges would be
converted into second homes, with dormitories, bunks, tables, and
other accommodations; the detectives were to receive five dollars a
day for their labors and to be deputized by the local sheriff once

they were inside the plant. Since it was illegal to transport a private army across state lines, pistols, clubs, rifles, and other paraphernalia of war would be sent on to Homestead separately.

A committee of the House of Representatives subsequently concluded that while Frick had a "legal" right to hire "watchmen . . . yet we do not think, under the circumstances, he should have done so." The committee was especially critical of the fact that the Pinkertons had been engaged "before the negotiations . . . [with] the Amalgamated Association were broken off," indicating that Frick never had any intention of coming to terms with the union. The men in the mill sensed this too, for on June 28 they hung Frick and superintendent Potter in effigy on plant grounds and physically prevented the effigies from being cut down. At this point the company began banking its furnaces—two days before the contract expired—and locking its men out. Though the lodges of the Amalgamated Association had taken no strike vote and still hoped for further conferences to effect a compromise, the decision was taken out of their hands. Whether or not they wanted it, they found themselves on strike.

One of the interesting and indeed ironic aspects of what followed was that the unskilled and semi-skilled workers, shunned by the craft-conscious Amalgamated, nonetheless threw in their lot with the skilled. At a mass meeting on June 30 they pledged solidarity with the strikers. An Advisory Committee of fifty, headed by an intelligent young Irishman named Hugh O'Donnell, took over direction of affairs, drafting plans to patrol the town, the mill, and, with a launch and small boats, the river. Any sign or movement indicating that the Pinkertons were coming—everyone by now knew of the Frick scheme— would be met with a set of signals, or at night, rockets, so as to mobilize one thousand workers in five or ten minutes.

On July 5, as planned by Frick, the Pinkertons were transported in darkened coaches to Davis Island Dam, a few miles below Pittsburgh, put on two barges—where they changed to their blue uniforms—and were given Winchester rifles. Despite all the complicated maneuvers to keep the massing a secret, the strikers learned of the Pinkerton "navy" before it had moved much beyond Pittsburgh. The little flotilla of union boats, led by the steam launch *Edna*, went out to meet the enemy. On shore, thousands of men, women, and children broke down the fifteen-foot fence that Frick had built and stormed to the river banks to prevent a Pinkerton landing. The first Pinkertons did try to embark at 4 A.M., and a shot rang out, then another and another. People were wounded on both sides. The Pinkertons, however, made the mistake of using the steamers they had to haul away injured detectives, thus leaving their barges immobile and stranded.

What followed was a day-long battle like those in wars between nations.

The detectives cut holes in the barges for occasional fusillades. From shore, the steel men put oil-soaked barrels on a flatcar, and after setting the barrels ablaze, pushed the flatcar toward the besieged Pinkertons. When this failed to ignite the barges, oil was poured directly on the waters and a small brass cannon shot off to set fire to the fluid. The wind was unfavorable and again the "enemy" was saved. By 5 P.M., however, it was obvious to the isolated Pinkertons that they were helpless. They ran up the white flag of surrender, were taken into custody, and paraded through town to the skating rink, taunted by strikers' wives and children along the way. Only the intervention of O'Donnell saved some of them from being lynched.

The toll in thirteen hours of fighting, from 4 A.M. to 5 P.M. was at least nine steelworkers dead, and three "guards." After the detectives were taken off the barges the proletarian "navy" set them afire. In a military sense it was a total victory for the workers, but it was only a preliminary engagement. Unions throughout the country rallied to the Homestead cause, a glass union in Pittsburgh demanding that the city council give back a million dollars Carnegie had donated for a library. Other unions held meetings, passed resolutions against the "hired thugs of the many times millionaire Carnegie," and sent thousands of dollars for relief. An AFL organizer in New Orleans expressed regret that the men at Homestead had "left a living Pinkerton man get away," and even in far-off England demonstrations were held to censure the steel magnate. Democratic members of Congress, in both houses, denounced the steel baron for asking his workers to take pay cuts while pocketing vast profits as a result of the recently passed McKinley tariff, which imposed levies of 55 per cent on iron imports and 70 per cent on steel. In free-trade papers, Carnegie was castigated as "Baron Carnage-y."

The press generally, however, reviled the strikers with the now customary epithets—beasts, traitors, murderers. E. L. Godkin's *Nation* trotted out its old prejudices against strikers who try "to deprive rich men of their property and poor men of their right to labor." Congressman William C. Oates, who headed an investigating committee, echoed these sentiments in a pontifical defence of the "right of any man to labor, upon whatever terms he and his employer agree, whether he belongs to a labor organization or not . . ." Neither of them, as Samuel Yellen points out, appreciated the striker's dilemma: "if he did not picket he was reduced to looking on while his job was given to a scab; if he did picket he transgressed the laws and ideals of the land."

On balance the weight of national opinion—despite the press and management-oriented legislators—seemed to be with the strikers. Republican Party leaders were so fearful that the little war on the Monongahela might jeopardize President Benjamin Harrison's chances for re-election that they sent vice-presidential candidate Whitelaw Reid to make a special appeal to Carnegie to come to terms with his workers. Another Republican luminary was sent to speak with Frick. Pressure on the steel firm was also exerted by a sympathy strike, in mid-July, of workers at three smaller Carnegie mills.

Frick and Carnegie, however, would not be intimidated. As the strike continued, they issued a statement "that the Homestead mill hereafter will be run non-union, and the Carnegie Company will never again recognize the Amalgamated Association nor any other labor organization." On July 10, they finally prevailed on Governor Robert E. Pattison, who had rejected previous appeals, to send in the troops, against their employees. Major General George R. Snowden mobilized eight thousand National Guardsmen and headed for Homestead, which in his opinion was consumed with "revolution, treason, and anarchy." The strikers had the queer notion, he said, that "the works are theirs as much as Carnegie's."

With troops patrolling the city, the company sent out seventy recruiters to hire "replacements." In its mill yard it built one hundred bunkhouses, kitchens, dining facilities, in preparation for the arrival of the expected strikebreakers. When they arrived—two thousand eventually—the striking steelworkers were helpless. In the face of militia bayonets, they could do nothing. Moreover, in addition to the militia and the Pinkertons, they had the courts to contend with—a typical united front in the labor wars. On July 18, O'Donnell and six other strike leaders were arrested on the charge of murdering a Pinkerton agent named T. J. Connors. The men gave themselves up and were released, after a night in jail, on $10,000 bail each. The union reciprocated by having murder warrants issued against Robert and William Pinkerton, Frick, and five other Carnegie officials, who also had to post $10,000 bail each though they did not spend a night in jail.

In August there were sixteen union leaders under indictment, and on September 22 a grand jury returned 167 true bills against thirty-four unionists for murder, conspiracy, and aggravated riot. And that was not the end of legal reprisal. A few weeks later State Supreme Court Justice Edward Paxson, on his own initiative and without a prior grand jury investigation, ordered the arrest of twenty-seven workers for "treason" against the state of Pennsylvania. Nothing ever came of any of these charges. The state, with a Carnegie lawyer helping the prosecution (much as Franklin Gowen had done in the Molly Maguire cases), put Sylvester Critchlow on trial after the strike was over, for the murder of Connors, but he was acquitted after only one hour of jury deliberation. In the next four months O'Donnell and another union man were similarly freed, and an agreement was reached to drop all other prosecutions, including those against the company and Pinkertons. But the harassment drained union funds and energies.

While the militia and the courts were engaged in these offensives, the strike boiled down to the usual question: could the men hold off the ravages of hunger long enough to outlast the company and the health of its finances. Relief funds were still coming in to the workers generously, but it cost $10,000 a week to feed 1,600 people in need of relief, a monetary drain that could not go on indefinitely. The company was having its troubles too. The scabs hired were inexperienced for the skilled tasks assigned them, requiring training that would take months. Frick therefore tried another gambit to get his old hands back. He posted a notice advising them either to return to work within five days or be permanently severed. No one returned.

The martial law, arrests, bail requirements, and influx of scabs, however, finally had its impact on the workers. By mid-October strike funds were dwindling, some strikers were calling for a return to work and others had left the city for jobs elsewhere. On November 5, the leaders of the Amalgamated Association came together in Pittsburgh to discuss a last, desperate measure—asking the AFL to declare a national boycott against Carnegie's products. But the union soon decided, to the relief of Gompers, only to request a more active solicitation of relief money.

On November 20, 1892, after five long months, the Amalgamated men voted by 101 to 91 (many among the eight hundred had forsaken Homestead for greener pastures or had lost interest) to reapply for their jobs. The strikers at Beaver Falls gave up at the same time, and though the lodges at Union Mills officially conducted their strike until August 1893, when only fifty-three men were left for picket duty, the mills had long since been in normal operation.

The plutocratic steelmakers could savor a major success. "Our victory is now complete and most gratifying . . . ," Frick wired Carnegie, vacationing in Italy. "Do not think we will ever have serious labor trouble again. . . . We had to teach our employees a lesson and we have taught them one that they will never forget." To which Carnegie replied an amen. "Life worth living again. . . ." read his return cable. "Surprising how pretty Italia . . . congratulate all around."

The sweet taste of victory was marred for Frick only by an incident that had occurred months before, on July 23. A young anarchist, Alexander Berkman, an admirer of the Haymarket martyr, Louis Lingg, and a lover of the flamboyant anarchist Emma Goldman, who was to leave quite a mark on organized labor herself, decided to settle accounts personally with Frick. He went to Homestead and burst into Frick's office where a porter tried to stop him—"Mr. Frick is engaged. He can't see you now, sir." But the undaunted anarchist dashed past the porter into another room to confront three men sitting at a long table. "Frick?" he called out, drew a revolver and shot wildly at Carnegie's black-bearded partner. The corporation chief fell to his knees, but the wound in the neck, though serious, was not fatal. Berkman, quickly subdued, was sentenced to twenty-two years in jail; he served fourteen. As had happened after Haymarket, six years before, the incident aroused a new red scare against anarchists—and not a few arrests. The steel strikers disassociated themselves from Berkman's act, but not a few labor leaders considered the shooting a manifestation of high idealism. Even Samuel Gompers, though bitterly hostile by then to anarchism and socialism, participated in the campaign that effected Berkman's release.

The results of the Homestead defeat can be measured by a few bare statistics. Membership in the Amalgamated Association declined from 24,000 to 10,000 in 1894 and to 8,000 in 1895. Profits of the Carnegie Steel Company, which had totaled $27 million in the seventeen years before Homestead, zoomed to $106 million in the nine years that followed.

6

The Debs Revolution

There have been no revolutions in the United States since the first one in 1776. The closest America has come to revolution has been in the labor wars, each one of which has been, in a sense, a revolution-in-microcosm. The strikers in these industrial flare-ups confronted not only the power of their employers but, ultimately, that of the State—the government, courts, police, militia. To succeed, they had to check or neutralize the administrative machinery of government, and in the process there was always the possibility of a widening and escalating of the conflict to a point where it might border on insurrection.

No event illustrates this point more vividly than the Pullman Strike of 1894, or, as it was called by some, the "Debs Rebellion." Each side escalated the war until it was only steps away from an actual revolution—and an actual counterrevolution. On one hand, a relatively small strike of 5,500 men in a single town became a nationwide strike in one industry and almost evolved into a nationwide strike in all industries—indeed only one step removed from insurrection. On the other hand a single employer was given organized aid by a gargantuan employer association, and through it the fulsome assistance of the federal government, its Army, Attorney General, and courts.

"The Pullman strike," writes Professor Selig Perlman, "marks an era in the American labor movement because it was the only attempt ever made in America of a revolutionary strike on the continental European model. The strikers tried to throw against the associated railways and indeed against the entire existing social order the full force of a revolutionary labor solidarity embracing the entire American wage-earning class brought to the point of exasperation by unemployment, wage reductions and misery . . ."

II

The "revolutionary strike" of 1894 was a contest not only of men but of philosophies, symbolized at one pole by George Mortimer Pullman, president of the Pullman Palace Car Company, and at the other by Eugene Victor Debs, president of the American Railway Union. Both had been born to poverty; both came from large families; both went to work at age fourteen and were self-educated; both were talented and able men who, befitting the saying, lifted themselves up by their own bootstraps. But Pullman, twenty-four years Debs's senior, emerged a paternalistic employer, paranoid and highly negative about unionism, while Debs became the most humanistic labor leader America has ever produced. According to Clarence Darrow, the outstanding civil libertarian lawyer of his day, "There may have lived some time, somewhere, a kindlier, gentler, more generous man than Eugene Debs, but I have never known him. Nor have I ever read or heard of another." James Whitcomb Riley, the Hoosier poet, said about Debs that he had:

> As warm a heart as ever beat
> Betwixt here and the Mercy Seat!

Six feet tall, lean, angular, with blue eyes and sensitive mouth, Debs had an affinity for the underclasses that he expressed often and practiced consistently. "Your honor," he told a court after being convicted for his pacifism in opposing World War I, "years ago I recognized my kinship with all living beings, and I made up my mind that I was not one bit better than the meanest on earth. I said then, and I say now, that while there is a lower class, I am in it; while there is a criminal element, I am of it; while there is a soul in prison, I am not free." Though idolized by workers, he once told a group of them: "I am not a labor leader; I do not want you to follow me or anyone else. If you are looking for a Moses to lead you out of the capitalist wilderness, you will stay right where you are. I would not lead you into this promised land, if I could, because if I could lead you in, some one else would lead you out."

One of ten children born to French-Alsatian parents in Terre Haute, Indiana, Debs was radicalized slowly by decades of personal experience, until he became the leading spokesman of the Socialist Party and five times its candidate for President. His first job, at fourteen, was scraping grease from freight engines of the Vandalia

Railroad at the munificent wage of 50 cents a day. A year and a half later, the boy with heavy brown hair and jutting jaw was promoted to locomotive fireman at a dollar a night, spending his afternoons at business college. He worked at the craft for a few years, but the job was dangerous and when a friend slipped under a locomotive and was killed, his mother prevailed on Debs to leave the railroad for a job in a wholesale grocery. His employer, like most people who came into contact with him, thought highly of the young man, and might have advanced him to a lucrative position. Debs, however, was already convinced that "business means grabbing for yourself."

In his free time he visited friends at the rail yards, and it was here one night in 1875 that he met Joshua Leach, Grand Master of the recently organized Brotherhood of Locomotive Firemen. Though he was no longer employed at the craft, he had enrolled as a member of the Brotherhood and was soon chosen as the secretary of its Vigo Lodge. By 1877 he had progressed to assistant editor of the union's magazine, and after 1880, when an officer of the organization disappeared with what remained of the treasury, he became the Brotherhood's secretary-treasurer and editor-in-chief of its newspaper. With the aid of his brother, Theodore, a lifelong helpmate, and two sisters, Debs rebuilt the BLF so that by 1883 it was out of debt and claimed 8,000 members. Typically, he worked a full year without pay, spending $800 of his own money to boot. According to J. P. Mac-Donagh of the Terre Haute Typographical Union, Debs also helped to organize brakemen, switchmen, and virtually every union in town as well as some in other places. He made friends easily and inspired confidence, so much so that he was elected city clerk in Terre Haute in 1879 and a member of the Indiana legislature five years later—both times, incidentally, on the Democratic Party ticket.

Perhaps because of his passion for and belief in the natural goodness of people, the man from Terre Haute held great hopes at first for resolving labor-management disputes through compromise. He did not believe, for instance, that the strike was a valuable labor weapon. "Our organization," he wrote in 1879, "believes in arbitration. All differences should be settled in this way, for no good has ever or can ever come from resorting to violence or bloodshed." It was not until 1886, after much unresponsiveness on the part of railroad employers, that his views on strikes came full circle. He did deny that "there is a natural, a necessary conflict between labor and capital," asserting that people who held such views "are very shallow thinkers, or else very great demagogues." But his ideas on this too were later modified.

After 1886 Debs began to nurture restless doubts about the craft structure of the railroad brotherhoods. The Brotherhood of Locomotive Firemen had grown under his stewardship from 2,000 to 20,000 members and its magazine from 3,500 subscribers to 33,000. Yet only one tenth of the 900,000 workers in the railroad industry belonged to unions, and they were making little if any progress. Pitting one brotherhood against another constantly, the carriers predominated over all. On a number of occasions Debs tried to weld the brotherhoods into a united force. In 1888, for instance, he brought them together in support of a strike on the Burlington line, but when the company threatened to seek injunctions one of the brotherhood leaders, P. M. Arthur, of the Engineers', deserted the others, causing the strike to collapse. Four years later the refusal of other railway crafts to aid the Buffalo Switchmen convinced Debs that it was time to take a new tack. "Justice to labor will never come in my judgment," he told the press, "until labor federates and wields its united power for the good of all."

Within a month after the Buffalo debacle Debs resigned his post in the BLF and gave up his $4,000 a year salary to devote himself to the formation of a single industrial union in the railroad industry. The sad results of the Buffalo Switchmen's strike, Homestead and Coeur d'Alene convinced the lanky ex-fireman of the urgency of labor unity. "If the year 1892," he wrote, "taught the workingman any lesson worthy of heed, it was that the capitalist class, like a devilfish, has grasped them with its tentacles and was dragging them down to fathomless depths of degradation." The point was made more poignant the following year when the nation once again succumbed to economic depression—the 1893 panic. Twenty-eight banks went bankrupt from January to April 1893, fifty-four more in May, 118 in June, and 642 for the whole year. Some 16,000 other business firms plunged to bankruptcy, putting hundreds of thousands of men out of work. Before the end of the year half of all blue collar workers were jobless, millions clamoring for relief. "We cannot disguise the truth," said Senator John J. Ingalls, before and after the panic, "that we are on the verge of revolution. . . . Labor, starving and sullen in the cities, aims to overthrow a system under which the rich are growing richer and the poor are growing poorer."

In the shadow of this malaise, fifty disgruntled railroad workers came together in a Chicago Hall on June 20, 1893 to establish the short-lived but portentous American Railway Union. Its stated purpose was to end once and for all the backbiting between the brotherhoods which had made labor in the industry impotent. The ARU was to be industrial in structure, to include in its fold all white employees (the exclusion of Blacks, traditional in the industry, was upheld by a small margin), men and women, conductors, brakemen, switchmen, engineers, firemen, even longshoremen, carbuilders, and coal miners associated with the rail corporations. Its dues were to be nominal—a dollar initiation fee and a dollar a year for the national office with supplementary dues to be paid in support of the local lodges.

The officers of the ARU chosen that day were men of considerable talent. George W. Howard had quit a supervisory job with the San Diego Street Car Company to head the Brotherhood of Conductors. L. W. Rogers, former editor of the *Railroad Trainmen* and Sylvester Keliher, secretary-treasurer of the Railway Carmen had key positions and—as the president—there was Eugene Debs. Looking at this array the *Machinist's Journal* made the enthusiastic assessment that "the new organization starts out with brilliant prospects ahead and under one of the brainest (sic) men of the present age." The "brainest" man, Debs, went to work at $75 a month—less than a fourth of the $333 he had earned with the BLF.

The American Railway Union was an instant success. As a fledgling just a few months old it conducted an eighteen-day strike against James J. Hill's Great Northern Railroad and forced the company to restore almost the entire amount of three wage cuts—$16 a month. "That a corporation of so gigantic proportions," said the Salt Lake *Tribune*, "had to yield so quickly to their men indicates that the day has already come when the voice of united labor has to be heard in the matter of wages." Victory against a rail system with 2,500 miles of track, as well as 9,000 employees, was so remarkable, especially in a depression period, that the ARU gained recruits at the rate of 2,000 a day. Within a year it had grown to 465 lodges and 150,000 members—not much smaller than the AFL at that time, and considerably larger than all the old Brotherhoods combined.

III

The other side in the 1894 clash was, as mentioned above, represented by George M. Pullman. Andrew Carnegie, in his book *Triumphant Democracy*, called Pullman the "typical American." It was the highest compliment the steel king could pay the sleeping-car king, but it was far from accurate. The round-faced Pullman with high forehead, intense brown eyes, brown hair, and a small chin-beard, lived in a $350,000 mansion on Chicago's fashionable Prairie Avenue, traveled in a specially built $38,000 railroad car, and was the friend and confidant of President Harrison, Marshall Field, and other luminaries— none of whom were especially "typical" of at least 99 per cent of the American public. The "model" town he built south of Chicago, called "a new departure and a new idea" by his publicists, and "a slave pen without an equal in the United States" by labor leader George Schilling, was also un-typical.

Pullman was "typical" only in the sense that like others among the favored few, he was the embodiment of the American success-story myth, the poor boy who rose from rags to riches. His father, a farmer turned carpenter, had provided adequately for a wife and eight children, but not lavishly. At fourteen George ended formal schooling and went to work in a store at $40 a year plus board. Later, after his family moved to Albion, New York, he became a cabinetmaker in his brother's shop, and when the Erie Canal was being widened, worked with his father moving houses from the Canal's banks—experience which proved valuable for George's later career in Chicago.

The midwestern mecca, to which Pullman traveled in 1855, was only a few feet above Lake Michigan's water level. Its cellars, consequently, drained poorly and it was sometimes necessary to raise the buildings. Pullman, with the knowledge gained in Albion, made a lucrative occupation out of it, his greatest feat being the elevation of the four-floor Tremont Hotel in 1858. After placing heavy beams in the cellar of what was then Chicago's best hotel, he used 5,000 jack-screws and 1,200 men, each turning the screws a few notches simultaneously to accomplish the job. Not a window was broken or a drink spilled in the bar. Subsequently Pullman performed similar service for a whole block of stores on Lake Street, between Clark and LaSalle. The work paid well, and with a $20,000 stake, Pullman at twenty-seven was now ready for bigger things.

The idea for building sleeping cars came to him, it is said, while he traveled on a train to New York during the winter off-season from house-lifting. Actually it was an idea that had occurred to many others going all the way back to 1829. Pullman, however, had the advantage of meeting a man named Benjamin Field in New York who had contracts with two Illinois railroads to run sleepers on their lines. After forming a partnership with Field he remodeled two passenger cars supplied by the Chicago and Alton Railroad. The result was a sleeper with important innovations—toilets at both ends, a linen closet, cherry-wood finishing and hinged chairs which could be raised to the ceiling when not in use. The two cars converted at a cost of $2,000, enjoyed a modest success as did others built by Pullman, but did not bring him the fortune for which he had hoped. Toward the end of the Civil War after a stay in Colorado where he operated a store twenty miles from Denver, Pullman had another try at the rail business. Investing $20,000 for equipping a plant, he built an extraordinarily luxurious car, with hinged upper berths that could be concealed behind wood paneling. It was to be the prototype for all sleeping cars thereafter.

The *Pioneer*, which won renown for carrying the body of Abraham Lincoln from Chicago to Springfield, was hailed as the "wonder of the age." It was bigger, roomier, higher than other sleeping cars, equipped with brocaded fabrics, beautiful mirrors, silver-trimmed lamps, red carpets, and wheels reinforced with rubber to make the ride smoother. Pullman was convinced that the riding public, sick of the discomfort of ordinary trains, would pay for an elegant sleeper, and he was right. The press toasted him as a "missionary of civilization"; General Philip Sherman called the *Pioneer* "the smoothest car I ever rode on." Within a year Pullman had forty-eight such sleepers on the railroads and in the next decade his patented palace cars, with their own conductors and Negro porters, were capturing the market. With the aid of men like Marshall Field, who supplied capital, he incorporated his company, bought a site in downtown Chicago and built a plant which in 1880 was capable of producing 114 cars a year and employing 1,000 men.

In the meantime the sleeping-car manufacturer also designed a dining car—the first one was called the *Delmonico*—with a six-foot kitchen, and a parlor car, all of which were attached to the trains of established lines, but owned and operated by Pullman. His products were so superior to that of other firms that the Pullman Palace Car Company became a virtual monopoly, growing with the railroads to mammoth size. According to Republican Senator John Sherman, author of the Antitrust Act of 1890, Pullman and the sugar trust were "the most outrageous monopolies of the day," earning "enormous profits, and [giving] their patrons little or nothing in return in proportion." But assertions of this sort did not inhibit Pullman's progress.

He was now a man of substance, with plants and repair shops in a number of cities and the owner of a great mansion on Chicago's Prairie Avenue, with a music room, pipe organ, library, and even a small theater. He belonged to the best clubs, was elected president of the Young Men's Christian Association, and with his friend Marshall Field (who believed that the nation needed a large standing army to ward off workingmen "riots" such as those of 1877) engaged in a number of philanthropic activities.

In 1880, when it became necessary to build a larger factory, Pullman decided to construct a "model" community for his workshops and workers that, like his sleeping cars, would be the talk of the universe. It would be a town, said a company brochure, where "all that is ugly and discordant and demoralizing is eliminated, and all that inspires to

self-respect is generously provided." If it were not entirely eleemos-
ynary—Pullman expected to earn a 6 per cent profit, in fair weather
or foul, on its tenements, stores and other facilities—it was to be "so
attractive as to cause the best class of mechanics" to seek it out as a
place of employment. Not surprisingly, the town would be called Pullman.

What arose on this 4,000-acre site, nine miles south of Chicago, was
indeed attractive—at least superficially. Thousands of visitors came to
view its wonders, 10,000 during four months of the 1893 Columbia
Exposition alone. Unlike other industrial sites, Pullman's streets were
wide and clean; its neat brick houses were arranged around a square,
landscaped with lawns and flowers. In its large Arcade were housed the
post office, stores, the opera house, town offices, a library, kindergarten,
and a YMCA. East of the Arcade building was a block of good-looking
nine-room cottages for the elite of the town, including the mayor, and
in the distance the Florence Hotel, named after Pullman's favorite
daughter. Sprinkled here and there were sites for churches, a Market
Hall for general merchandise stores, and finally the many streets—
each named after an inventor, Fulton, Stephenson, Morse, Watt, Pullman, etc.—of solid three-story brick tenements.

There was a universal and distressing homogeneity to the town of
Pullman. On each block lived three hundred to five hundred people
in identical two-, three-, and four-room apartments. In the southern
part of town, in addition, there were four big rows of shanties, sixteen
by twenty feet each, which rented for eight dollars a month and were
generally conceded to be the eyesore of the little paradise. There were
no saloons anywhere, since Pullman believed that "my children"—as
he called them—should be free of vice. Pullman was not only "my
children's" employer and landlord but the custodian of their morals;
and since every inch and every building of the town belonged either to
the Pullman Palace Car Company or the Pullman Land Association,
the sleeping-car king had a voice in that as well.

In any case, despite the incandescent image of Pullman, those who
peered behind the scenes found something less than utopia there. The
tenements, wrote Reverend William H. Carwardine, one of the minis-
ters in town, "are comparatively clean, having air and light; but
abundance of water they have not, there being but one faucet for each
group of five families, and in some cases the water is in the same
apartment devoted to the closets. There are no yards except a great
barren space in common." There was less family privacy, Carwardine
claimed, than in any community he knew of; in many of the houses
one had to pass through the apartment downstairs to reach the one upstairs.

Worse still was the predominance of the corporation over every-thing. Fifty-five hundred workers lived in Pullman's tenements, worked in his shops, prayed at churches rented from him, sent their children to schools built by him, relaxed in his park, and, as one worker put it, were "buried in the Pullman cemetery and go to the Pullman hell." Even the gas and waterworks belonged to the company, and the community's sewage was pumped into Pullman's 140-acre farm to be used as fertilizer. All of this, writes Gustavus Myers, "militated to hold the workers to their jobs in a state of quasi-serfdom, and it gave the company additional avenues of exploiting its workers beyond the ordinary and usual limits of wages and profits." Rents were 25 per cent higher than in neighboring communities. Gas, purchased by the company at 33 cents a thousand feet, was resold to the in-habitants at $2.25 a thousand feet. Water, bought from Chicago at four cents per thousand gallons, was resold at ten cents. To completely bind up the town under his authority, Pullman hired spies both in the shops and on the sleeping cars, and fined his serfs for the least infrac-tion. Conductors on the Pullmans received about $75 a month, out of which they paid $20 for meals, $4 for uniforms and an average of $6 in fines—for lateness, infraction of rules, etc. There was of course no avenue of appeal for such fines; Papa—the corporation—knew best.

But if Pullman lavished any hopes that his mecca of 12,000 would immunize him from labor disturbances, such as those that had ravaged Chicago, he was sadly mistaken. The town was not yet finished in February 1882, when 1,000 construction workers downed their tools because the company stopped paying half their commuters' fare from the big city. Wage cuts during the depression of 1883–85 brought a number of departmental walkouts and talk of a plant-wide strike. During the stoppages of the eight-hour day campaign of 1886 the Pull-man workers terminated work not only to win the shorter work week but in protest against a piecework system and in support of a change in policy relative to payment for industrial injuries. Other sporadic small strikes harried the town from 1887 to 1893, but all were broken by the threat of discharge, and the use of blacklists, spies, and strike-breakers. The town's denouement came with the panic of 1893 and the strike of 1894, just three years before Pullman's death.

IV

The Pullman Palace Car Company operated on the simplistic thesis of all the great corporations of the day that it was permissible to haul in heavy profits in good times, without sharing them with workers, but mandatory to lower wage rates in bad times. Since its formation in 1867 (capitalized at approximately $100,000) the company had always paid its stockholders a dividend of at least 8 per cent, in addition to which it earned large sums of undivided profits. As of 1894, with a total capitalization of $36 million, the firm had $25 million more in surpluses (which it distributed four years later, incidentally, in the form of a 50 per cent stock dividend and a 20 per cent cash dividend, in addition to the regular one of 8 per cent). Profits for 1892 and 1893, the two years before the strike, were so good they almost approximated the total wage bill. Dividends in 1892 amounted to $2.3 million, plus $3.3 million in undivided profit. Dividends in 1893 came to $2.5 million, with $4 million more in undivided profits, or a total of $6.5 million. The full wage bill for 5,500 workers for the year ending July 31, 1893 was less than a million dollars higher—$7.3 million—and for the year ending July 31, 1894 it was $4.5 million as against $2.9 million in dividends. Admittedly there was a sharp cutback in the building of new sleeping cars after the panic of 1893 got under way, but there was plenty of money in the Pullman exchequer to cushion the shock without cutting wages. Why, asked the *Daily Republican* of Springfield, Massachusetts, could not Pullman "dip back into the surplus of $4,000,000 made in the single previous year and keep up the wages of employees who are so carefully housed and otherwise looked after as so many dependents at Pullman?"

But in the summer of 1893 Pullman and his vice-president, Thomas H. Wickes, began a dual squeeze on their employees. The work force in the model town was trimmed to 3,100 men, and earnings of the remaining workers severely sliced. A table published by Stanley Buder in his book *Pullman* shows the number of journeyman mechanics falling from 2,625 in April 1893 to 1,950 a year later, and average monthly earnings from $59.33 to $40.07—approximately a one-third loss. Average monthly income in the largest department, carbuilders, fell from $60.71 to $39.52; in the second largest, painters, from $59.23 to $44.60. While the average wage cut for all American manufacturing that depression year was 12 per cent, at Pullman's it was 28 per cent—from $51.00 a month to $36.50. Yet, though he cut staff and wages, the car king refused categorically to reduce rents on his tenements or the charges for his utilities.

Lashed from a number of directions, workers fell behind in rent payments in the amount of $70,000. Reverend Carwardine cited the cases of three workers, who after deductions from their semi-monthly earnings, had pay checks of two cents, seven cents and forty-seven cents respectively. All refused to cash their largesse, one stating indignantly: "If Mr. Pullman needs the 47 cents worse than I do, let him have it." Generally, reported Carwardine, pastor of the Pullman Methodist-Episcopal Church, the workers "had only from one to six dollars or so on which to live for two weeks." Theoretically employees could have moved to nearby Kensington or Roseland, where rentals were a fifth to a quarter lower, but in practice the company gave first choice in employment to its own tenants, just as in the coal fields and other company towns. In the stark winter of 1893–94, then, the model town of Pullman was a town of extreme hardship, with children going hungry and laborers not knowing where their next meals were coming from.

In December 1893 there was a short strike of Pullman steamfitters and blacksmiths for higher wages; as usual they were given an ultimatum to return to their jobs, and those who did not, were blacklisted. In March and April the men started forming branches of the American Railway Union, proselytizing almost 4,000 members into nineteen locals within a matter of weeks. A committee of forty-six men were chosen to put the men's grievances before management, and in May, they, plus ARU vice-president George Howard met with Wickes in the Chicago offices of Pullman. Wickes listened politely and invited the committee to return two days later to talk with Pullman himself. Again the atmosphere of the meeting was amicable, but the palace-car mogul would not budge. He had taken on contracts, he said, at a loss just to keep the plant in operation and the men on the job. A raise in pay, therefore, was unwarranted. Insofar as rents were concerned, the company's role as landlord, he said, should not be confused with its role as employer. After all the company hadn't raised rents in good times; there was therefore no reason to lower them in bad times. Pullman assured the committee that he viewed the workers as his "children" and was just as concerned about their welfare as that of his own flesh and blood.

As the session closed George Howard, who hadn't said a word until then, asked for assurances that none of the committee members would be fired and promptly received them from Pullman. The meeting had been smooth and restrained, as befits a conversation between father and child. If the men felt disappointed, Howard and committee chairman Thomas Heathcoate nonetheless felt that the door had been opened a mite and there was room for further talks. Next morning, however, three committee members who worked in the iron department were laid off in clear violation of Pullman's pledge, and a meeting of the full committee that evening recommended that unless the men were returned to their jobs, everyone should strike. Before the nineteen locals could consider the issue it was learned through a friend at Western Union that the company—which probably had had a spy on the committee—had wired its supervisors to shut the shops as of noon,

May 11. The union leadership, thereupon, decided to beat management to the punch, calling its members out an hour and a half earlier.

From this relatively minor incident, a great conflict ensued. At the eleventh hour Pullman could have reinstated the three committeemen or agreed to have the matter settled by the arbitration of a third party. But one basic tenet of paternalism is that errant children must be taught stern lessons. Instead of yielding on so small a grievance Pullman instructed underlings to post a notice that "The works are closed until further notice." It was to be several months and many killings later before they would open again.

v

The mood of the Pullman workers was grim as they formed a central strike committee and placed a cordon of three hundred men around the plant. "We do not expect the company to concede our demands," said their leader, Heathcoate. "We do not know what the outcome will be, and in fact we do not much care. We do know that we are working for less wages than will maintain ourselves and families in the necessaries of life, and on that proposition we refuse to work any longer." The men waited for a miracle, the company for starvation to bring them crawling back. An earlier Pullman strike in 1886 had crumbled after ten days because the employees had no resources to fall back on. Pullman was so sure it would happen again that he sped away to a retreat in Maine and then met his wife and daughter, Florence, in New York, where he sequestered himself until the end of June.

But Pullman, wise as he was in business matters, miscalculated the tenacity of desperate workers—and the sympathy they evoked in places high and low. When all but one of the shops in the Arcade—the showcase in Pullman town—cut off credit on the first weekend of the strike, the men formed a relief committee to solicit food and cash. It was never able to keep up with the families' needs, but it did secure mountains of food and considerable money. Mayor John P. Hopkins of Chicago contributed tons of flour, meat, and potatoes, as well as $1,000 in cash and the use of a seven-room apartment in Kensington for strike headquarters. Typographical Union Local 16 gave $1,000; a painters' union $500. Even the Chicago Fire Department raised $900.75, and the Grand Crossing police $45. Someone in Anaconda, Montana, sent $250. Innumerable other sums ranging from a few dollars to hundreds —$15,000 in total were obtained not including provisions that ranged from "a bottle of ink to a carload of flour." Most important of all, early in June all sixty-two members of the Chicago City Council voted unanimously for a resolution asking the city's people to support the Pullman relief committee.

Not only the populace and its representatives, but much of the press, this time, was sympathetic to the strikers at Pullman. The Chicago *Daily News* provided a store for the relief committee's use. The *Times* and *Inter Ocean* flayed ceaselessly at the company's heartlessness. All that the "Marquis de Pullman" needed, wrote *Inter Ocean* on May 30, was "the knout, a liberal supply of shackles, and cheap transit to Siberia." A group of prominent ladies descended on businessmen in Chicago's Loop, seeking financial help for the strikers; several dozen doctors and nurses went to Pullman to furnish free medical service; and a number of pharmacists filled prescriptions without charge. Had the citizens of Chicago been asked to vote on the question of who was "right," the Pullman strikers would have won an easy victory.

For a month the strike remained localized and completely peaceful. "It is in evidence and uncontradicted," the U. S. Strike Commission stated, "that no violence or destruction of property by strikers or sympathizers took place at Pullman, and that until July 3 no extraordinary protection was had from the police or military against even anticipated disorder." But if the strike were peaceful, it was also ineffective. Pullman's palace cars were still making their runs, tacked onto trains of dozens of carriers. And the suspension of new car production was little more than an irritant because business was slow enough and profit margins small enough for the company to get by with the cars it had. Efforts to settle the dispute had all been of no avail. A committee of six, chosen by the reform-minded Civic Federation of Chicago, had written Pullman vice-president Wickes asking to discuss the matter with him, but their letters went unanswered. When the famous social worker Jane Addams walked into the vice-president's office uninvited, she was advised by Wickes that the company would not deal with any union and would not submit to arbitration since there was "nothing to arbitrate." Clearly, at this impasse, the choice for the strikers became simply to yield or do something drastic —it appeared certain that they would succumb to starvation long before the corporation began to feel any financial pinch.

VI

On June 12, 1894, the American Railway Union opened its first national convention at Uhlich's Hall in Chicago. After disposing of issues of high policy the four hundred delegates turned to their knottiest problem, the one in Pullman town—or as Debs called it "Pullemdown." A spokesman for the strikers began by reading a long appeal to the convention. "We struck," it said, "because we were without hope. We joined the American Railway Union because it gave us a glimmer of hope. . . . We will make you proud of us, brothers, if you will give us the hand we need. Help us make our country better and more whole-some. . . . Teach arrogant grinders of the faces of the poor that there is still a God of Israel, and if need be a Jehovah—a God of battles." A thin, worn-out seamstress who lived at Pullman told how the company had forced her to pay $60 back rent owed by her late father, an employee with thirteen years' service. Reverend Carwardine described the starvation in the "model town."

Sitting in the president's chair, Eugene Debs was torn between logic and emotion. His empathy with the strikers was total; he had walked through the town after the stoppage had begun, talked with its people, listened to their complaints, seen their travail. But like his associates among the union leadership, he was hesitant to commit a one-year-old organization to such a risky, crucial contest. He was not opposed to a national boycott or a national strike in principle, but he was aware that the moment was less than propitious. First, ARU, though 150,000 strong, was still frail, financially and otherwise. Second, there was the specter of depression staring *everyone* in the face, with thousands of unemployed ready to pounce on any available job, even if it involved strikebreaking. Third, there was the memory of so many defeated efforts. Jacob Coxey's army of 10,000 unemployed, which had marched on Washington demanding relief, was ending its venture in failure at approximately the same time that the ARU was considering the boycott against Pullman palace cars. A previous strike of the United Mine Workers of America, protesting wage slashes, had brought jubilation to the leaders of the union initially, when 180,000 coal diggers answered the call, but it had ended eight weeks later in the usual setback, with only minor adjustments.

Moreover, if the convention were to declare a boycott of Pullman cars there would be another and far more potent actor on the scene, the General Managers' Association. GMA, founded in 1886, had led a feeble existence until it was revived and reorganized in January 1892. Essentially its membership was an amalgam of railroad owners with terminals in Chicago—the nation's leading rail center—whose purpose was to establish a uniform policy on loading, unloading, car service, rates, switching practices, and above all wages. The twenty-four lines which comprised its membership owned 41,000 miles of track, $818 million in capital stock, and employed 221,000 workers. Among them were such giants as B&O, Santa Fe, Burlington, Northwestern, Rock Island, Northern Pacific, and Illinois Central.

To deal with union strikes GMA had formed two committees, with the prosaic names Committee No. 1 and Committee No. 2. Committee No. 2 was charged with ascertaining and setting wage schedules, Committee No. 1 with recruiting strikebreakers in emergencies. The previous year, 1893, when switchmen had threatened a walkout for higher pay, the request was referred to Committee No. 2 and the demand was flatly rejected. Committee No. 1 meanwhile began enrolling thousands of "replacements" in twenty cities, and against this formidable opposition the switchmen retreated. Ten days later, March 22, the baggage agents of the Lake Shore and the Michigan Southern railroads had applied for a raise, but Committee No. 2 approved it only for baggage masters and rejected it for all others. Again the men involved accepted the verdict sullenly, feeling incapable of finding any other alternative. Encouraged by such successes, GMA unanimously resolved that wherever a road involved in a labor dispute accepted the recommendations of Committee No. 2, GMA would throw all its resources into the fray. Costs would be borne by all the roads in "such proportion as may be assessed."

The United States Strike Commission, subsequently appointed by President Grover Cleveland, hinted that GMA was engaged in illegal activities. It questioned "whether any legal authority, statutory or otherwise can be found to justify some of the features of the association which have come to light in this investigation. . . . The association is an illustration of the persistent and shrewdly devised plans of corporations to overreach their limitations and to usurp indirectly powers and rights not contemplated in their charters and not obtainable from the people or their legislators."

But legal or not, the General Managers' Association was a reality. More, it considered ARU its worst enemy, and, as Almont Lindsey points out in his study of the Pullman strike, directed all its efforts toward the "complete annihilation" of Debs's organization. For Eugene Debs to contemplate a national action against such a formidable opponent was a cheerless prospect under the best of circumstances, and he used all of his influence and eloquence to try to head it off. When a delegate made a motion that all ARU members refuse to move a single Pullman sleeper beginning immediately, the ARU president suggested instead that a committee make another effort to talk sense to the company. Twelve men, six of whom were strikers who lived in Pullman, were sent to propose arbitration once more, but Wickes refused to meet with "outsiders." Next day the six strikers returned by themselves but were given Wickes's standard reply—there is "nothing to arbitrate." Setting wages was the exclusive prerogative of management, not to be impinged on either by the employees or any third parties.

On June 22 the convention finally voted to spread the strike to Pullman plants at St. Louis and Ludlow, Kentucky and to institute a nationwide boycott against all sleepers. Vice-president Howard pleaded that a strike against the Ludlow and St. Louis shops would be enough, but the delegates overrode him. Debs bowed to the will of the rank and file and threw himself into the battle with all his energies. Taking the floor he instructed the delegates on how the boycott, scheduled to begin at noon four days later, should proceed. Inspectors were to refuse to inspect the sleepers, switchmen to refrain switching them onto trains and, if already coupled, to sidetrack them. Engineers and brakemen were urged not to haul any train with a Pullman Palace Car on it. Debs predicted—correctly—that trouble would begin with the switchmen, who doubtless would be fired. In that event all members of the union and those who sympathized with it would walk out at once, transforming the boycott into a work stoppage. Setting up headquarters at Uhlich's Hall—from which 9,000 telegrams were dispatched in the next couple of weeks—Debs began to co-ordinate the great battle.

The boycott against Pullman vehicles began slowly. On the appointed day trains ran normally, palace cars still coupled to them. At 9 P.M. George Pullman visited the Twelfth Street Station of Illinois Central to watch the *Diamond Special* take off for St. Louis and was elated to see that the boycott was "ineffective." The next shift of switchmen, however, refused to handle the sleepers, and the day crew that followed did likewise. As anticipated, management reacted by firing those who would not switch the Pullman cars, and fellow workers in turn walked off the job. In a nonce 3,500 Illinois Central employees were out of work, and the boycott-strike had spread to fourteen other roads. After two days there were 18,000 railroaders on strike, on the third day 40,000, and on the fourth 125,000. With incredible speed the stoppage had immobilized such giants as the Burlington, Santa Fe, Northwestern and Illinois Central, had closed down the Union Stock Yards and Transit Company in Chicago, had halted the Southern Pacific and Northern Pacific out West, and had caused suspension or curtailment of traffic from the Far West to upper New York. According to the New York *Tribune* of July 3 there were 150,000 men involved in the first truly national strike in U.S. history. In the great expanse from Chicago to the Golden Gate only the Great Northern was able to maintain anything remotely resembling a normal train schedule. Despite open opposition by the old brotherhood leaders, such as P. M. Arthur of the Engineers, who threatened his members with expulsion and discharge, the response to Debs's appeal had far exceeded expectations.

In the first week of the boycott-strike, the ARU had more than held its own. Even John M. Egan, a former official of the Chicago and Great Western Railroad, who had been hired by the General Managers' Association to co-ordinate the anti-strike campaign, conceded on July 2 that the carriers had been "fought to a standstill." Testifying to the support won by Debs's union, hundreds of thousands of people were wearing the ARU white ribbon. "You cannot go a block," wrote AFL organizer William Boas to Samuel Gompers, "without you see some people wearing a white ribbon."

VII

For a strike that engulfed twenty-seven states and territories it produced an unusually small amount of lawlessness in its early stages, particularly and surprisingly, perhaps, in Chicago. Eventually twenty-five proletarians would be killed and sixty seriously injured nationwide, but the first outbreaks were, given the scale of protest, negligible. A crowd at Grand Crossing in South Chicago delayed trains for a few hours on June 26, but there was no property damage or vandalism. Illinois Central's Diamond Special was derailed not far from the same place a few days later. Here and there boxes or strips of metal were placed on tracks, switches were spiked, cars uncoupled. In the village of Blue Island outside Chicago on July 1 a throng gathered on the tracks. Reacting in panic, Marshall John Arnold swore in four hundred deputies and wired Washington: "I expect great trouble. Shall I purchase 100 riot guns?" The next day 2,000 people gathered on the same spot, ditched a mail train, upset a few baggage cars, and forced the Rock Island to suspend operations. But this was an atypical occurrence in the Chicago area at the time. It could have been handled, moreover, by Governor Altgeld, who in similar circumstances had sent in a few hundred militia to cool tempers in four downstate cities.

Out West there were other incidents. There were small clashes on the Santa Fe line between La Junta, Colorado, and Las Vegas. In Trinidad, Colorado, a large group of strikers disarmed fifty-two deputy marshals, and in Raton, New Mexico, hotel workers quit their jobs wherever the federal marshal and his eighty-five deputies stopped to find accommodations. Three miles from Raton, in the small mining town of Blossburg, rioters overturned sixteen cars. In California the railroads were so unpopular that militia, called out to contain the strikers, refused to act. There "does not seem to be a voice raised there," lamented *The Nation*, "in favor of law and civil government; and the inconvenience and losses to which the public are subjected seem to be accepted willingly, so long as the railroads suffer as much or more." But the situation, though tense, was manageable.

In any event, whatever problems there were elsewhere, there had not yet been a single riot in Chicago itself. If it was not quite as quiet as a monastery, it was not much noisier than usual. Mail cars were permitted to function without hindrance, for the most part, and if President Cleveland had been truly neutral about the situation and had ordered such cars coupled only to trains without Pullman sleepers, the amount of strike violence would have been next to nothing. Apart from the fact that Debs had counseled his followers to "respect law and order," there was no need for strong-arm tactics. The strike, clearly, was going in the union's favor. The carriers were unable to find sufficient men to run their trains, limited now, as they were, to old, portly supervisors who had not worked for years. Typically, after the governor of Michigan ordered the militia out, United Press reported from Battle Creek that "The Company has no men here that it can use to pull the trains if there were 1,000,000 soldiers here, and it is esteemed unwarranted. Then again the men have done nothing to prevent the company from moving its trains. The strikers say they will furnish all the men wanted for mail trains." Indeed, violence was unnecessary.

What tipped the scales in this stalemate—and aroused popular fury —was the federal government and its actions. It turned on the strikers with a vindictiveness never before seen on the American labor front. President Cleveland's administration identified so thoroughly with the Managers' point of view that it was impossible to tell where the activities of one left off and the other began. It was as if the GMA knew in advance that when its own resources were exhausted it would automatically be able to be resupplied by those of the Attorney-General, the courts, and the troops.

On the day before the boycott started, the Managers' called an emergency meeting in the Rookery Building, with Wickes of the Pullman Company in attendance, and unanimously resolved not to yield to the "unjustifiable and unwarranted" meddling by Eugene V. Debs. From then until the strike was broken, three weeks later, there was never the remotest thought of the Managers' negotiating, arbitrating, or compromising the dispute, and all requests by municipal and other authorities that the Managers' modify its position went unheeded. Egan was placed in charge of anti-strike activities, and immediately initiated operations on four or five fronts. A publicity bureau was opened to supply "information" to the press, and two dozen detectives were hired to ferret out—or manufacture—unfavorable news about the strikers and their organization. The mass media, some of which were friendly toward the workers when the strike was confined to Pullman, were now almost universally hostile. With spoon-fed "facts" at its disposal the commercial press, as early as June 27, was already decrying strikers' "anarchy"—a particularly sensitive charge just then because the President of France had been assassinated by a real anarchist three days before. "Mob is in Control," cried the Chicago *Tribune* of June 30, though as Debs noted there was as yet "no sign of violence or disorder."

The lead in one news story read: "Through the lawless acts of Dictator Debs' strikers the lives of thousands of Chicago citizens were endangered yesterday." Debs was pictured by the press throughout the strike as a tyrant who had called out the railroad workers without consulting them, and was enriching himself personally.

Among the sensational headlines in some of the nation's leading newspapers—often based on "news" leaked by the Managers' publicity bureau—were the following:

ANARCHISTS ON WAY TO AMERICA FROM EURÔPE

FROM A STRIKE TO A REVOLUTION

WILD RIOT IN CHICAGO—HUNDREDS OF FREIGHT CARS BURNED
BY STRIKERS—THE TORCH IN GENERAL USE

CHICAGO AT THE MERCY OF THE INCENDIARY'S TORCH

ANARCHISTS AND SOCIALISTS SAID TO BE PLANNING

THE DESTRUCTION AND THE LOOTING OF THE TREASURY

All of the above was either grossly untrue or greatly exaggerated, but it created a public climate so frenzied that the government could feel free to seek injunctions and send troops.

A second part of Egan's campaign was the drafting of strikebreakers. Committee No. 1 was instructed to hire replacements anywhere it could find them. Offices were opened in New York, Buffalo, Philadelphia, Cleveland, and Baltimore; between 100 and 250 men were enrolled nationwide every day, about 2,500 in all. If the number seems small it was only because each line did its own recruiting as well. Actually there were plenty of men clamoring for the jobs offered by Committee No. 1. Switchmen in New York who had been blacklisted since their own strike in 1886 told a reporter: "The men who are striking now are the men who helped to fill our places then. Now we are going to take their jobs." While these particular hired men, however, may have had the required skills, most strikebreakers did not, and both the effort to place substitutes on the trains and the threat made on June 29, by rail owners never to employ on any GMA railroad men who participated in the strike, could not by themselves have changed the situation.

As late as two weeks after the work stoppage began—on July 6—the Associated Press reported that "Despite the presence of the United States troops and the mobilization of five regiments of state militia; despite threats of martial law and bullet and bayonet, the great strike

. . . holds three-fourths of the roads running out of Chicago in its strong fetters, and last night traffic was more fully paralyzed than at any time since the inception of the tie-up." Of the twenty-four railroad lines feeding into Chicago, thirteen were all but immobilized, and most of the others were running only passenger and mail trains, and those irregularly. Statistics on the decline of freight by rail punctuated the point made by Associated Press: ten trunk lines that carried 43,000 tons of freight east-bound in the week ending June 20 hauled less that 12,000 during the following week. Four major lines did not carry a single ton and the Baltimore and Ohio only fifty-two tons. As Governor Altgeld noted in a telegram to President Cleveland: "At present some of our railroads are paralyzed, not by reason of obstructions, but because they cannot get men to operate their trains."

VIII

The Managers', however, had a trump card, the federal government, and a ready-made ally in the person of Richard Olney. A tall man, with graying brown hair, wide nostrils, a sort of Turkish mustache, and an aggressive walking gait, Olney had a streak of stubbornness and a volatile temper that were the last things needed in this crisis situation. He had been a corporation lawyer, specializing in railroads and estates, for three and a half decades before accepting Cleveland's appointment as Attorney General. Moreover, he owned sizable blocks of rail stock and had served as a director of several lines including the strike-bound Burlington, and the Boston & Maine, in which George Pullman was a co-director. Another Attorney General might have disqualified himself from entering in the dispute at all if for no other reason than that he had been closely associated with the Managers' and its affiliates. But Olney identified as totally with the corporations as Debs did with the workers in Pullman town. The strike, for him, was automatically illegal and any means used to smash it, justified. He was determined—as he himself put it—to apply "force which is overwhelming and prevents any attempt at resistance."

At the outbreak of the boycott, Olney wired U. S. Attorneys throughout the country to take prompt action wherever they considered the mail trains in jeopardy. The mail train was to become the synthetic excuse for repression of the Pullman strike. U. S. Attorney Thomas E. Milchrist, who read Olney's private telegram to the General Managers' Association meeting of June 28 in Chicago, was given a standing ovation. Almost immediately federal marshals were authorized to hire special deputies to "protect" the mails, and thousands were eventually enrolled, 5,000 in Chicago alone. In a crass show of bias, Olney permitted the railroads themselves to recruit two thirds of the deputies. Any road that wanted men assigned to its property was empowered to appoint one of its officials as a captain. He then was free to choose whom he wanted to serve; all he had to do was give their names to the federal marshal and they were, by that act, made deputies. Each deputy was given a star, paid $2.50 a day and $1.50 expense money, either by the government or the railroads. Most observers agreed, as a Chicago *Herald* reporter noted, that in general "they were a very low, contemptible set of men." Governor Davis H. Waite called them "desperadoes," hired "without any regard for their qualifications but simply for military purposes."

In fact, except in a few instances, the mail cars went unmolested. "Considering the scope of the strike," comments Almont Lindsey in his book *The Pullman Strike*, "it is remarkable there was not greater paralysis of the movement of mail." Debs publicly offered to assign union worker crews for any train with a mail car providing it did not have a sleeper on it. Both Olney and the Managers' disregarded the offer. Indeed, there were some occasions when the carriers deliberately coupled mail cars to Pullmans on trains which did not ordinarily carry them in order to both be able to taunt Debs and provoke striker obstruction of the trains' departures.

The exaggerated excuse that the strikers were obviously criminals for their alleged blocking of the federal mails, brittle as it may have been, clearly was a necessary stratagem for two other measures contemplated by Olney—injunctions and dispatch of troops. What other pretext could have been used to justify employing these extreme measures? Under the Constitution, President Cleveland was empowered to deploy federal forces against domestic violence *only* if requested to do so by a state legislature or, when the legislature was in recess, a state governor. Since the Illinois body was not in session, and since Governor John Peter Altgeld refused categorically at all times to call on Washington, Cleveland's hands were tied. But mail was a federal concern, and Olney found two Civil War laws, never until then used in time of peace, and with far-fetched relevance at best, to justify federal intervention. Under Sections 5298 and 5299 of the Revised Statutes of the United States, the President was authorized to take direct action when there was violence or an insurrection which challenged federal law. Mail delivery was of course covered by federal law; ergo, any interference in its handling justified deputization of marshals and the deployment of troops. The troops in turn would be used to enforce court injunctions—the ultimate strikebreaking weapons. With violence on the part of the strikers negligible, this course of action was like using a bulldozer to uproot crab grass. But Richard Olney, it must be remembered, had promised to use "overwhelming" force against the striking workers.

On June 30, the United States Attorney General designated Edwin Walker, a prominent lawyer who had represented the Chicago, Milwaukee and St. Paul Railway since 1870 and more recently the General Managers' Association, as special counsel for the federal government in Chicago. This was as outrageous an act by an allegedly neutral government official as it was unjustified, for Walker had been recommended by the Managers' and remained in the employ and on the payroll of his railroad throughout the dispute. His main task was to help the railroads secure injunctions.

An injunction is a tricky legal gadget whose origins go back to English law. Ordinarily a man is punished for a crime *after* he has violated a statute. But an injunction is an order which restrains him from committing an allegedly illegal act in advance. The presumption is that it would be too late to punish him afterward, since *irreparable* damage already would have been done. The first important use of such a device in labor disputes was around 1880, involving a financially strapped railroad being reorganized by a court-appointed receiver. The receiver complained that the walkout placed the property entrusted to him in jeopardy and an equity judge promptly issued an order restraining the walkout. Those who violated it did not have to be convicted as guilty by a jury of their peers, but were adjudged guilty of contempt by the judge alone, and packed off to prison without trial. "The whole transaction from strike to jail," writes legal expert Charles O. Gregory, "could be counted in hours rather than in the weeks and months required in actions at law."

The injunction as a handy legal tool was used only sparingly against unions until the Pullman strike, but the triumvirate of Oney, Walker, and the Managers' now adopted it as their primary strikebreaking weapon. On July 2 the Chicago *Tribune* appeared with the headline: STRIKE IS NOW WAR. On the same day, Walker and Milchrist applied for an injunction, using the strange argument that the strike was a violation of the Sherman Anti-Trust Act and the Interstate Commerce Act —two anti-monopoly bills passed on the initiative of labor and the farmers to curb big business, not unions. Olney never used these laws against big business, but by means of sophistry, his emissaries twisted them to apply to the Pullman strike, which, it was said, constituted a conspiracy "in restraint of trade." The application for an injunction was immediately granted by federal judges Peter S. Grosscup—who a few weeks before had stated that "the growth of labor organizations must be checked by law"—and William A. Woods—who was much beholden to the railroads for past favors. Without hearing a single witness on the union's side, and solely on the basis of "information and belief" affidavits by the government, offered without proof, the two jurists outlawed the great Pullman strike, and placed 150,000 workers at the mercy of their employers.

Under the omnibus injunction, the most severe ever issued before or since, Debs, George Howard, fifteen other leaders and "all other persons whomsoever" were prohibited "from in any way or manner interfering with, hindering, obstructing, or stopping" any trains entering Chicago, and "from compelling or inducing or attempting to compel or induce by threats, intimidation, persuasion, force or violence, any of the employees of any of said [twenty-three] railroads to refuse or fail to perform any of their duties as employees of any of said railroads, or the carriage of the United States mail by such railroads . . ." or "to leave the service of such railroads" engaged in interstate commerce. What this meant in effect was that *any* action to further the strike would be in contempt of court, with the people involved subject to arrest and imprisonment. It thus became illegal for Debs to send wires or otherwise communicate with his local unions. It became illegal for striking workers to picket, raise relief funds or open a strike headquarters. Worst of all it became illegal under the injunction to "persuade" a railroad worker to join the strike or stay on strike, even if the means of persuasion were peaceful and amicable. "It is seriously questioned . . . ," wrote the U. S. Strike Commission in its later report, "whether courts have jurisdiction to enjoin citizens from 'persuading' each other in industrial or other matters of common interest."

How far the courts had to go to tailor legality to the needs of management during the Pullman strike is evident from the decision of the Supreme Court upholding the injunction months later. According to the high tribunal, the government had to establish two criteria for a restraining order, first that the damage to the complainant's property would be irreparable unless checked beforehand, and second, that the alleged criminality was part of an illegal and malicious conspiracy. Now there was obviously no "conspiracy" (all the union's activity was and had been out in the open) and the amount of property damage until the injunction was a scant few thousand dollars. Undaunted, the Court devised a vague definition of "irreparable" beyond its normal meaning. It held that the "expectancy" of *future* business was as much a hallowed property right as a locomotive. So too the "expectancy" of retaining old experienced employees. By this odd logic the high court decided that Debs and his union men were inflicting "irreparable" damage on the helpless railroads. Moreover, it decided that damaging or deflating the "probable expectancies" of management for future business could be deemed "malicious conspiracy." It is interesting that the court never declared—then or later—that "expectancy" of future wages was also a property right, reparable by injunctions against strike-breakers.

Nonetheless, the Grosscup-Woods restraining order—and many others, from Michigan to California, that restated its essentials—stood sacrosanct. Railroaders were arrested, according to George Howard, for refusing to turn switches or fire up a locomotive engine. A fireman in Albuquerque who failed to carry out a company order to climb aboard an engine was held in contempt, and sentenced to fifteen days in prison. The injunctions and arrests derived from them, placed Debs and the ARU in an unenviable quandry. They could abide by court restrictions, in which case the ARU would be eviscerated, the strike lost. Or they could flout the court, go to jail, and see the strike smashed by federal troops. They decided not to abide by the injunction, to risk prison—in the hopes that somehow an infuriated labor movement would rescue them at the eleventh hour.

IX

On July 3, 1894, U. S. Marshal Arnold, as well as Walker, Milchrist, and Judge Grosscup wired Washington urging that armed forces be sent to Chicago—to protect federal property, prevent interference with mail and interstate commerce, and generally enforce the judicial edict. The telegram, intended to prod President Cleveland and his Secretary of War, Daniel S. Lamont (who opposed sending troops), was, like so many other aspects of the anti-union thrust, grossly misleading. It averred that there had been violence in Chicago when in fact it had been outside Chicago, in Blue Island. It implied that the violence still raged when it actually was over. And it falsely predicted an immediate general strike in the city with Chicago workers "joining the mob tonight, and especially tomorrow." Eventually such a strike was proclaimed, but it would be a week after the sending of the wire before it was even discussed seriously. The letter proclaiming its imminence that day was thus a brazen deception. Nonetheless, hysteria gripped the administration, which had been meeting regularly to discuss the strike, and when Secretary Lamont and General Nelson A. Miles withdrew their objections, President Cleveland ordered troops to Chicago from nearby Fort Sheridan. Eleven companies were on duty in Chicago on Independence Day and 1,936 federal soldiers by July 10.

Cleveland's action, like the injunctions, was of doubtful legality. Apart from the fact that he had disregarded the Constitution by by-passing the state governor and state legislature in Illinois, no federal property had been destroyed in Chicago—or even seemed to be in jeopardy. According to the Superintendent of Railway Mail Service, the mail cars were operating, and there was no pileup of mail in the post office. Governor Altgeld protested to Cleveland that the President had been misled, and that the action "is entirely unnecessary, and, as it seems to me, unjustifiable. . . . So far as I have been advised, the local officials have been able to handle the situation." Altgeld stressed the point that "if any assistance were needed, the State stood ready to furnish a hundred men for every one man required, and stood ready to do so at a moment's notice." Cleveland and Olney were undoubtedly aware of all this but they also knew that while Altgeld, a friend of labor, would alert the militia to keep order, he would not instruct them to actually crush the Pullman or any other strikes.

Similar dissent from Cleveland's actions and similar insistence that the states could handle their own affairs came from the governors of Kansas, Colorado, Texas, and Oregon. The militia had been called out in twenty states and was presumably capable of dealing with any emergency without federal troop support. Debs and James R. Sovereign of the Knights of Labor jointly warned Cleveland that "a deep-seated conviction is fast becoming prevalent that this Government is soon to be declared a military despotism." Reacting further, in fury, Debs cried out that "the first shot fired by the regular soldiers at the mobs here will be the signal for a civil war . . . Bloodshed will follow, and 90 percent of the people of the United States will be arrayed against the other 10 percent." He was to be proven wrong in his estimate of labor's strength and public support, but as the U. S. Strike Commission was to observe, there were no serious disorders until the federal troops arrived. Afterward there was a great surge of what Attorney-General Olney referred to as "anarchy."

On the evening of July 4 in Chicago, people congregated on railroad tracks, overturned some cars and set some aflame. Amid the explosion of firecrackers, citizens heard the clang of fire engines hurrying to and fro to douse the burning freights. Women and children constituted a large part of the crowds gathered at the rails, as did adolescents who found that the cars were perched on the tracks in such a way that thirty or forty men pushing back and forth could topple them. The next day the situation grew worse. Ten thousand people gathered at the Stock Yards, and as they moved east, on Rock Island property again, turned over and set fire to freights, threw switches, altered signal lights, burned down a signal house and tossed rocks. The troops did not use firearms in response to these actions, but they did attack the crowd with bayonets drawn, inflicting some injuries. The crowd, however, could not be dispersed entirely nor could any railroad cars be moved. When two hundred soldiers and three hundred deputy marshals tried to take out a trainload of livestock at Union Stock Yards they were halted by strikers after one mile and had to abandon the effort four hours later. In fact, from July 4 though 10 not a single carload of meat or livestock left these yards, so stubborn was the resistance of Chicago's militants.

July 5 was climaxed by a mammoth fire—of unknown origins—at the World's Columbian Exposition in Jackson Park that consumed seven buildings, leaving a blanket of black smoke over the city that could be seen miles away. That evening, at the request of Mayor Hopkins, Governor Altgeld sent five regiments of militia to Chicago. Lost in the shuffle of sensational news that day and almost irrelevant at that point was still another offer by Debs to Pullman to end the boycott at once if the latter would agree to arbitration.

Property losses to the railroads up to this point were only a few thousand dollars. But they multiplied by geometric progression the next day, July 6, when $340,000 of rail assets was demolished or went up in smoke. The crowds that roamed two and a half miles of track were somewhat smaller than the day before, about 6,000, but the havoc they wrought, especially against the Illinois Central, was much greater. In the evening an epidemic of fires took a toll of seven hundred cars at the Panhandle yards in South Chicago. One of the unique features of the day's events was the outbreak of street fighting for the first time; deputy marshals shot and killed two participants. Not far from Pullman, where freights were being toppled, a deputy shot an innocent bystander a hundred yards away and, in full sight of everyone, pumped a bullet into the victim as he tried to rise—killing him.

There were now 6,000 federal and state troops in Chicago, 3,100 police, and 5,000 deputy marshals, but the fury of the strikers and their supporters could not be checked. A peak of violence was reached on the seventh when Illinois National Guardsmen fired into a mob trying to stop the movement of a wrecking train at Forty-ninth and Loomis Streets. The Guard, assaulted by the protesters, began to shoot at will when four of its members were badly injured. At least four civilians were killed (one estimate put it at twenty or thirty) and twenty were wounded, including some women.

Though Chicago was the national center of the strike's storm, there were conflicts also in Denver and San Francisco, where federal troops were now on the scene, and grave situations in Iowa, Michigan, and California, where state militia were ordered to patrol impending trouble areas. On July 9 President Cleveland issued an order against assemblages of any kind in Illinois, and the next day applied it to

North Dakota, Wyoming, Idaho, Washington, Montana, Colorado, and California. The violence had begun to taper by then, but sympathy for the strike was so widespread that any small incident might re-kindle it. Symptomatic of the universal support for the strikers was a declaration, ironically by army officers, meeting in a small Chicago ho-tel, that the work stoppage was justified and that the Army had been called out solely for strikebreaking, not for maintaining law and order. All officers in attendance, including a colonel, were court-martialed. An equally interesting sign of support for the strike was shown by Chicago's newsboys, the majority of whom wore white ribbons and in-delicately tossed those newspapers hostile to the strike, such as the *Tribune,* into the sewers.

On July 10 two more people were killed by troops at Spring Valley, Illinois. As the week of rage ended, however, the military forces were gaining control of the "insurrection." Tonnage carried eastward by ten trunk lines for the seven days from July 8 to July 14 slipped to a rock bottom of 4,142—less than one tenth the normal load. But the tracks were being gradually, systematically cleared of human obstruction, and troops nervously rode shotgun on outgoing trains.

Meanwhile Judge Grosscup called into session a grand jury to in-vestigate this "insurrection" against the state of Illinois. The jury, after hearing one witness, E. M. Mulford of Western Union, who read into the record a selected sample of ARU telegrams, voted indictments on July 10 against Debs, Howard, ARU secretary Sylvester Keliher, and another officer, Louis W. Rogers. They were charged with criminal conspiracy to obstruct the mails, interfere with interstate commerce, and intimidate citizens in the exercise of their constitutional rights. After being arrested, the four strike leaders were released on $10,000 bail—supplied by two saloonkeepers because the union itself had no funds. Before their release, while they were still in custody, deputy marshals and deputy post office inspectors raided the ARU head-quarters, seized Debs's personal papers, unopened mail and books. Though the property was ordered to be returned the next day the headquarters had been ransacked so thoroughly that the attempted re-occupation had to be abandoned. The union no longer had an ade-quate place from which to work. Telegrams from locals asking instruc-tions or verification of rumors that there was a back-to-work movement could not be answered. Confusion was rampant, contributing in no small measure to the strike's defeat.

x

The anarchists convicted in the Haymarket affair of 1886 had preached the doctrine that the State—any State—was the unwavering enemy of the lower classes. In the Pullman strike, the Cleveland administration did its best to prove that thesis. It never once found fault with the railroads, the troops, or the deputies, though there was clearly good reason to challenge what they had done.

The name of the deputy who maliciously and with forethought killed a bystander near Pullman, for instance, was known to the authorities, but he was never arrested or prosecuted. Police Chief John Brennan of Chicago claimed that in at least one instance deputies fired into a crowd where nothing was amiss. "Innocent men and women were killed by these shots," he said. City police, he added, had been forced to arrest some of the deputies for theft and pilferage. "In one instance, two of them were found under suspicious circumstances near a freight car which had just been set on fire." Mayor Hopkins, according to Chicago reformer Henry Demarest Lloyd, had forty affidavits in his possession "showing that the burning of freight cars was done by railroad men; that the railroad men moved cars outside of fire limits, then burned them, inciting bystanders to participate." Sovereign of the Knights of Labor insisted that he had seen Chicago secret police reports "proving that some of the federal agents had been guilty of arson." Both Hopkins and Brennan asserted that the riots were not oraganized by the ARU but by others. Police Inspector Nicholas Hunt, who commanded 1,000 police, claimed that those "caught in the act of doing depredations" were almost never railroad workers or ARU members. At the conspiracy trial of Debs and his associates in February 1895, attorney Clarence Darrow had eighty-six witnesses ready to relate incidents in which the General Managers' Association had initiated or provoked violence. No effort, however, was made to prosecute miscreants on the government or employer side. By contrast, 190 strikers were indicted under federal statutes, and 515 others arrested by local authorities for everything from burglary and assault to murder.

With such one-sided administration of justice the strike was decidedly on the wane as of the tenth of July. Debs still believed it could be salvaged by the militancy of the workers in California and others in the West, provided the strike secured the support of Samuel Gompers' AFL. The final act of the Pullman drama was an attempt by the ARU leader to take the strike two steps further. Just as it had been necessary to spread the strike from a single town and a single sleeping car complex to the railroads of the whole nation, so it was now necessary to spread the strike to other industries, nationwide, and to as many big cities as possible. Only by paralyzing the whole economy, Debs believed, could the government be forced into a true neutrality on the over-all labor-management issue.

With that in mind, Debs issued an appeal for help. The first group
to respond was the Chicago labor movement, then and for years to
come the most militant labor center in the nation. On July 8 delegates
from every local union in the city, representing 150,000 workers, met
at Uhlich's Hall, and after an all-night discussion proclaimed that if
Pullman still refused to arbitrate they would call a city-wide strike.
A committee of three unionists, accompanied by three aldermen,
visited the company vice-president, Wickes, and were given again the
hackneyed answer that there was nothing to arbitrate. Thus rebuffed,
the Trades and Labor Council scheduled a city-wide strike for the
morning of July 11. There is little question that the city's proletariat
was thoroughly in sympathy with the Debs Rebellion, though only
25,000 suspended work. This low turnout occurred because workers
felt that with the area under virtual military occupation and the strike
leaders under judicial harassment, the strike was beyond salvage.
Others held off taking part because they knew that the AFL executive
council was meeting the next day to discuss a *national* sympathy
walkout—why not wait then for the bigger show?

And with the Chicago general strike thus a fiasco, this possibility
was the one slim hope left for the Pullman strikers. Soon more and
more trains were moving; the ranks of striking workers were even beginning to thin in California where the boycott had been, outside of
Chicago, most effective. Conceivably a nationwide general strike
might have been the adrenalin needed to revitalize the Chicago boycott. A call by the AFL, the Knights of Labor and the ARU for a
coast-to-coast walkout, even though these oganizations represented
only a half million workers among them, would undoubtedly have
brought to the streets several million working men, and might have
forced President Cleveland to retreat to a more neutral position.

At the urging of his Chicago affiliates, Sam Gompers called a
special meeting of his AFL executive council for Thursday, July 12.
Twenty-four of the nation's top labor leaders, including two from the
railroad brotherhoods, assembled at Chicago's Briggs House that day
to weigh the situation. Not unexpectedly, they concluded after a day
of deliberations, that "a general strike at this time is inexpedient, un-
wise, and contrary to the best interests of working people." Worse
still—for Debs—the assembled labor brass asked all AFL members engaged in sympathy walkouts to return to their jobs, and the Chicago
Building Trades Council immediately terminated its stoppage. Debs
was treated courteously when he appeared before the conference and
$1,000 was voted for his legal defense, but it was clear that Gompers
and his labor allies were lukewarm to the strike. They had been lukewarm in fact from the beginning when Debs had first wired the AFL

for assistance. Gompers' reply had been "Just received telegram signed your name. Verify same by letter giving full particulars." If Gompers showed no sense of urgency or solidarity it was because he recognized in the ARU a serious rival to his organization. Had the Debs Rebellion succeeded, there is little question that a new federation of labor would have emerged around the ARU and the remnants of the Knights of Labor considerably stronger than the AFL. Moreover, the little cigar-maker who headed the Federation could smell the fumes of imminent defeat if such a union battle materialized. Consequently, he would not risk the life of his organization on the touch-and-go gamble of a national walkout, especially on behalf of a man who, if the general strike succeeded, would become automatically his staunchest rival.

Following the Briggs House conference, the Pullman strike played out its sad, disappointing destiny. Through Mayor Hopkins, Debs submitted his proposal to end the stoppage on the single condition that old employees be given their jobs back, but the Managers' did not bother to reply, even to this essentially recognizable statement of defeat.

On the seventeenth the four ARU leaders were re-arrested, on a charge of contempt of court for violating the Grosscup-Woods injunction. The bail again was set at $10,000 for each man, but this time Debs and his fellow officers decided to remain in jail. Two days later, twenty-three new indictments were handed down, charging the same four and seventy-one others with breaching a host of federal statutes. During the week ending July 21, tonnage eastward on the ten trunk lines rose by 700 per cent from its low point the week before; it was now functioning at about two-thirds normal.

In the same week—on the eighteenth—George Pullman posted signs at the factory gates of his model town advising that "These shops will be opened as soon as the number of operatives taken on is sufficient to make a working force in all departments." The immediate response did not bring about a prompt reopening of the shops, since only 325 men applied for jobs and a minimum of 800 was needed to renew operations. By August 1, however, the required number of men were available, and ready to return to work.

The American Railway Union, a hopeful project just two months before, held a special convention August 2—with only fifty-three delegates present—and terminated its historic stoppage three days later. The remaining striking workers in Pullman, Illinois, conceded their defeat September 6, when the plants were already back in full swing. Everywhere, even in small rail centers, a few dozen men were fired or blacklisted. Illinois Central re-employed only two thirds of its old force. Union Pacific discharged all of its employees who had been active strikers. Southern Pacific introduced a "yellow-dog" contract, which returning employees signed, pledging they would never join a union.

The epilogue to the Debs Rebellion was written in the courts. With Edwin Walker assisting U. S. Attorney Milchrist, the four union leaders went on trial September 5 and were convicted of contempt. Debs was sentenced to six months at the county jail in Woodstock; the others to three months. The conspiracy charge did not come to trial in Judge Grosscup's court until February 9, 1895, and it ended in an indecisive and revealing fashion. Counsel for the defendants was Clarence Darrow, a former Chicago corporation counsel and for a while general attorney for the Chicago and Northwestern Railroad. Edwin Walker appeared on behalf of the government. Darrow's plan was to broaden the issue in the trial to reveal its social roots. With that in mind he subpoenaed Pullman and announced that he would call to the stand the members of the General Managers' Association to prove that the conspiracy was all on their side—not the union's. Pullman slipped out of town to avoid testifying. Representatives of the Managers' pleaded loss of memory about what had transpired at their meeting with Pullman. A demand by the defense for the minutes of the GMA's meetings became moot when the judge suddenly announced that one of the jurors had become ill—and adjourned the trial. Though Darrow offered to impanel another juror and read him the proceedings, the judge refused. The case never came up again. The government, having won its major objective—defeat of the strike—dropped the matter after a few continuances, like the proverbial hot potato.

7

War in the Rockies

Attesting to the vigor with which the American proletariat challenged "industrial feudalism" are some statistics on strikes and lockouts. No figures are available for the period before 1881, though one writer, George Gorham Groat, claims there are records of 1,491 walkouts prior to that time. By contrast, in the quarter of a century of enormous economic growth from 1881 to 1905, there were 38,303 strikes and lockouts, involving seven and a half million workers. Few, of course were as blood-soaked as the 1877 Railroad Men's War, but that they were not effete is indicated by an *Outlook* magazine study in 1904 of the previous thirty-three months. During that time, *Outlook* revealed, 198 pickets or sympathizers had been killed; 1,966 wounded; 6,114 arrested. The number of deaths in this relatively short span was about half of those on the battlefield during the entire Spanish-American war; the number of wounded slightly higher than American wounded in that war.

Large strikes like Pullman gained massive public attention, monopolizing the news for weeks because they blanketed the nation and struck at the nerve center of American capitalism, its transport system. In terms of militancy, however, they were matched by that of some of the smaller strikes. No strikes in American history, for instance, were so naked an expression of the class war, so akin to actual war, as those in the hard-rock mining communities of the West. Though fought by small numbers—a few hundred, a few thousand, and though their effect on the nation's economy was marginal, they embodied the extreme in labor-capital confrontation. In each case labor and its friends in local government stood arrayed on one side, capital on the other, with no one in between. Employers called on county sheriffs, hired guards, state and federal troops repeatedly; while miners grabbed instinctively for their Winchesters or sticks of dynamite. Shoot-outs, dynamitings, outdoor bullpens, injunctions, deportations were widespread and commonplace.

Some of the lesser-known labor wars were as savage as those in the more centrally located industries—perhaps more so. A case in point was that in metal mining out West, which like coal in an earlier day, was a nascent industry.

Though the California gold rush of 1848–49 and the discovery of the Comstock Lode near Carson City, Nevada, in 1859 spurred the production of gold and silver, it was not until the conclusion of the Civil War that hard-rock mining grew in astounding geometric progression. For example, only 8,000 tons of copper, the second most important metal ore, were mined annually before 1861, but 130,000 tons by 1890. Profits too, for the mine owners were sensational. To cite one case, from 1871 to 1886, the Calumet and Hecla Mining Company paid dividends of $28 million—an average of 144.5 per cent on investment per year. The lead, zinc, quartz, silver and iron-ore operations forged strongly ahead, parallel with the expansion in heavy industry, and before long scores of remote, inaccessible places in Colorado, Utah, Montana, Arizona, and Idaho burgeoned into sizable thriving towns.

Ordinarily, the first inhabitants of these new meccas were individual prospectors—primarily adventurers and fortune hunters. Then came the corporations—Anaconda, Phelps Dodge, Bunker Hill and Sullivan, and innumerable others, and with the corporations came labor-saving devices and class strife. The individual prospector could not compete with machine techniques. He became a miner working for wages, and as likely as not, reduced from skilled to semi-skilled tasks. A single man with an air drill, for instance, did the work formerly done by five hand-drillers, leaving four men relegated thereby to lesser jobs and lesser pay. And just as in other industries when times were good, management tried to hold the line on wages, gobbling up the extremely high profits for itself. But when the companies faced some adverse circumstance, such as an increase in freight rates or a decline in business, the adversity was immediately passed on to the miner in the form of still lower wages or added duties. The inevitable outcome of this situation as with other earlier ones in the East was, unsurprisingly, the emergence of trade unionism as a measure of worker self-defense. The laborers in the Rockies were almost entirely native-born or English-speaking, fairly homogeneous ethnically, and therefore quick to act in concert. The first modern organization was the one formed by the copper men of Butte, Montana, in 1878—a local that was to be the most stable and enduring of all metal miner unions. Others also budded throughout the West, some disappearing with the first blast of industrial war, but most achieving some measure of permanence, even when initially defeated.

Typical of the outbreaks which wracked the western region of the country for more than two decades were those of Coeur d'Alene, in northern Idaho. The Coeur d'Alenes, thirty miles long, a few miles wide, surrounded by mountains and filled with gulches and deep canyons, were almost untouched until 1882 when gold was discovered there. Then, with gold deposits there proving inadequate, the prospectors turned to silver and lead which were in greater abundance. By 1887, after the corporations had taken over and a narrow-gauge railroad had been chiseled through the main canyon, there were approximately 1,000 miners on company payrolls, the largest contingent employed by the Bunker Hill and Sullivan Company at Wardner. Purchased by a Portland capitalist named Simeon G. Reed, Bunker Hill was sold soon thereafter to a much larger combine—with offices in San Francisco and New York—headed by John Hays Hammond. The same fate befell most of the locally owned properties, converting the Coeur d'Alenes into an immensely profitable suzerainty of absentee owners.

In 1887 the Bunker Hill and Sullivan Company suddenly slashed the pay scale from $3.50 a day to $2.50, sparking a successful work-stoppage action which restored the cut, and coincidentally sired the first Coeur d'Alene union. In 1891 the firm had another try at cutting wages, again unsuccessfully. Then on New Year's Day 1892, it tried for the third time, shutting down its pits, allegedly to put pressure on the railroads to reduce freight charges. That this was not the real reason, or the only reason, was made evident in mid-March when they offered to reopen if the union would trim its previous pay rate. When the miners rejected this offer the Mine Owners' Association vowed "never to hire another member of the miners' union." This lockout became in turn a full-scale strike to save the union.

But from March to July 1892, Coeur d'Alene, if not entirely peaceful, was still far from riotous. Though the miners had been without pay for a full half-year, they were eking out an existence of sorts as a result of a five-thousand-dollar loan and other funds made available by the copper miners in Butte. They were disturbed by the influx of strikebreakers from California, but they were confident they could keep the numbers of them within reason. The Coeur d'Alene canyons were narrow, with only a few points of ingress; and these were carefully monitored by the union and a sympathetic sheriff. Some scabs were induced to leave voluntarily; a few were prodded at rifle point. On April 2, for instance, a group of non-unionists were marched along a gulch to the serenade of tin cans, and told to head for Montana.

In May the situation became more serious. A federal judge issued an injunction against interfering with the mine operations, and the companies brought in three hundred strikebreakers from Duluth, escorted by fifty-three armed detectives. The owners also combed the Idaho countryside looking for farmers willing to replace the strikers. Even so, more than half the scabs recruited were won over by fervid and peaceful persuasion to join the union—and the strike.

There is a limit to the retention of accumulated bitterness, however. In mid-July, with "blacklegs"—strikebreakers—now a distinct menace, the passions surrounding the situation erupted into serious violence. On the tenth there was a fist fight between a Bunker Hill and Sullivan guard and a striker in the town of Gem. Rumor spread that the worker had been killed, and hundreds of miners descended on the town with Winchesters. When they found they were misinformed, they drifted away. But on the eleventh, company guards did kill a striker and this time four hundred of his comrades stormed the Frisco Mill and its barracks. The strikers fired on the installation for some time, but were unable to dislodge the company men. While the fighting was under way, however, some miners managed to shove two fifty-pound boxes of dynamite down an unguarded water conduit leading into the mill, blowing it up. One guard was killed, twenty seriously injured.

From the Frisco Mill the strikers headed for the Gem Mill, a half-mile away. Again the resistance the workers met was fierce. In the exchange of fire, company police killed five strikers and wounded fourteen. Nonetheless, in this case, unlike at Frisco Mill, the guards were forced to surrender, yield their weapons to the attackers, and agree to leave the district; 110 scabs were paraded through the streets of Wallace, three miles from the mine. Much as the steel-workers in Homestead, Pennsylvania had paraded the Pinkertons to the local ice rink just a few days before. On the twelfth, the rampaging miners moved down the canyon from Wallace to Wardner Junction, twelve miles below, and forced the Bunker Hill and Sullivan, Sierra Nevada, and Last Chance mines to halt operations,

280 scabs were dismissed and escorted to the mouth of the Fourth of July Canyon near Cataldo, where they were ordered out of the area.

The violence had not been planned in advance. If it had been it would certainly have been reported to the Mine Owners' Association by a spy named Charlie Siringo, who had insinuated himself into the Gem local union as recording secretary. The violence flared from a sudden spell of fury, and might have abated as rapidly as it arose if there had been any effort to conciliate the dispute. Instead Governor Willey declared a state of insurrection on July 13 and requested federal troops from President Harrison. Almost 1,500 soldiers of the U. S. Army and National Guard arrived under the command of Major General J. M. Schofield, and at once instituted a reign of terror which an AFL organizer, stopping over at Coeur d'Alene, described as worse than anything practiced "in Russia, Siberia, or by a plantation Slave-Driver . . ." Every union member who could not escape to Montana—six hundred in all—was clamped in a hastily built stockade, a "bullpen." The rights of habeas corpus and arrest by warrant were thoroughly ignored by the troops. Only those strikers willing to turn state's evidence against their fellow workers, and forswear future union activity, were offered release. Meanwhile, General Schofield, with great military efficiency, set about on his own resolve to do what the employers had been unable to do—smash the union. Ranging far afield from re-establishing "law and order," the general issued an edict that no mineowner was to employ a union man in his pit. Two small mines, working with union men, were instructed to discharge them, and had no choice but to comply.

What Schofield left undone, the courts finished. Judge James H. Beatty sentenced a dozen strikers to terms of four to eight months for contempt of court and had them locked up in the Ada County jail. Thirty more were held on federal charges of criminal conspiracy, and fifteen, including Justice of the Peace George A. Pettibone (who would later figure in a sensational trial with Big Bill Haywood) and union lawyer James Hawley, stood trial. Four were convicted and sentenced to prison terms of fifteen months to two years, but were later released by the U. S. Supreme Court. Two men were tried for murder and acquitted. Scores of indictments had to be quashed finally when it became clear that the state could not muster the evidence to convict.

II

The Mine Owners' Association had hoped to destroy the union through military repression and court action, but, as often happens, its best laid plans not only went awry, but indeed fully backfired.

Though the union was battered and an injunction hung over its head, it went about re-recruiting old members, as well as some of those who had scabbed, with great persistence. The re-enlistment work had to be done sub rosa but in the end it was eminently successful; in one mine after another the men jointly demanded and were collectively granted a restoration of the wage cut. "Most all the men working in the Coeur d'Alene country," reported P. J. McArthur, secretary of the Butte Miners' Union, in February 1893, "are now union men. . . . We think before six months we will have better unions than ever before and the wages is the same as before the trouble."

Even more distressing for the owners were the circumstances leading from Beatty's court to the hatching of what professors Selig Perlman and Philip Taft have called "the most militant [labor organization] in the history of the United States."

Among those under the judge's sentence in the Ada County jail at Boise, was twenty-nine-year-old Edward Boyce, destined to become the national leader of the metal miners. A tall, thin, balding man with excellent features but protruding teeth—the result of a peculiar malady suffered by quartz miners—Boyce was born and educated in Ireland, and then emigrated to Boston, haven of so many Irishmen, in 1882. The city somehow did not fascinate him, and thus he moved westward, gradually, to Wisconsin, Colorado and eventually Idaho. Along the way he worked as a railroader and then a metal miner in Leadville where he joined the Leadville Miners' Union at that time affiliated with the Knights of Labor. In 1887, after drifting some more, he settled in Wardner, and when the strike there took place in 1892, he inevitably became one of its leaders, and one of those sentenced for contempt of court.

While in prison Boyce and the other unionists discussed endlessly the prospects for labor organization in the hard rock mines. In one of the sessions, James Hawley, their lawyer and once a miner himself, declared that there was a need to amalgamate the isolated metal mining unions into a single federation; the men agreed enthusiastically. On being released Boyce sold the idea to the leaders of the Butte Miners' Union, and on May 15, 1893, forty delegates from Colorado, Idaho, Montana, and South Dakota met in Butte to establish the Western Federation of Miners. Like the AFL at the time of its inception, the WFM did not flourish overnight. But when Ed Boyce became its president in 1896—after two chief officers had quit the year before—its membership expanded greatly and turned distinctly leftward politically. Before long it was forming union rifle clubs, and engaging in one militant strike after another.

The center of conflict was Colorado. There was eventually another labor war in Coeur d'Alene, 1899–1901, with the same scenario of dynamitings, troops, bullpens, rifle firing, arrests and union-busting. And there were others elsewhere in the West. But indicative of the degree and amount of turbulence in Colorado was the fact that state militia was dispatched to strike battlegrounds no fewer than nine times from 1894 to 1904, almost once a year.

Back in 1858 gold had been discovered in a mountainous region two miles above sea level and eighty miles (as the crow flies) southwest of Denver. The settlement there, Oro City, did not amount to much until 1878—two years after Colorado became a state—when lead and silver were also discovered. Oro City's name was changed to Leadville and within thirty-six months its population zoomed from 200 to 14,000, as both local capitalists and such outsiders as Marshall Field and Meyer Guggenheim formed corporations to reap the bonanza. Here the first Colorado mining union came into being in 1880, and the first strike—of 3,000 men—was smashed by a Committee of Five Hundred (prototype of later Citizens' Alliances), the declaration of martial law, and the dispatch of sixteen companies of hastily organized militia. The union leaders were deported from the county, and the only flicker of unionism that survived for a decade and a half after this occurrence was the ineffective Knights of Labor.

Meanwhile in 1891, gold was also discovered in a barren district with arid climate not too far away, and within two years, the town of Cripple Creek boasted 5,000 inhabitants. Together with six or seven adjacent villages carrying esoteric names such as Anaconda, Altman, Goldfield, Victor, and Independence it became the locale of 150 operating mines. Not even the panic of 1893 dampened the boom at Cripple Creek; every freight brought an influx of jobless men seeking work. They found it at Cripple Creek—and found a strong union too. In December that year the already established Free Coinage Union No. 19 affiliated with the Western Federation of Miners, and elected as its leader a tough, cool Scotsman who once had studied at the McKeesport School of Mines—John Calderwood.

Calderwood had barely been installed when the union faced its first severe crisis—one of many to follow. In Cripple Creek, Colorado, as in Pullman, Illinois, the producers understood the significance of a surplus labor supply. Taking advantage of the unemployment caused by the depression, they unilaterally proclaimed in January 1894 an increase of the working day from eight hours to nine and ten—at the old pay. As an alternative they offered to retain the eight hours, but at fifty cents a day less pay. The union, of course, rejected both plans. Early in February roving pickets closed all the mines except the Pikes Peak, Gold Dollar, Portland and a few smaller ones which agreed to continue the old wage standards. For a few months the strike dragged on with few problems for the union. Those men who stayed at work assessed themselves 10 per cent of their wages to aid the strikers, and with money from the ever-generous Butte miners and those of the San Juan district in Colorado, the union fed its men at soup kitchens. An injunction against the union action was granted by a malleable local court but none of the companies could recruit more than a few men to oppose the union members. And the military or semi-military force needed to protect scabs just was not available, either from local or state authorities.

Typically, when Sheriff Frank Bowers of El Paso County sent a team of six deputies to Victor to defend a mine from would-be-dynamiters, they were surrounded by the city marshal's "special police"—all sympathetic to the strikers—at a ravine near Altman, and captured. Governor David H. Waite, a colorful Populist in his late sixties, with a booming voice and a long white beard, did send in three hundred militia after the Altman incident, but refused to permit them to act as agents for the companies, and soon withdrew them completely. A back-to-work movement begun by an *agent provocateur* at Anaconda aborted when the agent, William Rabedeau, was severely beaten by the local unionists.

In desperation the corporations called a secret meeting in Colorado Springs to which they invited Sheriff Bowers. Could he raise an army of deputies to protect strikebreakers? Yes, said the sheriff, but he had no money to pay them. The managers thereupon agreed to foot the bill and the sheriff to prosecute their little war.

Whatever philosophic virtues there may be to non-violence, neither the bosses of Cripple Creek nor their employees were willing to test it. A grim mood permeated the Creek towns. The strikers had been willing to accept a compromise made by Winfield S. Stratton of the Independence mine, for a nine-hour day at $3.25 and an eight-hour day at $3.00, but the other owners had rejected it. They also rejected a suggestion by the governor for arbitration. Clearly, another labor war was imminent, and small bands of unionists began to raid hardware stores for rifles and ammunition. Junius J. Johnson, a former West Pointer who had been left in charge of the strike while Calderwood beat the bushes in Colorado for relief money, prepared for Bowers' assault by organizing the strikers into a military cadre. A camp was established on a high, precipitous bluff overlooking Altman, called Bull Hill; primitive boardinghouses and a commissary were set up; and the strikers were given training in the art of war.

On May 25—four months after the strike began—the first group of deputized gunmen arrived from Denver on two flatcars of the Florence and Cripple Creek Railway. Commanded by an ex-police chief and including for the most part ex-policemen and ex-firemen, the 125 members of the strong-arm delegation were not ready for the greeting that awaited them. The miners clambered down the hill to the Strong mine, right near the railroad tracks, warned everyone out of sight, and set dynamite to the property. As the deputies alighted from the train, the shaft house blew three hundred feet into the air and another explosion a few seconds later plummeted the steam boiler toward the sky. Showered by debris of wood and metal, the human imports from Denver jumped back on the flatcars and backed away to safer confines several miles from Bull Hill.

In the bedlam that followed, with many men on drunken binges, including two hundred railroaders who had been laid off the day before by the Florence and Cripple Creek, a boisterous character named Jack Smith assembled a group of miners, loaded two wagons with dynamite, and vowed he would blow up every mine and every superintendent's house in the area. It took all of Johnson's persuasive power to dissuade him, but sometime in the wee hours of the morning, Smith caught up with the Denver gunmen and fought a bloody half-hour battle near Wilbur in which one man was killed on each side and five miners captured. At daybreak, after Calderwood had returned and incarcerated Smith, a semblance of peace prevailed. But the tense mood was obviously building for bigger battles. Two hundred miners from Leadville started toward Cripple Creek; one hundred armed diggers at Rico captured a train and traveled one hundred miles toward the seat of hostilities. Calderwood meanwhile arranged for the saloons to close in Cripple Creek, for strict discipline to be enforced at Bull Hill, and for daily armed drills. In Colorado Springs a Law and Order gathering called by the operators empowered Sheriff Bowers to arm more deputies. They were recruited from all sections of the state and stationed at the Colorado & Midland Railroad yards in Divide.

With civil war imminent Governor Waite issued a double-edged proclamation ordering the contending armies to disband, and placing his militia on full alert. At Altman the governor pledged he would do all in his power to settle the dispute on terms acceptable to the workers, and then set out with Calderwood for Colorado Springs in a howling storm to talk with representatives of management. After a few harrowing experiences, in which both the governor and the union leader were almost lynched on the Colorado College campus, the meetings were shifted to Denver and an agreement reached for an eight-hour day and a three-dollar wage—a stunning victory for the Western Federation of Miners.

There was still the serious business at hand, however, of aborting the incipient war at Cripple Creek. By the time General E. J. Brooks arrived with his militia, the brigade of company-paid deputies was already out of control. It had broken into small groups, cut telephone and telegraph wires, seized newspaper reporters, and engaged in a series of minor skirmishes. Had things progressed much further the bloodshed would have been considerable and property damage monumental, because the miners were well organized. Though they had no cannon they improvised a bow-gun capable of throwing beer-bottle missiles, filled with dynamite, to the foot of the hill. At various places electric wires were connected to explosives ready to blow up mines at the push of a button. Every striker was given five dynamite cartridges, each the size of a pencil and fitted with percussion caps, to carry in his vest pocket.

On June 7 the deputies began to march on the strikers. The latter scrambled to their posts on Bull Hill. Had General Brooks not thrown his forces between the adversaries the human death toll in shootings and from dynamitings would have been enormous. The militia, however, stopped hostilities before a single shot was fired, ordering both deputies and miners back to their respective camps. The strikers yielded to Brooks, permitting him to occupy Bull Hill and the town of Altman. The deputies had to be subdued with sterner measures. Frustrated by not being able to settle scores with the miners, they fanned out into Cripple Creek town, arrested a considerable number of people, and caused general havoc. Finally, Brooks was able to round them up and place them on a train for Colorado Springs.

III

The Cripple Creek strike was unique in that the forces of the state remained benevolently neutral. Thus, while the pall of defeat was cast over organized labor efforts elsewhere, such as at Pullman, in the Rockies the Western Federation of Miners recorded a tremendous victory. Its momentum carried the Federation into areas both not yet touched by unionism and those in which the debilitated Knights of Labor still presided. In the few years following the Cripple Creek triumph, scores of new WFM locals dotted the hard-rock mining areas, and most were able to come to terms with employers without strikes. Just as defeat has a domino effect, so does victory. With memories of the Cripple Creek strike still fresh, the mine owners in many communities, rather than face a similar prospect, responded to the WFM's gentle prodding.

Not that every WFM campaign led smoothly to reconciliation; far from it. In a strike of 2,500 miners at Leadville in 1896, Governor Albert W. McIntire sent in ten companies of infantry and one of cavalry after an oil tank at one mine and a shaft at another were blown up, presumably by the strikers. Together with 350 members of a businessmen's corps the armed forces eviscerated the union and forced its members to return to work on management terms. A similar fate befell strikers in Coeur d'Alene, Idaho, in 1899 after they had blown up the Bunker Hill and Sullivan mill and set fire to company offices and boardinghouses. Governor Frank Steunenberg, a Populist elected with the help of miners' votes, turned on his political allies and, with President McKinley's troops, smashed the union with much the same tactics as those used in the same area in 1892. One union official was sentenced to seventeen years for second-degree murder, eight others to two years for interfering with U.S. mails. It was almost two years before the soldiers were withdrawn.

Yet, despite these setbacks, the over-all prospects for the future of the Western Federation were definitely good. It had struck a resonant chord in its approach to the inter-mountain diggers. Its policy of direct action seemed to fellow miners like the ideal response to the cold, unresponsive attitudes of management. The unionists of the mining camps of the Rockies showed little disposition for niceties. They were not shocked or alienated when Ed Boyce, at the 1896 WFM convention, called on them to arm at least 25,000 members within the next year. Nor did they bridle at Boyce's personal belief in socialism or at a later, more firm commitment by the WFM to the "principles of socialism without equivocation." They concluded from their experiences that there were two irreconcilable classes in society, and that direct action and socialism, as propounded by the WFM leadership, were the only proper worker responses to that stalemate.

The Western Federation truly exuded an aura of power. Its campaign for the eight-hour day was imaginative—and generally successful. Its friendly relations with innumerable local, and some state, officials helped buttress the organization's feeling of power. So too did the formation in 1898 of the Western Labor Union as a WFM satellite to enroll workers outside the mines, and as a competing labor counterforce to the AFL, which many, if not most, miners considered both tepid and treacherous. Unlike the anthracite union of the 1870s or that of the railroaders in 1877, WFM provided the hard-rock miners with a stable, tough, and reliable base and a fair treasury. In less than a decade, then, it grew from fifteen local unions in five states to two hundred in thirteen states, Alaska, and Canada.

As the new century began, the Federation seemed to be headed toward even greater things. It won a sensational victory in 1901 against the gold companies of Telluride, in the southwest corner of Colorado. The mineowners there had introduced a unique system of payment based on the number of fathoms a worker mined, a fathom being defined as six feet high, six feet long, and as wide as the vein. It was an unjust system because the veins varied considerably in width, but the evil was compounded by the fact that the corporations repeatedly reduced the price per fathom and also imposed additional chores on workers, such as breaking the ore into specified sizes or shoeveling it down the chute. Since there were no wage or hour guarantees for the miners either, earning the union's minimum rate of $3 a day or completing the tasks in eight hours became increasingly difficult, often impossible.

In May 1901, after the owners of the Smuggler-Union mine, which employed 400 men, refused to change the fathom system, the diggers struck. Their leader was twenty-five-year-old Vincent St. John, of whom much more would be heard in ensuing years. Six weeks after the stoppage action began, the company's manager, Arthur L. Collins, managed to get 50 scabs into the pits, and in the next two weeks, 40 more. The union's position of strength was thus seriously endangered; St. John decided to strike back. On July 3 at 5 A.M., while the night shift was leaving the mine and the day shift was going in, 250 strikers, armed with shotguns, revolvers and rifles took positions behind boulders and trees—like the Minutemen of the American Revolution—and attacked the equally well-armed strikebreakers and deputy sheriffs. The next few hours were bedlam, with one striker killed in the first fusillade and the company buildings under siege. When the battle was over, 3 other men lay dead, six wounded; 88 scabs had surrendered to the union and been escorted out of town where they were told to head for Ouray County. A few were beaten severely and one man shot in both arms as the strikers took revenge for their slain comrade. The strike was won. Late the same day, St. John signed a three-day "armistice," and in those three days Lieutenant-Governor David M. Coates (once a union official himself) helped work out an agreement that guaranteed the $3 a day minimum. A subsequent pact in November with all the area's mineowners established the eight-hour day for underground mine workers.

That same year the Western Federation widened its horizons by launching a drive to unionize thousands of workers in Colorado's smelters. The smelter industry, which reduced—separated—the gold-bearing ore after it left the mines, was dominated by such giants as American Smelting and Refining, and United States Reduction and Refining. Its employees were still working ten to twelve hours a day, as against eight now quite firmly established as standard in the mines. An eight-hour law, passed by the legislature had been adjudged unconstitutional by the Colorado Supreme Court. But even when a constitutional amendment, adopted by popular referendum, effectively reversed the courts, the smelter companies blithely disregarded the statute. Moreover, not only were the smelter workers' hours longer but their wages were barely half those of the diggers—a minimum daily pay of $1.80 out of which was deducted five cents for compulsory insurance. Living conditions for the workers were so poor that many mill families lived in tents—winter and summer—because they could not afford to rent a house.

After months of preparatory work, in August 1902 the Western Federation chartered the Colorado City Mill and Smelterman's Union No. 125. The drive augured a considerable expansion of WFM's ranks. And it was also the prologue to the second Cripple Creek strike, the most contentious in WFM's entire, stormy history.

IV

The leading figure in the smelter unionization campaign and the strike that followed, was a hulking miner who typified the spirit of proletarian struggle and resistance more than any man of this period, and was soon to head the most radical union the United States has ever produced, the Industrial Workers of the World. William D. (Big Bill) Haywood, stoop-shouldered, blind in one eye, but square-jawed and strong as an ox, was six foot two and 225 pounds of muscle. He could, and sometimes did, knock a man unconscious with a single blow. He was a living legend and no angel. After his wife, the former Nevada Jane Minor, fell from a horse and was permanently incapacitated, he sometimes went on sudden drinking binges, and just as suddenly quit. But if he loved a good brawl, he loved Shakespeare too, whom he read avidly, and he could cry like a child while reciting poetry. He enjoyed enormous popularity with the miners, not only for his manliness, but because of his ability to reduce complicated concepts to bare essentials. Typical was this characterization of the "barbarous gold barons," who, he said, "do not find the gold, they do not mine the gold, they do not mill the gold, but by some weird alchemy all the gold belongs to them."

Haywood was born in Salt Lake City in 1869, of a Scotch-Irish mother who came from South Africa, and a father whom he described as a member "of an old American family, so American that if traced back it would probably run to the Puritan bigots or the cavalier pirates." The elder Haywood, a Pony Express rider, died when Big Bill was three; the only memory of him that lingered in the boy's mind was of being taken to a Main Street store in Salt Lake for a new velvet suit. At seven, after his mother had remarried and the family had moved to a mining town called Ophir, Bill saw one man kill another in a gun fight, a scene he was to witness many times in the future years. "I accepted it," he wrote in his autobiography, "as a natural part of life." He himself was in endless brawls with youngsters his own age who called him "Squint-eye" or "Dick Dead-eye" because of his one-eyed blindness. But it did not faze him: "I used to like to fight," he records.

While still at school Haywood was indentured to a farmer during summer vacation time at a dollar a month and board. When the boss whip-lashed him for idling over a nest of field mice, he ran ten miles to his home. It was his first "strike" and the first of many odd jobs. At twelve Big Bill saw a Black, accused of killing a policeman, turned over to a mob and lynched. The incident left him limp with tears. At fifteen, mother Haywood decided that her son should learn a trade, and the young man outfitted with a pack consisting of "overalls, jumper, blue shirt, mining boots, two pairs of blankets, a set of chessmen, and a pair of boxing gloves," set out for Humboldt County, Nevada, where his stepfather was superintendent of the Ohio Mine and Milling Company.

Though there were some mining towns with 5,000 and 10,000 population by this time, many others were hardly more than dots on the desert. Eagle Canyon, where Big Bill alighted, was one of the latter, a desolate place, which housed its miners in a single wooden building twenty-eight feet long and fourteen feet wide. The nearest town of any size was sixty miles away, and the only youngster in the area Bill's age, four miles away. The spell of loneliness was broken for the future labor leader only by a dog he acquired, and by the oldest man in the camp, a tall, gaunt, red-whiskered chap named Pat Reynolds, who regaled him with stories of the Knights of Labor. Reynolds also loaned him books by Darwin, Marx, Burns, Voltaire, Byron, and above all, Shakespeare.

Bill Haywood was still in Eagle Canyon in May 1886 when he learned through the newspapers about the Haymarket Riot in Chicago—it was to be, he wrote, "a turning point in my life." Discussing Haymarket with Pat Reynolds every night, Big Bill found himself adopting the same anti-capitalist position as his mentor. He was convinced that it could not have been Albert Parsons or his anarchist friends who threw the bomb—"if it had been, why did Albert Parsons walk into court and surrender himself?" When Parsons and three others were hanged, Big Bill repeated over and over again the last words of August Spies: "There will come a time when our silence will be more powerful than the voices you are strangling today."

The next ten years in the life of Bill Haywood were much like those of many thousands of other working Westerners—rootless, uncertain, sometimes despairing. After leaving Nevada he went to work at the Brooklyn lead mine in his native state, Utah, where he saw "men going to and coming from the hospital all the time suffering from lead poisoning." Another indelible memory for him was of a miner killed when a slab of rock fell from the roof and crushed his head against the air drill. Big Bill married at nineteen, had two children with Nevada Jane, one of whom died, and he tried to settle down—but could not find his own work niche. He did some assessor work and prospecting, tried his hand as a cowboy, surveyor, and as a farmer on a deserted army post at Fort McDermott, Nevada—which he enjoyed most because it gave him a sense of independence. But when the government returned this land to the Indians, Haywood was forced to uproot again—in the midst of the 1893 depression. Circulating far and wide through the West, riding the freights, hitching rides with ranchers, he somehow managed to earn a few dollars to keep his brood together—once even by operating a poker game for a month. It was not a stable existence.

Finally in 1896 Big Bill returned to the pits, taking a job at the Blaine mine in Silver City, Idaho. Here he was to find his calling. While his wife was giving birth to a second girl and he himself was recovering from an accident which smashed his right hand, Ed Boyce, the new WFM president, came through town on an organizing tour. Crippled hand and all, still living off collections made by fellow workers to keep him going, Big Bill threw himself into the union campaign with characteristic gusto. He became the sparkplug of a drive that recruited 1,000 members in Silver City—only two of whom had to be persuaded with a little muscle—and he was soon the president of the Silver City Miners' Union. Two years later he was on the WFM's national executive board, and the following year "turned off the air on the machine drill for the last time" as he left for Denver where WFM convention delegates chose him as the organization's secretary-treasurer. It was while sitting in his office, at the new post, that Big Bill suggested to Ed Boyce that they unionize three nearby smelters. They did.

v

The second Cripple Creek strike was a small-scale replica of the Pullman strike nine years earlier. It did not actually begin in

Cripple Creek's mines, but in the reduction mills at Colorado City, and in the shadow of Pikes Peak.

WFM Local 125 in Colorado City was quite moderate in tone in expression of its demands. "We . . . desire the prosperity of the company," said one of its letters to a corporate official, "and so far as our skill and labor go will do all we can to promote its interests." But the managers of the Portland, Telluride and Standard smelter plants (the latter a subsidiary of United States Reduction and Refining), considered a moderate union just as repulsive as a militant one. They plain and simply did not want to deal with any kind of union. Pinkertons were hired to infiltrate the new local, and as the names of new union recruits were uncovered by the detectives the men were discharged one by one. When Big Bill Haywood went to talk about these peremptory firings with J. D. Hawkins, the Standard mill general superintendent, the company official bluntly admitted that the dismissals were for union activity—and he promptly fired twenty-three additional union men. The Western Federation of course could not tolerate such a situation, and in mid-February 1903, declared a strike for such modest demands as reinstatement of those fired, a $2.25 minimum daily wage, a shorter work day, and union recognition.

The stoppage proceeded according to the established pattern: the companies, reacting to the strike, recruited strikebreakers, and in turn, the strikers established picket lines to intercept them. Then with the plea from Standard's manager, Charles M. MacNeill, that the strike posed a "grave danger" to his property, Governor James H. Peabody sent in six companies of state troops to clear up the conflict. Within three days picketing was curbed, union camps torn down, the homes of union men searched, the union hall placed under surveillance. The battle, however, was fortunately not yet beyond resolution. With public sentiment heavily on the side of the smelter workers and the Denver newspapers snapping at the companies for their obduracy, Governor Peabody called a conference and effected a settlement with two of the mills. Portland and Telluride agreed to the eight-hour day, union recognition, and reinstatement of the strikers. Had MacNeill of Standard followed suit, a costly labor war would have been averted.

Haywood and Charles Moyer, the South Dakota smelter worker who had replaced Ed Boyce as WFM president, had another weapon they could use against management—they could shut off Standard's supply of ore by calling out the nearby Cripple Creek diggers who mined it. First, however, they made a public appeal for arbitration. They encouraged businessmen of the district to act as go-betweens as well as a state commission which tried to mediate in the disagreement. When these gambits failed, the Cripple Creek mines furnishing ore to Standard were closed down for two weeks. Later after the commission worked out a compromise whereby MacNeill agreed to abide by the eight-hour law and to reinstate union members as rapidly as circumstances allowed, Moyer called off the Colorado City strike and declared an armistice until May 18—to see if Standard would carry out its promises. It did not. Of the 102 strikers who reapplied for jobs forty were turned down, sixty others were offered work at lower grades than they had had before. MacNeill refused to raise his minimum pay of $1.75 a day, though his two major competitors had already come to terms with the union for $2.00 and $2.65. On July 3, after further procrastination by Haywood and Moyer, the strike was renewed at Colorado City, and on August 8, District Union 1 at Cripple Creek declared a sympathy strike.

There is good reason to believe that the ensuing conflagration at Cripple Creek would have erupted regardless of what Haywood did. Colorado and its union-management relations that year were in an uproar: coal miners were on strike in Trinidad and Pueblo; teamsters, butchers, cooks, and waiters in Denver; 250 WFM members at the Sun and Moon mine in Idaho Springs; and another, more bellicose strike was in the offing at Telluride.

On the management side, employers had been planning counterstrategy against the WFM ever since the first Telluride strike in 1901. What they needed, they felt, was their own man in the governor's chair, and a semi-military movement capable of combatting the miners with physical force. In Jim Peabody they had as bitter an anti-union advocate as it was possible to install in the statehouse. A former shopowner and banker, Peabody was determined to set aside the eight-hour day, as he wrote the Los Angeles *Times*, "if it requires the entire power of the State and the Nation" to do it. He also favored legislation to outlaw strikes and boycotts.

The second facet of employer strategy was implemented late in April 1903, when six hundred businessmen met in the offices of the Denver Chamber of Commerce and formed a Citizens' Alliance. Within six months almost every mining town had its chapter, and the state-wide membership spiraled to 30,000 pro-management people, dedicated to eviscerating the WFM by whatever means necessary. As the head of the Alliance in Denver put it cryptically: "unions should not strike; striking unions are not legitimate; the [Western] Federation must be destroyed."

The mineowners, who of course were the backbone of the Citizens' Alliance, could have avoided the dispute with the WFM by agreeing to withhold ore going to the Standard mills. Instead they remorselessly broadened the battle. The strike was only three days old when local merchants in Cripple Creek, pressured by the Alliance, announced they would no longer advance credit to the miners, as in the past. Haywood countered by opening four stores which redeemed strikers' relief coupons and sold meats and groceries to others at cost. The union emporiums functioned throughout the strike and were immensely successful. Simultaneous with the merchants' gambit canceling credit, the owners declared that they would reopen their mines with scabs one at a time, beginning with the El Paso.

A stockade and ten-foot wooden fence was built around the El Paso shaft house—for which carpenters were paid the unheard-of high wages of a dollar an hour—and seventeen armed guards were employed to patrol the property. On August 18 the mine reopened with seventy-five scabs. Two weeks later a second mine, the Golden Cycle, repeated the process—built a fence, hired armed guards, recruited replacements—but was unable, unlike the El Paso to resume work until troops arrived. Meanwhile help-wanted ads for miners were placed in many newspapers, as far away as Duluth, which pointedly omitted the fact that the men were to be used as strikebreakers.

For three weeks or more the strike was a standoff. Only the Portland mine in Victor, which the union permitted to operate to supply its mill at Colorado City—which was not on strike—and the El Paso showed any signs of life. Violence by either side was negligible, and, according to the sheriff, easily contained. On September 2, however, businessmen in Cripple Creek petitioned the governor for armed forces, and on the fourth—after an investigating committee had talked with the owners, but carefully avoided contact with the union—700 troops (later expanded to 1,000) disembarked near Goldfield and set up six camps in the vicinity. Since there was no money in the state Treasury for such adventures, the mineowners graciously agreed to advance Governor Peabody as much as a half-million dollars. It was money well spent, for in General Sherman Bell, who commanded the soldiers, they had a champion as fervid as themselves. "I came," said the general, "to do up this damned anarchistic federation." He would "take no further orders from the civil authorities," permitting himself to be guided only by the laws of "military necessity." His credo was best expressed in a retort to a union lawyer seeking habeas corpus for his clients: "Habeas corpus, hell! We'll give 'em post mortems!" One of his aides, when reminded of transgressions on the Constitution, said: "To Hell with the Constitution. We are not going by the Constitution, we are following the orders of Governor Peabody." According to the Boston *Transcript*,

Bell was receiving $3,200 a year from the mineowners in addition to his state salary.

The militia deployed sentinels along the roads, guards at the mines, and at night lit the skies with a portable searchlight. If their equipment at first was sub-par, it was soon remedied by the secret arrival from Wyoming of 1,000 Krag-Jörgensen rifles and 60,000 rounds of ammunition, which Haywood charged was a gift of the federal government. Western Union telegraph lines connected Bell's headquarters with Denver and his auxiliary camps.

This was war, and Bell might as well have been back in Cuba where he had fought the Spaniards with Teddy Roosevelt. Almost at once the soldiers began arresting union officers and union militants, who were placed in the old wooden jail at Goldfield, popularly called the "bullpen." The first man caught was Charles Kennison, president of the Cripple Creek Miners' Union Number 40, soon to be followed by Sherman Parker, secretary of the Free Coinage Miners' Union Number 19. No warrants were issued for the arrest of these men, no bail set, and no charges levied—other than the one of "military necessity." For good measure, the soldiers tossed the county commissioner, the justice of the peace, and city marshal of Independence into the same bullpen as the strikers.

The union hired a respectable Denver law firm to institute *habeas corpus* proceedings on behalf of the incarcerated men. When the case came up for hearing on September 21, ninety cavalrymen formed a ring around the courthouse and the prisoners were marched into jail by a company of infantrymen with bayonets drawn. After some delays, because the judge refused to consider the case in an atmosphere of virtual martial law, the men were granted their freedom. The militia, nonetheless, refused to accept the decision, and to everyone's amazement marched the prisoners back to the bullpen, where they were finally released a few hours later on the governor's direct order. Bell evidently had strayed a mite too far, but Governor Peabody's conscience was not particularly hurt by other acts committed under military rule. The *Victor Record,* for instance, was raided on September 29 and every member of its staff carried off to the bull pen because Bell took exception to one of its editorials.

Simultaneous with the repression of union activists and their friends, the militia escorted strikebreakers into the mines. WFM members were not permitted to talk or communicate with them in any way. Stranded far from home, under the watchful eye of soldiers and guards day and night, many workers who might have responded to union pleas not to work continued to scab. Thus, behind fences and barricades, the managers opened up the Golden Cycle six days after the guardsmen arrived, and in rapid order the Findlay, Strong, Ajax, Tornado, Elkton, and Thompson shafts started up again too. The Western Federation and its cause clearly were being hurt, yet the strike was far from broken. The stores and relief program gave the strikers financial help. Adequate monies were coming in not only from Colorado, but from as far away as Utah, Oregon, Nevada, Idaho, Montana, and British Columbia. The Federation was still a functioning organization. Its members, disregarding an order by General Bell that every citizen register his weapons, were well-armed. The substitution of strikebreakers for strikers was clearly not enough to break the union. As General Bell clearly understood, it was necessary to stop the strike "to do up this damned anarchistic federation."

An incident in mid-November gave Bell, Peabody, et al the pretext for assault on the union that they had been waiting for. An explosion at the 600-foot level of the Vindicator mine—while under military guard—took the lives of a foreman and superintendent. Ordinarily an accident of this sort would have been shrugged off as a relatively minor affair. In the period of labor upheaval, 1903–4, there was a spate of mine disasters far more costly than the one at Vindicator, including one in Wyoming which claimed 338 lives, and another at the Daly-West mine in Utah which killed thirty-five diggers. The decision of the coroner's jury, moreover, was that the explosion had been due to causes "unknown." According to Haywood and the union it was an act of provocation by company detectives. Strikers charged with the explosion were adjudged innocent in later court proceedings. Nonetheless four union leaders were arrested by the military and the governor used the occasion to declare that "a state of insurrection and rebellion" existed in Teller county. Civil authority was placed in limbo, habeas corpus suspended, and the military assumed governing power. Bell issued a vagrancy order (as he also did in the Telluride strike) declaring that "idle men [strikers] will find employment or face deportation from the district." Cripple Creek became a military dictatorship. Local police were deposed, their places taken by the militia. Newspapers were forbidden to carry any material unfavorable to the military. Union men were pursued into union halls and arrested by the score. A member of the Western Federation executive board, who came to open a cooperative store at Goldfield was told by the colonel in charge to leave town or go to jail. Teachers were stopped on their way to school and told to go home. Drunken soldiers became a common sight, carousing, fighting, beating, jailing anyone they could lay their hands on.

By February 2, 1904, Cripple Creek had returned to what was euphemistically called "normal" and the troops were withdrawn—

for five weeks. Meanwhile the Mine Owners' Association consolidated its mounting victory by introducing the "rustling card" system. Anyone who wanted work first had to fill out a card giving his personal history and stating that he would not accept membership in the Western Federation of Miners. Only then was he permitted to gain employment. In effect this was a massive blacklisting system aimed at rooting out the WFM altogether. "The avowed purpose of this association," said the Mine Owners' group with naked candor, "is to drive the disturbing and dangerous element of the WFM from the district and from the state . . ."

Despite all these efforts, the strike continued. Haywood was stubborn as a bulldog, as he went about reorganizing his forces and trying to swing public opinion. When the Mine Owners' Association issued a "Red Book" detailing the "Criminal Record of the Western Federation of Miners," he countered with a 27,000 word "Green Book," stating the "Category of Crime of the Mine Owners' Association." He printed a flag poster which was plastered on thousands of poles and billboards around the state. On each stripe of the flag was a slogan revealing the state's violations of liberty: "Martial Law Declared in Colorado!" "Habeas Corpus Suspended in Colorado! "Free Press throttled in Colorado!" "Corporations Corrupt and Control Administration in Colorado!" "Militia Hired by Corporations to Break the Strike in Colorado!" etc. Haywood also prevailed on the Colorado Federation of Labor to denounce "the presence of an armed soldiery in Teller and San Miguel counties . . . for the sole use and benefit of the Mine Owners' Association in their warfare against organized labor"; the Federation, in addition, threatened a statewide strike.

While all this was going on, WFM president Moyer was arrested in the Telluride area, where the union was engaged in an equally vicious strike, and harried by General Bell with the same tactics as those used at Cripple Creek. Moyer was charged with "desecrating the flag"—his name appeared on the union's flag poster which Haywood had printed—and was held in jail for three months despite efforts by his attorneys to secure his release on bail. Haywood himself was saved from deportation to Telluride—on the same charge—when a friendly sheriff incarcerated him in a Denver jail and set up a special prison office from which he continued to direct union affairs.

As of June 1904 the strike, in its various stages, had been under way for sixteen months. On June 6 another dynamiting presaged its final act. The town of Independence was in a deep valley below Altman and a half mile from Victor. Here on a hillside, at the station of the Florence and Cripple Creek Railroad, non-union men of the Findley mine were waiting for a train due at 2:15 A.M. to take them home when a massive explosion occurred, filling the air with flying timber, earth, and dismembered bodies, some of which were blown straight up 150 feet. Thirteen men were killed outright, sixteen injured, six of them requiring amputations. The holocaust might have been even worse but for the fact that men from the Shurtloff mine were a minute late in running for the station when the dynamite went off.

Subsequently a coroner's jury ascribed the blame for this disaster to "members and officials of the Western Federation of Miners." But when bloodhounds arrived from Trinidad that same day and were taken to the roped-off station, one of them drew a trail straight to the home of a Citizens' Alliance detective, and another to the powder magazine of a non-union mine. There were other suspicious circumstances pointing to the owners and Citizens' Alliance as responsible for the explosion. A boss at the Findley mine had urged his men to wait fifteen minutes before going to the depot—the fifteen minutes during which the explosion occurred. A banker at Victor had pleaded with a neutral police chief to resign, because "There is work to be done that you won't want to do."

Perhaps what the banker was referring to apart from the explosion itself was the lawlessness that began immediately after the incident. All mines were closed as a great mob gathered at the square in Victor, where the union hall and union store were located. C. H. Hamlin, secretary of the Mine Owners' Association made a rabble-rousing speech blaming the WFM for the explosion and calling the strikers a gang of cutthroats. He called on the assemblage to take the law into their own hands and not to rest until fifty union men had been shot down, another fifty hung on telegraph poles, and the rest driven over the mountain peaks. Someone in the crowd heckled Hamlin and someone else punched him with a fist. In an instant a small riot was on and two scabs killed, three wounded. Union men who took refuge in their headquarters were peppered by volley after volley of bullets from the rifles of the militia which had come to the square from their armory. Four were seriously wounded and the rest forced to surrender after a continuing exchange.

It was now the turn of the militia and the Citizens' Alliance to wreak their vengeance. No sooner were the strikers taken off to the bullpen than the mob rushed into the union hall, wrecked every piece of equipment and furniture and even shredded the books in the library. Union halls in other towns were similarly invaded and destroyed. On the blackboard of the engineers' union, after it had been ruined, was written: "For being a union man, deportation or death will be your fate. Citizens' Alliance." Every one of the four

WFM stores—in Anaconda, Goldfield, Victor, and Cripple Creek—
—was demolished and tons of commodities carted off by the rioters,
who included in their ranks the leading businessmen and citizens of
the area.

Again a state of insurrection was proclaimed, and again General
Bell was called to the scene. At Dunville, twelve miles from Victor,
one man was killed, fourteen others brought in as prisoners. On the
night of June 8 a gang of eight men invaded the *Victor Record* press
rooms, smashed its linotype machines and presses with big ham-
mers, and carried its employees to the bullpen. (The state later paid
the *Record* $4,206 in damages.) Still the anti-union fury was unap-
peased. Citizens' Alliance mobs continued to destroy property, arrest
inhabitants—including the city marshals at Anaconda, Independence,
and Goldfield—and remove local officials deemed friendly to the
union. Warrants were served in Denver on Moyer and other union
officials (Haywood hid in the home of the mayor's secretary and no
further attempts were made to arrest him.) Over the protest of
the manager of the Portland mine, which it will be recalled was
permitted to operate with union men, the shaft was closed by
militia and the company instructed to hire only non-union diggers.

What little union-busting these measures did not achieve was
completed by General Bell's wholesale deportations. Twenty-seven
strikers were shipped to Colorado Springs at once. To determine
who else was eligible for exile, Bell convened a makeshift commission,
mostly of Citizens' Alliance men, to interrogate the 1,569 prisoners
in his custody. At least 238 were ordered banished, and 42 held for
trial on various criminal charges. On June 10, 72 men were put on a
Santa Fe train, taken to a point near the Kansas line, and marched
out of the state. A volley of shots was fired over their heads as they
ran off—leaving wives, children, and homes behind—to remind them
what their fate might be if they dared return. "I don't want these
men in Colorado," said General Bell, and that evidently was the only
"law" needed to execute the policy. Other union men and supporters
were deported to New Mexico, and elsewhere, among them lawyers,
a former state attorney, a general who had served in the Civil War,
a county attorney, a judge, and a county clerk. Five union men who
returned to their families were gathered up by a band of 25 masked
men and again run out of Victor. One man was so badly beaten he
could not walk. Not even strike relief was permitted to remain in
union hands, the militia leaders insisting that it operate only under
their aegis.

The strike continued desultorily for a few months—and nominally
for a few years—but in fact the Western Federation had been beaten.

Hundreds of its members took out the employer "rustling cards" to go back to work, and though they secretly continued allegiance to the Federation, it was years before they reorganized openly. As late as December 1904 the mines in Telluride, now non-union, had to be patrolled night and day by guards armed with rapid fire guns, for fear of a union resurgence. But here too the Federation was in tatters.

Under these circumstances the vindication of the union in the courts was an anticlimatic, slight victory. On November 18 charges against the forty-two men accused of murder in the Victor riot were thrown out. A month and a half later the courts dismissed indictments against the national leaders of the WFM accused of complicity in the depot explosion. Further exculpation for the union came when some of the deportees filed suit against the state of Colorado and collected $60,-000 in damages.

In the aftermath of the over-all defeat, the Colorado State Federation of Labor organized a Liberty League to work in the 1904 elections using the slogan "Anybody but Peabody." The Democrats of the state incorporated the Liberty League program into their own, and though the Republican national standard-bearer, Teddy Roosevelt, carried the state handily, Peabody was massacred at the ballot box. In the aftermath, too, the WFM became the fulcrum for a movement even more radical, the Industrial Workers of the World.

But the war in the Rockies was over, the union in disarray. Harry A. Floaten, a socialist sympathizer of the WFM who had been deported and re-deported by Bell's minions, composed a parody that carried the flavor of defeat:

> Colorado, it is of thee,
> Dark land of Tyranny,
>   Of thee I sing;
> Land wherein labor's bled
> Land from which law has fled
> Bow down thy mournful head,
>   Capital is king.

8

Halfway House

The adversities suffered by the Western Federation of Miners occurred, ironically, at a time when unions generally were making great strides. The six-year period from 1899 through 1904 is recorded in labor history, in fact, as the "era of good feelings." Negotiated agreements on wages and hours were concluded in a host of industries inadequately or only partly covered before—the building trades, railroads, printing, machine shops, Great Lakes shipping, pottery, and above all in the coal pits. Prosperity returned to America coincident with the Spanish-American war, and with it, labor plunged into another round of struggles for industrial democracy—more successful than previous ones. The number of strikes, which in the early and mid-1890s averaged 1,000 to 1,300 a year, jumped to 1,779 in 1900, to almost 3,000 in 1901, and almost 4,000 in 1904. But, unlike results in the preceding period of depression, nearly half the stoppages ended in tangible gains. By 1904, the labor movement more than quadrupled in size—from 447,000 members in 1899 to 2,072,000 in 1904. The AFL, hub of the movement by now, saw its membership increase from 350,000 to 1,650,000. The growth of some individual unions was even more sensational, the Carpenters and Joiners advancing from 20,000 to 155,400, the Hotel and Restaurant Employees from 2,000 to 49,400, and the United Mine Workers from 40,000 to 260,300. The railroad brotherhoods, despite so many setbacks in their industry, nonetheless boasted a total of 200,000 members.

The over-all surge of organized labor had an effect both on the character of unionism and the nature of industrial relations. In the hegira from impotence to expansion many unions, such as those in the building trades, achieved arms-length accommodation with management, and one or two, such as the United Mine Workers, were able to establish an armed truce. No union gained its objectives without some duty on the picket line, some violence, arrests, killings. But in certain fields, mainly the decentralized industries, management recognized that it could not destroy its nemesis, and concluded that some sort of collaboration was preferable to war. Indeed, under some circumstances, collaboration could be profitable.

The contractors' association in Chicago, for instance, entered into an agreement with Martin (Skinny) Madden's carpenters' union in 1897, granting the closed shop in return for the union's pledge not to supply labor for *non*-association members. Thus, competitors who refused to join the association were, with the union's help, driven out of business. On occasion "Skinny" would call a strike against a recalcitrant employer to force him into the contractors' association. This cozy collusion was obviously in contrast to previous relations in the industry. In 1890–91 the National Builders' Association had used every conceivable device to abort the carpenters' movement for an eight-hour day. It imported strikebreakers, prevailed on material suppliers not to sell materials to union contractors, and hauled local unions into court. Strikes in Newark, Pittsburgh, Portland, Wheeling, San Francisco, New Orleans, Seattle and a half dozen other cities were smashed; one in Chicago, where pickets roamed a sixty-five mile radius to head off strikebreakers at railroad stations, terminated indecisively. By the end of the decade, however, the contractors found that wide-open, harsh attacks on unionism were too costly and often futile. They concentrated instead on taming the beast —and if possible using him for management purposes—rather than obliterating him. Pacts by industry similar to the one made with Skinny Madden were reached with bricklayers, steamfitters, plumbers, printers, and other craft organizations.

Some of these relations bordered on racketeering, or crossed its threshhold. For instance the Stonecutters' Union of Brooklyn received 10 per cent of the $600,000 in excess profits earned by the stonecutter association members as a result of the union's policy of striking independent corporations that failed to accept association membership or abide by its price-fixing. To take another example, by virtue of a 1902 agreement between the coal association of Chicago and the teamsters' union to strike or otherwise harass non-association members, the owners were able to drive up coal cartage costs from $1.40

to $2.00 a load. The labor leadership was so solicitous of the welfare of the coal association that it drove a whole competitive industry—the natural-gas industry—out of the city. By threatening to withhold coal from large office buildings in winter weather the union officials forced realtors to cancel their natural-gas contracts.

The spirit of "accommodation" that prevailed between labor and management was not limited to racketeers and industrial associations. There was in fact a far more important segment of capitalism that recognized its benefits. Testifying to the desire for substituting a form of reconciliation for warfare was the formation in 1900 of the National Civic Federation. The key figures in this organization were Ralph M. Easley, a Chicagoan who had already sired a local group with these objectives, and Marcus Alonzo (Mark) Hanna, an Ohio businessman associated with the Rockefellers. Hanna had helped McKinley into the White House in 1901 and was the leading spokesman of big business in the political arena. As president of the NCF until his death in 1904, he confidently predicted that under the NCF's ministrations there would be a "total abolition of strikes in the United States." By acting as the liaison between "reasonable" labor leaders—as opposed to radical ones—and the corporations, Hanna felt that unions would soften their militancy. He had no desire to advance the union cause, but given a choice between labor leftists and labor moderates, he considered it practical to undercut the former by giving a boost to the latter.

Associated with Hanna on the NCF roster were such industrial titans as J. Ogden Armour and Louis F. Swift of the meat-packing empires, Elbert H. Gary of the steel trust and Cyrus H. McCormick, the harvester king. Almost all of them fought their own unions hammer and tong, refusing them recognition for decades, but collectively they tried to fashion an image of moderation—especially in strikes that affected other entrepreneurs. To give the Civic Federation a tripartite character, Hanna added to its councils leaders of labor and representatives of the "public." On the labor side there were many union officials, such as the high-ranking AFL president, Sam Gompers, who were anxious to pad their security by enlarging the area of collaboration. Gompers was chosen NCF vice-president. John Mitchell of the United Mine Workers, P. J. McGuire of the carpenters' union, and leaders of the railroad brotherhoods also played a prominant role in NCF affairs. Rounding out the NCF list were former President Cleveland, banker Isaac N. Seligman, Oscar S. Straus, president of the New York Board of Trade and Transportation, and a bevy of men with strong business connections whose claim to "third party" status was that they had no record, except for Cleveland, of personal strikebreaking. With this blue-ribbon assemblage Hanna and the Civic Federation tried their hand at mediating the 1901 steel strike (which went down to utter defeat), the two anthracite coal strikes (where a stalemate was achieved), the threatened strike of 20,000 New York teamsters (which was averted) and similar struggles in twenty-two states.

Even in the "era of good feeling," however, individual battles between labor and capital continued as savage as in the past. During the 1902 coal strike, for instance, there were fourteen people killed, forty-two seriously wounded, sixty-seven cases of aggravated assault, twenty-two buildings and houses burned down and sixty-nine "riots." It was as though the labor movement were proceeding simultaneously along three non-contiguous tracks. In the seesaw between collabora-tion and war, some unions attained stability, status, and considerable power; others at the farthest track declined to insignificance (for example, the Amalgamated Association of Iron, Steel and Tin Workers after its 1901 strike). In the middle road some unions developed a stable structure after years of battle, but were never more than a hairsbreadth from a new labor war. In the latter category was the United Mine Workers of America, which was to be a pivotal force in the house of labor for the next half century.

II

It says something significant either of the tenacity of the miners or the enduring nature of their oppression—or both—that they never let up on efforts to gain control over their working conditions. Their strikes were often defeated, their organizations disbanded, yet they always put themselves back together and drove on. The American Miners' Association, formed in 1861 to organize what one of its leaders, Daniel Weaver, called "this heterogeneous concatenation of genus homo," died off a decade later to be replaced, on the initiative of John Siney, by the Miners' National Association of the United States. But after the Long Strike of 1875, and the uproar over the Molly Maguires, this association too dissolved in impotence. Yet, a decade later the miners were at it again, this time forming the Amalgamated Association of Miners of the United States. Led by the energetic and dynamic John McBride, a dedicated follower of Siney's, it was hastily assembled to meet a new challenge—the introduction of the Lechner mining machine, which caused the corporations to reduce wage scales for miners from sixty cents per ton dug to forty cents. The Association had hardly raised its banner when its member miners in the Hocking Valley of Ohio—McBride's bailiwick—downed their tools, and after the usual clashes with Pinkertons, company police, vigilantes, and two years on the picket line, were vanquished. Their whole new Association was destroyed in the same battle.

Still, McBride and a few equally rugged figures, such as Chris Evans of Straitsville, Ohio, and a bearded miner from Braidwood, Illinois, Daniel McLaughlin, would not give up. By the very nature of the industry all the bituminous mines or all the anthracite mines—or both—had to be struck simultaneously for a miners' union to be effective. It was futile for a single local to pit itself against a single mineowner, since the slack in coal supply could easily be taken up by the unaffected mines. Thus, without a national organization the miners were as ineffectual as an ant trying to move a mountain. McBride and his associates, therefore, put together yet another alliance of mine unions. On September 9, 1885, in Indianapolis, thirty-five delegates from the seven leading coal-producing states launched the National Federation of Miners and Mine Laborers.

Almost at once the National Federation received an assist from an unexpected ally, an Ohio mine operator named W. P. Rend, who urged his fellow capitalists "to stop this war upon their poor employees." With Rend's help the National Federation was able to secure arbitration of its demands and to win an award reinstituting the sixty cents tonnage rate. Spurred on by this success the union met with owners from six states and in late February 1886 signed the first interstate contract in the industry. It set a wage scale ranging from sixty cents per ton in Hocking Valley to ninety-five cents per ton in Illinois, and more important, established the pattern for all future collective bargaining in the coal industry.

This was the foundation on which the United Mine Workers of America was built four years later in 1890. This amalgamation of the National Federation and a rival group in the Knights of Labor was the first union in the coal fields durable enough to withstand depression or defeat—and fight again. For the next dozen years UMWA was a frail reed blown by harsh winds always threatening to uproot it, but never quite succeeding. The 1894 strike, as already related, was beaten down, leaving the organization with a dispirited membership of only 10,000 and a treasury of $600. But in 1897 there was another strike, and with the aid of Eugene Debs, who toured the coal fields for a month, and Sam Gompers, who sent organizers and funds to the embattled men, UMWA scored a clean-cut victory against the bituminous operators. After twelve weeks on the picket line and a shower of injunctions and arrests, the diggers had earned a decent contract. Under the guiding hand of a militant thirty-seven-year-old Irishman, Michael D. Ratchford, the union's membership rolls and fortunes both climbed significantly—to 33,000 members and $11,000 in the till. In 1898, after a rash of strikes in West Virginia and Illinois, UMWA forced operators in the Central Competitive Field—Illinois, Indiana, Ohio, and western Pennsylvania —into granting the long-cherished eight-hour work day.

At this juncture, the destiny of the United Mine Workers was placed in the hands of a young man in his late twenties who was to be its guiding spirit for quite a while. John Mitchell, according to McAlister Coleman, had "the physiognomy of the poet or priest," with "hair growing low on his high forehead, dark, brooding eyes and . . . sensitive mouth." Born in the tiny town of Braidwood, Illinois, in 1870, Mitchell went to work at the age of eleven in the pits as a helper to his stepfather. Brought up on the Calvinist dogmas of his Presbyterian stepmother, and imbued with the spirit of unionism that pervaded Braidwood—where the mayor was almost always a coal miner—John applied for membership in the Knights of Labor four years later. Its uplift philosophy seemed to blend the two strains that made up his personality, religion, and labor solidarity.

Three years later Mitchell was joining with Italian, Polish, Hungarian, and Austrian immigrants in one coal strike after another aimed at eliminating the system of year-long contracts, which the foreign-born were forced to sign as a condition of employment. The strikes were ineffective, but they brought Mitchell to the attention of the older union leaders, and when in 1897 trouble brewed in southern Illinois and West Virginia, Ratchford put him on the payroll as a full-time national organizer. A year later he was elevated to vice-president of the UMWA and in 1899, when Ratchford resigned to become a member of the United States Industrial Commission, Mitchell was chosen as UMWA president at a salary of $1,200 a year. He took over the union at a time when the coal patches were consumed in turmoil. In his first report, the new president noted that in the previous year there had been no fewer than 260 strikes in the industry, the union winning its objectives in 160 instances, compromising 29, losing 36—and 35 still under way.

Mitchell was no Big Bill Haywood—Haywood, indeed, considered him a "jackass." He was ministerial in mien, like a parson more than a labor leader, and philosophically a moderate, two traits which endeared him to the press and to men like Mark Hanna. But he was honest, he understood mining and the miners' plight, and he had an inordinate knack with facts and figures which he could call on to upset management arguments. When he became the UMWA's leader, the organization, despite successes in the bituminous field, was woefully weak in the anthracite mines where 145,000 diggers

were employed. The spirit of Franklin Gowen hovered over the
pits of eastern Pennsylvania, where the Reading Railroad still dominated the industry. If anything, management's anti-union attitudes
had become more rigid, because both the railroad and its mines
were now a suzerainty of the House of Morgan. George Baer, the
Reading's president, a strange combination of intractability and
Christian devotion, believed that unions had no place in the industrial firmament. "The rights and interests of the laboring man,"
he wrote a stockholder during the 1902 strike, "will be protected
and cared for—not by the labor agitators, but by the Christian gentlemen to whom God has given control of the property rights of the
country . . ."

Mitchell's task was to make Baer and his colleagues accept collective
bargaining. It was no simple assignment. As UMWA organizers
walked the little towns built around the hard-coal collieries, they
gained a deeper insight into the foibles of the "Christian gentlemen"
entrusted by God with "control of the property rights of the country."
Wages in the anthracite mines were still substantially at the levels
of 1880. Children under fourteen were still employed in the dark pits,
despite state laws to the contrary. The diggers were still cheated at
company "pluck-me" stores; they still paid high rents for little blackened shacks owned by management, and still were victimized by
short-weighing of the coal they mined. As the union drive moved
toward a climax, Mitchell prepared himself with affidavits and statistical charts on all these matters, hoping understandably for public
sympathy. In August 1900 he presented to the operators the union's
demands for recognition and a 10 per cent boost in pay—but received
no reply.

Baer was not only itching for a fight but was convinced it would
lead to an easy victory. His spies had informed him that the two-year
union drive had netted a mere 9,000 members. How could the
UMWA call out all 145,000 miners in the anthracite fields? To his
consternation when the strike began in mid-September 1900, 112,000
miners responded. To make matters worse, the Republican boss,
Mark Hanna, quickly put his grubby fingers in the pie. Sensing that
a prolonged and bitter battle would prejudice the re-election prospects
of President McKinley, then campaigning on the intriguing promise
of a "Full Dinner-Pail," Hanna went over Baer's head to J. P. Morgan
himself to discuss the strike. The monarch of Wall Street, like the
National Civic Federation president, concurred readily that while
losing a strike might be unfortunate, losing a presidential election to
the likes of William Jennings Bryan would be a disaster. Morgan
agreed to the 10 per cent raise, and the imperious Philadelphia

and Reading Railroad executive, Baer, was forced to pin notices on colliery bulletin boards finally giving recognition to the hated union.

An exuberant Mitchell, having conquered a whole, large industry at age thirty, cried out that this was "the only great contest in which the workers came out entirely and absolutely victorious." Membership in the UMWA skyrocketed to 232,289 by the next convention. Nonetheless the UMWA leader's assessment was on the optimistic side, as events soon proved. Baer and his friends had not given up, they were simply biding their time. Despite the agreement for union recognition they refused to deal with the UMWA or put into effect other provisions they had conceded. As unsettled grievances piled up and wildcat strikes broke out here and there, owners of the larger collieries began their preparations for Act Two. They built stockades, blacklisted militants and enlarged private police forces.

Mitchell by now was hounded by the radicals in his union, demanding a second strike, but he was unwilling to yield. Regional stoppages in West Virginia and Alabama had already collapsed under attacks by state troopers and the coal and iron police. The UMWA's treasury of $100,000 seemed inadequate to meet Baer's challenge. Hoping that the 1900 experience could be repeated, Mitchell appealed to Hanna and Easley of the Civic Federation to arrange "a conference with the proper people in New York"—namely, J. P. Morgan. This time, however, Hanna's magic did not work. There was no presidential election in the offing, and though McKinley had been assassinated, the White House was secure for the interests of big business under his successor, Teddy Roosevelt. Hanna did arrange for a face-to-face meeting between Mitchell and J. P. Morgan, but the august financier brushed him off: if the union leader wanted to meet with the operators he would have to arrange it himself. Even when Mitchell trimmed the union demand for a 20 per cent wage increase down to 5 per cent, the pit owners, sensing that the union was on the defensive, spurned his concession offer.

The UMWA under Mitchell—and subsequently under John L. Lewis —was a strange combination of militancy and radicalism at its base and moderation at its apex. During the ensuing strike, for instance, the Socialist Party was able to form as many as three or four locals per day in the colliery regions. "The Coal Strike," reported one of the party's organizers, "has done more for the cause of Socialism than all the events that ever happened in the United States before." But Mitchell was neither a socialist nor a firebrand. At the convention of miners called in Hazleton on May 15, 1902, he fervently urged the delegates to postpone a walkout, and to trust mediation via the Civic Federation once more. The diggers, however, were sick of the protracted delays this route would bring and were much more influenced by an appeal from Eugene Debs "to cut loose from the Civic Federation . . . and fight it out yourselves," than by the more moderate appeal. The vote for a strike was almost unanimous, and early in June some 145,000 Pennsylvania miners deserted the pits. In Hungarian, Polish, Italian, Irish, and a dozen other accents they sang a little ditty to the tune of "Just Break the News to Mother" that expressed their sentiments:

Just break the news to Morgan that great official organ,
And tell him we want ten percent of increase in our pay,
Just say we are united and that our wrongs must be righted,
And with those unjust company stores of course we'll do away.

The operators were ready and waiting for the strike and, in fact, eager to be provoked. Within two days there were 3,000 coal and iron police, garbed in blue uniforms and shiny buttons, plus 1,000 "special operatives" less flashily dressed, guarding the mines, as well as strikebreakers rolling in on freight cars from Boston and New York. Some of the owners, notably the Lehigh Valley Coal Company, evicted strikers from their shacks. At the end of July, 1,200 National Guardsmen arrived in the colliery areas and before long 7,800 more. A Citizens' Alliance of company and company-minded men wreaked its typical havoc, and under employer pressure, credit was cut off from the strikers by local retail stores. Though the miners in the non-striking soft-coal areas voted a dollar a week assessment to provide relief, hunger in the area of the strike was rampant. George Baer, in customary fashion, disparaged reports of starvation. "They don't suffer," he told a newspaperman, "why, they can't even speak English." But whether they spoke English or not, the miners and their families were indeed living at bare subsistence level. There were, in addition, the usual arrests, beatings and killings, characteristic of all labor wars. As already noted, 14 men were killed, 42 badly injured, and the coal patches ablaze with violence: 69 riots, homes, and stockades burned down, 6 rail trains wrecked, 4 bridges dynamited. Even schoolchildren in 14 schools went on strike because the fathers or brothers of their teachers were scabbing. Through all this tumult and hunger, and despite the great intimidations of company police and National Guard, the miners held out.

The "Christian gentlemen to whom God had given control of the property rights of the country" could not mine coal; nor could they enlist enough skilled strikebreakers to do it. The months ticked away, but the strike remained a deadlock. Winter approached, factories in many places were forced to close for lack of "black gold."

Pressures generated on behalf of the strikers by such intellectuals as Henry Demarest Lloyd, Walter Weyl, Clarence Darrow, and John R. Commons began to have their effect. In New York the Democratic Party convention called for nationalization of the hard coal mines, and a rally of 10,000 sympathizers in Madison Square Garden echoed this sentiment. Finally President Roosevelt, who was busily cultivating a "progressive" image, intervened to effect an agreement. It is testament to the changed relationship of forces both in the mine towns and nationally that on this occasion—unlike Pullman eight years before—the federal government did not mobilize for an all-out fight against the strikers.

Instead Roosevelt sent Secretary of State Elihu Root to talk with J. P. Morgan aboard the latter's yacht and won his assent for arbitration. At subsequent White House meetings between representatives of the coal industry and the UMWA's John Mitchell (of whom Roosevelt later said "They didn't come any finer") the machinery was established to implement the banker's agreement. Baer, boorish to the end, shouted that "Government is a contemptible failure if it . . . [compromises] with the violators of the law and the instigators of violence and crime." But by mid-October Morgan re-emphasized that "the operators will arbitrate," and ten days later the strike was over. The award of the arbitration commission, handed down on March 22, 1903, was a profound disappointment to the more militant miners. It granted the desired 10 per cent wage hike but rejected the proposal for eight-hour work day and union recognition. After five months on the picket line, tens of thousands of workers felt betrayed. The United Mine Workers of America, however, had crossed the threshhold. In future years it would win some battles and lose some, but unionism in the coal fields had been transformed from a wraith to a reality. It could be maimed but no longer could it be smashed.

III

The truce between the coal miners and the coal operators, tenuous as it was, would probably not have even occurred at all if a new factor had not been added to the American social equation, the beginning of what historians have called the "Age of Reform." Theodore Roosevelt was no champion of the lower classes. On the contrary, his previous record had been extremely conservative politically. As a member of the New York legislature he damned a bill for a shorter workday for streetcar workers as "socialistic and un-American." His prescription for radicalism was "taking ten or a dozen of their leaders out, standing . . . them against a wall and shooting them dead." He had fought against pensions for teachers and warmly hailed President Cleveland's suppression of the Pullman strike eight years before. If Teddy Roosevelt therefore chose to mediate the coal strike rather than break it, it was only because the social climate in America was in the process of being modified. This indeed was a major factor in the "era of good feelings"—making it a sort of halfway house in the history of the labor wars.

The union battles, it should be recalled, followed immediately upon the heels of the rush toward industrialization and were an effect of the unbridled power accumulating in the hands of business-men and financiers as a result of that industrialization. Though over-whelmingly defeated, they nonetheless had left behind pockets of proletarian power which eventually converted a flock of isolated unions into a union *movement*. Thirty years after they began, labor had a national federation, the AFL, with two million members—and there was a considerable area around the fringes of capitalism where ongoing collective bargaining prevailed.

Nor was that all. The labor wars were integrally related to and paralleled a broader revolt by agrarians and some elements of the middle class against the robber barons and their entrenched wealth. This revolt too suffered defeat far more often than it enjoyed victory, but it ground away at injustice until it smoothed the rough edges of capitalism and coated them with at least a veneer of reform.

While John Siney was building a union in eastern Pennsylvania to fight the railroads which owned the anthracite mines, a former government clerk named Oliver Hudson Kelley was expanding his National Grange of the Patrons of Husbandry (the Grange) into the country's most remote agrarian corners. By 1874 there were 20,000 local granges in thirty-two of the thirty-seven states, with one and a half million members crying "Down with Monopoly." The Grange sponsored a host of bills to tame and regulate the railroads, commonly called the "Granger laws," and fostered a wide variety of co-operatives—to undersell and undercut the monopolies. Though pre-sumably apolitical, the Grange sponsored and helped form third-party movements in eleven states.

Overlapping the activities of the Grange, which started to decline in 1875, was the Greenback movement. Originally conceived as a means of undermining capitalism by making low-interest loans avail-able to "agriculturists, manufacturers, mechanics, planters," it was adopted by the leftist National Labor Union of William H. Sylvis after the Civil War and by the rural radicals. Under the NLU's complicated plan, private banking would be abolished, and govern-ment banks would loan money at nominal interest to those who could not afford the rates of the private banks. In this way working people would secure the credit to establish thousands of producer—worker-owned—co-operatives which finally would undermine private capitalism. Though the rural radicals did not go so far, contenting themselves with the cheapening of money, their goal too was a redistribution of income, wealth, and power in favor of the poor. During the 1878 elections the National Independent (Greenback) Party polled a million votes and elected fourteen members to Congress, including Adlai E. Stevenson, the father and grandfather respectively of a presidential candidate and a senator in this century.

The alliance of reformers surrounding the Greenback Party enlarged itself in 1880–82 to include Susan B. Anthony, the suffragette monopolies. The Alliances too put forth third-party tickets under leader, as well as the Marxist Socialist Labor Party. It added a new plank to its program, the then radical idea of a graduated income tax, also aimed at redistributing income toward the lower classes; and it ran General James B. Weaver for President in 1880. Weaver's speeches had the unmistakable flavor of class conflict: "The corporations and special interests . . . created during the past twenty-five years by various species of class favoritism, have grown rich and powerful. They are now pleading to be left alone. . . . The world has heard similar lamentations before." Though he polled but 3 per cent of the vote, Weaver verbalized the malaise of millions.

Following the Grange and the Greenback parties, rural resistance by farmers, with union labor support, expressed itself in a network of "Alliances" which by 1892 had a million members and was publishing eight hundred papers promoting such plans as federal ownership of the telegraph, abolition of national banks and breakup of land such headings as Independent Party, People's Party, Industrial Party and in the South wrested control of the Democratic Party in a number of states.

Finally, the agitation of a quarter of a century culminated on July 4, 1892, when 15,000 shrieking delegates met at Omaha to inaugurate the People's Party—the Populists. The preamble to the program adopted by these "hay-seed socialists," as denigrators called them, is worth quoting: "We meet in the midst of a nation brought to the verge of moral, political and material ruin. Corruption dominates the ballot box, the legislatures, the Congress, and touches even the ermine of the bench. . . . The fruits of the toil of millions are boldly stolen to build up the colossal fortunes for a few, unprecedented in the history of mankind; and the possessors of these, in turn, despise the republic and endanger liberty. From the same prolific womb of government injustice we breed the two great classes

—tramps and millionaires." Among the planks in the Populists' program, in addition to the "free and unlimited coinage of silver and gold at the present legal ratio of sixteen to one," were government ownership and operation of the railroads, telephones and telegraphs, the graduated income tax, and the reclamation of land held by railroads and corporations "in excess of their actual needs." General Weaver was the Populist candidate for President again in 1892, polling 1,041,028 votes. It was a disappointing figure, considering the forces behind the People's Party, though it was 9 per cent of the total. In 1896 the Populists combined with the Democratic Party to run the erratic William Jennings Bryan for President and Adlai E. Stevenson for Vice-President. This was the apogee of Populism in America, its fusion candidates losing the election by only 600,000 votes against Republican McKinley.

Hayseed socialism, however, left its mark on America. Though suffocated at the ballot box, it blended into the "Progressive Era" of the first decade and a half of the twentieth century. The Progressive Era was a cacophony of middle-class dissent, accompanying a rise in socialism and syndicalism which manifested itself in many ways. Mavericks in a host of cities and states dislodged predatory political machines and agents of corporate wealth from power. Reformer Tom L. Johnson took over the administration of Cleveland; Seth Low, president of Columbia University, New York; Ben Lindsey, Denver; Robert M. La Follette went into the governor's chair of Wisconsin; Joseph W. Folk in Missouri; Albert B. Cummings in Iowa; Hiram Johnson in California; Charles Evans Hughes in New York. To take party nominations out of the hands of the bosses they passed legislation for "direct nomination" by the people through primaries. To checkmate legislative power they introduced the referendum and initiative in fifteen states.

Muckrakers like Lincoln Steffens wrote of the corruption in St. Louis; Ida Tarbell on the peculations of Standard Oil; Charles E. Russell on the beef trust; and writers like Upton Sinclair produced an avalanche of muckraking novels, the most famous being *The Jungle*, about conditions in Chicago's meat-packing plants. Social workers, such as Jane Addams, Robert Hunter and Julia Lathrop, organized settlements for the immigrants and the poor and rent the skies with cries for reform. The momentum carried over to Teddy Roosevelt's "Square Deal" and Woodrow Wilson's "New Freedom" and reforms that had been advocated for decades suddenly saw the light of day. Persistent suffragettes won the right for women to vote. Twenty-five states enacted legislation limiting the work day; thirty-eight states passed laws restricting child labor. The Pure Food and

Drug Act gave the public a measure of protection against unscrupulous hucksters. The Clayton Act closed loopholes in the regulation of monopolies and specifically exempted unions from prosecution as conspiracies.

There was, of course, a seamy side to the Progressive Era that matched its sunny one. There were unsanitary sweatshops, unsafe working conditions, two million children still working in factories and mines despite changes in the law, and a continuing round of labor wars.

Nothing could be so heartbreaking as the "Ludlow Massacre" which occurred on Easter night 1914. Coal miners striking against John D. Rockefeller's Colorado Fuel & Iron Company in Ludlow, Colorado, were awakened that night to find company men and National Guardsmen drenching their tents with oil. They had moved into these improvised homes when agents of the oil tycoon had evicted them from company-owned dwellings. Regularly harassed by soldiers' bullets they had taken the precaution of digging a cave, where they placed thirteen children and one pregnant woman. All fourteen were burned to death that night, and six other adults were shot to death, as the tent community went up in flames. Equally tragic was the death of scores of Jewish and Italian immigrant girls in the sweatshop owned by the Triangle Shirtwaist Company in New York on March 25, 1911. Poorly ventilated, with girls crowded back to back, the floor littered with garbage and inflammable material, and with toilets outside the factory, Triangle was an inevitable firetrap, particularly when the employer bolted the steel door leading to the stairway in order to prevent "interruption of work" by employees going to the toilet. The only means of exit when the fire broke out was through the freight elevators, and before the girls could jam into them, 143 had perished, some jumping to their death, others burned in the overwhelming flames.

Yet in this age of reform, politicians had to pay some obeisance to the outcries of the underprivileged. Their solutions usually were more rhetorical than real, but the lower classes, with middle-class support, obviously had achieved some small measure of power. There was no enormous breakthrough, no end to the strikebreaking and anti-unionism of the industrial goliaths. But there was an opportunity for a few militant unions, in addition to conservative ones, to gain a degree of stability. The United Mine Workers of America was one of these. Others included the unions in the needle trades' industries, under heavy socialist and anarchist influence. They fought hard and paid for their strikes with innumerable arrests and deaths. In the general strike of New York's shirtwaist workers, 771 Jewish and Italian girls were arrested. During the 133-day walkout by 41,000 men's clothing workers in Chicago, 874 strikers were jailed and 7 killed on the picket line. But like the coal miners, these militants too won union recognition and the closed shop and were able to forge sound and enduring organizations.

A halfway house, nonetheless, is by definition a point along the way. Whatever gains labor made in the "era of good feelings" (and the Progressive Era generally), there was still a massive employer resistance to contend with. The National Association of Manufacturers was engaged in an intense drive against the closed shop, hundreds of Citizens' Alliances continued to sprout throughout the land, and above all, the major industries were insulated from unionism by the traditional methods of strikebreaking. In steel, oil, textiles, meat packing, and scores of other fields, labor had either a tenuous foothold or none at all. Tens of millions of workers, mostly the unskilled and the foreign-born still had no means of defense against industrial tyranny.

In the absence of assistance from the AFL, someone had to build a home for these disinherited. The Wobblies tried it after 1905; a team of William Z. Foster and John Fitzpatrick tried it again during and after World War I; and finally came the Congress of Industrial Organizations in the mid-1930s. After a host of new labor wars, the first two failed. But the third finally achieved a decisive, if incomplete, breakthrough.

9

The Wobblies

At 10 A.M. on June 27, 1905, Big Bill Haywood, secretary-treasurer of the Western Federation of Miners lumbered onto the platform at Brand's Hall on Chicago's near North Side, picked up a piece of wood and gaveled a historic meeting to order. On the podium with Haywood was the Socialist Party's leading personality, Eugene Debs; the widow of the Haymarket martyr, Lucy Parsons; the irrepressible, pert, white-haired lady, "Mother" Mary Jones, who was still walking picket lines for the coal miners and others at age seventy-five. Sprinkled through the audience were Charles Moyer, president of the WFM, the most important force represented at the conference; Daniel De Leon, an intellectual giant, but personally difficult leader of the Socialist Labor Party; Father Thomas J. Hagerty, a tall, bearded Catholic priest who had embraced socialism and now edited the American Labor Union's *Voice of Labor;* William E. Trautmann, editor of the German-language publication of the United Brewery Workers; Charles O. Sherman, general secretary of the United Metal Workers—a split-off from the AFL's International Association of Machinists; socialist publicists Ernest Untermann and A. M. Simons. Conspicuously missing were Victor Berger, spokesman for the Socialist Party's right wing, who controlled the Central Labor Union in Milwaukee, and Max Hayes, another socialist unionist, who represented the center of the party. Having just won a surprisingly good vote at the AFL convention for a resolution urging "the overthrow of the wage system" Berger and Hayes considered a new labor federation unnecessary, even counterproductive.

In the hot, overcrowded room, Haywood explained to the 203 delegates the aims and purposes of the conference. "Fellow workers," he began, "this is the Continental Congress of the working class. We are here to confederate the workers of this country into a working class movement that shall have for its purpose the emancipation of the working class from the slave bondage of capitalism. . . . The aims and objects of this organization should be to put the working class in possession of the economic power, the means of life, in control of production and distribution, without regard to capitalist masters." Thus was born the most colorful and most radical labor movement in American history, the Industrial Workers of the World.

After making a pilgrimage en masse to the graves of the Haymarket victims buried in Chicago's Waldheim Cemetery, and passing a resolution endorsing the Russian Revolution then in progress (the first one, of 1905), the delegates wrote a constitution. "The working class and the employing class," said its preamble, "have nothing in common. There can be no peace so long as hunger and want are found among millions of working people and the few who make up the capitalist class have all the good things in life." Between the rival classes "struggle must go on until all the toilers come together . . . and take and hold that which they produce by their labor . . ." Instead of containing isolated, self-centered craft unions, the IWW was to be divided into thirteen industrial groupings— agriculture, mining, transportation, construction, railroad, and so on— thereby "forming the structure of the new society . . . within the shell of the old." Hopes ran high, as the delegates departed, that the "one great industrial union" would "smash all labor fakers and traitors" in the AFL and emerge as the rallying force for the downtrodden. Father Hagerty—soon to disappear and end his days as a derelict on Chicago's skid row—confidently predicted that the IWW would become "the dominating union influence in this country within two years at the most." For an organization that officially represented only 52,000 workers (three fourths of them in the Western Federation of Miners and its non-miner satellite, the American Labor Union), this was a tall order.

II

In actual fact the IWW's first years were difficult ones. One of the first blows it received was the loss of Big Bill Haywood. Seven months after the convention at Brand's Hall, Haywood, Moyer, and an old friend of the Western Federation of Miners, George A. Pettibone, were arrested in Denver and charged with conspiring to murder Frank Steunenberg in Caldwell, Idaho. The former governor of Idaho, who, it may be recalled, had broken the union's back in the second Coeur d'Alene strike, was returning from a daily one-mile stroll to the center of town, when he opened the gate to his home and was blown to bits. A bomb had been carefully connected on a fishing line to the gate so that when the entrance way was jarred it detonated. The assassination of so prominent a citizen naturally brought forth rewards—of $15,000—and special measures for apprehending those responsible for the crime.

By an odd quirk, the authorities hired James McParlan, the man who had "exposed" the Molly Maguires thirty years before and was now manager of a Pinkerton agency office in Denver, to direct the search. McParlan went West and there extracted a confession from Harry Orchard, an occasional bodyguard for Moyer, that he had been hired for Steunenberg's murder by Haywood, Moyer, and Pettibone. Furthermore, Orchard said that this was not his first crime on their behalf, that over the years he had killed twenty-six mining bosses for his three mentors. Another man, Steve Adams, was arrested a little later, and according to the Pinkertons, fully corroborated Orchard's confessions.

On February 12, 1906, a county attorney in Idaho filed complaints against the two labor leaders and Pettibone, but there was a problem in finding a way to get the accused from Colorado to Idaho without long court proceedings over extradition. The governor of Colorado solved the matter by signing extradition papers secretly on a Saturday evening, when the defendants could not get to a court, and having them arrested—without warrant—and hustled to a railroad car bound for Idaho, without anyone knowing about it. "They will never leave Idaho alive," boasted McParlan to a Chicago *Tribune* reporter.

To the Wobblies, as IWW members were called, to socialists, and even the AFL these proceedings had the stench of a frame-up. The three men had in fact been kidnaped, and flagrantly denied their judicial rights. In the pages of the socialist sheet *Appeal to Reason* Eugene Debs wrote with passionate fury: "Nearly 20 years ago the capitalist tyrants put some innocent men to death for standing up for labor. They are now going to try it again. Let them dare! There have been 20 years of revolutionary education, agitation, and organization since the Haymarket tragedy, and if an attempt is made to repeat it, there will be a revolution." Seldom have Americans been so stirred by a civil-liberties case as by this one. When President Roosevelt called the three men "undesirable citizens" at a White House press conference, thousands of college students put buttons on their lapels that read "I am an undesirable citizen." Demonstrations on their behalf were held in all corners of the land. In Boston, 50,000 union men paraded, chanting:

> If Moyer and Haywood die; If Moyer and Haywood die:
> Twenty million workers will know the reason why.

As the trial neared, 20,000 citizens of New York marched to Grand Central Palace to hear a tirade on the injustice of the arrests by a socialist leader, Morris Hillquit. *Appeal to Reason* published special editions of a million copies each. Samuel Gompers, certainly no friend of Haywood's, rose at the 1906 AFL convention to excoriate the authorities in Colorado and Idaho for kidnaping. Unions all over the country contributed considerable sums for the three men's defense.

On May 9, 1907, fifteen months after he had been spirited out of Denver, Bill Haywood, first of the defendants, was put on trial. Clarence Darrow appeared for the defense, William E. Borah, just elected to the U. S. Senate, and James H. Hawley, for the prosecution. Dozens of reporters from as far away as London jammed the courtroom. The case itself, though it lasted a couple of months, proved to be anticlimactic. By the time the case came to court, Adams had repudiated his confession, blowing a gaping hole in the prosecution's case. Orchard, the state's main witness, was thus without corroboration and his own testimony didn't help the state's case either. It turned out his real name was Alfred Horsely, that he had a long career—even before joining the WFM—as a bigamist, thief, and arsonist. In addition, several defense witnesses testified that Orchard had previously threatened Steunenberg over another matter, completely unrelated to unionism—Steunenberg had forced him to sell a share in a mine which later yielded a rich strike. The defense also showed that Orchard had committed perjury in court before, as well as having confessed to crimes he had not committed. After a masterly eleven-hour speech by Darrow which ended at 10 P.M. on July 28, 1907, the jury deliberated through the night and returned a verdict of not guilty. Pettibone, who went on trial next, was similarly acquitted; the case against Moyer was dropped.

When Big Bill Haywood emerged from jail in Boise he was a proletarian hero of grand stature. But while he had been incarcerated, the IWW had consumed itself in factionalism. At the 1906 convention the heterogeneous forces that had fashioned the organization divided into "conservatives" and "radicals," the former led by delegates from the WFM, the latter by De Leon, Trautmann, and St. John. The conservatives, though quite radical by AFL standards wanted to emphasize day-to-day unionism rather than "revolution." The radicals clung to the spirit of the preamble. In a bedlam of polemic and recrimination, president Charles O. Sherman bolted the ranks and by 1907 the WFM, main bastion of the IWW, voted by a two-to-one margin to disaffiliate.

The feuding within the now considerably smaller IWW did not end here, however. At the 1908 convention deep fissures came to the surface between Left Wing socialists and the syndicalists. In part this was a matter of temperament, in part philosophy. The western migratory workers who poured into Chicago in blue denim overalls, black shirts, and red ties, singing "Hallelujah, I'm a Bum" were not particularly enamored of the ballot box. They accepted Marx's doctrine of the class struggle, and many carried joint memberships in the IWW and Socialist Party. But they considered electoral action an effete trap, and wanted to confine IWW's work to the economic front. Vincent St. John, the metal miner from Telluride, expressed their misgivings, as did Haywood, who had been converted to syndicalism on a trip to France. Daniel De Leon, on the other hand, insisted on both efforts on the part of the union, economic and electoral. The sage of the Socialist Labor Party, referring to his adversaries as "slum proletarians" and a "bummery," finalized his split with the IWW at the 1908 convention, leaving the organization to the syndicalists. Eugene Debs, caught between the two factions, alienated by the apolitical trend of his brain child, but nonetheless warmly sympathetic to its industrial and revolutionary approach, refused to attack the IWW publicly, but he did permit his membership to lapse.

III

Father Hagerty's prediction that the IWW would become predominant in the ranks of labor "within two years at the most" couldn't have been more incorrect. Indeed, with the various factional losses it had sustained, it should, by rights, have disintegrated completely and quickly. Yet there was something special that kept the Wobblies afloat even at their lowest ebb. They maintained a labor solidarity unequaled, except perhaps by the American Railway Union and the Western Federation of Miners. Thus, when sailors in Crescent City, Oregon, went on strike against a large lumber company, it was the IWW millhands and woodsmen who helped them win their demands. Unlike the American Federation of Labor, which the Wobblies called the American *Separation* of Labor, the IWW offered to organize anyone—foreign-born, unskilled, even the Japanese and Chinese. "We are going down into the gutter," Haywood said, "to get at the mass of workers and bring them up to a decent plane of living."

The Wobblies were among the most imaginative strategists the labor movement has ever seen. They organized, for example, the whole town of Goldfield, Nevada, from 1906 to 1908—3,000 engineers, miners, clerks, waiters, common laborers, dishwashers, newsboys, etc. —and with that kind of solidarity attained what St. John called "the highest point of efficiency . . ." Underground miners won a $5 daily pay scale, bakers $8 a day plus board, clerks $5 a day for a ten-hour day, bartenders $6 for an eight-hour day. The Goldfield *Gossip,* a paper so incensed at the Wobblies it proposed they be hung to telegraph poles, nonetheless conceded that the industrial union had vastly improved the lot of the lower classes. "Where these men and women had previously been called upon to work for twelve or fifteen hours a day for a small wage, they found themselves, as members of the IWW, commanding a higher wage, enjoying a union scale, and working only eight hours a day." The techniques of the Wobblies were refreshingly simple. As described by St. John: "No committees were ever sent to any employers. The union adopted wage scales and regulated hours. The secretary posted the same on a bulletin board outside the union hall, and it was the LAW. The employers were forced to come and see the union committees." This idyllic situation did not survive a management counteroffensive—abetted and assisted by the AFL—but it did reveal the IWW's ingenious ability to organize.

Another manifestation of that unique, creative talent was the sitdown strike at General Electric's complex in Schenectady, in December 1906. The Wobblies had enrolled 3,000 of GE's 17,000 workers, ranging from draftsmen to sweepers. When the company fired three of the draftsmen, employees at the power plant—almost all Wobblies —pulled the switches. Instead of leaving the factory, to set up outside picket lines, the IWW members conceived of the highly original tactic of sitting at their benches for the next sixty-five hours. It was the first sitdown in U.S. history, prototype of the sitdowns which three decades later would spark labor's greatest surge.

Another imaginative venture, enacted on the other side of the continent, in Portland, Oregon, a few months later, was "so startling," wrote Philip Foner, "that it commanded attention all over the country." A walkout over wages at one of the sawmills was extended by the Wobblies to all of the other mills until 2,300 of the 2,500 millhands in the city were on strike. As the workers left work or came in during shift changes, they were met by mass picket lines, handed red ribbons, and marched to the IWW headquarters to sign union cards. Oddly enough there was little resistance. According to the Portland *Oregonian,* there was "no drunkenness or violence and only one arrest . . . The men are directed by the strike leaders to preserve order and the peaceful conduct of the strikers is causing surprise." The same paper noted that "where the AFL has failed, the IWW at one leap is succeeding. The Federation is slow to organize unskilled workers, the IWW is quick to do so. This is why the sawmill men are joining the numerically weaker organization."

The Goldfield, Schenectady, and Portland efforts ended untriumphantly, but they demonstrated the drama, and color of the Wobblies, which sprang from the depths of their idealism. Wherever there was trouble, there one could find the IWW zealots battling it out with police and scabs, going to jail and paying the price for free speech and industrial justice. They were typically American crusaders, riding the rods, tramping the roads, marching off to prison defiantly. They talked scornfully of "Scissor Bill" who "wouldn't join the union," and of "Casey Jones, the Union Scab." They sang endlessly a book full of lyrics, written by fellow-workers to old tunes, many of religious origin. "Dump the Bosses Off Your Back," for example, was a verse composed by John Brill to the music of "Take It to the Lord in Prayer." The hue and cry of the worker seeking a fair share was captured in this chorus of Ralph Chaplin's "Solidarity Forever"—the union song still most often heard on picket lines to this day:

> It is we who plowed the prairies; built the cities where they trade;
> Dug the mines and built the workshops; enless miles of railroad laid;
> Now we stand, outcast and starving, 'mid the wonders we have made;
>   But the Union makes us strong.

Despite the ideological turmoil at its conventions, therefore, the IWW was able to insinuate itself in the lumber fields, agriculture, and one or two mass-production industries. In the first fifteen months of its existence, it issued 384 charters, most of them to small nuclei, waiting for the propitious time to synthesize a massive organization. It was after the purge of the De Leonists in 1908, that the "one big union" began to recruit members on a grand scale. The time was ripe: the millions of immigrants arriving in the United States and the millions of unskilled workers already there, could find no solace in the AFL. They were looking elsewhere, and the IWW was blessed with a large number of remarkable visionaries who were willing to share their sacrifices and advance their cause.

Typical of these was a frail, graceful, and very pretty Irish girl in her teens who mesmerized audiences with her resonant voice and impassioned eloquence. Elizabeth Gurley Flynn, the "rebel girl," was a gray-eyed, lovely woman with dark hair who made her first speech at sixteen to the Harlem Socialist Club, and at eighteen was agitating in New York, Philadelphia and elsewhere against an economic system which tossed the unemployed aside with abandon. That same year, 1908, a depression year, the IWW broadened its campaign on behalf of the jobless and Gurley Flynn was inprisoned in New York; Missoula, Montana; Spokane, Washington. Charged with conspiracy in Spokane, she was tried with a man named Charley Filigno. He was convicted; she was freed, whereupon an angry prosecutor demanded of the jury foreman: "what in hell do you fellows mean by acquitting the most guilty . . ." The foreman replied with interesting candor: "If you think this jury, or any jury, is going to send that pretty Irish girl to jail merely for being bighearted and idealistic, to mix with all those whores and crooks down at the pen, you've got another guess coming." A dynamo of charm and fervor, Gurley Flynn later applied her talents to the struggles in Lawrence, Paterson, Everett, among others.

The man who left the deepest imprint on the IWW, as much as Haywood perhaps, since he handled day-to-day operations, was the former leader of the Telluride miners, Vincent St. John. "The Saint," as he was called by intimates, was born in Kentucky in 1876, of Irish-Dutch parents with sustained wanderlust. From 1880, when Vincent was four, to 1895, the family migrated variously from New Jersey to Colorado, Washington State, and California. When he was nineteen, St. John set out on his own and settled in Colorado, to begin a flamboyant career as prospector, miner, and unionist. At twenty-five he was president of the Telluride miners' union, leading men considerably older than he in the 1901 strike. For two years thereafter the authorities tried to pin the murder of a mine manager on the Saint, but failed. Pinkerton agent McParlan sought to implicate him in the assassination of Frank Steunenberg, but again there was no evidence on which to base an indictment. Blacklisted, arrested many times, shot in the hand—and permanently crippled—during the Goldfield strikes, he became the spokesman of the syndicalist faction in the IWW, and after 1908 with Big Bill, its leading figure.

St. John generated universal trust and respect, especially among young radicals. "I never met a man I admired more," Elizabeth Gurley Flynn wrote of him. "He radiated sincerity and integrity," according to James P. Cannon, future leader of the American Trotskyists—a man not given easily to praise. And from 1908 to 1915, while he served as general organizer and secretary of the IWW, the Saint fashioned "an organization in his own image." Quick to act, modest, unselfish, he built a movement that responded swiftly to crisis and evoked self-sacrifice from its members. "The air was clean in his presence," Cannon says of St. John, and that was also true of the IWW. It did not manipulate people as so many other leftist groups, before and since, have done. It made no fetish of leadership, it developed no bureaucratic pyramids.

Indeed the IWW's uncompromising dedication to workers' freedom

of choice was probably its undoing. The "one big union" organized
at least a million workers in its heyday, and won its demands in a
sizable majority of its strikes. Even in its years of anguish 1905–8, it
did well on the picket lines. At the 1907 convention Trautmann reported that the IWW had conducted twenty-four stoppages in the
previous twelve months, only two of which had been "flat failures."
"All other strikes ended either in compromise, or in complete attain-
ment of what the strikes had been inaugurated for." Yet at no time
did the IWW number more than 100,000 to 120,000 members. While
the AFL held its membership in tow through collective agreements
and the closed shop, the IWW considered the closed shop and the
check-off of dues repugnant instruments of coercion. A man should
remain in the union and pay his dues, said the Wobblies, out of an
inner conviction, not by the compulsion of a written pact with the
employers. Noble as were these purist views of freedom, they
proved, in the end, impractical. Proletarians joined the IWW in great
spurts of enthusiasm, by the thousands, participated in the victorious
strikes that affected them, then left it. A year after the sensational
triumph of 25,000 Lawrence, Massachusetts, textile strikers—which
St. John said was "the start that will only end with the downfall of
the wage system"—the IWW local in town had fallen to a slender
membership of 700 adherents.

But if the IWW remained numerically small, it was always agitating, distributing leaflets, newspapers, bulletins, and ready to join a
labor cause whenever the opportunity presented itself. Its strikes
ran the gamut from agricultural laborers to mass production workers,
from one end of the nation to another—a list much too long to document here. Typical of its activity, however, were the class struggles of
steelworkers at McKees Rocks, six miles below Pittsburgh, the free-
speech fights in the West, the upheavals among harvest and lumber
workers that went on constantly, and most notable, the Lawrence
textile strike of 1912 (see Chapter 10).

IV

The Pressed Steel Car plant at McKees Rocks in 1909 was a
microcosm of American industry. Included among its 5,000 to 8,000
workers were fourteen different nationality groups, the most numerous being Hungarian, each speaking its own tongue, and each clinging
firmly to antagonisms carried over from the old world. Some of the
immigrants at McKees Rocks had been prominent political figures
at home: Russians who had served in the 1905 Duma, Italians who
had led resistance strikes, Germans who were active in the metal
workers' union. But because of the language barrier they were easily

divided, and thoroughly exploited. "When all's said and done," the company's president, Frank Hoffstot, was wont to say, wages are fixed by "supply and demand . . . the same as everything else. . . . We buy labor in the cheapest market."

Wages at the car plant were already low, having been reduced during the 1907 panic, and reduced still further in 1909, despite a general economic upturn. But nothing rankled the employees so much as the introduction by Hoffstot of a pay scheme called the "pool system." Under this plan, men with specific occupations, such as riveters or heaters or helpers, were lumped together into 52 gangs of 10 to 150 each, and compensated on the basis of total gang output rather than individual effort. It was a system that lent itself both to confusion and corruption. The foreman was given the pay for the entire gang. In turn, he doled it out as he saw fit, rewarding favorites willing to speed up the work, penalizing others. A social worker who made a survey in the area was shown checks of $6.50 earned by a riveter for twelve work shifts, $1 by another for three shifts, $3.50 for four, $15 for two weeks. To make matters worse the foreman, to pad his pocket, extorted $5 to $50 each from job applicant —of whom there were many—and often fired workers in his crew solely to hire others. Safety conditions were abominable—one plant was called "Slaughter House," another "Last Chance," signifying the toll of dead and maimed workers from accidents. Added to these tribulations were the company stores—which though illegal were operated through agents—and the company-owned hovels, without running water or toilet, which were rented for $12 a month.

After months of these painfully intolerable conditions, on Saturday July 10—payday—forty riveters at the "Last Chance" advised the company they would not work unless told specifically what their rates were, and unless their former pay cuts were rescinded. On Tuesday, as they returned to work, the forty were fired, along with sixty others in the erection department who had made a similar demand. Within forty-eight hours 5,000 un-led and unorganized workers were on strike. Only a few hundred men stayed at their jobs, including a handful of AFL electricians. Before the stoppage was a day old, violence broke out. Strikebreakers, hastily assembled in Cleveland and Pittsburgh, were loaded onto a company steamer, *Steel Queen,* and brought to the bank of the Ohio River leading to the plant. As the ship came toward the shore three hundred strikers let loose volley after volley of rifle fire, much as steel workers at Homestead, not far away, had done seventeen years before. No one among the strikebreakers was hit, but the *Steel Queen* was forced

to flee to the opposite shore, where it discharged the scabs that
management had counted on.

Undeterred by this setback, the company, in feverish haste, tried
another tack. The plant was surrounded by 300 deputy sheriffs and
200 state constables, while 50 mounted constables—"cossacks"—began
evicting workers from company houses. To be dispossessed so unceremoniously on the second day of a strike was too much for the working-class families. "Kill the Cossacks," cried wives of the strikers as
their men literally defended their homes with rocks and whatever
else was on hand. It was an unequal fight; the constables wounded
about 100 and arrested 25 more on charges of inciting to riot. But the
evictions stopped. Meanwhile in Pittsburgh, Hoffstot announced that
no picket would ever again be employed by the Pressed Steel Car
Company. "They're dead to us," said the company executive. "There
are more than enough idle men in Pittsburgh to fill every vacancy."
The Pearl Berghoff Agency of New York had already been hired to
do the recruiting.

The strike had broken out without central leadership, but Hoffstot's defiant attitude convinced the laborers they had better organize.
C. A. Wise and American-born workers in the axle department
brought together a committee of representatives of the main ethnic
groups employed at the plant, called the "Big Six." Because the group
had little knowledge of how to handle the situation, it enlisted the
aid of a Socialist lawyer in Pittsburgh. Parallel to the "Big Six,"
and more radical, was a group within the plant of foreign-born who
needed no outside help. They already had been exposed to the
revolutionary and labor struggles of Russia, Poland, Germany, France,
Austria, Italy—and three of them were members of the IWW. The
Unknown Committee designated groups to meet trains and ferries,
established twenty-four-hour picket lines and a special warning system
to call out the pickets in an emergency. The foreign-born radicals
knew what they were doing; their committee was so effective in fact
that the sheriff, on July 26, temporarily prohibited further introduction
of strikebreakers. If the Big Six, led by Wise, was ready to accept a
compromise, the Unknown Committee was determined to use any
means, including dynamite, to gain every labor demand.

After a brief lull in the war, skirmishes broke out again when
constables tried to evict forty-seven families on August 7, in order to
turn their homes over to scabs. The next day there were more battles,
this time in front of the plant, and on the eleventh a striker was
killed as he tried to stop strikebreakers headed for the plant entrance.
Five thousand mourners marched behind the coffin of the slain man;
the Unknown Committee sent a letter to the constables warning

that "for every striker's life you take, a trooper's life will be taken."
On August 15 the militants, now in full charge of the strike, prevented
another steamer, the *P. M. Pfeil*, from landing Berghoff replacements.

At this juncture, a month after the strike had begun, its direction
was officially placed in the hands of the IWW. Great posters in five
languages announced that William Trautmann, IWW general organizer, would address a meeting on Indian Mound, a hill near the Ohio
River. At the appointed hour 8,000 people were present to hear a
battery of speeches in nine different languages, including Trautmann's
German and English. At another mass meeting three days later the
Car Builders' Industrial Union, IWW, was born, 3,000 men joining
immediately, and vowing they would never "return to work unorganized and unprotected."

Until then the strike had attracted little national attention. But in
the week of August 22 McKees Rocks became front page news. That
Sunday an IWW squad, performing its normal function of boarding
streetcars to discourage scabs, was met by a deputy sheriff, Harry
Exler, widely known for his anti-union sentiments. After an acri-
monious verbal exchange Exler pulled out a gun and began firing.
The strikers returned the fire, killing Exler on the spot. Almost at
once there were troops on the scene and a new gunfight flared,
during which eleven men died, eight of them on the union side, two
scabs and one Cossack. Forty strikers were injured, and many more
arrested, while the troops wreaked their vengeance by tying strikers
behind horses and pulling them along the cobblestones. The next day
the troopers invaded "Hunkeyville" to drive more union families
from their homes, and launched attacks on union meetings.

The two-day explosion brought indignant protest from the liberal
and socialist press and some even from conservative sheets which
decried a company announcement that it did not care what happened
to its "former" employees. Of the few defenders of the "law and
order" prevailing at McKees Rocks, Frank Morrison, secretary-treasurer of the AFL, stood out like a sore thumb. He blamed the debacle
on "ignorant foreign labor, aliens who do not speak our language
and understand our institutions . . ." There was thus little wonder
that so many unskilled and foreign-born turned their backs on Gompers' Federation. Morrison possibly even wished for a defeat of
"ignorant foreign labor" at McKees Rocks, but if so he was to be
sorely chagrined.

The strikers refused to be disheartened. They decided to hold
meetings despite the threat by troops to break them up. Eugene Debs,
though threatened with "bodily harm" if he appeared, addressed
10,000 Pressed Steel Car employees and their friends on August 25.

The leader of the Pullman "rebellion," fifteen years earlier, hailed the stoppage as "the greatest labor fight in all my history in the labor movement." It would be "a harbinger," he said, "of a new spirit among the unorganized, foreign-born workers in the mass-production industries who can see here in McKees Rocks the road on which they must travel—the road of industrial unionism." In a final flourish, he predicted total victory, a prophecy that would come to pass two weeks later.

Despite the presence of armed forces, picketing of the streetcars was so determined that motormen refused to haul scabs and a Pittsburgh railway company was forced to suspend transport to Mc-Kees Rocks. The strikebreakers inside the mills soon began to desert in sizable numbers, even though the company tried forcibly to restrain them. Life inside the former scabs reported, was like a prison. Since many of these men were Hungarians, hired at Castle Garden, the Austro-Hungarian government demanded an investigation. An inquiry by the U. S. Department of Commerce and Labor confirmed what the IWW was saying, namely that a system of "peonage" existed in the mills.

On August 28, sixty strikers permitted themselves to be hired as scabs; once inside the plant they persuaded three hundred strike-breakers to come out with them. In addition, a committee from the Brotherhood of Railway Trainmen came to McKees Rocks on September 1 to inform the IWW that trainmen on the only lines leading into the city would no longer transport strikebreakers. By now it was obvious that the mills could no longer operate. According to the New York *Sun* there were "less than one hundred workmen within the [company] stockade."

The company was defeated; on September 7, 1909, Hoffstot yielded. He agreed to end the pool system, raise wages by an immediate 5 per cent and 10 per cent more in sixty days, fire the remaining scabs, and rehire all strikers. It was a victory of towering proportions, in an industry dominated by J. P. Morgan, where labor had suffered nothing but frustration since 1892. And, very importantly it was followed by union successes against Inland Steel and Republic Steel at East Chicago, Indiana, and the Standard Steel Car Company of East Hammond.

v

If McKees Rocks was a traditional—though not traditionally con-ducted—struggle of factory workers, an indication of the universal concern of the IWW for *all* problems of the downtrodden was their sensational free-speech fights, most of them in the West. "Quit your job," read the *Industrial Worker* of September 30, 1909, "Go to Missoula. Fight with the Lumber Jacks for free speech." Thus did the Wobblies proclaim one of approximately thirty free-speech fights from 1909 to 1917. Unlike the free-speech campaigns of such organizations as the American Civil Liberties Union, the IWW's efforts were usually a byproduct of other drives against social injustice and were always conducted through direct action rather than legal tests in the courts. The first consequential free-speech fight—in Spokane, 1909—resulted from a drive against thirty-one employment sharks who had the habit of fleecing the last dollar from casual laborers, supplied to the farm, lumber, and railroad industries. They sold jobs that did not exist or others that, by prearrangement with the foreman, were to last a short time. The more discharges, the more new men could be placed— and the more fees for the employment agencies. Reaction against the swindlers was so intense that in January 1909 a mob of two to three thousand men hurled rocks and ice through the windows of the Red Cross Employment Agency, preparatory to demolishing it. It took all of the persuasiveness of IWW organizer James H. Walsh to deter them: "All they wanted you fellows to do," he told the crowd, "was to start something and then they would have an excuse for shooting you down or smashing your heads in. . . . You can gain nothing by resorting to mob rule." The Wobbly prescription was a collective campaign not to patronize the sharks—"Don't Buy Jobs"—and it was publicized in the time-honored fashion of radicals, at soapbox meetings on street corners. Evidently it had considerable appeal, for within a few months the small and inactive IWW local membership rose to 1,200 members and the organization opened a larger headquarters, with its own library and assembly hall.

True to form, the city fathers in Spokane took no action against the unscrupulous agencies, but instead passed an ordinance prohibiting further outdoor meetings. Their good citizens, they felt, should not be subjected to the unpatriotic and anti-religious blasphemies of the "I Won't Work" brigade, even if it took an unconstitutional piece of legislation to effect it. The Wobblies ignored the law, continuing their demonstrations through January and February 1909 until the police specifically forbade IWW meetings. Now it was decided to test the ruling by tactics which future Gandhian pacifists would call "nonviolent resistance." Walsh mounted his soapbox to address a street-corner crowd. He had no sooner finished with the salutation, "Fellow workers and friends . . ." then police dragged him down and escorted him to the paddy wagon. Another Wobbly immediately jumped up in his place and another, and another, until forty-eight radicals were arrested. The charges against all but Walsh were discharged, and though the IWW organizer was found guilty no attempt was made to have him serve his sentence.

Little happened during the summer when most migrant workers were dispersed in the fields or lumber camps. When September came, however, the city quietly amended its ordinance to exempt the Salvation Army from its strictures. Infuriated by the discrimination, the Wobblies again held an outdoor meeting, and another organizer, James P. Thompson, was arrested. The judge freed him on the charge of violating the second ordinance—the one exempting the Salvation Army—on the grounds it was unconstitutional, but convicted him under the original ordinance. While the case was pending on appeal the IWW decided on an all-out fight. Letters were sent to all "lovers of free speech" to come to Spokane, and meetings were organized around the clock.

For the next five months there was pandemonium in the city. No sooner had one man or woman been taken away to jail, then another rose in his place. Eight editors of the *Industrial Worker* successively put their paper to bed and then betook themselves to the soapbox—and prison. Elizabeth Gurley Flynn chained herself to a lamppost, continuing her speechmaking until she was cut loose by police. Frank Little, asked by the magistrate what he was doing when arrested, replied "reading the Declaration of Independence," and was promptly sentenced to "30 days." On the first day of the campaign alone 103 were beaten and imprisoned. Within a month there were 500 crusaders for free speech locked up, living on bread and water, refusing to accept bail, singing "Red Flag," "Hallelujah, I'm a Bum," the "Marseillaise," and other revolutionary songs.

Each week the jailers marched their prisoners through town to take an ice-cold shower and marched them back again to the unheated jail in frigid weather. During the 110 days that they were held there, 334 men required emergency hospital treatment, an average of five times each. Some lost their teeth, many were permanently weakened—but the protest went on. The prisons became inadequate to house the great number of prisoners, and the overflow had to be put up in a school and at Fort Wright, generously contributed by the War Department. All of it was made to order for national headlines, particularly such lurid charges as those of Elizabeth Gurley Flynn that the women's cells were being used as a brothel, with police soliciting customers. When, on top of this, Vincent St. John announced another free-speech rally day for March 1, 1910, the authorities beat a retreat. On March 3, civil liberties returned to Spokane, the prisoners were released, and 19 of the more dishonest employment sharks had their licenses revoked.

The fight in Spokane was followed almost immediately by another in Fresno, California, where Frank Little was trying to organize fruit pickers. At the behest of the fruit growers in the immensely rich San Joaquin Valley, police arrested one hundred Wobblies while they were holding meetings. Thereupon a couple of thousand "blanket stiffs" embarked from Portland, Seattle, and as far away as Denver to the scene of hostilities. Faced with the choice of finding new prison space—since their own jail was full—or acceding to free speech, the authorities relented. As the men were released in small groups, they sang a new verse of "Hallelujah, I'm a Bum":

> Springtime has come and I'm just out of jail
> Without any money, without any bail.

From 1909 to 1913 there were almost two dozen major free speech fights conducted by the Wobblies—and more afterward.

The battle for civil liberties at Everett, for example, a medium-sized lumber city thirty miles from Seattle, introduced new tactics on both sides. Three AFL unions were on strike in this non-union town in 1916, when the IWW Lumber Workers' Union No. 500 decided to open a headquarters to unionize the area. To head them off, the sheriff employed the tidy tactic of arresting the Wobblies—as they came into town or as they ascended the hallowed soapbox—and deporting them out of the city. All told, three or four thousand IWW members were treated in this fashion before the denouement.

Ever ready to accept a challenge, the revolutionary unionists decided that if they could not come into Everett by land, they would try it by water. Forty-one of them took a boat from Seattle but were met by the sheriff and his vigilantes of Everett, were beaten and finally driven to the outskirts of town. On November 5 three hundred determined free-speechers tried anew. They boarded two ships headed for Everett, their voices raised lustily to the words, "Hold the Fort":

> We meet today in Freedom's cause.
>   And raise our voices high,
> We'll join our hands in union strong,
>   To battle or to die.
>
> Hold the fort for we are coming
>   Union men be strong.
> Side by side we battle onward,
>   Victory will come.

At the docks, one of the boats, the *Verona*, was met by a reception committee of two hundred vigilantes, who fired at the crusaders for fully ten minutes from the cover of a nearby warehouse. Some of the leftists fired back because when the battle was over and the ship had been backed out, two vigilantes and five IWWs lay dead, with thirty-one workers and nineteen vigilantes wounded. Seventy-four Wobs were held on charges of murder, but when Thomas H. Tracy, the first one tried, was found not guilty in May 1917, the other seventy-three were released.

Overlapping the free-speech fights, the IWW gave guidance to scores of other working-class struggles, each handled with inspiring improvisation. During a 1912 strike of construction workers against two railroads, the Wobblies put up a "thousand-mile picket line" from San Francisco to Minneapolis to prevent the transport of strike-breakers. IWW missionaries boarded trains headed for strike sites and induced potential replacements for the striking workmen not to work as scabs.

Another interesting technique was employed in unionizing harvest workers. Migrants of course did not stay long enough at any job to be enrolled in a union; the effervescent Wobblies had to find a way around this problem. The field hands usually rode the freight trains from one job to another, or congregated in "jungles" near the tracks in between assignments. The Wobblies, therefore, concentrated their re-cruitment efforts on the trains. Armed committees greeted the farm laborers and convinced many of them to accept the red card of the IWW. That card was the equivalent of a railroad ticket, for without it the migrant could not ride Wobbly-controlled freights. Through the use of this technique the revolutionaries were able to build the Agri-cultural Workers Organization, IWW, to 18,000 members by October 1916, and with this as a base, sent organizers into the lumber areas of Montana, Washington, and Idaho, construction camps throughout the West and oil fields in Kansas and Oklahoma.

Another ingenious Wobbly technique was the "strike on the job" conducted by IWW lumber workers during walkouts in 1917. In-stead of laboring a full ten hours, they stopped work at the end of eight; or they slowed down operations so that they performed eight hours' work in ten hours' time. It was enough to drive management berserk, but it worked. When one crew was fired, a new crew, already indoctrinated by the "one big union," adopted the same tested methods. Faced with inefficiency and the high cost of labor turnover, the employers gave in to the workers' demands for an eight-hour day.

Ablaze with idealism and class solidarity, the ragged enthusiasts of the IWW challenged the capitalist system wherever they thought they had a chance for a victory for labor. Though they believed in ultimate revolution that would torpedo the capitalist system, their methods were tailored to win immediate concessions: the revolution would come in due course when enough workers were in motion. Unlike the "long-haired preachers," whom they damned in one of their songs for promising "pie in the sky," their own feet were sturdily planted on the earth. Had they been able to hold their ranks together through the organized discipline of signed agreements and closed shops, their battles might have consolidated a "one big union" and perhaps even become, as Hagerty had predicted, the predominant force in the labor movement. But this never came to pass.

10

Bread and Roses

The outstanding and certainly the most publicized IWW strike before World War I and before IWW's decline was that of 23,000 textile workers in Lawrence, Massachusetts, in 1912. It was a local happening, rather than national, and it did not evoke as much violence as many other labor wars. But it was unique in proving that an amalgam of foreign-born and unskilled workers, more than half of whom were women and children, could challenge great and inaccessible corporations—and win. It proved too that there was a deep vein of idealism in the underclasses that could be tapped under the right circumstances by a leadership with which they could identify. "It was not short of amazing," wrote Ray Stannard Baker in the *American Magazine*, "the power of a great idea to weld men together. . . . There was in it [the strike] a peculiar, intense, vital spirit, a religious spirit if you will, that I have never felt before in any strike." By all odds this labor war should have collapsed at its inception, for how could anyone expect that twenty-seven different ethnic groups, speaking dozens of different languages, and filled with suspicion of each other, would fuse into a cohesive force? The answer lay in leadership and commitment. "They are always marching and singing," a sympathetic writer, Mary Heaton Vorse, said of the picketers; and they marched and sang until they revolutionized Lawrence.

This industrial city, thirty miles north of Boston, in the Merrimac River Valley, boasted a population of 86,000 in 1912 and was known as "the worsted center of the world." It was a one-industry town, with 32,000 operatives working at its twelve woolen and cotton mills, and 60,000 more dependent on them for their daily bread. Its leading corporation, the Morgan-controlled American Woolen Company, was also the leading textile firm in the nation, with a capitalization of $60 million and thirty-four plants spread throughout New England, three of the larger ones situated in Lawrence. Back in 1845 when the city was founded by a business syndicate called the Boston Associates, its organizers had visions of a paternalistic paradise much like the future Pullman, Illinois, with clean streets, fine little homes, good schools and better-than-average cultural facilities. At that time, textile technology was in its infancy, and the composition of the factory work force was fairly homogeneous, consisting primarily of skilled native Americans or other English-speaking workers. But great technical advances in the 1880s left the dream of paternalism far behind, changing not only the character of production and the composition of the work force, but the tone of life. By 1912 Lawrence was a mean and ugly little city, no different from other urban blights—worse in fact. Immigrants from Italy, French Canada, Poland, Russia, Syria, Lithuania, and twenty other countries composed 48 per cent of the population and their offspring another 38.

In the long run America may have been a haven of opportunity for these immigrants and their children, but in the short run it was a daily, living hell. Wages, even by 1912 standards, were at the starvation level. For a full fifty-six hour week, according to a survey by Charles P. Neil, U. S. Commissioner of Labor, workers averaged $8.76—with one third earning $7 per week or less. Since almost no one worked full weeks throughout the year, the breadwinner who took home $400 a year was doing quite well. Half this sum went for housing. A five-room flat in the most congested area of town, where four-story tenements were built two to the lot and toilets were in the hallway, had to be rented for $4 a week, a six-room flat for $5. "The normal family of five . . ." said a U. S. Senate report, "is compelled to supply two wage earners in order to secure the necessities of life." Three out of every five households were forced to take in one or more boarders, all crowded into small, dank rooms, with windows so close to the next building—"15 to 20 inches"—they offered almost no light.

This was man-made poverty, induced not by poor times or poor corporate conditions—American Woolen's dividends in 1911, for instance, were twice what they had been in 1902—but by heartless unconcern. As a leading stockholder of American Woolen told Reverend Harry Emerson Fosdick: "Any man who pays more for labor than the lowest sum he can get men for is robbing his stockholders. If he can secure men for $6 and pays more, he is stealing from the company."

Boston brahmins insisted that wages in the South were even lower than in Massachusetts. Presumably this justified their own low scales, the exacting speed-up, and other abuses.

Management cried that "competition" barred better conditions, but this was small consolation to families whose main food staples were bread, beans, and molasses. Meat (a cheap cut of stew beef that sold for ten to fourteen cents a pound) was a rarity reserved for Sundays; milk at seven cents a quart, and new clothing, especially overcoats, were virtually inaccessible luxuries.

"Often," one witness told a congressional committee, "the children went hungry; there were days when only bread and water kept them alive." The famous birth-control advocate Margaret Sanger, who came to Lawrence to take charge of a group of 119 children, commented that she had "never seen in any place children so ragged and so deplorable . . ." Walter Weyl, a leading Progressive and adviser to Teddy Roosevelt, noted that he had "rarely seen in any American city so many shivering men without overcoats as I have seen in the cloth-producing town of Lawrence." Living in cramped quarters under abysmal conditions, it is not surprising that the mortality rates were so high. Of every 1,000 infants born 172 died before age one. A study of thirty-four select cities by the U. S. Census office showed that only six had higher incidence of death than Lawrence, and of these, three were also textile towns in New England. Eight hundred people suffered from tuberculosis, of whom 150 died annually. According to one Lawrence physician, writing for the Socialist Call, "thirty-six out of every 100 of all the men and women who work in the mill die before or by the time they are twenty-five years of age." The figure sounds high, but there is no question that malnutrition, disease, and death were frequent and widespread.

The immediate cause of the uprising at Lawrence was a new law that reduced the work week for women and children from fifty-six hours to fifty-four. Ordinarily a two-hour reduction in laboring time should have brought workers jubilation, but in this case it provoked widespread anxiety, not only among women and children but among men whose hours were also being reduced because it was impractical to have two sets of work schedules. Would the operatives be paid the same amount for fifty-four hours as for fifty-six, or would the shorter hours constitute a 3½ per cent wage cut? In a similar situation in 1910, when hours were trimmed from fifty-eight to fifty-six, the hourly wage rates had been adjusted upward to compensate for the shorter week. This time, as the first payday approached after the shorter week was put into effect on January 1, 1912, people were unsure. Company officials refused to give a committee of IWW members a firm answer as to whether pay rates would be changed. A special delivery letter on the matter from the IWW to American Woolen's president, William M. Wood, went unanswered.

On January 11, a cold, bleak Thursday, the Battle of Lawrence began. No union instigated it, perhaps none could have. The AFL's United Textile Workers of America had a small base among skilled mule-spinners. In addition there were nine independent local unions, all representing the better-paid and English-speaking craftsmen, none substantial enough or willing enough to unite the mass of unskilled and foreign-born. The IWW, by contrast, did have a following among these masses. Local 20 of the National Industrial Union of Textile Workers, chartered in 1906, had gained some momentum and respect in 1910 and 1911 by conducting a few brief slowdowns and a four-month strike of cotton weavers at the Atlantic Mill. Still, the IWW numbered locally only a thousand adherents, of whom only three hundred were paid up in their dues—a small contingent, considering that there were 32,000 workers altogether in the twelve mills.

The afternoon of January 11, as the pay envelopes were passed around in the Everett Cotton Mill, Polish weavers counted their money and began shouting "not enough pay, not enough pay." Company officials tried to explain, through interpreters, the economics of a fifty-four hour week, but the women were adamant. They sat at the machines, refused to work, and finally left the plant. By nightfall, 1,750 operatives had deserted their looms at the Everett mill and another one hundred at the Arlington Mills, determined, as they said at a hastily called demonstration, not to return until each of their shrunken pay envelopes were padded out by about thirty-two cents.

Next morning the fury spread from the one mill to others, by that peculiar type of osmosis typical of labor wars. Italians at American Woolen's Washington mill bellowed that they had been short-changed "four loaves of bread," and went on a rampage that was anything but effete. Going from room to room in the plant they shut off the power, cut belts, shredded cloth, smashed electric bulbs, and pulled those who continued to work from their machines. Here and there they brandished knives and saluted recalcitrants with a hail of bobbins and shuttles. Men and women, normally peaceful and restrained, were suddenly uncontrollable. It was not only the thirty-two cents "short pay," but the accumulated miseries and grievances now producing a single grand hostility. "Better to starve fighting," they cried out, "than to starve working." A force of 110 policemen were called to quell the disturbance, but by 11:30 A.M. the mill was silent.

From the Washington, the strikers, with Italian and American flags flying, marched on the Wood mill a few squares away, to repeat the damage, and from there to three others. The toll for a day of spontaneous outrage was a few workers injured, six workers arrested, and assorted machinery smashed or disassembled. But after all the window-breaking, rock-throwing and other acts of violence there were 10,000 men, women, and children on strike. In a single day four times as many people had been unionized as in the previous six years.

Having "hit the bricks," the strikers faced formidable tasks beyond their immediate competency—setting up a picket system, raising relief funds, dealing with the press, holding mass meetings, calling out the workers from the rest of the mills. That expertise had to be found somewhere, and there were few people to turn to at the time except the Wobblies. Sam Gompers of the AFL was unfriendly to the Lawrence strikers, as indicated by his later derogation of the affair as "a passing event," "a class-conscious industrial revolution." John Golden, leader of the AFL's textile affiliate, not only refused to have his few skilled craftsmen join the strike but worked mightily to keep them on the job in hopes that the millowners as a *quid pro quo* would grant his union recognition. His jabs at the "anarchistic" strikers were sometimes more fierce than the rhetoric of the manufacturers. Thus, clearly, no help could be expected from the AFL. In the afternoon, then, while turmoil still reigned in the mills, a mass meeting at the Franco-Belgian Hall voted to send a telegram to Joseph J. (Smiling Joe) Ettor, a member of the IWW's executive board, to come to Lawrence.

Events proved this step decisive, for without the IWW to inspire and mold the unskilled and foreign-born workers into an effective fighting unit, the strike would have collapsed within a few days.

II

Heeding the summons of the Lawrence workers, Joe Ettor arrived in the city on the banks of the Merrimac in time to address a mass meeting Saturday afternoon. Ettor, though only twenty-seven, was one of the most brilliant tacticians of the labor movement. Born in Brooklyn, reared in Chicago, he had inherited a radical philosophy from his father, an Italian immigrant who could recite revolutionary tales endlessly. As an adolescent employed as an iron worker in San Francisco, Joe joined the Socialist Party, then the IWW when it was formed, and spent his free time on the soapbox, as well as organizing construction men, lumber jacks, and miners up and down the West Coast. Short but husky, with jet black hair and dusky brown eyes, he had a ready smile and youthful charm that belied his considerable experience in the class struggle. If he did not look like a typical worker—with his immaculate blue suit, Windsor tie, and hat tilted to the side

—he nonetheless cast a magnetic spell on laborers. He could speak English, Polish, and Italian fluently, and got along in Yiddish and Hungarian, which made him the perfect person to mobilize the foreign-born. After his activities on the West Coast, he moved back East, participated in the McKees Rocks strike of 1909, unionized coal miners, and led a strike of Italian shoemakers in Brooklyn. Though quick to make decisions he was always practical. "Make this strike as peaceful as possible," he told the Lawrence workers. "In the last analysis, all the blood spilled will be your blood."

Accompanying Ettor to Lawrence was Arturo Giovannitti, a tall, robust man, also under thirty, who was a recent convert to the syndicalist thesis of "propaganda of the deed," and the editor of *Il Proletario*, organ of the Italian Socialist Federation. Where Ettor was pragmatic, Giovannitti was romantic, passionate, poetical. Ettor took charge of the strike, Giovannitti of strike relief.

The first order of business was to assemble a leadership. At Ettor's suggestion that Saturday, each of the fourteen most numerous ethnic groups elected four members to a committee of fifty-six, plus an equal number for a back-up committee, to take the place of the original fifty-six in the event that they were arrested. It was an interesting organization in three respects: first, the committees were not asked or required to affiliate with the IWW; second, no one had to be a Wobbly to serve on them, and third, they unanimously chose IWW member Ettor as chairman. As exponents of what today would be called "participatory democracy," the Wobblies asked no one to join their organization except out of conviction and commitment. Yet, through daily meetings for each ethnic group and other means of communication, the IWW managed to involve everyone in the decision-making process. "Never before," observed the New York *Sun*, "has a strike of such magnitude succeeded in uniting in one unflinching, unyielding, determined and united army so large and diverse a number of human beings."

The salient feature of the Lawrence walkout was its picketing. No large-scale picketing had ever been seen in New England before. On January 15, two days after he arrived, Ettor had literally thousands of people walking en masse in front of the mills, twenty-four hours a day. Without that picketline, old hands would have gone back and replacements brought in at a much faster clip. Pickets carried placards reading "Don't Be a Scab," and called out to friends to join them. They engaged the non-committed in endless discussions and booed boisterously when someone went through their line.

Within a week after mass picketing began, the number of workers on strike reached 22,000. Not everyone was enlisted through organized verbal persuasion, or because they responded to appeals by friends. Many were intimidated by the large numbers in front of their mills, or by house calls, and, in some instances, by physical coercion. But it testifies to the meticulous planning of the Wobblies that even these workers, hesitant to strike, were soon won over to full participation in the picketing. At the peak of the strike it was estimated that 23,000 operatives were out; almost all of them must have been involved in direct activity, since there were occasions when as many as 20,000 men, women, and children were on the line at one time.

To halt the picketing became the main concern of the corporate coalition headed by American Woolen's William Wood, and of the local and state authorities who were on its side. The Lawrence police force had been strengthened on Saturday by the appointment of twenty-five firemen as "special police," and a few companies of state militia were already prepared for action by Sunday. Monday, the first confrontation took place. After doing a stint in front of some mills, thousands of pickets marched to others which were still working. As they sought to cross bridges over a canal, which separated these plants from the Washington mill, police and militia blasted them with water from high-pressure hoses. The crowd retreated but some of the stalwarts threw chunks of ice at their antagonists. And, a few were able to cross the canal and infiltrate into the mills. Thirty-six strikers were arrested, twenty-nine charged with "rioting" or carrying dangerous weapons. Though the New York *Times* next day reported "Bayonet Charge on Lawrence Strikers," and the Socialist *Call* that scores had been shot, it had been in fact a minor skirmish. But it suited the purposes of the local government, for it created a climate of crisis. The Commission of Public Safety thus proclaimed that there would be "no more toying with these lawless strikers"—henceforth the troops would "shoot to kill." Every few days, nonetheless, the Committee conducted parades, ranging from 3,000 to 10,000 people, marching through the center of town with flags flying, bands playing, and workers singing the "Internationale," "Solidarity Forever," and other Wobbly tunes. "It is the first strike I ever saw," wrote Ray Stannard Baker, "which sang." The singing and the large turnouts gave the mill workers a sense of power they had never felt before and a sense of commitment seldom seen in strikes up until that time. Workers who were ordered away from a picket line sat down or lay spread-eagled on the sidewalks in a tactic of non-violent resistance, challenging the police to arrest them. To supplement the picketing and parades, squads were formed by the Committee to visit scabs at their homes. If the male or female worker proved intractable after a long session, the home would be daubed in red with the word "scab." Occasionally sterner measures were taken such as the dispatch of a letter warning that the "traitor" might be found in the gutter with his throat slashed. This kind of thing never happened, but the combination of persuasion and intimidation was effective. Though 2,500 troops were called to the scene, not to mention Pinkertons and police forces, the number of strikers swelled. On July 19, 1,000 skilled workers, most of them American-born, joined the walkout.

Every device imaginable was used to throttle the picketing. Three hundred and fifty-five strikers were hauled into court on various charges, 54 of them sentenced to jail terms, 220 given fines. In an outbreak of judicial fury one local judge sentenced 34 strikers to a jail sentence of one year each, after brief five- or ten-minute trials. Their sentences were later changed to small fines by the State Superior Court, but in the meantime the union had to raise $27,200 bail to win their release pending appeal. In addition to the formal arrests, many hundreds of strikers were picked up, held in jail briefly, and released without being charged. Toward the end of January the militia was placed in full charge of the situation and promptly forbade picketing, parades, or congregations of three or more people. Owen R. Lovejoy of the National Conference of Charities and Correction reported that "three peaceable citizens are not permitted to stand at a corner long enough to say, 'Shall we turn up or down the street?'" Militiamen he interviewed frankly admitted that "we were fighting on the side of the mill owners" to break the strike.

Yet despite all the harassment, some form of picketing continued. Groups of a few dozen strikers linked arms and tramped down the width of a sidewalk, driving everyone from their path. Similar groups "invaded" stores, walking in and out, creating turmoil by their mere presence but using no violence and doing no shopping. Police and troops often clubbed, sometimes bayoneted pickets. The beatings were so bad that on one occasion, at the suggestion of a pregnant Italian woman, only women manned the picket lines. "Soldier and policeman no beat woman, girl," said the originator of the scheme, but both she and another pregnant mother were so brutally assaulted by police that they lost their babies and came close to losing their lives. Despite such violent opposition to the strike, it was simply impossible to repress 20,000 active people. They continued to march and sing and march and sing some more. Expressing their mood was this special lyric, written for the occasion:

> In the good old picket line, in the good old picket line,
> The workers are from every place, from nearly every clime,
> The Greeks and Poles are out so strong, and the Germans all the time,
> But we want to see more Irish in the good old picket line.

In the good old picket line, in the good old picket line,
We'll put Mr. Lowe in overalls and swear off drinking wine,
Then Gurley Flynn will be the boss,
O Gee, won't that be fine,
The strikers will wear diamonds in the good old picket line.

The "good old picket line," like the front trench in a shooting war, had to be sustained from the rear—by publicity and propaganda, by fund-raising and relief. Here, too, large numbers of people were involved. There were, for instance, eighteen committees—each serving a particular nationality or craft. There was also a central relief committee made up of the leaders of the eighteen committees. Since neither Local 20 nor the National Industrial Union of Textile Workers had any funds, national appeals were made to unionists and socialists through leaflets, circulars, letters, and tours undertaken by Giovannitti, Haywood, and Elizabeth Gurley Flynn. An average of $1,000 a day, and sometimes as much as $3,000 was solicited from various sources. With a total figure of about $75,000 obtained, fifteen relief stations were opened as well as soup kitchens that fed 2,300 pickets daily. No effort was made to pay rents, except in extreme cases where evictions were imminent. But families, depending on their size, were given $2 to $5.50 a week in food orders, plus $1 for coal and 50 cents for wood every two weeks. Two volunteer doctors provided medical attention. The sums were barely enough to allow the strikers to hold out, but it was a well-organized operation, "undoubtedly," as the U. S. Bureau of Labor observed, "the all-important factor in enabling the strikers to enforce their demands to the extent that they did."

III

Two people were killed in the nine-and-a-half-week walkout, both of them strikers. The number doubtless would have been higher if Ettor and later Haywood had not repeatedly implored strikers to avoid combat. "The public as a whole," wrote the Lawrence *Evening Tribune*, "realizes that the strikers are peaceably inclined . . ." Yet the corporations and their henchmen, in an effort to thwart the strike leadership, tried constantly to fabricate an aura of violence around the "anarchist revolutionaries." The first such try was the "Dynamite Conspiracy." On Friday, January 19, a local newspaper spread the word that dynamite had been bootlegged into town. Next day, acting on an anonymous tip, the state police uncovered three caches of explosives, one in a cemetery, one in the tailor shop of a Syrian who sympathized with the strikers, the third on the premises of a shoe cobbler next to the socialist printer who did leaflets for the union. Authorities were quick to claim that the dynamite had been smuggled in by two New York Italians with the specific purpose of blowing up the larger mills and the bridges leading to them. Seven strikers were arrested for the "plot," and Ettor was briefly held while police went through his briefcase looking for evidence. In a quick counterclaim Ettor accused the companies of planting the explosives to discredit the union.

Subsequent events proved he was not far wrong. Nine days later John J. Breen, a prominent Lawrence citizen and member of its school board, was picked up by the state police and charged with the actual crime. He was tried in May—long after the strike was over—convicted, and fined $500. In August a rich contractor, Ernest W. Pitman, who was a friend both of Breen's and the American Woolen president, William M. Wood, admitted to the Suffolk County district attorney that he, Breen, one of Breen's friends, and one of Wood's associates had hatched the plot, and that Wood had paid for it. Pitman committed suicide the day he was summoned to tell his story to the grand jury, and though Wood and the other two were brought to trial in 1913, it was impossible, without Pitman's testimony, to make the charge stick. The jury was divided and the case was never tried again, but there were few workers who doubted that the dynamite plot had originated with Wood and his friends.

Another attempt to discredit the rebel labor directorate occurred a few days later. Governor Eugene N. Foss had suggested that the Strike Committee accept arbitration, but was turned down. A conference with Massachusetts city and state officials, including the militia commander at Lawrence, Colonel E. LeRoy Sweetser, was similarly futile; the union also rejected a plan to meet with each company separately and insisted on city-wide negotiations. On the 25th, Foss proposed a thirty-day truce, during which the mill owners would be *requested* to grant fifty-six hours' pay for fifty-four hours' work. This too was turned down, and two meetings of Ettor and five others on the Strike Committee with President Wood in Boston resulted in a flat rejection by American Woolen of all demands. Somehow, after the second of these meetings, word got around that the strike had been settled. To counteract this rumor the committee called a series of parades beginning early morning Monday, the twenty-ninth.

Ironically, the day began with an address by Ettor at Lawrence Commons, urging the vast assemblage not to be goaded into violence. This had been the IWW position throughout, but a sixth sense told "Smiling Joe" that the authorities were waiting for an excuse to do something drastic. He was determined not to give them the pretext. Taking his position at the head of the parade he led it through the textile district, and when the militia stopped it from further advance at one of the mills, he detoured it—to the cheers of the strikers—down a side street. As the picketing continued, the police herded the crowd up and down various streets until it was pushed into a knot so tight it could hardly move. Meanwhile, as an ugly mood built up, some of the strikers pelted streetcars, carrying those still at work, with rocks, smashing a few windows and prompting the New York *Times* to report "Real Labor War Now In Lawrence." But compared to McKees Rocks, Homestead, or Coeur d'Alene it was less violent. No striker had tried to arm himself; none had weapons more lethal than rocks picked off the streets. And there had been no actual fighting.

In the evening, during another parade, however, police set up barricades and with clubs flailing, charged into the marchers. Inevitably a fracas broke out. From windows nearby, chunks of coal were thrown at the police, followed by snowballs and ice. After a sergeant was hit by one of these missiles, he ordered police to draw guns, and in the ensuing melee shots rang out. One of them killed a striker named Annie LoPezzi. The union later produced nineteen witnesses who said they saw Oscar Benoit, a policeman, fire the fatal bullet. The government, however, had another version of the event, claiming that the murder was committed by a "man in a brown overcoat" named Salvatore Scuito, assisted by another Italian, Joseph Caruso, both union sympathizers. Scuito was never apprehended, and in a subsequent trial Caruso produced an unimpeachable alibi, sworn to by three witnesses, that he had been home eating at the time of the murder—and he was acquitted.

Scuito and Caruso, however, were not the game the authorities were after. On the thirtieth, Ettor and Giovannitti were taken into custody as "accessories." They had been at a gathering of German workers three miles away the night of the incident, but they were accused of inciting, provoking, and counseling those who did "commit the said murder." In a statement composed behind bars, Ettor asserted he was being held not because of anything he had done or not done, but because the employers felt he was the "backbone of the strike." "Be of good cheer," he advised his comrades, "and remember that the watchword is 'no arbitration, no compromise.'"

With the two IWW agitators safely incarcerated and (as it happened, for the next eight months), the mill magnates considered they had the strike on the skids. Another show of force would conclude matters. The owners' henchmen in the city government, using the LoPezzi tragedy as justification, now imposed what amounted to martial law. Colonel Sweetser became *de facto* ruler of Lawrence, twelve more companies of militia were called in and all street gatherings of three or more, as already noted, were proclaimed illegal.

Arrests, tear-gassing, and harassment grew; even non-strikers were driven from the streets. A woman and her two younger sisters were hauled out of bed at midnight to face a police magistrate on the charge of "intimidation." An eighteen-year-old Syrian boy, John Ramy, member of the drum and bugle corps of the strikers, was bayoneted to death by a squad of militiamen as he tried to run away from them. The town's mill section soon resembled a city awaiting war. Soldiers guarded the bridges with rifles and fixed bayonets, electrically charged iron fences surrounded the factories, great flashlights swept the region, and barricades of cotton were placed here and there, with sharpshooters ready behind them.

If this prescription of bayonets, electrified fences, and arrests was designed to break the back of the adversary, it was a grave miscalculation. Bayonets, as Ettor and Haywood stated many times, could not weave cloth. All the machines at the Washington mill were turned on, for instance, to give unionists the impression that everything had returned to normal. But as the New York *Times* reported, "not a single operative was at work, and not a single machine carried a spool of yarn." That week the number of scabs, usually about 7,000 to 8,000 reached its low point, and the number of strikers its peak.

While removal of Ettor and Giovannitti from the scene, was a blow, it had its beneficial side, because it focused national attention on events in Lawrence. Moreover the strike did not fall apart without Ettor, as the employers had confidently expected. He was ably replaced by Big Bill Haywood, assisted by Trautmann, Gurley Flynn, James P. Thompson, and Gido Mazzerrella. The hulking one-eyed Haywood, veteran of a dozen industrial wars and internationally toasted after being acquitted in the Idaho case, was the subject of boundless adulation when he first came to Lawrence on January 24. Three bands, a drum and bugle corps, and 15,000 people gave him the greatest welcome anyone had ever received in this city. He had departed after a few days for a speaking tour to raise funds, but returned immediately to take charge of matters when Ettor was jailed. In fact he acted as the leader of the strike for most of its duration.

The militia's restrictions on picketing were circumvented by the simple technique of picketing the whole mill district rather than individual mills. An "endless chain," often of 7,000 to 10,000 people, walked along sidewalks without stopping, each one bedecked with a white ribbon reading "Don't be a scab." The soldiers might pick people off for "congregating," but it was not possible to sweep everyone walking from the streets without silencing the whole city's business.

Thus, for the next month, the status quo prevailed; strikers neither lost nor gained much ground. At Governor Foss's suggestion a committee of five representatives and three state senators, including future President Calvin Coolidge, was appointed to make another try at conciliation. When it came to town Haywood showed it pay envelopes of $6.99, $5.45, $6.30, on the backs of which were printed, with unintended irony, advertisements urging workers to put their savings in a local bank. Haywood's exhibits made good publicity, but conciliation failed again; the owners refused to negotiate as a unit, insisting on separate negotiations for each mill.

IV

If little was happening either on the picket line or in negotiations, something was afoot on another front. On February 5, the Italian Socialist Federation in New York conceived a plan to lighten the relief burden, and simultaneously gain wide publicity: by the placing of Lawrence's children in foster homes in other towns. It was a tactic that had been used in Italy, France, and Belgium, but never in industrial warfare here. The plan was accepted by the Strike Committee and Gurley Flynn put in charge of finding reliable homes for the youngsters.

On February 10, 119 children aged four to fourteen, accompanied by four women, including Margaret Sanger, made their way from Lawrence to Grand Central Station, New York, where they were greeted by a massive crowd of 5000 socialists and Wobblies, singing the "Internationale" and the "Marseillaise." Every one of these children, according to movement physicians who examined them, was suffering from malnutrition. In Haywood's words: "Those children had been starving from birth. They had been starved in their mothers' wombs. And their mothers had been starving before the children were conceived." The youngsters would certainly be assured better food and housing than they had enjoyed in Lawrence.

A week later another 126 emaciated children were shipped out, 103 to New York and 35 to Barre, Vermont, each contingent's departure causing a furor in the press, pro and con. The Boston *American* called the practice inhuman, and demanded it be stopped. Fashionable Beacon Hill ladies asserted that such children "would become in time veritable breeders of anarchy." John Golden of the AFL United Textile Workers denounced the exodus as a trick "to keep up the agitation and further the propaganda of the Industrial Workers of the World." The Strike Committee rebutted its detractors by showing that in every instance parents had given their consent to the removal of the children in writing, and impartial observers noted that the offspring were living under much better conditions than at home. But on the twenty-second, the police chief, relying on an old statute that defined a child as neglected if he were not under "salutary control," announced that "there will be no more children leaving Lawrence . . ." Seven tots who were headed for Bridgeport that day were tossed into a paddy wagon, taken to the police station and their parents told that the city would provide for them if they needed help.

The climax came on the twenty-fourth of February, when 200 more youngsters were scheduled to leave for Philadelphia. Parents of most of the children were frightened into canceling the trip, but the families of the remaining forty were determined to go through with the plans for it. When they arrived at the railroad station, police and militia barred the way. As described by the Women's Committee of Philadelphia to the House Committee on Rules, this is what happened: "When the time approached to depart the children, arranged in a long line, two by two, in orderly procession, with their parents near at hand, were about to make their way to the train when the police, who had by that time stationed themselves along both sides of the door, closed in on us with their clubs, beating right and left, with no thought of the children, who were in the most desperate danger of being trampled to death. The mothers and children were thus hurled in a mass and bodily dragged to a military truck, and even then clubbed, irrespective of the cries of the panic-stricken women and children." Thirty adults and youngsters were arrested on charges of "congregation" and 14 children sent to the city farm by the juvenile court.

News of the event sent shock waves throughout the nation. "It is an outrage. . . ." said America's leading literary figure, William Dean Howells. "I cannot think of any more outrageous thing that could have been done at Lawrence than for the police to prevent these innocent sufferers in the strike from being taken away from the scene of industrial strife to places where they could be properly cared for . . ." The event was so startling even Governor Foss, through his secretary, issued a public apology for the cruelties of Lawrence' officialdom. Progressive U.S. senators joined the chorus for an investigation, and such well-known figures as Mrs. William Howard Taft and Mrs. Gifford Pinchot journeyed to the strike scene to observe the situation for themselves. Scores of reporters, reformers, and writers made similar pilgrimages, creating a tremendous amount of notoriety for the textile city.

Resolutions were passed in innumerable unions and petitions drafted asking a Congressional investigation. Big Bill Haywood had already written to Socialist Congressman Victor Berger of Milwaukee, asking for such a probe, and though the two men were at opposite ends of the spectrum within the Socialist Party, Berger renewed his plea for congressional investigation on February 26, declaiming that it was "incredible that children should be practically imprisoned and starved with their parents in order to bring about the capitulation of workingmen and workingwomen fighting for better conditions." To the preliminary hearing before the House Committee on Rules, the Strike Committee, in another grab for favorable publicity, sent sixteen adolescents to present the strikers' side of the story. On the day the youth arrived, Sam Gompers was on the witness stand making his usual charges against the IWW and its anarchy and revolution. One of the boys, of Polish extraction, could not restrain himself:

"You old son-of-a-bitch! You're telling a god-damned lie!"

"Young man," cried the Chairman as he gaveled for order, "that sort of language will not be tolerated here. Do not attempt it again!"

The boy refused to be chastised: "It's the only kind of language I know, and I'm not a-goin' to let that guy lie about us and get away with it." One of the high points in the hearings from March 2 to 7 was the testimony of Camella Teoli, aged fourteen, who told how she used to go to school until "a man came up to my house and asked my father why I didn't go to work." Since she was under fourteen the man agreed to take $4 to have papers forged stating she was of legal working age. Two weeks after she started work at American Woolen's Washington mill, her hair got caught in a machine and "pulled the scalp off." She was in the hospital seven months, and still under treatment when she testified, though she was at work again, at another mill. When asked why she went out on strike, she replied "because I didn't get enough to eat at home."

The unsavory publicity from such testimony and the over-all "children's crusade," as well as a pile-up of spring orders that could not be filled with skeleton crews, finally caused the textile companies to surrender. On March 1, American Woolen made a proposal to increase pay rates by at least 5 per cent. The offer was accepted within a few days by the United Textile Workers and craft unions affiliated with the Central Labor Union, but rejected by Haywood's Strike Committee as too "vague." Nonetheless, through the auspices of the State Board of Conciliation and Arbitration, meetings were arranged with William Wood and after more than a week of bargaining an agreement was hammered out. It provided for increases of 5 to 21 per cent in inverse order of earnings, those earning twelve to twenty cents an hour receiving a penny raise, those at the bottom of the ladder, nine and a half cents an hour, two cents, and a flat five per cent for all pieceworkers. Other improvements included time and a quarter for overtime, payment of premiums and bonuses every two weeks instead of four, the fifty-four-hour week, and a pledge to reinstate strikers without discrimination. It was as close to a total victory as a strike could be expected to gain.

"Passive, with folded arms," Haywood noted, "the strikers won." At the meeting of 15,000 workers which ratified the agreement on March 14, Big Bill noted "that this is the first time in the history of the American labor movement that a strike has been conducted as this one has. . . . You have demonstrated that there is a common interest in the working class that can bring all its members together." The affair concluded with the singing of the "Internationale" in a dozen languages. When the Strike Committee was liquidated ten days later, Local 20 of the IWW proclaimed that the strike had been a "preliminary skirmish" that would "end only when the working class has overthrown the capitalist class and has secured undisputed possession of the earth and all that is in and on it."

In the wake of the Lawrence triumph, a quarter of a million workers whose employers did not want to be caught in the IWW whirlwind, gained similar benefits. One writer, unfriendly to the IWW, bemoaned the fact "that today in old New England some 250,000 people . . . look with gratitude from the heart to William D. Haywood," and warned that the newfound prestige of the IWW "represents an amount of harm which only years of educational effort can overcome."

V

Even with the strikers' victory, there was one final act in Lawrence yet to be played: the Ettor-Giovannitti trial. In adjourning the spectacular ratification meeting on March 14, Haywood asked the workers not to parade—"wait till Ettor and Giovannitti are out of jail." With the strike over, the IWW applied its full resources to the months' old civil-liberties case. An Ettor-Giovannitti Defense Committee was formed, with Haywood as chairman, which promptly organized branches in a few dozen cities. On May 1, 5,000 Lawrence textile workers marched past the prison where the two IWW leaders were lodged, with a great banner reminiscent of those carried in the Haywood-Moyer-Pettibone case, reading: "If Ettor and Giovannitti are to Die, Twenty Million Working Men Will Know the Reason Why." Protest meetings were held not only in America but in Germany, Sweden, Italy and France, where some proposed a boycott of American woolen goods, and if necessary a strike against ships headed for the United States. Giovannitti was nominated by citizens in three sections of Italy for the Italian Chamber of Deputies. The sharp contrast between the $500 fine imposed on the dynamite plotter, Breen, and the threat of death that hung over the strike leaders sparked an impressive wave of protest, and produced a defense fund of $60,000. Adding fuel to the fires, the authorities indicted Haywood, Trautmann, and six other members of the defense committee on charges of conspiracy to intimidate the textile workers. Though the charges were never tried, they pinpointed the double standards of Massachusetts justice.

On September 30, the day the trial was to start, the Second Battle of Lawrence broke out. Against the advice both of Ettor and Giovannitti and of their own Local 20 leaders, 12,000 textile workers walked out of the mills in a twenty-four hour protest strike. City and state police were again at their worst, arresting 14 protesters, clubbing people indiscriminately. The mill owners contributed to the stormy atmosphere by firing and blacklisting 1,500 of those who participated. Haywood had to threaten them with another shutdown before they agreed to rescind their action. It was wise that they did, since workers at Lowell, Haverhill, Lynn and other textile towns had already voted that unless the courts "open the jail doors . . . we will close the mill gates." A renewed textile battle would have been a political strike, fought on a much wider front.

The trial was held in Salem, site of the famous witch trials of colonial times. It lasted fifty-eight days and ended in acquittal, although six hundred veniremen had to be examined before a jury could be constituted. The district attorney called Ettor and Giovannitti "labor buzzards" and "social vultures" who came to Lawrence "of their own volition, seeking the lust of power, the lust of notoriety, if not the lust of money." But the evidence consisted primarily of speeches by the defendants, none of which proved that they had conspired in a murder, or indeed that the murder had been committed by their alleged accomplices, Scuito and Caruso. Two detectives of the Callahan Detective Agency testified that they had taken notes of a particularly incendiary speech in Italian by Giovannitti, urging his listeners to sleep by day and prowl for blood by night. But the private detectives' testimony was grossly discredited when they could not produce the notes. The defense, for its part, showed with one witness after another that the IWW officials had constantly counselled and practiced peaceful tactics.

The proceedings, of course, centered not so much on the murder of Annie LoPezzi as on the political views of the two Wobblies; and in his summation to the jury Ettor emphasized this point: "My ideas are what they are, gentlemen. They might be indicted and you might believe, as the District Attorney has suggested, that you can pass judgement and that you can choke them; but you can't. Ideas can't be choked." Alluding to Spartacus, Christ, Wendell Phillips, and John Brown, he urged the jury not to "believe for a moment that the cross or the gallows or the guillotine, the hangman's noose, ever settled an idea . . ." Giovannitti gave an impassioned speech that in the words of a writer for *Current Opinion* "held all hearers spellbound." It stressed the ethical side of a "nobler humanity where there shall be no slaves, where no man will ever be obliged to go on strike in order to obtain fifty cents a week more, where children will not have to starve any more, where women no more will have to go and prostitute themselves . . . where at last there will not be any more slaves, any more masters, but just one great family of friends and brothers." "Let me tell you," he said toward the end, "that the first strike that breaks again in this Commonwealth or any other place in America where the work and the help and the intelligence of Joseph J. Ettor and Arturo Giovannitti will be needed and necessary, there we shall go again regardless of any fear and of any threat. We shall return again to our humble efforts, obscure, humble, unknown, misunderstood—soldiers of this mighty army of the working class of the world, which out of the shadows and the darkness of the past is striving toward the destined goal which is the emancipation of human kind, which is the establishment of love and brotherhood and justice for every man and every woman on earth."

On November 25 the jury of four carpenters, one hairdresser, one leather dealer, one sailmaker, one stock fitter, one grocer, one truckdriver, one Morocco dresser and one lamp worker, delivered a verdict of not guilty. Caruso was freed in another proceeding.

The laborers of Lawrence had proven that with unity, organization, and militancy they could tame the untamed corporations and defend their martyrs. They had also shown once again that the government was as much their adversary as the employers, and that the underdog could only win if he flouted the false legality wielded by anti-labor officials in order to circumvent justice.

11

First Round in
Mass Production

Late in 1911, a couple of months before the dam burst at Lawrence, a minor schism developed within the IWW over its slow rate of growth. It did not thoroughly split the organization as had the Sherman and De Leon faction fights, and it was of little historic importance, except that it publicly introduced a radical leader, William Z. Foster, and an issue, "boring from within," both destined to figure prominently in the labor wars.

The IWW had made some progress from 1908 to 1911 and had brought unionism to industries previously considered untouchable, but for Foster the pace of advance, measured against the potential, was ridiculously slow. Where others ascribed the IWW's difficulties to its failure to engage in electoral politics, Foster had his own reason. He had recently returned from a tour of Europe where certain syndicalist groups had achieved great success by working inside rather than outside the established labor movement. He did not disagree with the general program of the IWW; he ascribed its weakness, instead, to the fact that it had isolated itself from the mainstream of labor. Syndicalism in France had enjoyed considerable success by working inside the established labor movement. He proposed that the IWW do the same here; that it dissolve as a union, transform itself into a propaganda league solely to disseminate revolutionary teachings, and send its members into the AFL—to radicalize the old unions. It was an idea scorned by St. John, Haywood, and Trautmann, and it made no impression on the thirty-one delegates at the September 1911 convention. But Foster pursued it.

That the "one big union" was not quite as impotent as Foster claimed was soon proven by the strikes in Lawrence, and those of 18,000 textile workers at Lowell and 15,000 at New Bedford. On the other hand, it was wrong to say that the AFL by contrast was always and everywhere in league with the bosses and the government. From 1900 to 1910, for instance, it conducted hundreds of boycotts against anti-union firms, and in one of them, the Buck Stove boycott, Samuel Gompers himself was sentenced to a year in jail for defying an injunction. Neither he, nor secretary-treasurer Frank Morrison, given a nine month sentence, nor John Mitchell, given six months, ever served their terms, but the incident indicated there was some fight, even in the old stalwarts.

Moreover, there was a strong minority of socialists and liberal-minded progressives in the AFL. Many AFL unions were led by Marxists, such as the Brewery Workers, or had large socialist segments, such as the United Mine Workers. When Max Hayes, a socialist leader in the typographical union, ran for president of the AFL in 1912, he polled a respectable 5,073 votes to Gompers' 11,974. An outstanding progressive, John Fitzpatrick, was president of the Chicago Federation of Labor, and in Milwaukee the central labor body was headed by socialist Victor Berger.

Over-all AFL philosophy was certainly moderate, but there were individual AFL leaders and rank and file members who did not hesitate to use violence and dynamite to gain desirable union settlements. Glaziers broke plate glass in disputes with their employers; linemen cut telephone and telegraph wires; carpenters mutilated expensive woodwork. The McNamara brothers, John J. and James B., leaders of the Iron Workers, confessed to dynamiting the Los Angeles *Times* building on the morning of October 1, 1910, as retribution for the viciously anti-union policies of General Harrison Gray Otis who owned the paper. Twenty people were killed in the bombing. Evidence indicated that 150 buildings and bridges were dynamited by members of the Iron Workers in their running quarrel with the National Erectors' Association over the hiring of non-union labor. Thirty-eight men were convicted in federal court for some of these actions, including the president of the union, the vice-president, the secretary, and the secretary of the California Building Trades. Nor were these men particularly penitent about their actions. Anton Johannsen, who was implicated in the McNamara affair but not tried, and who later became vice-president of the Chicago Federation of Labor, made this defense:

"If a man says to me the McNamaras should be condemned, my reply is: All right, we will condemn the McNamaras; but we will also condemn the Carnegies and the Steel Trust. If a man says to me that the Iron Workers' Union should be condemned, I say; All right, but we will also condemn the National Erectors' Association. Before the union began to use dynamite their men lived on starvation wages, some of them on less than $400 a year, with families! . . . Put on the searchlights, and we are willing that our sins should be compared with the sins of the employers."

If Foster did not identify with moderate socialists like Victor Berger or with dynamiters who were militant but not really politically radical, he nonetheless saw an element of flexibility and hope within the AFL that could be cultivated. With patience and good planning, revolutionaries might capture the AFL as the syndicalists had done with its counterpart in France. There were twenty million unorganized workers to be organized, especially those in the mass-production industries, and anyone who could enroll a large number of them would inevitably overtake the Federation leadership. In any event, the IWW, Foster believed, had proven to be a flash in the pan. Something different had to be tried to gain greater union strength and Foster made his attempt. With a small band of followers he formed a propaganda group called the Syndicalist League of North America, and brought himself and his friends into the soiled confines of the AFL to win converts for industrial unionism and revolution. Using a device called "amalgamation" he was able five years later to win an outstanding if brief victory for industrial unionism in the packing-house industry, and in 1919 he led the first and most bitterly fought national strike in the steel industry. No one knows what might have happened to the AFL had the steel strike triumphed.

II

At first glance William Zebulon Foster seemed an unlikely figure to lead what Philip Taft calls "One of the greatest organizing feats in American labor history." For the twenty-six years before 1919 he had wandered about from coast to coast in the U.S. and over four continents, holding down literally dozens of jobs. From the time he went to work for a sculptor at the age of ten, for $1.50 a week, he had shifted from locale to locale, industry to industry—agriculture, lumber, the building trades, chemical, mining, railroads, meat packing, and three years on trading ships to Latin America, Africa, and Australia. He had been a hobo and an occasional panhandler, a man one might expect to be flighty or disorganized. Yet he was of strict personal habits, disciplined, stable, soft-spoken, and one always felt in his presence that his mind was always in motion, filled with plans for the next foray. Tall, wiry and good-looking, he was not as exciting or charismatic as Haywood, nor as humanistic as Debs. But he was an immensely resourceful organizer, a description confirmed by virtually everyone, including Sam Gompers. Though his formal education lasted only three years, he was the articulate author of scores of pamphlets and books, as well as an effective speaker, especially with working-class audiences.

Bill Foster was born in Taunton, Massachusetts, near Boston, in February 1881. His father was an Irish immigrant, a worker at a variety of jobs, who hated and plotted against the British. His mother, a devout Catholic, bore twenty-three children, most of whom died early. The family moved to Philadelphia just before the great blizzard of 1888, and here at Seventeenth and Kater, (as Foster himself described it, "a noisome, narrow sidestreet, made up of several stables, a woodyard, a carpet cleaning works, a few whore-houses and many ramshackle dwellings") he received his baptism in slum life. While at school from age seven to ten, he sold newspapers and joined the "Bulldogs," a gang which at that precocious age was already engaged in drinking, shooting craps, smoking, petty stealing, "and also considerable sex perversion. They broke street gas lamps, pilfered hucksters' trucks and stoned the 'horseless carriages' that ventured into our lawless neighborhood."

In 1894, the thirteen-year-old Foster was clubbed down by police during the strike of Philadelphia streetcar men, his first such experience. He was "profoundly stirred," he writes, by the Homestead strike, Coxey's unemployed army, and the struggles of the Western Federation of Miners. Had he been able to vote in 1896, he says, he would have cast his ballot for William Jennings Bryan and the Populists. In 1901, just twenty, he joined the newly formed Socialist Party, and had he not become consumptive as a result of working in fertilizer plants, he might have played a role in Debs's organization. Then after three years at sea, Foster returned to the West Coast, helped split the local Socialist Party branch in Seattle—because it was too moderate for his taste—and as a reporter for the *Workingman's Paper*, went to Spokane in the fall of 1909 to cover the growing free speech movement. He was so enamored of its methods, he submitted to arrest, became one of its leaders, and while in jail serving a two-month sentence, joined the IWW. It was the first of many arrests for Bill Foster—jailings in Kansas City, Missoula, Newark, Chicago, Denver, New York, and in eight Pennsylvania towns during the 1919 steel campaigns were still to come.

Eventually—in the 1920s—Foster would become a communist, and follow unwaveringly the twists and turns of Soviet policy. But in the intervening decade he was a spirited individualist, letting his curiosity lead him down various paths. In 1910 it led to France, where the General Confederation of Labor (CGT) was embroiled in a multitude of local and nationwide strikes. He was immensely impressed here by the syndicalist success in "fighting for their policies within conservative unions, rather than withdrawing from them and trying to construct new, ideal, industrial unions on the outside." Conversely he was repelled by the tactics of the syndicalists in Germany, which dictated separation from the bureaucratized social-democratic unions. He returned to the United States, after a year and a half abroad, having learned some French, Italian, and Spanish—to guide the IWW toward the French-inspired policy of "boring from within."

Foster's Syndicalist League of North America, the propaganda vehicle he forged in 1911 after leaving the Wobblies, never attracted more than 2,000 adherents and lapsed into inaction in 1914. His International Trade Union Educational League, which followed in its wake in 1915, was an even worse fiasco, though Foster made a 7,000-mile hobo trip around the country trying to pad its ranks. As its only legacy it left behind a cadre of one hundred unionists in Chicago who were able to gain some influence in the Chicago Federation of Labor. Foster himself took a job as car inspector on the Soo Line, joined Local 453 of the Brotherhood of Railway Carmen and became its delegate to the Chicago Federation of Labor. He was obviously well liked, for he was chosen business agent for the thirteen carmen locals, and when he refused a second term was unanimously asked to reconsider.

After five years he could show few dividends for the policy of "boring from within." Even the IWW, despite a painful setback in the textile mills of Paterson, and the disintegration of its forces in Lawrence, had been able to grow during those years. As of 1917 it claimed 110,000 members; federal authorities a year later, in what was probably an exaggeration to inflate the IWW's threat to national security, put it at 250,000. The AFL itself had added 600,000 recruits. But Foster, at thirty-six, had no progress to report. His comrades had captured no bases of support in the conservative unions, and he personally was doing nothing more productive than working twelve hours a day, seven days a week, inspecting freight cars, and feeling —as he put it—"quite helpless."

Then on July 11, 1917—Foster pinpointed the date almost as if he
had experienced a religious vision—he conceived of a plan, while
walking to work, for unionizing the Chicago packinghouses.

The meat packers were Chicago's most formidable capitalists, employing about one eighth of its blue-collar laborers. They had established, in two generations, a mass production system that was still
another marvel of the industrial age. As late as 1870, the pioneers
of meat packing, Philip Armour, Gustavus Swift, and Nelson Morris
were still slaughtering cattle only in the winter months, because they
had not yet discovered a means of refrigeration other than natural ice.
Armour's firm was then valued at $200,000. Two impressive technologi-
cal and organizational advances, however, suddenly gave the industry
the needed adrenalin for a great leap. One was the construction by
nine railroads in 1865 of the 300-acre Union Stock Yards, with facilities
for unloading five hundred cattle cars simultaneously. It was the
largest and most modern of such yards in the world. An even more
important advancement, was the design by one of Swift's engineers
of a freight car which used the principle of air circulation for refrigeration, thereby making it possible to ship dressed meat all year
round.

By 1875, the industry was shipping 250,000 cattle a year, and by
1890, one million. The plants enlarged apace, introduced division of
labor methods, and branched out in a dozen directions, producing
such byproducts as fertilizer, glue, combs, bristles, felt, buttons, oleo-
margarine, glycerine, and 600 or 700 other items made of what was
formerly considered waste material. The refrigerated cars, owned
by the packers because the railroads refused to manufacture them,
were also used to transport fruit, vegetables, butter, eggs, and cheese
West on return trips. By 1917 there were 200,000 employees in the
industry, 60,000 of them in Chicago, and Armour alone was netting
profits of $40 million. The war in Europe gave the packers a further
boost as meat exports jumped from $143 million in 1914 to $354 million in 1917.

Foster's plan for bringing the giant industry into the AFL was an
ingenious crossbreeding of craft and industrial unionism, which he
called "amalgamation," or "federated" unionism. While permitting the
craft organizations to continue their separate existence, it would feder-
ate them for the packinghouse operation into a single council, with
its own executive board and business agents, and a central office.
Each craft local would temporarily subordinate itself to a Stockyards
Labor Council, which would distribute circulars, hold meetings, enroll

members, and set strategy on the promise that at a future date it would return the members to their appropriate locals according to their particular craft and jurisdiction. Meanwhile, the council would function in effect as an industrial union, under a single, unified leadership.

Amalgamation, Foster realized, was not the ideal approach to unionism, but it was the only one feasible within the confines of the AFL. It was a qualitative advance over the compartmentalization that had resulted in the defeat of the 1904 packinghouse strike and the decimation of the Amalgamated Meat Cutters and Butcher Workmen of North America from 56,000 members to 7,000 or 8,000. Formed in 1896, with jurisdiction over both the meat-packing plants and the retail butcher shops, the Meat Cutters and Butcher Workmen seemed headed for a strong, stable future in 1904 when 50,000 stockyard workers in nine cities responded to its strike call. The workers were militantly determined to win an 18½ cent per hour minimum wage. They stayed out for nine weeks, and like most participants in the labor wars, were shot, clubbed, and arrested by the score for their efforts. After the second week, clashes with police and strikebreakers (1,400 of them blacks imported from the South) were daily and violent occurrences.

But the union had been fashioned for the horse-and-buggy days of the industry, before it had become mechanized. The typical worker many years before had been the skilled butcher, proficient in a dozen tasks which he performed by himself. Now the work was subdivided into 120 separate operations, two thirds of them performed by unskilled people along a "chain" much like the future assembly lines in automotive production. The "chain" system required an integrated form of unionism. Instead the Meat Cutters and Butcher Workmen had chartered fifty-six locals in the packinghouse plants, each representing a single department, each with its own executive board and business agents, each bargaining separately. Moreover, skilled personnel, such as the stationary engineers, stationary firemen, horseshoers, hair spinners, electric-line men, etc., had their own locals in other internationals. It was an unwieldy kind of organization, without central direction, and certainly incapable of matching economic power with the great beef trust. The disparate unions made a valiant effort in their 1904 strike and displayed remarkable solidarity, all things considered, but they drowned in the undertow of structural weakness.

Foster resolutely sought to avoid this pitfall. Having formulated his plan for "amalgamation" on July 11, he had it approved by the district council of his own union, the Railway Carmen, that same evening, and by the "half-dead" Butcher Workmen Local 87 two days later. On the fifteenth he introduced a resolution in the Chicago Federation of Labor calling for a joint drive in the industry by all of its trades, and with the help of the CFL president, John Fitzpatrick, won a unanimous mandate. Thus was born the Stockyards Labor Council, with representatives from a dozen organizations—the Butcher Workmen, Railway Carmen (who produced the refrigerated freights), Carpenters, Machinists, Office Workers, Steamfitters, etc. Foster was elected secretary, and a rank-and-file butcher named Martin Murphy, president, in what was to be the first significant test for "boring from within."

Circumstances were auspicious for the drive. The meat-packing employees had received no general wage increase for thirteen years and though they nursed a suspicion of the AFL for its past lack of vigor on their behalf, they were ready for a new showdown. The supply of labor to feed the packers' war-time booming business was tight, because the government had cut off immigration during hostilities, thus enhancing American proletarian bargaining power. Moreover, the federal government, which had intervened so often against labor, was avidly wooing Gompers and the conservative AFL leadership to assure uninterrupted war production. Woodrow Wilson, himself took a night train to Buffalo the following November to pay tribute to the AFL, and thus became the first President to take the trouble to address a Federation convention.

In the Chicago Federation of Labor, which sponsored his plan, Foster had an ally. It was the most independent and powerful central labor body of any city in the nation. Its president, John Fitzpatrick, a bull-necked man with a rugged face and gentle blue eyes, was one of the outstanding humanitarians of the American labor movement—and a true believer in the cause of unionism. Where so many of the leaders of the AFL were turning toward an opulent style of life befitting their status, "Fitz" continued to reside in the poor neighborhood near the stockyards where he had lived before becoming a union official. At lunchtime he usually ate sandwiches at his desk prepared for him by his wife, an ex-schoolteacher.

The youngest of five brothers born in Athlane, Ireland, to a strict Catholic—and Anglophobic—family, Fitzpatrick experienced in his life the same adversity that had made socialists out of Foster and Haywood. His mother died when he was a year old, his father before he was ten. An uncle brought him to Chicago in 1882, when Fitz was eleven, but the uncle also passed away soon thereafter, leaving the youngster to fend for himself. With only five years of schooling he had no alternative but to seek a mundane occupation. He worked on the killing floor of the Chicago stockyards, then as a blacksmith and horseshoer, and in due course as business agent, treasurer, and president of the Horseshoers' union. He was moved deeply by the anarchist strikes of 1886, participated in the Pullman strike of 1894, and at the turn of the century became head of the Chicago Federation of Labor—and a vigorous enemy of the racketeering elements in its ranks. Five feet ten in height, with muscular arms and torso, a man who, like Haywood, could lay someone out with a single punch, he nonetheless eschewed drinking or swearing, was as gentle as a lamb in personal relationships, and incapable of resisting a request for a handout. He never joined a leftist party, perhaps because his most fervid political feeling was Irish nationalism. But he never indulged in the socialist-baiting of Sam Gompers, and he was a close friend of the Irish socialist, James Larkin. Fitz was truly a phenomenon in the AFL, a diamond in the rough, and but for a twist or two of fate he might have replaced Gompers as the foremost figure in the house of labor. He was the ideal sponsor for William Foster's program.

Indeed, without Fitzpatrick's support and encouragement, the Stockyards Labor Council would have aborted. The national AFL gave it neither funds nor organizers; officials of the Meat Cutters and Butcher Workmen were hostile to it. But Fitzpatrick put Foster's close associate, Jack Johnstone, on the CFL payroll, and arranged for two black organizers to be appointed by the Illinois Federation of Labor. Foster himself was employed by the Railway Carmen, his own union, for a trial period of ninety days. With this nucleus and episodic help from friendly business agents in some of the craft unions, the Stockyards Labor Council, formed on July 23, 1917, began its crusade.

In the first six weeks its development was incredibly slow. Thousands attended mass meetings of the council and cheered lustily, but only 500 signed application cards. The stockyards workers certainly wanted the eight-hour day (with ten hours' pay) and the right to bargain that the council demanded, but they had little faith in the AFL's competence or power. Faced with this general attitude, Foster took two bold steps. He called together unionists from the large western packing centers—Sioux City, Kansas City, Denver, St. Louis, St. Paul, Omaha—where concurrent membership drives had been sparked by the Chicago effort, and formed them into a loose national committee, with Fitzpatrick as chairman and himself as secretary. What started therefore as a local campaign was now nationally co-ordinated and thus inherently dramatic. Second, Foster announced to the press that a strike was imminent. Action evidently was what the workers wanted, for on the heels of the announcement, as newspapers blared in big headlines that "Strike Looms at Yards," tens of thousands flocked into the packinghouse unions across the country. For example, at the first meeting of the formerly weak Local 87 in Chicago, 1,400 new recruits enrolled.

To put muscle behind the strike threat, the Foster-Fitzpatrick team conducted a strike vote on Thanksgiving eve, securing a 98 per cent favorable response in the nine largest meat-packing centers. The strike, however, never took place. Before it could begin, Sam Gompers, without consulting either Fitzpatrick or Foster, referred the matter to President Wilson's Federal Mediation Commission. As it turned out, the strike could not have accomplished any more than what emerged from the commission's deliberations. A preliminary agreement in December, under the commission's auspices, called for a 10 per cent raise, seniority rights, machinery to redress future grievances and non-discrimination on account of "creed, color, or nationality." Six other demands, including the one calling for a shorter workday, were turned over to arbitration by Judge Samuel Altschuler. On March 30, 1918, the judge handed down a historic decision which even Foster conceded was highly favorable. It awarded to the 125,000 employees of the five major packers, another 10 to 25 per cent raise, the eight-hour day with ten hours' pay, a guarantee of five days' work each week, equal pay for men and women doing similar work, and paid time off for lunch. In the wake of this landmark decision, hundreds of small packers signed on the same terms with little resistance. Only the Union Stockyards management in Chicago held out, and it was brought around quickly by a short strike of 3,000 stockhandlers. The labor movement, at last, had won a major victory in a mass-production industry. "It's a new day," Fitzpatrick told jubilant workers in Chicago, "and out in God's sunshine, you men and you women, black and white, have not only an eight hour day, but you are on an equality."

IV

Having proven the viability of "amalgamated" unionism, William Z. Foster shifted his organizing efforts from meat packing to the steel industry. While waiting for the Altschuler decision, he had drafted a blueprint for operations in America's leading industry, and a week after the judge made his determination, presented a resolution to the Chicago Federation of Labor, for a federation of all unions with some jurisdiction in steel "into one mighty drive to organize the steel plants of America."

No one had to tell Foster that his adversaries were Herculean, or that their power reached into every sinew of business and politics.

In the background was the House of Morgan, which in 1901 had put together the United States Steel Corporation, a $1.4 billion conglomerate of twelve large firms. With almost a quarter of a million employees, Big Steel now built nine tenths of the nation's bridges, produced half its pig iron, steel rails, and coke, three fifths of its structural steel, and nearly all of its barbed wire, wire nails, and tin plate. Together with Bethlehem Steel and three or four other companies it had a stranglehold on the single most basic product of the American economy. And with the help of J. P. Morgan, who handled wartime purchases for Britain and France, U. S. Steel had earned the fabulous profits of $108 million in 1915, $303 million in 1916, and $254 million in 1917.

In the foreground was Judge Elbert Henry Gary, chairman of the board of the corporation as well as president of the American Iron and Steel Institute. The judge, a meticulous dresser and an ardent churchgoer, was a gentleman of the old school. Youngest of three children born in Wheaton, Illinois, to Erastus and Susan Gary, both of upper-class families, the judge had been untouched either by poverty or great hardship. He was educated in a Methodist college which his father had helped found, served two months in the Northern army during the Civil War, read law with a Naperville law firm, studied at the Union College of Law in Chicago, and graduated in 1868 at the head of his class. With his brother and another associate, Gary formed a law firm with the melodic name, Gary, Cody, and Gary, acquired numerous wealthy clients and in due course was sitting on the board of directors of important railways and other industrial corporations. Gary became mayor of his beloved Wheaton (for which he later built a lavish Methodist church), served as county judge for two four-year terms, and as president of the Chicago Bar Association for two years. Then in 1898, he gave up his legal work and moved to New York to become president of the Federal Steel Company. The elder J. P. Morgan was so enamored of his professionalism in this and other ventures that he assigned him the task of organizing the first billion-dollar corporation in American history.

Judge Gary, for whom a $50 million mill and a city were named on the shores of Lake Michigan near Chicago, was seventy-three and a man of fixed habits and firm philosophy, when Foster's big steel drive began. Back in 1901 his firm's members had proclaimed the policy that "we are unalterably opposed to any extension of union labor," and on this principle he was as adamant as the Pope on the subject of abortion. Echoing phrases used by George Baer during the 1902 coal strike, Gary contended that the job of taking care of the workingman must be left to "the employers, the capitalists, those having the highest education, the greatest power and influence"—not by "outside" unions. To offset any influence the "outsiders" might win, he fashioned for his workers an elaborate program of paternalism, which he claimed cost U. S. Steel $65 million from 1912 to 1919, and which included recreational facilities, options to buy stock, accident prevention measures, improved sanitation, and 25,964 housing units. Like George Pullman he was convinced that such provisions were all his "children" required. Other firms, notably Youngstown Sheet and Tube, Bethlehem, and Inland, felt the same purpose could be achieved through "employee representation" plans and company unions. By permitting employees to let off steam by airing grievances, they felt they were preventing the steam from being piped into legitimate unions. Gary and the rest of the steel magnates were even willing to grant wage increases in order to remain immune from the spread of organized labor. As of August 1918 they had instituted seven general raises in the industry and more than doubled the pay scales for common labor.

None of these moves sufficed, however for the workers. There was a malaise in the mills that could not be placated with paternalism or employee representation. The loudest and most universal cry, heard in a dozen foreign languages, was for "eight hours." Workers who felt they were giving their all to the war effort were incensed that the steel corporations refused them equitable hours of work. Whereas building trades workers enjoyed a forty-four-hour week, railroad men forty-eight hours, and coal miners fifty-two hours, half of the iron and steel employees labored twelve hours a day, six days a week. Every second week, when they changed over from day to night shifts, there was a "long turn" of eighteen to twenty-four hours without rest. Some put in eleven hours on the day shift one week, thirteen hours on the night shift the next. Less than 25 per cent were lucky enough to toil under sixty hours. According to mill officials, the schedules were both reasonable and necessary, since steel was produced in a continuous operation. Many employees, they said, relaxed or went to sleep on the job during three or four hours slack time each day. But the workers were not appeased by such arguments; the continuous operation, they pointed out, was necessary only for working the blast furnaces, and if there were any men who slept on the job, they were few and far between. Even the Senate Committee on Education and Labor, by no means in the employee's corner, was constrained to say that "the policy of working men 10 and 12 hours per day in the steel mills is, it seems to the committee, an un-wise and un-American policy."

Weekly wages in the steel industry, it is true, were higher than the average in other industries, and there was an elite of about one per cent among the skilled workers who earned $20 to $30 a day—a very high wage in 1918. Yet a study by the Commission of Inquiry of the Interchurch World Movement, representing forty-two of the largest Protestant denominations, indicated that 38 per cent of the steel workers earned less than a "minimum of subsistence," and another 34 per cent less than a "minimum of comfort." If the wages of common laborers had doubled, so too had prices in the war years. Actually on an *hourly* basis steel wages were no higher than those in industry generally.

In any case, the main complaint of the mill workers was long hours, a policy on which the corporations refused to budge. Machinists at Bethlehem, for instance, were awarded an eight-hour day by a ruling of President Wilson's National War Labor Board, set up to cool industrial strife during hostilities. But Bethlehem defied the order for many months, and when the war was over, simply forgot it. In light of such inflexibility on the part of management, Foster was convinced that an organizational blitzkrieg "would catch the workers' imagination and sweep them into the union en masse." There was indeed a slow fuse burning under mill smokestacks.

Without aid from any union, immigrant workers at a Republic Steel plant had hit the bricks, on Christmas of 1915, and spread their strike to other Republic shops, as well as to Youngstown Sheet and Tube. At Youngstown, Ohio, on January 7, 1916, guards fired at a mass assemblage of strikers, who retaliated by burning and demolishing four square blocks of property. There was rioting at a U. S. Steel subsidiary and at a Westinghouse works a few months later, which prompted the call for troops. None of these individual efforts brought the strikers involved the concessions they sought, of course, but the fuse in the industry as a whole was set to explode, and in Foster's view, a "hurricane drive simultaneously in all the steel centers" would succeed within six weeks. Given one hundred organizers and a twenty-five-cent per member assessment by the twenty-four national unions which had a stake in organizing the mills, the old syndicalist felt he could beat the nine-week time it had taken for the major victories that had been gained in the packinghouses. By using techniques such as "huge mass meetings, noted speakers, brass bands, parades, full-page newspaper advertisements," the toilers of iron and steel, Foster felt sure would join up in large blocks.

In Foster's mind at least, this was an ambitious but not unmanageable project. There was plenty of money in union coffers—the Railway Carmen for instance held a $3 million treasury. And there was no dearth of capable organizers. All that was needed was a bit of daring and vision. The twenty-four national unions certainly had much to gain within the structure that Foster had proposed. It was to be a "free will federation" of those who wanted to participate, with workers assigned to a common pool after paying a $3 initiation fee, then reassigned to the various craft unions as quickly as they could be formed into locals. The locals in any given area, regardless of which national union they belonged to, would be assembled into iron and steelworkers' councils and a national committee representing all the national unions would function as the single spokesman for the whole. The Amalgamated Association of Iron, Steel and Tin Workers, now down to a handful of adherents, and the Mine, Mill and Smelter Workers (formerly the Western Federation of Miners), would receive the bulk of the new recruits, since they held jurisdiction for about three quarters of the potential half-million members.

Foster's plan was carefully devised not to scare too many entrenched labor forces, and, by all reckoning should have gladdened the hearts of Sam Gompers and his fellow potentates. The former railway carman put his resolution before the Chicago Federation of Labor in April 1918 and was instructed, as its delegate to the forthcoming AFL convention, to ask the national body to implement it. This was a departure from the plans for action against the meat packers which had been initiated by the CFL itself, but opposing Big Steel was a greater venture and besides, the core of the industry's operations were around Pittsburgh, not Chicago.

The syndicalist-turned-regular soon learned, to his dismay, that "boring from within" was like trying to move a mountain with a pitchfork. It could be done perhaps, but it was not an easy task. If there was gold at the end of the rainbow, even for craft union leaders, there was also the risk that the uncorralled immigrants might inundate the feudal baronies of AFL officials. It was not without motive that Gompers had observed in 1903 that "industrial organization is perversive of the history of the labor movement, runs counter to the best conception of the toilers' interests now, and is sure to lead to the confusion which precedes dissolution, and, disruption." When the plan was put to Gompers preliminary to its introduction at the convention, he was considerably less than excited about it; and Michael F. Tighe, president of the Amalgamated Association was even more hesitant. Both men slowed Foster's blitzkrieg down to a crawl.

Gompers referred the matter to Tighe's convention where it was conveniently pigeonholed. Undaunted, Foster reintroduced his resolution at the CFL, won endorsement once more, and then placed it before the AFL convention at St. Paul in June. It was given pro forma approval, as many such resolutions were, but it seemed destined for discard. Gompers failed to call a meeting of the unions which were to

form the amalgamation, and when Foster's bullishness finally did force
a meeting, it was held during a hectic lunch hour in a corner of the
hall without any accommodations or amenities for transacting business.
A campaign to unionize a half-million workers was in effect being
relegated to the status of an inconspicuous side show. It took all of
Foster's skills of persuasion to convince Gompers to attend a session
the following day, and that one did nothing more than to plan a conference on the matter for Chicago in early August. Thus, four decisive
months were lost before a National Committee for Organizing Iron
and Steel Workers was finally launched.

In tribute to his status, Gompers of course was designated chairman (he later resigned in favor of Fitzpatrick), Fitzpatrick vice-
chairman, and Foster, secretary, the key administrative post. Most
of the fifteen unions (later expanded to twenty-four) that attended
the conference agreed to trim initiation fees for new members to
$3, $1 of which would go to the organizing committee. The national
unions later were to receive a small bonanza of about a half-million
dollars from such fees, but they balked in this initial meeting at assess-
ing themselves even a few dimes per member. Instead each union
contributed the sum of only $100 each; and, the AFL itself gave
nothing. Also, instead of receiving one hundred organizers for a simultaneous campaign in fifty to seventy-five steel towns, the AFL auto-
crats assigned a total of only six men to Foster and instructed him to
concentrate on a single area—if necessary, a single mill. "I daresay,"
he comments in his recollections, "that when the Chicago conference
adjourned few of the labor bureaucrats attending it thought that
much more would be heard from the annoying steel campaign."

V

The AFL officialdom did not reckon on Foster's perseverance however, or the spirit of the steelworkers. If the war had to be waged on
two fronts, against the employers overtly and against the enervating,
conservative AFL officials, covertly, they were equal to the dual
challenge. Foster accepted the limits imposed by Gompers and early
in September 1918 initiated operations in four cities in one small area
near Chicago—Gary, Joliet, South Chicago, and Indiana Harbor. He
secured the loan of organizers from the more socially minded unions,
such as the United Mine Workers and eventually assembled a staff
of one hundred. He held meetings and put out leaflets in a variety of
languages. The results were electrifying. Fifteen thousand workers
attended the first mass gathering in Gary and 749 paid their $3 fee.
Five hundred joined after a similar session in Joliet. David Brody, in
his book on the steel strike of 1919, quotes an elated Gary unionist:

"You talk about spirit, why, that is all these men out here are breathing. They have been hungering for the chance to get in and at last the Macedonian call was answered." Within a month the federation of steel unions had the power, if it wanted to, to fully paralyze all the mills in the vicinity of Chicago. But, that city, as important as it was, was not the hub of the industry; much more proselytizing would have to be done, especially in the Pittsburgh-Youngstown area, before any mass work stoppage could be considered.

Nonetheless the first assault bore some fruit. Alarmed by the danger signals of steelworkers meeting together, and prodded to an extent by the War Labor Board, Judge Gary ordered into effect on October 1 what he called a "basic eight-hour day"—with time and a half thereafter. This did not cut the workday, since the men were required to continue on the job for twelve hours. But it did add two hours' pay each day—no small achievement for a one-month organizing drive.

Encouraged by these results, Foster moved his headquarters to Pittsburgh, the nerve center of the industry, and broadened the campaign. Organizers fanned out along the Monongahela River, and to steel towns in Ohio and West Virginia; in Pueblo, Colorado, news of the great drive encouraged spontaneous organization by employees of the Rockefeller-controlled Colorado Fuel and Iron Company.

But the element of surprise, of shocking iron and steel management was now gone. The flu epidemic of October-November 1918, which forced suspension of meetings for many precious weeks, delayed matters further and gave the employers a breathing spell to fashion a multilateral counteroffensive. By the time the steelworkers' main thrust got under way the war was over and the corporations more arrogant. Judge Gary had correctly foreseen that management would be in a much stronger position if the "labor question" could "be postponed until after the war and until the difficulties surrounding the war have passed away." The corporations no longer could be shackled by appeals to their patriotism; they could once again act without inhibition.

The first obstacle Foster's legions had to contend with was the denial of their rights of free speech and assembly. Company-minded mayors and town councils, all through the state of Pennsylvania, in Monessen, Braddock, Duquesne, McKeesport, Homestead, Clairton, Bethlehem, either passed ordinances requiring permits for mass meetings—which they then refused to issue—or instructed police to attack the workers in attendance. The National Committee meeting of July 20, 1919 records that McKeesport had finally granted a permit for a meeting after considering it for seven months, but "in

Clairton and Duquesne, the authorities still refuse to allow the American Federation of Labor to hold any meetings." Typically, at Homestead a union organizer, after renting a hall found the lease canceled under pressure by burgess P. H. McGuire, who had himself engaged in the dramatic 1892 strike but had long since turned against unionism. So hard-nosed were the local officials about any assemblage that a speaker for a federal agency who came to Duquesne in February to deliver talks on Abraham Lincoln was accosted and held in jail for three days. This kind of indiscriminate incarceration was illegal and unconstitutional, but the mill owners knew full well that it would be months or years before there would be judicial redress, and by that time the campaign would be over.

Foster defied the ban on free speech by forming flying squadrons of ten organizers each to invade the steel towns. They were repeatedly arrested and their meetings broken up, but they always came back to the same towns to try again. Organized labor's protests to the U. S. Secretary of Labor and the governor of Pennsylvania led to ineffective investigations and faint promises to look into the matter. The organizing committee was forced to take sterner measures. In April William Feeney of the United Mine Workers led 10,000 coal diggers to Monessen, forty miles from Pittsburgh, and accompanied by this collection of muscle, Foster, Phil Murray, president of District 5 of the UMWA, the eighty-nine-year-old Mother Jones, and James Maurer, president of the Pennsylvania Federation of Labor, were able to deliver their speeches. In Donora, Feeney rented vacant lots out of town and was able to campaign for the union by such improvisation for a couple of months. When businessmen drafted a petition demanding that the meetings be stopped, Feeney organized a boycott that all but ruined local trade, and thereby won an apology from the town fathers and a reversal of policy. In each case, opening of a territory to free speech also opened it to rapid unionization.

Little by little Pennsylvania was forced to pay obeisance to democracy, but never entirely, especially as the strike drew near. In August, a forty-nine-year-old grandmother, Fannie Sellins, who served both with the coal miners and the steel committee, was killed at West Natrona, Pennsylvania, when she tried to remove children from the scene as "deputy peace officers" began shooting. "Kill that goddamn whore," shouted one of the "peace officers," and kill her they did, pumping a bullet into her body as she lay on the ground. Many people witnessed the cold-blooded assassination of a woman whose son had been killed fighting in France "to make the world safe for democracy," but no one was ever prosecuted. Speaking at Homestead that same month, old Mother Jones demanded to know "whether

Pennsylvania belongs to Kaiser Gary or Uncle Sam." She was not
given the same treatment as Fannie Sellins but she was pulled from
the podium and sent to a local prison. That month too the burghers
of Duquesne denied a permit for a meeting to be addressed by
Rabbi Stephen Wise of New York. "Jesus Christ himself could not
speak in Duquesne for the AFL," blurted out the mayor. The fight
for free speech won considerable public support in many places, but
the continuing lack of civil liberties hobbled efforts to fully organize
the Pittsburgh district—a weakness that severely hampered the ensuing strike.

Another obstacle confronted by the organizing committee was an
unprecedented wave of worker discharges. The unions claimed 30,000
active members were fired or blacklisted. "We don't discharge a man
for belonging to a union," insisted the president of Illinois Steel before
the Senate Committee, "but of course we discharge men for agitating
in the mills." The Gary *Union News* noted that "company officials
are picking out men here and there for the pink slip and invariably
it is the union worker of some consequence." When there was a cut-
back of production at the Cambria Works in Johnstown, Pennsylvania,
hundreds of union men with ten to thirty-five years of seniority were
singled out to be fired. The Interchurch Commission found a memo
in the "labor file" of a Monessen plant that contained a list of
elected local union officers with a cross put through the names of five
of them, scheduled for the pink slip. In Johnstown, the Commission
said, "literally thousands of men were summarily discharged." In such
circumstances, immigrant workers of forty different nationalities
joined unions with understandable trepidation.

VI

It took some incredibly artful dodging to explain away the fierce
anti-union gambits of the corporate leaders. They were able to get
away with their own derelictions by trotting out a new bogey—
communism. What was afoot, they said was not a genuine effort to
organize the steel mills but an un-American stab at bolshevizing the
whole United States—with an avowed "red," labor leader William
Z. Foster in the vanguard of the movement's leadership. In the press
and through hundreds of provocateurs hired from the Sherman Service and the Corporations Auxiliary Company to cause division and
dissension, they mounted this attack. The nation was then already in the grips of an anti-communist hysteria, backlash from the
Russian Revolution, and it was worse in many respects than the
McCarthy brand which followed World War II. Thousands of IWW
members had been arrested, including Haywood, Giovannitti, and

Gurley Flynn, for their opposition to the war, and in one four-month trial, Judge Kenesaw Mountain Landis (later to become commissioner of baseball) sentenced ninety-three Wobblies to terms ranging from ninety days to twenty years, and levied fines totaling $2.3 million. A socialist, Rose Pastor Stokes, was given ten years for writing a letter to the Kansas City *Star* in which she said that "No government which is for the profiteers can also be for the people." Five members of the national executive committee of the Socialist Party, including Victor Berger, were jailed for twenty years by Judge Landis, who regretted very much that he could not have had them "lined up against a wall and shot." Debs was thrown into prison at Moundsville, West Virginia in April 1919 for an anti-war speech made the year before.

In this climate it was convenient, as well as simple, to draw a bead on the ex-Wobbly who had written extensively on revolution before he began "boring from within." A sheet considered servile to management interests, the Pittsburgh *Labor World* dug up some of Bill Foster's writings and publicized them in a special edition. A reporter for *Iron Age* repeated the charges, focusing especially on a 1911 pamphlet called "Syndicalism" in which the leader of the old Syndicalist League had stated that his movement "in addition to fighting the everyday battles of the working class, intends to overthrow capitalism . . ."

All of this ideology was of little interest to workers who were not being seduced by words of revolution, but by the promise of shorter work hours. Nonetheless the various "exposés" made for titillating reading in an age of anti-communist phobia. In vain did Gompers assure everyone that Foster was now a "regular." He was so "regular" in fact that he made dozens of speeches to sell Liberty Bonds during the packinghouse campaign and told the Senate Committee on Education and Labor that "my attitude towards the war was that it must be won at all costs." Many radicals, in or on their way to jail, might have considered these the words of a turncoat. But to an inflamed public, and in spite of his patriotic remarks Foster was still a fiery revolutionist.

The initial effect of all the anti-communist propaganda—as distinguished from its cumulative effect later on—was probably small, for despite it, and despite the curb on free speech, and the hiring of thousands of spies and armed guards, the organizing campaigns maintained a steady forward pace. On May 25, 583 delegates, speaking for 80,000 organized steel laborers from Pueblo to Birmingham, met in Pittsburgh. They were dissuaded by leaders of the National Committee from calling a strike then and there only with great effort. At the AFL convention in June, Fitzpatrick announced that 100,000 men had joined the crusade, and more were coming in daily. That this was not synthetic optimism churned out for public consumption is evidenced by a private letter from Foster to Fitzpatrick, dated July 28. "The campaign," he wrote, "is going along like a house afire now. In Monessen, they signed up about 600 in the last couple of days. In McKeesport we segregated 1,000 applications on Saturday. Now they have about that many more for division [amongst the affiliated unions in the National Committee]. In Vandergrift, they are piling in heels over head and in Homestead a steady stream is joining." At the end of the drive Foster reported that about half of the organizable workers in the steel industry had been enrolled; 156,702 had paid initiation fees, and 100,000 more had signed application cards, though they had not yet contributed any monies.

Winning the allegiance of the workers, however, was only part of Foster's battle. The full test would be in securing recognition of the union. "Eight hours and the union" was the slogan under which the campaign was conducted. But while Judge Gary had shown he might bend on an issue of hours or wages, he held a taut line against dealing with a labor organization. On May 15, Mike Tighe of the Amalgamated Association broke ranks and asked Gary to deal with his union separately—a step that Foster described as treachery. But even this prospect of dividing his adversaries failed to ease the judge's stubbornness. He rebuffed Tighe's advance with an acid reply that "as you know, we do not confer, negotiate with, or combat labor unions as such. We stand for the open shop." A month later, with the labor pot boiling and rank and filers demanding "action," Gompers too wrote to Gary suggesting he meet with a committee of six, including himself, Fitzpatrick and Foster to discuss the over-all situation. This time the U. S. Steel chairman did not bother to reply. He was convinced, as he told Bernard Baruch, head of the War Industries Board, that the AFL represented an insignificant minority of workers and that if the union was foolish enough to call a strike, it could not muster—by his private poll—even fifteen per cent of the mill workers. Thus instead of submitting to mediation or negotiations, Gary and his fellow capitalists responded by firing still more union men.

With militants losing their jobs by the thousands and no machinery available to resolve disputes, local steelworker councils began outcries for immediate strike action. "The men are in a state of great unrest," Foster reported to the National Committee in mid-July. A council in Johnstown threatened to "strike alone," and here and there members stopped paying dues in protest against the AFL's hesitations. Faced with this pervasive mood, the National Committee, though more than a little uneasy about what the course of events would be, had no alternative. After elaborating twelve demands—including union recognition, the eight-hour day, a wage increase, seniority rights, reinstatement of those discharged for union activity, and the checkoff of dues—the committee sent its members a strike ballot in English and five foreign languages. The result was a rousing 98 per cent response in favor of "stopping work."

There was something overwhelmingly depressing about the position of tens of thousands of laborers asking little more than to be allowed, through chosen representatives to talk with their employers—and being refused. Foster and Fitzpatrick appeared at Judge Gary's office in New York, August 26, to try to do some bargaining but he did not even deign to exchange greetings. President Wilson and Bernard Baruch tried to arrange a meeting of the disputing parties, but the judge held his ground. After a month of this sort of jockeying, the strike became inevitable.

At the eleventh hour Wilson asked the National Committee to postpone it from September 22 to October 6. The request came at an unfortunate moment, just a day or two after police had killed three strikers in a work stoppage at the Standard Steel Car Company of Hammond, Indiana. Gompers nonetheless issued a public statement, without consulting anyone, endorsing the President's appeal. Telegrams also came to the Pittsburgh headquarters from the presidents of the machinists' union, the bricklayers', plumbers', railway carmen, and a half dozen others, likewise asking for a postponement. But the rank and file worker was not to be so easily appeased even by a President of the United States. Local steel councils, such as ones in Gary, South Chicago, and Youngstown warned that "unless you call the strike before Friday morning we will be forced to take matters into our own hands." Caught between the fear that a strike could not be won and the danger that so many organized steelworkers would break out of control and against their leaders, Gompers and the National Committee begrudgingly approved Foster's recommendation that there be no further postponement. The strike was on.

VII

The steel strike of 1919 was part of a larger strike wave which included a city-wide strike in Seattle, a walkout by the Boston police, national stoppages in the coal and clothing industries, and more than 4,000 individual walkouts, involving one of every five workers in America. But the labor war in steel was by far the most important of these events.

From prison, Eugene Debs commented to an interviewer that while he did not expect a "prearranged" general strike, yet "in the heat of

passion men may lay down their work and be swept into a revolution
with cyclonic fury . . . Anything is possible as an outcome of the
present situation." The belief that actual national revolution was a
realistic possibility was shared that year by many left-wingers in addition to Debs, as artificial comparisons were made with events elsewhere. "The trade union," wrote the *Union Record* of Seattle, while
the city was in the hands of labor, "is to the American workers what
the Council of Workmen and Soldiers is to Russia, Austria, and
Germany. The labor council is the central soviet . . ." Two days after
the Seattle strike another "soviet" was proclaimed in Butte, and in
May still a third one in Toledo. And though the immediate issue in
steel was the more limited one of collective bargaining, its underlying
implications were far broader. When J. P. Morgan wired Gary "heart-
iest congratulations on your stand for the open shop," he understood
full well that what was at stake was more than the eight-hour day. On
that he and Gary might have yielded. But the showdown, as they saw
it, in truth was a war between two classes, in which Gary and Foster
were merely the symbols. The management actions that followed had
the flavor of that war.

"A historic decision confronts us," read the circular distributed to
hundreds of thousands of iron and steelworkers by the National Committee, "if we will but stand together like men our demands will soon
be granted and a golden era of prosperity will open for us in the steel
industry. But if we falter and fail to act this great effort will be lost,
and we will sink back into a miserable and hopeless serfdom. . . .
STOP WORK SEPTEMBER 22." The primary concern of the federated
unions was to get the men off their jobs, that of the corporations and
their hirelings to keep them in or drive them back. To get the men out
the unions needed little more than access to them—through meetings
and other kinds of personal contact. To keep them in, the corporations
had to prevent contact between union organizers and steelworkers by
making meetings illegal, and by terror, whispering campaigns, and
propaganda.

"In anticipation of the steel strike," read an editorial in the New
York *World* of September 22, 1919, "what do we see? In the Pittsburgh
district thousands of deputy sheriffs have been recruited at several of
the largest plants. The Pennsylvania State Constabulary has been concentrated at the commanding points. . . . At McKeesport alone 3,000
citizens have been sworn in as special police deputies subject to instant call. It is as though the preparations were made for actual war."
Along the Monongahela River, from Pittsburgh to Clairton, less than
two dozen miles, 25,000 men were picked, paid for, and armed by the

steel corporations, but designated "deputies" so they could operate against the strikers under the cloak of official authority.

An omen of what was to come was the repressive actions that had been taken the day before the walkout. In North Clairton that Sunday afternoon, state police rode their horses into a crowd of 3,000 steel-workers and their families, engaged in nothing more menacing than listening to a speaker in an open field—a gathering for which the union had secured a permit. After clubbing and kicking almost everyone in sight, shooting off a revolver which fortunately hit no one, and ripping the American flag from the speaker's platform, they dragged two union organizers and fourteen others to jail on the ironic charge of "disorderly conduct." Dozens who were injured failed to report it or go to the local hospital for fear that they too would be arrested. A similar attack took place in Glassport, adjoining McKeesport, and the "rioters"—who also had a permit—were held on $1,000 to $3,000 bail each. News media reported clashes in Pittsburgh between state police and a "mob bent on holding labor mass meetings." In an incredibly short time all of the gains won by labor in its fight for free speech during the previous months were ruthlessly reversed. The simplest communication between men was impeded, and normal picketing became a virtual impossibility.

The subsequent behavior of the supposed proponents of law and order was nothing short of criminal. They broke up meetings where there were no disturbances. Special police and the state constabulary invaded homes, beat up occupants, forced people off the streets, and even robbed strikers in broad daylight. Foster produced hundreds of affidavits of such criminal behavior, but no one was ever prosecuted, and neither the governor of Pennsylvania nor President Wilson ever intervened to restore to workers their civil liberties. For example, Trachna Yenchenke of Homestead made a deposition on October 3 that two state policemen, without warrant, entered his home while he was asleep, kicked him, punched him, and took him half-naked to jail. The next day he was fined $15.10. James Trook of Butler, a store-keeper described how state troopers ran down a cripple for sport then chased three strikers home. When they protested, a trooper shouted "Get the hell out of here, you sons of bitches, or I will kill you." At Monessen, state police rounded up groups of foreign-born strikers at the mill gates. Those who said they were willing to go to work were freed. The others were jailed in rickety, unlighted building, and threatened with hanging. In Gary, after the troops came, a favorite technique of harrying striking workers was for a company superintendent to take a squad of soldiers to the home of a striker,

and go into the home himself to warn the man that this was his last
chance to return to work. Unless he did, said the superintendent,
pointing to the troops at the window, he would be immediately jailed
or deported to the old country.

Widespread harassment of all kinds by the "cossacks"—state constabulary—and the deputies was reported almost daily in the ensuing
months. "The state police keep everyone moving or club them down,"
was the word from Donora. "Reign of terror in Newcastle, caused by
deputies in uniform of soldiers. Women and children arrested for
nothing," read a telegram to the U. S. Labor Department from that
city. The investigation of the non-partisan Interchurch World Movement was filled with "the arresting and holding of men and women for
long periods in the jails and police stations without provocation, and
even without definite charges being lodged against them . . ." Two
strikers at Monessen related how constables attacked them, put them
in a cellar, and told them "you fellows are going to be hung about
8 o'clock."

Equally ominous as such incidents was the fact that armed deputies
and the constabulary became the instruments for another attempt at
extinguishing free speech. Two days before the walkout, Sheriff
William S. Haddock of Allegheny County, Pennsylvania prohibited—
on his own motion—any outdoor congregation of three or more people. This step was necessary, he explained, to prevent "agitators" from
"attract(ing) the workingman's attention." Indoor meetings would be
tolerated, providing they received advanced sanction, and were conducted in English. The insistence on English was an interesting demand. Experience showed, said Haddock, that "practically 90 per cent
of the offenders against the law in matters of this kind [strikes] are
either aliens or naturalized citizens of foreign extraction, who are
easily led into attacks upon our Government." In this revival of nine-
teenth-century Know-Nothingism, a steel-town paper made the incredible claim that the strikers were "ignorant foreigners unable to
understand the truth and blessed only with the belief that in some
magical way they are to be put in possession of the mills."

In practice, of course, meetings were not permitted in any language
in this widespread strike along forty-one miles of the Monongahela,
the very heart of the industry. The area included such towns as Monessen, Donora, Clairton, Wilson, Glassport, McKeesport, Duquesne,
Homestead, Braddock and Rankin. Not only mass meetings but even
union business meetings were proclaimed illegal. When labor attorney
W. H. Rubin sought an injunction against interference with the regular meeting of the Amalgamated Association in one of these towns, the
judge denied his motion on the grounds that while no violence had

yet occurred, the situation was so tense that it might. During the whole three and one half months of the strike almost no meetings of any kind were held in this district. One exception was in Pittsburgh where the authorities magnanimously allowed meetings to be held in one spot, the Labor Temple, a considerable distance from the struck mills. Another was in Homestead where the officials relented and sanctioned one meeting a week—as long as it was conducted in English and uniformed constables could sit on the stage during the proceedings.

There were a few other towns where the officialdom was more tolerant—in Gary and Youngstown, for instance, at the outset—but even in such places conditions tightened perceptibly as the weeks dragged on. In Bethlehem, under the aegis of Charles M. Schwab, meetings were outlawed, as they were in Natrona, where a union organizer, J. McCaig, was arrested for "inciting to riot." Workers in the Sharon-Farrell district had to walk many miles into the state of Ohio to assure their rights under the U. S. Constitution. Where a sympathetic clergyman, such as the Reverend Adelbert Kazincy of Braddock, opened his church to the strikers, other forms of harassment were found. In this instance the bank suddenly foreclosed the mortgage on Kazincy's Catholic Church, and the constabulary beat strikers as they left the sanctuary.

VIII

Yet despite the terror the turnout on Monday the twenty-second was most impressive. Foster claimed 275,000 men had walked out, or more than half the mill workers. On Tuesday he reported 304,000 off the job and by the end of the week 365,000 (the U. S. Department of Labor put the figure at 367,000). Except for the mills in four small outpost towns the iron and steel industry was either closed or curtailed in *seventy* major centers. In the Chicago and Buffalo districts the strike was 100 per cent effective, in Wheeling and Steubenville, all the furnaces were abandoned. There were weaknesses in such places as Birmingham, Alabama, and Duquesne, Bethlehem, and McKeesport, Pennsylvania but even in the Pittsburgh area, three quarters of the mill hands had left their posts.

Because of a shortage of organizers the strike was confined essentially to the smelting and rolling branches of the industry. But in pockets here and there fabricating plants and coal mines, associated with the mills, were also shut down. At Youngstown railroad workers in the yards joined the walkout, giving the strike a decisive lift. Enthusiasm was so contagious that despite orders by some craft union leaders that their members stay on the job, skilled men such as the steam and operating engineers, voted to go out with the unskilled. It was the most solid expression of working-class discontent America had yet seen.

Judge Gary and his fellow steelmakers obviously had misjudged the determination of their employees, but they continued to whittle away at worker solidarity using a combination of force and fear. The scope of management's attack was evident on the first day. The strike, said Mayor John A. Toomey of Buffalo, was an attempt by "bolsheviks" to spread the "red" doctrine among foreigners. The Chicago *Tribune,* after reporting on the first page that between 75,000 and 80,000 workers were out in the Chicago area, carried an inside story headlined "U. S. Agents Act to Control Reds," The subhead read: "Foster's plan of a social revolution is revealed," and quoted again from his old pamphlet *Syndicalism.* There was also that first day, a rash of violence and arrests, as authorities in various places tried to contain or suppress union picketing. Near the American Steel & Wire plant in Farrell, Pennsylvania, one striker and one scab were killed, and two state troopers injured. Seven unionists were shot at New Castle. All told, twenty-two people would die in the long struggle, twenty of them strikers, and many hundreds would be injured. In that first outburst seven men were arrested at McKeesport, sixteen at Clairton, dozens more elsewhere. All this evidently was according to plan and assumed so by the public since steel shares which should have declined, forged upward on the New York Stock Exchange.

The second day was a repetition of the first—more fatalities (four in the Pittsburgh and Buffalo areas), sixty wounded by gunfire, and the first melee in the Chicago district where 450 strikers chased twenty-five scabs at Indiana Harbor. The violence prompted Governor Alfred E. Smith of New York at this early date to send troops to Lackawanna, near Buffalo, hub of the industry in his state. On this day too Ohio Congressman John G. Cooper, in a style that would be made famous many years later by Senator Joseph McCarthy, rose in the House of Representatives to wave an ominous brochure in everyone's face. "I hold in my hand here," he shouted "a pamphlet entitled 'Syndicalism.' I charge that Mr. Foster's own words in this book show his unfitness as a labor leader and disqualify him from the name of an American citizen or the protection of the American flag!" The next day Congressman Julius Kahn, chairman of the House Military Affairs Committee, conferred with Attorney General A. Mitchell Palmer to urge that Foster be prosecuted for the deaths that had already taken place.

The aim of this move obviously was to weaken worker—and public —support by painting the national stoppage as a foreign conspiracy rather than a legitimate labor struggle. "If the strike succeeds," Judge Gary told an audience at the Ritz-Carlton in New York, "it might and probably would be the beginning of an upheaval which might bring on all of us grave and serious consequences." There could be no compromise with this foreign menace, he said; it was a "fight to the finish." On Saturday, September 27, the newspapers in Pittsburgh began carrying advertisements (and there were to be thirty in the next two weeks) echoing this refrain. The one in the *Chronicle-Telegraph* read: "Yesterday the enemy of liberty was Prussianism. Today it is radicalism. Masquerading under the cloak of the American Federation of Labor a few radicals are striving for power. They hope to seize control of the industries and turn the company over to the 'red' rule of Syndicalism . . . American is calling you. The steel strike will fail. Be a 100 percent American. Stand by America. . . . GO BACK TO WORK MONDAY." The pastor of the Holy Cross Church, Thomas Devlin, in a letter to the editor, proclaimed that "The Kaiser, Hindenburg or Von Tirpitz have nothing on Foster. He is in the class of Trotsky, Lenin, and the Bolsheviki. . . . Why do not the civil authorities arrest and imprison a professed anarchist worse in his teachings than [Alexander] Berkman, [Emma] Goldman, or any of the Russian Reds."

Legislative and administrative agencies not only echoed these sentiments but acted on them as well. After an appearance by Foster before the Senate Committee on Labor and Education in early October, the Committee issued a report that "behind this strike there is massed a considerable element of IWW's, anarchists, revolutionists, and Russian soviets . . . [who] are attempting to use the strike as a means of elevating themselves to power within the ranks of organized labor." Based on this assessment the Committee urged that aliens among the strikers be deported, a cry already heard in many places.

The Wilson administration, despite its liberal posture, also inflamed anti-red and anti-foreign passions. Though the Justice Department continued to refuse to take a single step to restore workers their civil liberties, its agents swooped down on steel centers to arrest hundreds of aliens, lest, as the New York *Times* put it, "the strike be used as a means of advancing Bolshevism." Colonel W. S. Mapes, stationed in Gary, broadcast the sly innuendo that if the government were to release all the facts it knew about the "reds," the "strike would break at once." General Leonard Wood, commander of the troops sent to Gary, believed it his duty, as he stated in a private letter to George W. Perkins of U. S. Steel, to do "my part in rounding up the Red element." Newspapers reported bloody battles between "Bolsheviki" and the authorities, such as the one leaked by U. S. Steel about a gun fight in Sharon in which six men were allegedly killed. All of this was either pure fabrication or at best gross exaggeration. The Interchurch Commission of Inquiry concluded subsequently that the "excitement over Bolshevism" was "baseless." But there is no question it had its impact. Foster and Fitzpatrick themselves conceded, as they stated in a letter to the commission, that "the men in active charge of the strike have been thoroughly discredited," as a result of the "tremendous power and influence . . . of the United States Steel Corporation over the newspapers of the country . . ."

The press not only joined in promoting the red scare but did yeoman's work to give the impression that the strike was collapsing. As early as September twenty-third and twenty-fourth the *Gazette-Times* in Pittsburgh carried blaring headlines such as: "Situation improving, Carnegie Steel Co. asserts: Mills here running," or "21,000 said to have gone back to work." The *Leader,* on the twenty-fourth, reported "Pittsburgh Mills Running Full," and on the next day that "Workers flock back to jobs, Braddock reports three times as many working today as yesterday." This was simply not true. In fact almost no one took Judge Gary's advice to "Go back to work Monday"; on the contrary there were more men out the second week of the strike when Bethlehem plants joined the walkout. In the first month, steel production fell precipitously, and in some places ceased altogether. Yet the mass media, with few exceptions, continued to give prominent space to corporation claims that closed plants were reopening. One wag observed that if all these claims were put end to end the mills would have forty-eight times their normal contingent of employees.

Foster and his National Committee tried to counteract newspaper misstatements by hiring a professional publicity man to give its side of the story and by distributing a weekly strike bulletin in four or five languages. But the union with all its efforts could not match resources with U. S. Steel. Even Fitzpatrick's offer on the fourth day of the strike, to send the men back to work if the corporations would agree to arbitration, made little impression. The offer was scorned by Gary, and played down by the newspapers, which had more industry-biased reports for their readers. "Without a single exception worthy of note," concluded an investigator for the Interchurch Commission, "the statements, demands, grievances and testimony from the strikers were printed under headlines or in a context tending to give the impression that what the striking steelworkers sought was something unwarranted and that their grievances were unfounded."

IX

The ultimate goal of the corporations was to erode morale. The red scare and public reaction to it did this in part. Fictitious stories of plants resuming operations added to the workers' confusion. And a whispering campaign carried on by hundreds of management spies completed this aspect of the corporate offensive. For example, instructions given by the Sherman Service to its secret agents in South Chicago on October 2 were typical of what the steel firms expected: "We want you to stir up as much bad feeling as you possibly can between the Serbians and Italians. Spread data among the Serbians that the Italians are going back to work. Call up every question you can in reference to racial hatred between these two nationalities . . . Urge them to go back to work or the Italians will get their jobs." The Corporations Auxiliary Company had five hundred spies in the field spreading defeatism. The Interchurch Commission uncovered six hundred reports by these agents describing their techniques. When a worker at Monessen told one of the spies, "Z-16," that he intended to go back to work the agent tried to stampede his companions by stating that he too would return because "I am in pretty poor shape financially and have a family of my own to support." According to S. S. Dawson, manager of the Corporation Auxiliary Company office in Pittsburgh, his spies had worked their way into leadership posts in some of the twenty-four federated unions and into some city central bodies, e.g. in Akron. Not infrequently the undercover men went beyond whispering and information-gathering to provoke violence and riots. One Sherman Service official in Chicago, R. V. Philips, was indicted for a scheme to "kill and murder divers large numbers of persons," the blame for which, as planned, would fall on the strikers.

With all the weapons in Judge Gary's arsenal, however, the first few weeks of the strike was a stalemate—an impressive testimony to the tenacity of the foreign-born workers especially, who must have been bewildered by the slurs on their patriotism and the uncertainty of their future. The first back-to-work pleas failed completely, raising Foster's hopes and causing him to comment that "the only way to beat [the strikers] is to starve them out."

For this was the Achilles heel of the National Committee: it had no money. The twenty-four federated unions, all-told, contributed $101,-047 to the Committee—less than thirty cents for each worker on strike. The Amalgamated Association of Iron, Steel and Tin Workers, which received more than $150,000 in initiation fees alone as a result of the organizing drive donated less than $12,000 to the strike fund. Indeed three unions far removed from the steel industry, the Ladies' Garment Workers, the Furriers, and the Amalgamated Clothing Workers, were considerably more generous than the participating craft unions, contributing $180,000 to the cause. The AFL itself gave nothing, though it did issue a call for funds which netted $418,000 for strike expenses

and relief, $150,000 of it raised at a meeting at Madison Square
Garden, on November 8.

But even such large sums were insufficient given the over-all need.
According to Foster the committee required two million dollars a
week for cash-relief payments to strikers. This need was impossible to
meet. The best he and Fitzpatrick could do was to open forty-five
"commissariats" which distributed food to those in need twice a week.
By the estimate of labor historian, Samuel Yellen, this came to nine
and one-third cents per week for every striker during the fifteen
weeks the commissariats were in operation—enough perhaps to prevent outright starvation, but hardly enough to sustain morale indefinitely. This inadequate supply of strike funds was without question the single most important cause for the steel strike's failure. The
defections of some of the unions, most notably the Amalgamated Association, were painful blows. But nothing hurt so much as the lack of
money to pay weekly cash strike benefits.

Foster, Fitzpatrick, and Gompers were fully and sadly aware of
this weakness and tried to end the walkout as quickly as possible
through arbitration or mediation. At the Industrial Conference initiated by President Wilson on October 6, Gompers proposed a six-man
arbitration committee, two each from business, labor, and the public.
He even offered to send the strikers back to work pending arbitration.
But Judge Gary, who attended the session, was so patently opposed to
that suggestion that it never was put to a vote. Foster and Fitzpatrick
applauded the intervention of the Interchurch World Movement,
which began an investigation of the strike October 3, and the labor
leaders later asked it to apply its prestige toward mediation. But these
efforts too came to naught. The strike had to be fought on Gary's
terms, "to a finish."

X

After the first indecisive weeks, the strength of the employers began to show. On October 4, strikers returning from a meeting in Gary,
where the walkout was almost one hundred per cent effective, met a
small group of homeward-bound black scabs and engaged in a small
tussle. It was a trivial incident in which only one man was injured
slightly, but it brought the inevitable call for the militia. The governor
of Indiana responded almost by reflex action, assigning eleven National Guard companies to Gary and 1,000 militiamen to nearby
Indiana Harbor. In vain the union tried to circumvent the move by
offering to supply from its own ranks seven hundred war veterans who
had just finished fighting for their country to keep the peace, but the
state administration was in no mood for simple solutions.

A day or two later the strikers, including the veterans, staged a parade in violation of militia orders. Thereupon the governor petitioned for federal troops and General Leonard Wood arrived with a regiment from Fort Sheridan, north of Chicago. The general, who had ambitions for the presidency, immediately limited picketing and declared martial law. "The [U.S.] Steel Corporation," writes Foster, "now had the situation in hand; and the Gary strike was doomed." Strike leaders and pickets were arrested and put to work sweeping streets or splitting wood. Picketing was restricted, union meetings suppressed, and the government showed a sudden zeal for midnight raids to unearth "red plotters." Even more important, the army became a shield behind which strikebreakers could be imported and protected from unionist wrath. And as the number of strikebreakers grew, demoralization mounted, causing some of the strikers to desert.

By the end of October this defection had become a serious problem for the unions in Gary. It was compounded by the fact that a sizable portion of the strikebreakers were black. Though the steel companies recruited from whatever ethnic groups they could, black workers turned out to be their best source, for despite Foster's efforts to woo them, the blacks felt little kinship for the AFL. All they knew of it was the experience of being placed in segregated locals or excluded entirely—a fate even worse than that accorded the foreign-born. Thus the blacks who had begun to find jobs in the mills during the labor shortage occasioned by the war, were lukewarm to the union's pleas to join when the strike broke out. Their number was not yet large, but except in Wheeling and Cleveland, they refused to honor the union cause. And in the months that followed 30,000 to 40,000 other blacks were recruited by the steel companies to replace whites in every major steel center. It was an opportunity for them to find a niche in an industrial haven from which they had so long been barred, and they took it. Had it not been for General Wood's troops, Gary strikers might have dissuaded the strikebreakers black and white, from their actions, but under martial law it was not possible. The same was true in other steel districts, where either company armies or the local deputies also prevented communication between strikers and scabs.

By the end of October the labor ranks were beginning to crack. This was when the Executive Council of the AFL issued its appeal for funds and the commissariats were opened to ward off the extreme widespread hunger. For a brief moment in early November there was a ray of hope for the steelworkers from another quarter—a national stoppage by the United Mine Workers' calling for a six-hour day and a 60 per cent raise in pay. The steel strike was now six weeks old and the steel companies still had a supply of coal. Yet had the miners remained out for any length of time, the pinch undoubtedly would have affected both industries and probably brought government pressure for a compromise. Wilson's Attorney General, A. Mitchell Palmer—who would soon become famous for the "Palmer raids" against radicals—was able to secure an injunction from Judge Albert B. Anderson of the U. S. District Court in Indiana on November 8 ordering the miners back to work in the bituminous fields. Faced with the injunction, John L. Lewis, new president of the UMWA, called off the strike; "we cannot fight the government," he said. And though the miners, as determined in their cause as the steelworkers, refused to heed their president's instructions and stayed away from the pits for another month, the union finally accepted a government proposal for a 14 per cent raise and arbitration. With their return to work, another bastion of support for the beleaguered steel strikers collapsed.

Nonetheless Foster and Fitzpatrick were determined to fight on. They had a few more cards to play. The Pennsylvania Federation of Labor, at a special convention, voted to call a general strike to re-establish in the Keystone state the rights of free speech and assembly. The resolution, however, was never implemented, and this hope for support of the steelworkers too faded away. Another possibility for buttressing the strike was to call out railroaders in the mill yards around Pittsburgh. Had the men of the Union Railroad, and the McKeesport and Monogahela Railroads suspended operations, the steel companies would have been driven to compromise. The National Committee sent representatives to Washington to ask the railroad brotherhoods to conduct a strike vote, but the brotherhoods—as in the Pullman strike of 1894—were unreceptive. A vote was permitted much later; by then, however, the strike was clearly on the downgrade and another opportunity had been lost.

As of mid-November, Foster estimated that the steel mills around Chicago—except in Joliet and Waukegan—had reassembled 50 to 85 per cent of their labor complements, including strikebreakers and those strikers who had decided to go back to work. Mike Tighe made a tour of the area and judged that Gary was operating at 75 per cent strength and Indiana Harbor at 90 per cent. Everywhere the ranks still holding out were thinning appreciably. Foster and Fitzpatrick tried one more ploy. They asked the Interchurch Commission to contact Judge Gary and settle the strike on any terms it thought just—disregarding, if necessary, "our old original demands." Fitzpatrick went to New York on November 27 to discuss the matter further, and the commission agreed to serve as an intermediary providing it was understood that it was acting on its own behalf.

On December 5, then, three nationally respected clerics, Bishop Francis J. McConnell of the Methodist Episcopal Church, and Dr. Daniel A. Poling, and Dr. John McDowell, representing the Interchurch Commission, met with Judge Gary for two hours. As a devout churchgoer, the steel potentate could hardly refuse such an interview. To do so would have been out of character. But sitting in his New York office, the seventy-three-year-old Gary bristled with scarcely disguised anger. He had a report from an anonymous source, he told the three religious leaders, that their own movement was tinged with "red radicals." Before he would consider anything they had to say, he insisted on questioning them at length on this subject. When the talk finally came around to the issues at hand in the strike, Gary told them there was nothing to discuss. The steelworkers were at work, he said, and pleased with their conditions; the few still out were "nothing but a group of red radicals whom we don't want anyhow." The three churchmen never got to present their plan for "a permanent mediation body." "There is absolutely no issue," said the judge, in conclusion.

With this futile discussion, all hope for a negotiated settlement vanished. As of December 10, according to Foster's statistics, only 109,300 of the original 365,600 strikers remained out of the mills, and the number dwindled further in the weeks following. Even by the secretary's figures, steel production had returned to 50 or 60 per cent of normal, an estimate that probably was on the conservative side. On January 8, 1920, after three and a half months, the National Committee suspended the strike. There were still, it said, tens of thousands who refused to concede, but except for isolated areas the major steel regions were rapidly approaching normalcy. In a telegram to affiliates, the National Committee stated: "All steelworkers are now at liberty to return to work pending preparations for the next big organization movement." This was an idle expression of optimism, for it would be fifteen years before the next serious labor drive in steel. On July 1, 1920, the National Committee for Organizing Iron and Steel Workers was formally disbanded.

12

The Lean Years

The "golden" 1920s was a dreary decade for the American labor movement. Normally unions flourish in good times when labor is in short supply and employers can afford concessions. But the golden twenties, that hectic age of prohibition, jazz, and flappers, was an exception to the rule. Times were indeed economically good. After a brief slump, the national income climbed from $61 billion in 1921 to $87 billion by 1929, and with prices relatively stable (because of a lingering depression in agriculture) this represented a great increase in per capita income from $553 to $716.

The eyes of America in that era were on material comforts, on gadgets and contrivances. Young boys played games identifying the make of automobiles, and the horseless carriage was in such demand that it added four million jobs to the labor force. Radio sales spurted from a mere $11 million in 1921 to $412 million eight years later. The electrical industry tripled production; building construction skyrocketed from $1.2 billion in 1919 to a peak of $6 billion in 1926.

"The business of America," said Calvin Coolidge, "is business," and who could quarrel with the stony-faced man who had set a path toward the White House by breaking the Boston policemen's strike. *True Story* magazine bought a full-page ad in the New York *Times* on May 7, 1929, which lauded business for "making a fairy tale come true. Within ten years you have done more towards the sum total of human happiness than has ever been done before in the centuries of historical time." Herbert Hoover, with undiluted exuberance, noted that "we in America today are nearer to the final triumph over poverty than ever before in our land. The poorhouse is vanishing from among us." Hoover's theory of "percolation"—that if you fed more profits to corporations, some of it would trickle down into proletarian pay envelopes—seemed to be working. Despite slashes in the early part of the decade, real wages went up 4.5 per cent overall.

The AFL, however, did not expand with this boom, as it had in the one from 1914 to 1920 when its ranks grew from two to four million. In the backwash of the steel fiasco, its affiliates lost one major strike after another, as capital mounted an offensive similar to the one of 1903–8, but far more savage.

The mood of America, as the golden twenties opened, was solidly conservative. Though radicalism had been given a shot of adrenalin by the Russian Revolution and though a host of progressive and labor parties had emerged after the war, there was a countercurrent of rightist repression and synthetic "Americanism" which swung the pendulum in the opposite direction. On November 7, 1919, while the recently formed communist movement was holding meetings to commemorate the second anniversary of the Soviet revolution, Department of Justice agents, aided by local police, raided leftist headquarters in more than a dozen cities. Almost two thousand people fell into the dragnet in New York alone. Two months later, on January 2, 1920, simultaneous assaults were made against the Communists and the IWW in thirty-three cities. Seldom had America witnessed such police state tactics. Five hundred men and women were arrested in Boston, shackled and driven through the streets. Five hundred fifty-six aliens with radical backgrounds were unceremoniously deported, with the peak reached when 249 men and women of Russian descent, including Alexander Berkman and Emma Goldman, were placed aboard the ship *Buford*, bound for the Soviet Union.

In the next two years so many radicals were indicted and convicted—mostly on charges of criminal syndicalism—that neither the Communists nor Wobblies could function in any capacity resembling normalcy. In Chicago twenty communists received sentences of one to five years. In New York, Benjamin Gitlow, Charles Ruthenberg, and three others were given terms of five to ten years. In California there were 264 convictions. Though the vast majority of radicals never served their terms, winning reversal in the upper courts or being pardoned by liberal governors such as Alfred E. Smith of New York, the arrests, trials and deportations enervated the radical movement. The socialists were now a cipher, having lost three fourths of their membership in the split which had created a number of communist parties. The IWW had been decimated by the conversion of innumerable adherents to communism and the flight of Big Bill Haywood to the Soviet Union. The communists, meanwhile, rent with factionalism themselves and harassed by continuing raids which made the Party at best semi-legal, failed to gain a strong, stable, foothold.

The climate thus was ripe for an employer assault, and management took full advantage of it. Under a patriotic-sounding label, called the "American Plan," capital jabbed at the heart of unionism, questioning its very right to exist. From a thousand different but co-ordinated forums, the disciples of "Americanism" shouted that unions desecrated the worker's right to "free choice." Hundreds of "American Plan" organizations were formed to proclaim the virtues of the non-union "open shop," as against the "closed shop" which was designated "un-American." If the employee himself were not sufficiently patriotic to resist the blandishments of union "pinks" and radicals, management itself intended to save him from that subversive fate.

In accordance with this high principle, the American Banker's Association, representative of 23,000 organized financiers, trumpeted the laborer's right "to work out his own salvation and not be bound by the shackles of organization . . ." The National Grange at its 1920 convention defended the option of any individual "to work where his industry is needed at any time and at any wage which is satisfactory to him"; no union should be permitted to curb that God-given prerogative. A. M. Glossbrenner, of the Indiana Manufacturers' Association, announced that "we will not employ an individual in any part of the plant that does not sign an individual contract in which it is expressed that he is not and will not become a member of a labor organization while in our employ." The unions called this a "Yellow Dog Contract," but in the spirit of the so-called freedom that pervaded the industrial scene, employers imposed it as a condition of employment on thousands of workers. Eugene Grace, the chieftain of Bethlehem Steel, went one step further: he refused to sell steel to contractors in New York and Philadelphia who were so unpatriotic as to hire union labor.

By late 1920 there was hardly a nook or cranny in the United States that did not boast an "American Plan" organization. In New York State alone there were fifty. Massachusetts had eighteen, Connecticut twenty, Illinois forty-six, Michigan twenty-three. The National Open Shop Association, an amalgam of many of these groups, offered to supply spies and strikebreakers wherever needed to suppress a union. Sensing that its true activities might not be too popular with the public, despite the Americanism tag, the association urged its affiliates, however, to operate "with the utmost secrecy, as we have found that publicity usually beats our purpose."

At a January 1921 meeting in Chicago, twenty-two state manufacturers' associations coined the name, the American Plan, and pledged not to enter into any agreement with a labor union. "Never before," wrote Savel Zimand in a brochure on the subject, "has America seen an open shop drive on a scale so vast as that which characterizes the drive now sweeping the country. Never before has an open shop drive been so heavily financed, so efficiently organized, so skillfully generated. The present drive flies all the flags of patriotic wartime propaganda. It advances in the name of democracy, freedom, human rights, Americanism." Even United States Attorney General Harry Daugherty was enlisted in the crusade. "So long, and to the extent that I can speak for the government of the United States," he said, "I will use the power of the government within my control to prevent the labor unions of the country from destroying the open shop."

The employer attack at its inception coincided with the postwar depression of 1921, in which industrial production slumped 15 per cent and the number of factory wage earners fell by about a quarter. It was an opportune moment for employers to cut workers' pay and increase hours. Early that year the American Shipowners' Association proposed a new contract to two seamen's unions, calling for 25 per cent pay slashes and the abolition of overtime. As negotiations dragged on, the moguls relented slightly, dropping the 25 per cent to 15 per cent, but added other provisions such as abolition of preferential hiring for union members, which would have gravely weakened the organized forces. The ensuing strike, beginning at midnight May 1, was the largest in shipping history, tying up three hundred vessels in the New York Harbor alone. Aided by the United States Shipping Board, however, the employers secured a series of injunctions, had hundreds of strikers arrested in Atlantic and Gulf ports on the charge of "vagrancy," and hired the usual contingents of strikebreakers, many, oddly enough, off university campuses. After fifty-two days the strike was shattered, and though the unions did not disappear they were fragmented by serious schism.

At approximately the same time, hundreds of small strikes broke out in the well-organized printing trades, when some of the employers reneged on an agreement for a forty-four-hour week that was to go into effect May 1, 1921. For the next four years it cost the International Typographical Union $16 million for strike benefits, and the International Printing Pressmen and Assistants' Union a million dollars. These two unions survived, but the Stockyards Labor Council, built so assiduously by Foster in 1917–18 was caught in the economic bind and totally demolished. On December 5, 1921, after three wage cuts and the coercion of meat-packing workers into a company union, 45,000 packer employees in thirteen states walked off the job. Discord between Dennis Lane, secretary-treasurer of the Amalgamated Meat Cutters and Butcher Workmen, who formed a dual council to the Stockyards Labor Council after the 1918 victory, and Jack Johnstone, who succeeded Foster in the latter's leadership, was a major factor in the abject defeat that followed this strike. Feelings were so bitter that two organizers were killed in the internecine war, and on one occasion Johnstone had to shoot it out with a gang of raiders who tried to take over his headquarters. In any event, this first bastion of mass-production industry to have been taken by the AFL was now a rampart of company unionism.

Wherever one turned in the aftermath of World War I, labor's road was rocky; victory often was a compromise in which it simply won a reduction of a wage cut, rather than a wage increase. Thus 100,000 workers in the cotton mills of New England, after seven months of bloody picket-line clashes, had nothing more to show for their effort than a chipping away of the original 42.5 per cent wage cut to 22.5 per cent. Sixty-five thousand members of the Amalgamated Clothing Workers in New York fought a successful six-month battle to retain union control of jobs, but had to agree to a pay cut of 15 per cent. Not even the building trades unions, fortress of the AFL, were immune from attack—and defeat. After a spectacular public investigation of union practices in New York and Chicago, builders in the latter city sliced pay by one fifth; and with a $3 million slush fund, the aid of a Citizens' Committee and imported strike-breakers, they thoroughly vanquished the Chicago Building Trades Council. A lockout of craftsmen belonging to fifteen unions in San Francisco also terminated in a rout, with the unions accepting both wage cuts and the "American Plan's" open shop.

The most important strike of this period, setting the tone of the hard times, was that of hundreds of thousands of railroad shop craftsmen. Under the Transportation Act of 1920, which ended federal operation of the railways and established a nine-member Railroad Labor Board, the government became, in effect, the arbiter of wages and conditions. Its first decision in July of that year granted a thirteen-cents-per-hour raise to shop employees, and was of course heartily endorsed by the craft unions belonging to the AFL's Railway Employees' Department. The next decision ten months later, however, deflated wages by five to eighteen cents an hour, and caused industry-wide worker consternation. And the six shop craft unions, which were part of the Railway Employees' Department, had additional woes; not only was premium pay abolished for work on Sundays and holidays, but the carriers introduced a system of "contracting out" their jobs to outside firms which put their men on piece work. In many instances the "outside contractors" were secret subsidiaries of the railroads that hired them. When the board, at the request of the corporations, instituted another wage cut in May 1922—12 per cent for the shop crafts, a penny to five cents an hour for the maintenance-of-way workers—the unions sent out one million strike ballots, and received an overwhelming mandate to strike.

Had the four operating brotherhoods and the maintenance-of-way union joined the work suspension, the outcome might have been very different. But the brotherhoods stood aside, in another testament to the folly of craft unionism, and the maintenance-of-way leadership, despite a membership vote to strike, simply asked the Labor Board for a rehearing. Nonetheless 400,000 shop craftsmen from coast to coast did walk out in July 1922, and stayed out for more than three months. The chairman of the Railroad Labor Board branded them "outlaws" and threatened to revoke their seniority rights, but the ranks held firm through July and August.

Finally in September, Judge James H. Wilkerson issued an injunction that was so far-reaching it left even the railroad magnates breathless. The judge's order prohibited union members, their leaders or their attorneys, from writing, speaking, telephoning, or in any way communicating with fellow workers to dissuade them from scabbing. Union meetings were barred, and unions instructed not to use their funds for strike purposes of any kind, including picketing. In vain the AFL protested that the Clayton Act exempted unions from antitrust injunctions, and that the Transportation Act did not forbid strikes against a Board decision. With the gun at their head in the form of an injunction, the shop craftsmen were lucky to salvage anything from the assault on their organizations. On the initiative of the Baltimore & Ohio, however, about a hundred roads employing 225,000 shopmen did enter into separate agreements at least restoring seniority rights. But the other 175,000 strikers were deprived of any independent union representation to voice their claims and were forced into company unions.

II

Indicative of labor's slump in the golden twenties was the twin war in the coal industry—between labor and management, on one hand, and between factions of the union on the other. The United Mine Workers of America was then the most dynamic and important labor organization in the country. Weakness in the anthracite fields, once the union's Achilles' heel, had been overcome in 1912, when the UMWA was at last accorded full recognition and its hard-coal membership grew fantastically, from 18,000 to 105,000. Only one geographic area, around Connellsville—the coke section—remained outside the union fold. The soft-coal fields, except for those in the important state of West Virginia, were also solidly unionized. Indeed so all pervasive was the union organization in coal, that it was no longer even necessary to put picket lines around shafts when there was a strike in such places as Illinois.

The power of the miners' union was an important factor for the government to consider, as the nation entered into the war that President Wilson had implied he would keep America from joining. To meet the needs of the war effort, new shafts were being opened, many old ones re-opened. Production of soft coal eventually reached 579 million tons, in 1918, and corporate profits in that field $149 million. This industry had to become and remain stabilized, i.e. kept free of strikes, or the war effort would be jeopardized.

To face this necessity Wilson established a United States Fuel Administration, and one of its first acts was to sponsor, in September 1917, what became known as the Washington Agreement, covering the competitive coal fields originally, and later the whole industry. The agreement provided wage increases of up to $1.50 a day, and was to expire either at the "end of the war" or on April 1, 1920, whichever came first. Unfortunately, the Washington Agreement was far from adequate to offset the balloon-like rise in the cost of living—almost 50 per cent from 1917 to 1919, and another 30 per cent the following year. By the time hostilities ended, November 11, 1918, miners in the pits were chafing at the bit, barely subsisting with their families and demanding action. The government and the UMWA leadership as well, however, insisted that the "end of the war" did not mean the end of hostilities, but instead the date that President Wilson *proclaimed* that the war was over. No strikes were to be permitted until April 1, 1920. For rank and-file diggers this proclamation was intolerable. In Illinois, 75,000 union insurgents went on strike despite appeals by their district president, Frank Farrington, that their action was illegal. So dissatisfied were the diggers with the dilatory tactics of their leaders that they held a rump convention in August, representing the vast majority of the membership in District 12, and supplanted the incumbent officials with a committee of their own. For this insurgency, twenty-five of the local unions had their charters lifted by the national organization.

In Kansas, the miners' malaise took another form. To short-circuit

militancy in the pits, Governor Henry J. Allen initiated legislation for
compulsory arbitration of labor disputes. The miners, led by a powerful, tough district president, Alex Howat, challenged the law repeatedly. Though president John L. Lewis opposed compulsory arbitration, he nonetheless disciplined thirty-three Kansas locals which
went out on "unauthorized" strikes, and Howat was removed from
office—the first of dozens of such removals by Lewis.

A tight situation, in which the pit men were determined both to
make up for their losses in real wages and to organize non-union
mines, sparked wildcat strikes and near civil war on a broad front.
The labor war in Mingo and surrounding counties of West Virginia
was so fierce that at one time the miners formed an army of 4,000
men to confront 2,100 federal troops. West Virginia in 1919 employed 92,000 soft-coal diggers, less than half of them unionized.
Companies which had recently opened pits in the area imposed
yellow-dog contracts on their miners, and when the latter went on
strike, took the issue to court and secured injunctions on the ground
that the men had violated their pledge not to join a union.

In May 1920 a strike broke out in Mingo, and the operators'
association brought in detectives of the Baldwin-Felts agency to evict
miners from their company homes. In the little town of Matewan,
Police Chief Sid Hatfield, who was friendly to the miners and a member of the feuding Hatfield and McCoy families, tried to head off the
detectives. In the ensuing shoot-out Albert and Lee Felts and four
of their detectives were killed, as were the town mayor, a miner,
and a young boy. Hatfield himself was subsequently gunned down
on the steps of a courthouse at Welch. But the guerrilla war did not
let up, even when the governor sent in state troops. On both sides
shooting continued that summer, as deputies drove past tent colonies
firing their revolvers, and strikers took refuge behind laurel bushes
near the mines to shoot at strikebreakers. At Fairmont, on one occasion, one hundred women stood fast on a picket line while troopers
and deputies arrested their husbands, and then were themselves
hauled off to a bullpen when they refused to move. They sang a lusty
little ditty which expressed their sentiments:

> Just like a mule,
> A goddam fool
> Will scab until he dies.

On August 21, in Mingo County, West Virginia, six people were killed
in a three-hour battle and five hundred federal troops were called in.

While the strike spread to other counties of West Virginia and
into Kentucky, a peace of sorts prevailed for a few months until

violence flared again in May 1921. It reached its peak in August when thousands of miners decided to march on Logan County, where there was a particularly obnoxious sheriff, and on Mingo County, then under martial law. Trains and automobiles transported the motley, "citizens' army," carrying all kinds of guns and attended by nurses in white uniforms with the emblem UMW of A on their caps. The "army" advanced without opposition for some miles and might have dispersed without incident if the word had not come down that five miners had been killed at one of the union camps. Fighting then broke out in five places, and it seemed for a while that there would be a wholesale battle between 4,000 members of the "citizens' army" and 2,100 federal troops hastily rushed to the scene. At this juncture some of the miners surrendered; others went home. Afterward 325 people were indicted for treason, 200 others for "conspiracy" and carrying weapons. William Blizzard, leader of the march and head of the subdistrict where it had occurred, was put on trial in May 1922, but after five weeks was acquitted. All the other cases were dismissed. Meanwhile the strike, however, had lost most of its momentum, and was finally called off in October 1922, after more than two years.

This situation, as described above, illustrates the tenor of the times in the coal patches during the postwar period and reveals the workers' pervasive feelings that there was nowhere for them to turn for relief, either to the operators, the government, or to their own officials. Had the diggers been sustained by a leadership matching their own militancy they would have met the challenge of a difficult time without *fratricide* or wildcat strikes—and they might have fared better. But dominating the union from September 1919 on was an imposing conservative figure who reserved his best fights for union opponents—such as Howat, Farrington, John Brophy, Powers Hapgood, George Voyzey—more than for the coal companies.

John Llewellyn Lewis, six feet tall, stocky, busy-browed, square-jawed, was, as his 1969 obituary described him, "a giant of the American labor movement." For good or ill, or something of both, he certainly was the most important man on the moderate end of the labor spectrum, as Debs, Haywood, and Foster were on the radical end. Distinguished by a leonine head of black hair and a thunderous voice that would wake the dead, he was a magnificent orator, slow and deliberate in style, eminently capable of turning a brilliant, clever phrase. When asked during the 1930s why he included so many communists in the organizing staff of the CIO, he quipped back, "Who gets the bird, the hunter or the dog?" Gruff, unsmiling, theatrical, he had a devastating way of characterizing an adversary. Roosevelt's

Vice-President John Nance Garner, for example, was referred to as "a labor-baiting, poker-playing, whisky-drinking, evil old man." When Lewis broke with William Green, the man who had been vice-president of the UMWA and whom he had elevated to the presidency of the AFL, he said: "I have done a lot of exploring of Bill's mind and I give you my word there is nothing there." He described Walter Reuther as "an earnest Marxist chronically inebriated, I think, by the exuberance of his own verbosity," and George Meany as "an honest plumber trying to abolish sin in the labor movement." In the 1930s he became a hero to millions by forming the Committee for Industrial Organization and leading it in its greatest days of triumph. But in the 1920s he was considered by many, if not most, coal miners an undiluted scoundrel, a heavy-handed dictator who would balk at nothing, not even violence, to keep control of the union—and, above all, a sellout of the mineworkers' interests.

Lewis, the oldest of four boys and two girls born to Welsh immigrants, was born on Lincoln's Birthday in 1880, in the small mining town of Lucas, Iowa. His father, Thomas Lewis, was a member of the Knights of Labor who was blacklisted for many years after the miscarriage of a strike in 1882. Unionism was daily conversational fare at the Lewis table, and from his father, John L. imbibed its principles from the time he learned to understand English. Because the older Lewis had to shift to other cities for work outside the pits, John L.'s formal schooling was completed in three different places. He was a husky, tough youngster, who enjoyed a good fist fight, but was bright, popular, and in ensuing years a voracious reader. After seven years in the classroom he had to go to work to help contribute to the family finances, and in 1897, when the blacklist against his father was lifted, he returned with him to find work in the Lucas pits. In his spare time he formed baseball teams and debaters' clubs and read Shakespeare and the classics avidly.

For five years after reaching the age of majority, the future "giant of the American labor movement" wandered the byways of the West, mining copper in Montana, silver in Utah, gold in Arizona, coal in Colorado. He was working in Hannah, Wyoming, in 1905 when a mine accident took the staggering toll of four hundred lives, an event that left enduring impressions on his mind and emotions. Returning to the pits of Lucas in 1906—and to his schoolteacher sweetheart, Myrta Edith Bell, daughter of a doctor, whom he married the following year—Lewis became active in the UMWA and was elected by acclamation as a delegate to its convention. Though this was a minor step on the ladder, unionism was now John L. Lewis' career. In 1909, having moved to Panama, Illinois, he was elected president of the mine local there, and then state legislative agent. "It was impossible to ignore him anywhere," writes his biographer Cecil Carnes. "Platforms trembled when he mounted them and he always timed his entrance like an actor . . ." Sam Gompers was impressed by Lewis too, for in 1911 he designated him a member of his field staff, and assigned him to organizing for the AFL in various parts of the country—where among other things he consolidated a following in the UMWA. By 1917 he was the mine union's chief statistician and vice-president. Then in September 1919, when the incumbent, Frank J. Hayes, became ill, John L. Lewis ascended to the UMWA presidency.

In this thirteen-year climb to power, Lewis had never been infected by radicalism. Experience had molded Eugene V. Debs from a good Democrat to a left-wing Socialist, and Bill Haywood from a metal miner to a Wobbly, but Lewis would have nothing to do with "the daydreams of visionaries." He damned the Wobblies, who in his opinion held the "fantastical ideas of misguided enthusiasts and mercenary enemies of the trade union movement." He hated the communists. If his own rhetoric sometimes sounded "visionary" it was persiflage for a deeply embedded conservatism. He often bellowed and was sometimes rebellious, but when the chips were down he was a good Republican who placed limits on any challenge to the free enterprise system.

This characteristic became evident in the first crisis faced by Lewis as president of the UMWA. In defiance at first of a warning by President Wilson that a national strike against the Washington Agreement would be "not only unjustifiable but unlawful," Lewis called 400,000 soft-coal diggers off the job on November 1, 1919. But when Judge Albert B. Anderson of the U. S. District Court in Indiana issued an injunction—which the AFL called "so autocratic as to stagger the human mind"—he retreated: "I will not fight my government, the greatest government on earth." The miners did not come out empty-handed from this foray—they received immediate pay adjustments of 14 per cent and 20 to 31 per cent later. But UMWA radicals felt much more could have been gained, and almost a third of the soft-coal members, unappeased by the settlement, continued a wildcat strike for a short period.

III

Whether this first act of leadership was or was not a "victory," as claimed by Lewis, it was to be the last one for a dozen years. Having vastly expanded production capacity during the war, the coal industry was now capable of satisfying the nation's needs even with part-time operation. The point was brought home with great impact as negotiations with the operators began in 1922.

There was more surplus coal above ground than ever before in U.S. history. Overproduction bred unemployment, and unemployment cut deeply into the union's bargaining power, since there were jobless available to replace those who might strike. One solution to this problem was offered by John Brophy, president of District 2 in Clearfield, Pennsylvania, and one of the best loved figures in the union. A devout Catholic and a Fabian socialist of unquestioned integrity, the English-born Brophy proposed that the government buy the nation's coal mines for $4.5 billion, and work out a national agreement with the union. The planned use of black diamond facilities would eliminate the economic evils springing from overcapacity, as well as ease the cacophony that always arose in collective bargaining.

There were of course many radicals in the UMWA ranks who seconded Brophy's scheme for nationalization; the coal union was always a haven for large numbers of leftists. But Lewis, the simple unionist, suspicious of visionary ideas, preferred the old, mundane route to worker triumphs. The result was a string of strikes, almost all rear-guard actions to retain what had been won, for most of the decade. In 1922, with high unemployment rates strongly affecting the coal patches, the soft-coal operators demanded wage cuts of 25 to 35 per cent, whereas the miners demanded a 20 per cent hike. More important, Lewis insisted on a single interstate agreement. Unless there were one agreement and one pay scale, the operators in one district would hold a competitive advantage over those in another, forcing the latter to lay off still more miners. When the operators of the Central Competitive Field balked at negotiating a uniform pact, a nationwide strike started on April 1, 1922. For good measure the anthracite diggers were included—since negotiations there had been held up—thus making it the first time in history that both sections of the industry had gone out together, 600,000 strong. In addition, on Lewis' call, 75,000 men in the unorganized Connellsville, Pennsylvania, coke region who had not engaged in a strike or belonged to a union for thirty years, joined the common effort. From the point of view of numbers of strikers the stoppage seemed to have awesome possibilities; but if so, they were never realized.

As labor wars go, the 1922 strike was a mild affair. Except for Connellsville, there were few attempts to bring in strikebreakers and in most places there was no organized picketing; it was not necessary. The stoppage settled down to a contest of wills, until June 21–22, when a startling incident occurred in Egypt, near Herrin, Illinois.

The "Herrin Massacre," which brought much opprobrium to the miners' cause, might not have happened if the union had not accommodated one employer in a special situation. William J. Lester of the Southern Illinois Coal Company, owner of a strip mine in Egypt, proposed to the UMWA sub-district that he be permitted to bring in a massive Bucyrus shovel to dig the coal bed on the unequivocal promise that he would not ship the fuel until the strike was over. To supervise the work he assigned C. K. ("Old Peg") McDowell, whose right leg had been smashed in strikebreaking activities back in Kansas, and who along with Lester had no intention of living up to the understanding.

McDowell began his work by importing "finks" from Chicago's skid row, guarded by detectives of the Hargreaves Secret Service agency. The crew of the Bucyrus shovel was composed of members of the independent Steam Shovel Men's Union, a group expelled from the AFL, already engaged in strikebreaking in a number of strip pits in Ohio. Both the sheriff, a former miner, and the state militia tried to dissuade McDowell from his obvious course. But holed up with sixty armed men in an improvised stockade, and with a storeroom of shotguns, hand grenades, and rifles at hand, McDowell closed off the road leading to the mine, and for some unexplained reason sent the goon squads out in trucks to fire at farmhouses and cattle. On June 13 he began loading coal on rail cars. Eight days later, on the afternoon of the twenty-first, a striker talking with friends at a farmhouse a half-mile away, was killed by a bullet from the high-powered rifle of a McDowell guard.

Immediately the whole mining community was in an uproar. More than 1,000 miners came from near and far, invaded hardware stores and American Legion halls for arms, and launched an attack on the small band at the Southern Illinois Coal Company mine. According to Colonel Samuel Hunter of the National Guard: "It was a seemingly well-organized, remarkably sober, determined, resolute aggregation of men and boys fighting as they put it in their own words, 'to preserve the union.'" From the cornfields around the mine the shooting continued until the sun came up next morning when McDowell finally raised the flag of surrender. But too much hate had been generated for the incident to end quickly and peaceably. Cheering strikers blew up the Bucyrus shovel, set dynamite to loaded coal cars, and disarmed and took the guards in tow. By now most of the attackers had gone home to sleep, but among those who remained were some bent on mischief. McDowell was dragged down a lane and riddled with bullets. Other prisoners were handed over to a mob that had not been involved in the fighting but now were wreaking vengeance on their captives. Six of Lester's men had a rope placed around them and were systematically gunned down in an open trench. Other detectives and "finks" escaped to the woods, but by nightfall there were nineteen bodies at the local morgue.

National reaction to the gruesome event was of course blisteringly hostile to the workers. Two hundred and fourteen unionists were indicted for the murders and the cry for their blood reached high levels. But Herrin, Illinois, was not the eastern Pennsylvania of Molly Maguire times. The whole community had lived through the bleak days when miners who now earned $7 to $15 a day had worked for $1.25 and $2.00. The slain men were foreign invaders trying to upset those gains, and there was no jury in the county that would convict the miners. The coroner's jury, without flinching, charged that "the deaths were due to the acts, direct and indirect, of the Southern Illinois Coal Company," and all union men put on trial subsequently, eleven in all, were acquitted. Lewis, in his best red-baiting style, blamed it all on the "Reds" and instituted a small pogrom of suspensions and charter revocations against men he said were under the orders of "revolutionary masters in Moscow." Illinois miners, however, did assess themselves a million dollars to pay for the company's destroyed equipment and the costs of defending their two hundred brothers.

Outside the coal communities, the Herrin massacre cost the UMWA considerable public support, but the strike was not destined for glory anyway. In June operators offered to reopen the mines at the old wage scale. The union rejected it. A month later President Warren G. Harding wired twenty-eight governors asking them to call out militia to protect the mines—i.e. to escort strikebreakers in to work. In August, after eighteen weeks, Lewis came to terms with the operators of Ohio, Indiana, and Illinois—as he did eventually with others—in which the old wage scale was to be retained until March 31, 1923. The agreement conflicted so strongly with rank and file wishes, that the union lost its hold on the mines in Virginia, West Virginia, Alabama, Texas, Colorado, and Utah. Worse still, Lewis deserted the 75,000 miners in Connellsville, Pennsylvania, who had responded to his summons with such high hopes four months before. With only John Brophy to help them, they were left to fend for themselves, until their strike petered out in August 1923—after sixteen months.

Following 1922 the UMWA descent was precipitous. For one thing, mechanization hit the coal patches. Every day now new machines were being placed in the shafts, raising productivity from four tons a day per man in 1920 to five tons in 1924, and as a consequence placing vast numbers of miners among the ranks of the unemployed. U. S. Steel bought 100,000 acres of mining property in West Virginia and Kentucky, all non-union operated. The day rate negotiated by Lewis might be $7.50 in union mines, but south of the Ohio River there were tens of thousands in Virginia, Kentucky, Tennessee and Alabama working in non-union pits for as little as $3 a day.

This inequitable situation demanded some drastic action. But Lewis chose instead to renew the bituminous pact in 1923 for another year, and in 1924 signed the "Jacksonville Agreement," extending the same pay scales for three more years. If it was a "victory," as Lewis contended, it was one only in the sense that the operators had asked that rates be cut back to those prevailing back in 1917, before the Washington Agreement. In any case, the ink had barely dried on the Jacksonville Agreement, when unionized operators in complete violation of the pact began instituting one wage cut after another. The Pittsburgh Coal Company, with 17,000 miners controlled by the Mellon family, the Rockefeller-owned Consolidation Coal Company, and one hundred lesser firms tore up their pacts, reduced pay to approximately $6 a day and returned to the open shop.

It is unpleasant and for the most part unnecessary to recount the rest of the coal miners' tale in the 1920s. It was a sad one. By October 1927, for instance, the Illinois diggers were forced to accept a cut from $7.50 a day to $6.10. In 1930, the proud union which had reached a peak of 450,000 members was down to 150,000. At least two thirds of the nation's coal was now mined by non-union men.

In addition to the disaster in relations with management, there was a holocaust of gigantic dimensions within the union. There was no talent that John L. Lewis exercised more than this talent for fully controlling the union. Every convention was carefully rigged with Lewis stalwarts, some from "blue sky" locals that existed only on paper. Every election was carefully manipulated, and Lewis henchmen always counted the votes, so that John L. would emerge victorious. No one could gavel a delegate out of order with such finality. When delegates challenged him at one convention by one hour of jeering, Lewis cried out majestically from the platform: "May the Chair state that you may shout until you meet each other in Hell, and he won't change the rule!" In quick order, after 1924–25, the right to elect organizers was taken out of the rank and file's hands—by the slim vote of 2,263 to 2,106—and placed in Lewis'. One district and one local after another was placed under the president's trusteeship, giving Lewis a mechanical control of the whole organization.

The progressives, around Brophy, Powers Hapgood, a well-to-do socialist, Howat, George Voyzey and Frank Keeney of West Virginia,

formed caucuses and tried to unseat Lewis, but always failed. Voyzey, an opposition candidate for the union presidency in 1924, polled
66,000 votes, John Brophy, in 1926, 60,116 votes—in each case about
one third of the total. Both insisted that they had been given "the fast
count." In 1925, the progressives, together with the communists,
formed a "Save the Union" committee, but were denounced by Lewis
as "dual-unionists" and communists, and expelled from the UMWA by
presidential fiat. The progressives, with a considerable base in Kansas
and Illinois, sent squads to Ohio and Pennsylvania to recruit for
their cause. In response, Lewis sent his henchmen to southern Illinois,
and not infrequently bloody battles between fellow unionists broke
out with fists and guns. By the time such struggles had waned,
the communists had established an independent National Miners'
Union, under the guiding hand of Pat Toohey, claiming 40,000
members. An opposition force in southern Illinois had formed the
Progressive Miners of America. And Keeney has established his own
organization in West Virginia. What remained of the United Mine
Workers was an enervated organization under a one-man dictatorship.

IV

Not every segment of the labor movement was lashed by mechanization, unemployment, reduced bargaining power, and internal friction as was the UMWA. But the decline of the unionist drive was all
but universal. The AFL lost one fourth of its membership by 1923—
down from 4,078,740 in 1920 to 2,926,468. The Seamen's Union fell to
50,000 by 1921, and the Brotherhood of Maintenance of Way Employees lost 125,000 card-carriers as a result of its role in the 1922
strike. The independent Clothing Workers' enrollment lapsed from
200,000 members to just slightly more than 100,000.

The return of prosperity after 1921 pushed workers' wages to higher
levels, both nominally and in real terms, but it did little to improve
the status of organized labor. More than a million workers were now
conscripts of company unions, at Bethlehem Steel, Eastman Kodak,
Westinghouse, the Pennsylvania Railroad, International Harvester,
and elsewhere in a variety of industries. The yellow-dog contract was
a feature of many corporate personnel policies.

In a lukewarm effort to reverse the trend, AFL unions sought to
curry favor with management by co-operating in joint efficiency
drives. For instance, under the B&O plan, originally instituted by
the International Association of Machinists and the Baltimore & Ohio
Railroad, the union was granted recognition in return for collaboration with management to improve the "quality and quantity" of pro-

duction. The plan resulted in ten or twelve more work days per year, but little else. It was, in any case, no panacea to arouse the millions of workers waiting to be sold on unionism. The AFL itself ventured into a few new organizing drives, but it lacked the necessary spark to ignite a massive worker movement toward unionization. At the 1926 convention a resolution was carried proposing an amalgamated campaign in the automobile industry, similar to the one that union leaders organized in steel in 1919. But it collapsed when the AFL refused to go ahead without the consent of General Motors and Ford employers. A thrust into the textile town, after a sensational year-long strike led by the communists, at the woolen mills of Passaic, New Jersey, was costly and bloody, but spent itself by September 1930. For all practical purposes the AFL was immobilized, on the defensive, trying to stay intact, nothing more.

The only important challenge to the AFL hierarchy in the golden twenties was from its old nemesis, William Z. Foster, who clung tenaciously to his notion of "boring from within." With Jack Johnstone and other old associates, Foster formed still another left-wing grouping, the Trade Union Educational League (TUEL) in November 1920. Though shunned by the AFL, and ignored by the recently formed communist parties for having sold out the revolution during the war, "E. Z. Foster," as his enemies called him, was still the steel strike leader with a national reputation to capitalize on. His name was a byword to be cursed or lauded, depending on one's viewpoint. Moreover, the slogan of his TUEL, "Amalgamation and a Labor Party," was captivating to innumerable unionists trying to head off a postwar reaction.

Literally thousands of local unions, seventeen state federations of labor, and twenty international unions including the railway clerks, meat cutters, bakers, lithographers, textile workers, maintenance-of-way employees, typographers, machinists, brewery workers and bookbinders, as well as scores of city federations of labor, would endorse the program for amalgamation in the next few years. Four hundred delegates of railroad workers founded the Railroad Workers Amalgamation Committee in December 1923, and two hundred miner delegates from twelve of the thirty mine districts, including the largest one, Illinois, formed the International Committee of Progressive Miners. The left wing of the International Ladies' Garment Workers' Union gained control of three of the largest New York locals—2, 9, and 22—with 30,000 members, plus locals in Philadelphia and Chicago. In the United Mine Workers, where there was unquestionably a majority for "Amalgamation and a Labor Party," Voyzey and Brophy, as already noted, received about one third the vote in elections against John L. Lewis—and had the votes been counted honestly, probably much more.

"Under our leadership," Foster said in 1925, "fully half of the whole labor movement demanded an amalgamation." That may have been an exaggeration but it was not terribly inaccurate. The contest between the left and right was taking place even in such rock-ribbed old-line organizations as the carpenters' union. The TUEL ran candidates in the metal trades, and swept elections against Mike Tighe of the Amalgamated Association in many of the large centers, though they lost nationally by approximately three to two. Hard line left wingers opposed the socialists and simple unionists in the Amalgamated Clothing Workers, the International Ladies' Garment Workers, the Furriers, the Machinists, and in many city federations of labor, including those of Minneapolis and Buffalo. At a time when the AFL numbered about two and a half million, a group that could muster this kind of support was not inconsequential. At its peak the TUEL claimed 300,000 adherents, more than a tenth of the Federation's membership.

The TUEL, however, led no spectacular struggles on the scale of the 1919 steel strike and recorded no dramatic victories such as the IWW's at Lawrence in 1912. In part this could be attributed to the general slumber of unionism in the 1920s, and in part to the manipulative methods of the communists, who controlled the TUEL after Foster secretly joined the Party in May 1921.

The communists, at first, had spurned "boring from within" in favor of dual, revolutionary unionism—sponsoring unions outside the AFL, and with a program calling for revolution. But in 1920 Lenin published his famous pamphlet *Left-Wing Communism, an Infantile Disorder,* in which he berated as an "unpardonable blunder" the strategy of trying "to create new, *fantastic* forms of labor organization!" The "task of the communists," he suggested, "is to be able to *convince* the backward elements, to be able to work *among* them, and not *fence themselves off* from them by artificial and childishly 'Left-wing' slogans." This was what Foster was also saying, and it suddenly made both him and his policy of "boring from within" extremely palatable to the American communists. They adopted TUEL as the "IWW idea within the AFL," and Foster and his colorless assistant, Earl Browder, as their new labor messiahs.

The IWW idea within the AFL, however could not overcome the clumsy tactics which "fenced off" the TUEL as effectively as if it were a dual union. The slogan "amalgamation and a labor party," highly attractive in itself, was surrounded with less alluring ones such as "defend the Soviet Union," and "abolish capitalism," which isolated the TUEL from less radical workers. Even Foster himself criticized the "strong tendency to consider the Trade Union Educational League groups as Party fractions and hence to restrict them to Party members alone." Another factor in the emasculation of the TUEL was the break between Foster and Fitzpatrick in 1924, when the latter supported the presidential candidacy of Robert M. La-Follette and the Progressive Party, while the communists, after much back-and-forth movement between endorsing and withdrawing endorsement from LaFollette, ran Foster and Benjamin Gitlow on their own ticket and polled a mere 33,361 votes.

All of the above made it simple for the AFL leaders to quarantine the TUEL militants and expel them by the thousands. William Dunne, of Butte, Montana, was thrown out of the 1924 AFL convention, and the TUEL—Foster's protestations notwithstanding—declared a "dual union." The socialists who headed the needle trades unions (except for the Furriers) were similarly able to make short shrift of TUEL adherents, and Lewis in the UMWA conducted a vicious, though successful, purge of progressives and communists, replete with violence and killings. The textile strikes in Passaic, New Jersey, and Gastonia, North Carolina, led by the TUEL were militant and imaginatively conceived, but ended in a rout. TUEL made more of an impact than Foster's Syndicalist League and International Trade Union Educational League of 1912 and 1916, but it remained a segregated appendage to the house of labor, far removed from center stage. On September 1, 1929, it was quietly interred by the communists, with the Trade Union Unity League, dedicated to work outside the AFL, taking its place.

V

The stock-market crash of October 1929 and the Great Depression that followed immobilized the labor movement generally and the AFL in particular. The AFL did not die out, as other federations had done in the past. Neither, however, did it keep pace with the challenges of the time.

The 1929 depression was the most traumatic in the American experience. The value of all stocks listed on the New York Stock Exchange fell from $87 billion on October 1, 1929 to $19 billion on March 1, 1933. From 1929 to 1932 the total physical output of goods was reduced by 37 per cent, and the total income of industrial workers dropped from $15 billion to $6 billion. Iron and steel production, a fairly accurate barometer of good times, slumped by more than four fifths. Everything was chaos and despair. Within two and a half years 4,835 banks had failed, costing depositors more than $3.25 billion. Millions of families watched their life savings disappear. In 1931 alone, 17,000 retail stores closed their doors. Many Goliaths of the business world went under—Van Sweringen, Insull, Krueger, the United States Bank, to name a few—and with them they pulled under hundreds of thousands of small investors and members of the middle class. Through it all the most glaring symbol of the era's social sickness was the increasing army of the unemployed. By March 1933 the number of jobless workers was at least thirteen million, and with just about the same number working only part time. By 1934 there were two and half million workers who had not been employed for two years or more, and six million who had not received a pay check for at least a year.

In these circumstances, large-scale unionization was out of the question. Those workers who still clung to jobs were morbidly fearful of being replaced by thousands ready to work at almost any wage for almost any number of hours. The focus of insurgency, as the Great Depression veiled the nation in gloom, was outside the AFL and the other segments of the House of Labor. On March 6, 1930, the communists led a national demonstration for "Work or Wages" which attracted almost a million unemployed workers in more than a dozen cities, a hundred thousand each in New York and Detroit. Two months later another national protest brought out only about a third as many people, but helped in the formation of the National Unemployed Council. As a parallel organization to the council, the socialists established their Workers Alliance, and an unaffiliated radical who was to become the nation's anti-war leader in the 1960s, A. J. Muste, organized the National Unemployed League. Before long the three groups, as well as many local ones, were conducting guerrilla warfare against the Depression, involving literally millions of people in small acts of resistance—such as sitting in at a relief station to secure aid for an unemployed family, demonstrating in front of city halls, occasionally raiding a food warehouse, and in thousands of instances preventing marshals or police from evicting tenants who could not pay their rent. Typically, as reported by an Associated Press dispatch of January 20, 1931, from Oklahoma City: "A crowd of men and women, shouting that they were hungry and jobless, raided a grocery store near City Hall today. Twenty-six of the men were arrested."

Reminiscent of Coxey's Army forty years before, thousands of World War I veterans bivouacked in Washington, demanding early payment of a bonus promised them for 1945. Their placards dramatized the popular disenchantment: "Heroes in 1917—Bums in 1932," "We Fought for Democracy—What Did We Get?" President Hoover could think of no better answer to this outcry than to order the men and their families home, and when many had left, sending in General Douglas MacArthur, with tanks and cavalry to burn down their camp. Fifty-five people were injured.

On farms too, the high degree of discontent brought mass action and violence. At its extreme the agricultural protest took two forms —"strikes" to withhold produce from the market, and forceful resistance to foreclosure sales. A Farmers' Holiday Association in Iowa sprang to life in Sioux City, Council Bluffs, and other cities in 1932. With guns, clubs, and fists the farmers declared themselves "on strike" to prevent milk and produce from reaching an already depressed market. The effort was not successful, but it led to a nationwide movement which engendered similar action throughout the farm belt. More effective was the farmers' campaign against foreclosures. Sometimes repossession sales were stopped entirely. More often the technique was to turn the forced sale into a farce. For example, the farm of Charles Grady of Champaign County, Illinois, with a $2,750 mortgage on it, was put on the block and "sold" for $4.75. No one dared bid any higher. An indebtedness of $1,200 on another farm was paid off for $16.46, tractors "sold" for twenty-five cents, horses for a dime, wagons for fifteen cents. After the "sale" the property was leased free to its former owner for ninety-nine years.

America was ablaze with social protest of many kinds in the first few years of the 1930s, but little of it involved either workers still on the job or the AFL. Most workers were understandably shy about taking militant action against the innumerable wage cuts of the period. But they probably would have received no help from the AFL even if they had decided to speak out. The philosophy of the Federation stressed "co-operation" with the industrial goliaths more than conflict, just as it had in the early part of the century when Gompers and Mitchell were part of Mark Hanna's Civic Federation. There was little about the AFL or William Green, who succeeded Gompers, that any segment of the working class, employed or unemployed, could find attractive. Its first reaction to relief for the jobless was that "labor wants jobs, not a dole." It considered unemployment insurance "a hindrance to progress," just as the extreme right did. It was still unwilling to modify its craft unionism and form industrial unions, the only feasible structure for mass production industry workers.

This insistence on craft unionism was inexplicable in terms of naked reality. During the 1920s, according to Professor Ernest J. Eberling, productivity went up by 7 per cent a year. Technological advancements were astounding. One man and a helper could do as much with a ditch-digging machine as forty-four men had done previously with pick and shovel. The Ford Motor Company announced in 1926 that it had 7,782 separate jobs. Forty-three per cent of them required only one day's training, and another 36 per cent less than a week. Even some employers were quicker than the AFL leadership to recognize that craft organization was outmoded. Gerald Swope, president of General Electric, discussed with William Green the confusion that would take place in his plants if fifteen craft unions tried to organize them. Couldn't the AFL, he asked, assign the men to a single, industrial union? Green consulted with his executive council and came back with the expected negative answer.

That this position was maintained was all the more remarkable because of the approximately thirty-six million workers who were candidates for union membership, less than 10 per cent belonged. Even the craft unions were painfully weak compared to their potential. Out of 559,259 painters in the United States in 1933, only 59,300 carried a union card. Little more than one fifth of the 991,461 carpenters were in Bill Hutcheson's Brotherhood of Carpenters and Joiners. Of the eight million retail clerks and salesmen a mere 7,200 belonged to the union of their craft, the Retail Clerks International Protective Association. Among a half-million steelworkers a mere 8,600 were organized.

If the AFL hierarchy could not stir itself to change policies of organization, however, there were thousands of young radicals ready and willing to do so. As the wheels of industry began to get rolling again under New Deal ministrations, laborers in turn regained a measure of self-confidence, and began to organize on their own—or under the leadership of Communists, Socialists, Trotskyites and Lovestoneites. This time their efforts would not be in vain.

13

Impending Victory

Alfred Renton Bridges (christened "Harry" by American co-workers) defiantly proclaimed during the 1934 waterfront strike that "I neither affirm nor deny that I am a Communist." The statement was characteristic of the Australian-born longshoreman who more than any single individual gave West Coast unionism its vital impetus during the 1930s. He did not disavow his leftist views or his close association with the Communists, but he refused to feed the red-scare and insisted he was responsible only to rank-and-file dockworkers.

Lank and slim, with a prominent hooked nose, a long, narrow head that seemed to fit his spare body, thin lips, and perceptive eyes, Harry Bridges identified so closely with the rank and file that not even the anti-red crusade of the Joe McCarthy days could have driven him from leadership of his union. Not a great theorist, he nonetheless had an inordinate capacity to break down and express complicated ideas in their most essential terms. He could also enjoy a drink with the boys in the saloon of San Francisco's famous Embarcadero and spoke in a cockney accent that carried a certain fascination and earned him the nickname "Limo." He was quick, witty, and above all, bold.

Why Bridges became a radical is hard to say. He certainly was not denied financial opportunity; had he remained in Melbourne he would have become a prosperous real estate dealer like his father, and perhaps just as conservative. First son to an Irish woman of pious Catholic background and an Australian real estate agent father,

Harry Bridges, born in July 1900, spent the first sixteen years of his life rather uneventfully, particularly in comparison to the stormy youth of other labor leaders. He had an adequate education, between the ages of five and sixteen at St. Brennan's parochial school, and he was a good student. His father, who proudly wanted his son to join him in the real estate business, sent him to the tenements to collect rents, but Harry hated the chore. After St. Brennan's he went to work as a clerk in a stationery store, but found that just as dismal. He had the urge for adventure in distant places, and despite his father's misgivings signed on for a ketch that sailed between Australia and Tasmania. Twice he was shipwrecked, once washed overboard, hanging onto a mandolin until rescued.

Small incidents and a spirit of rebelliousness characteristic of so many seagoing people, propelled Bridges toward the United States and participation in its labor struggles. On a trip across the Pacific in 1920, he and some of his friends got into an argument with the captain about working Easter Monday, a normal holiday for Australian workers. Angered by the event, Bridges signed out when the *Ysabel* docked at San Francisco, paid an $8 tax to enter the United States and took employment with an American vessel traveling the Coast and Gulf ports. A year or so later, when his ship tied up in New Orleans where a maritime strike was in progress, Bridges, in his usual spirit of adventure, joined the picket line, was arrested, and was held overnight. After the strike he went to work as a quartermaster on a government ship pursuing rum-runners, but by October 1922 he had satisfied his wanderlust. He went to work as a longshoreman in San Francisco.

Shoreside workers in 1922 were still reeling from the defeat of their strike in 1919, when the seamen had gone blithely through their picket lines to man the ships, and teamsters had continued deliveries to the docks. The local of the International Longshoremen's Association in the San Francisco bay area was in ruins, and in its place was a company-controlled organization popularly known as the Blue Book Union, after the color of its membership card, with whom all of the employers were happy to sign a closed shop agreement. One of Bridges' first experiences with Blue Book was being fired for taking up a grievance with the Luckenbach company about short pay. And the company union, of course, having no intention of putting up too vigorous a front against the employers, did not support him.

The biggest complaint of the longshoremen then and for years to come was the pernicious hiring system called the "shape-up," portrayed so vividly in the film *On the Waterfront*. They would form a line at the docks each morning hoping that a benign foreman would pick them for his gang. Since supply was invariably greater than demand, some waited hours before being chosen, others waited totally in vain. No one was assured steady employment unless he was exceptionally competent, had an "in" of some kind with a foreman, or paid a regular bribe. It was a system that lent itself to favoritism and corruption, and caused a variance in earnings from $40 a week for the lucky ones chosen to work fairly steadily down to $10 to $12 for the vast majority.

Bridges fared better than most, not because he bribed his supervisors, but because he was a capable winch driver, part of a "star gang" much in demand. It was not his own economic condition, then, that spurred him to organize the stevedores, but rather an over-all idealism visible in hundreds of young men of this period—the Reuther brothers, Farrell Dobbs, Harold Gibbons, Emil Mazey and James Cross, to name a few. Only in his twenties, a stable and a serious man, with a family to support after his marriage in 1925, Bridges never tired of preaching the sermon so commonly heard in communist and socialist organizations. On the shape-up line, in the saloons, wherever he had the opportunity, he talked endlessly of the need for united action with the seamen and teamsters, and of union democracy and rank-and-file control of union leaders. Unionism for men like Bridges was a waystation toward over-all social and economic liberation, and he promoted it with a passion that the old-line, business-oriented unionists could not muster. In 1924 and again in 1926 he tried to revive the International Longshoremen's Union in San Francisco, but the small groups he was able to assemble quickly broke up. Workers' fear of reprisal and blacklisting still hovered over the waterfront long after the disastrous strike of 1919.

At the low point of the Depression Bridges tried again. With kindred spirits he had accumulated in a decade on the docks, he published a mimeographed paper, *The Waterfront Worker,* with a circulation of about a thousand. Its four pages, though sometimes ink-smeared and illegible, bristled with the stevedores' grievances and won converts to a rank-and-file "Committee of 500" that Bridges formed in the spring of 1933. Someone else beat the irrepressible Australian in applying for a charter in the AFL's International Longshoremen's Association, but he convinced his followers to join it, and soon was its leading figure. Interestingly, the communists who were committed at the time to dual-unionism opposed joining the AFL and lamely urged their friends to support the Marine Workers Industrial Union, one of the affiliates of the communist-led Trade Union Unity League. But Bridges had no taste for such experiments, and the communists in due course joined his group, rather than the

other way around. In a whirlwind drive during July and August
1933, the ILA local in San Francisco lured away the vast majority
of the Blue Book union and immensely swelled its own ranks.

II

Apart from the influence of Bridges and his talents, the ground
was fertile in 1933 across the whole nation for a big union spurt.
"The country is full of spontaneous strikes," wrote commentator
Benjamin Stolberg. "Wherever one goes one sees picket lines." As it
became evident that the Depression had hit rock bottom, working
men and women regained their confidence and initiative. Almost
1,200,000 took strike action, six times as many as in 1930. A radical
mood replaced the synthetic joy of the 1920s and the despair of the
very early 1930s. The Communist Party grew from 8,000 to 24,000
members, and greatly influenced the hundreds of thousands of
people in such satellite organizations as the League Against War
and Fascism, Friends of the Soviet Union, Workers Ex-Servicemen's
League and the United Council of Working Class Women. The
Socialist Party, all but defunct in the 1920s, recovered so well by
1932 that its presidential standard-bearer, Norman Thomas, polled
884,781 votes. Groups such as the Trotskyites and A. J. Muste's
American Workers Party numbered only a few thousand, but they
exercised an influence well beyond what one might expect from
their numerical strength. One or two leftists among a thousand
workers was enough to give the group direction and stimulus, and
there were plenty of young leftists around. A new generation, active
at first in the battles of the unemployed, and then in the plants,
talked openly of revolution as if it were the first order of business
on the historical agenda, and studied left-wing uprisings and defeats
in Austria and Germany as if they were germane to their own
circumstances. "Fear of a revolution," wrote David A. Shannon, an
historian of the Great Depression, "was very widespread during the
last several months of President Hoover's administration, and much
of the politics of the period can be understood fully only by viewing
political events against the background of anxiety about violent revolt."

If America was not close to revolution in 1932 it was only because
it still had considerable resources to ease the plight of the hungry
and destitute. But the situation was not one to be regarded lightly,
and the New Deal, when President Roosevelt took office in March
1933 could not risk the kind of frontal assault against labor, which
included the poor, that other administrations had conducted in the
past. This kid-glove treatment was to be a major factor in the success

of the organizing drives and labor wars of the 1930s, for the sentiments of the times required a government that would still the
economic and political storms with reforms and reconciliation, not
repression. If Roosevelt had tried to smash embryonic unions with
naked strikebreaking, the New Deal would have collapsed. He needed
the moderate labor leaders as a counterweight to the reactionaries
who nagged him from the other end of the political spectrum, and
he could not have held them with an outright anti-union stance.
Some historians have concluded that it was Roosevelt who gave
unions their impetus in the 1930s, but the actual facts do not reflect
this conclusion. Though there was an interplay of cause and effect,
it was the irresistible pressures of millions of people, flailing out of
frustration, that drove the New Deal to the appeasement of unionism.

One of the measures adopted as a sop to labor was the inclusion in
the National Industrial Recovery Act of June 1933 of a provision,
popularly referred to as Section 7(a). Since the bill contained a
number of sections which were a bitter pill for labor to swallow—such
as a provision giving employers authority in each industry to raise
prices in concert—it had to be in part, at least, sugar-coated. Section
7(a) granted workers "the right to organize and bargain collectively
. . . free from the interference, restraint, or coercion of employers,"
and made it illegal for an employer to require his employees to
join a company union "as a condition of employment."

The NIRA was no Magna Charta, as some contended. It did not,
for example, dissolve company unions, nor grant legitimate ones
sole collective bargaining rights, but it was interpreted by many
workers to mean that the government was behind them. Using the
momentum unleashed by 7(a), John L. Lewis gambled the United
Mine Workers' $75,000 treasury on a blitzkrieg organization drive,
and within a few months enrolled hundreds of thousands of coal
diggers who had drifted away from the union before and during the
depths of the Depression. The needle trades unions also swelled
their membership rolls under the spur of Section 7(a). Altogether
about a million new workers entered the ranks of organized labor.

On the other hand, Section 7(a) was totally ineffective in auto,
steel, and basic industries generally where employers simply refused
to abide by its provisions. According to Philip Taft "the evidence
shows in the months after the enactment of the NIRA, at least as
many company unions were organized as those not controlled by
the employers." General Hugh Johnson, placed in charge of administering the Act, ruled that corporations could hire and fire workers
"on merit," an ambiguous clause which the automobile moguls used
as justification for the discharge or laying off of literally thousands

of unionists. Whenever business slowed down they fired the union
members, pinpointed by company spies, alleging that they were not
as hard-working as company union and non-union workers. The National Labor Board, set up to cope with the problems of worker
representation and illegal discharge, was disregarded by the larger
employers, as was its successor in 1934, the National Labor Relations
Board.

Nonetheless, if Section 7(a) was only a secondary spur to the
surge of unionism in the 1930s, it did help Harry Bridges re-establish
the International Longshoremen's Association on the San Francisco
docks. A Labor Board order reinstating four workers discharged in
September 1933 for joining the ILA gave additional momentum to
the organizing drive. Despite the Blue Book, discontent among the
dockworkers could no longer be contained. If the hourly wage of
eighty-five cents was high by comparison with rates elsewhere, still
the shape-up system and the surplus of laborers made it impossible
for all but a few longshoremen to take home a full pay check. "At
the present time," noted Boris Stern of the U. S. Bureau of Labor
Statistics in November 1933, "a very conservative estimate would
probably place more than 50 percent of all the longshoremen on the
relief rolls." If a quarter of the men earned as much as $40 a week,
the remaining three quarters took home $10 or $12 for a job that
was as backbreaking as it was unsafe. Both Section 7(a) and Harry
Bridges gave these dispirited men hope. Section 7(a), however, did
not win for the stevedores the right to "bargain collectively," despite
its explicit guarantees to that effect. That right, like so many others
in hundreds of subsequent instances, had to be won on the picket
line.

III

The radical unionists of the 1930s brought to their work a number
of *a priori* political concepts. They opposed in principle any collaboration with capital, such as that Samuel Gompers, for instance, had
practiced with the National Civic Federation, or that William Green
had in his attempt to win support from General Motors for unionizing
the auto industry. The employer and the state were, to the radicals,
implacable enemies to be fought to the death. Moreover, the new
radicals felt that the "labor fakers" who had headed the old unions
were concubines of that enemy and that unless challenged would
undermine any legitimate labor struggle. The ultimate defense, then,
against employers and labor fakers was to vest control of the affairs
of unions in their rank-and-file membership. The rank and file

surely could be trusted to safeguard its own needs, to pick its own leadership.

As a first step in moving the ILA in this direction, Bridges promoted a convention of delegates from all the docks on the West Coast in February 1934. But he was leaning, he knew, on a weak source. ILA locals in Seattle, Portland, Tacoma, and other ports had had a tenuous existence since the 1919 strike; they were limbs without a head and would be as long as San Francisco was shackled to company unionism. They had little internal dynamism. Most of their paid officials and their district president, William J. Lewis, were men of conservative political convictions and accustomed to entering into binding agreements for the workers they represented without consulting them. With Bridges' permission, these men were allowed in the meeting hall but excluded from the deliberations of the ten-day convention. The delegates, workers not yet sure of themselves, chose the old officialdom for an executive committee to co-ordinate the West Coast organizing campaign, but neutralized their influence by resolving that no agreement could be deemed valid unless and until approved by a rank-and-file vote. They also put forth five objectives, more militant than anything the ILA had ever proposed: companies' full recognition of the union, union-controlled hiring halls to replace the shape-up, a raise in pay from eighty-five cents an hour to one dollar, a thirty-hour week, and a coast-wide agreement covering all U.S. ports and expiring on the same date. Three other significant resolutions were carried. One called for a waterfront federation going beyond the longshoremen to include all marine workers, as well as teamsters; another for rank-and-file gang committees to handle grievances, rather than business agents; and a third, opposing arbitration, on the grounds that it invariably led to defeat.

The employers, seized by a fit of sudden patriotism, refused to deal with the convention—though it represented 12,000 longshoremen —on the grounds that it was communist-dominated. Sixteen of the twenty delegates from San Francisco, they said, were members of the Communist Party. And when on March 5 the shipowners did meet with representatives of ILA, their only response was a flat rejection of the union's proposals. They were banking on William Lewis, national ILA president Joseph C. Ryan and the federal government to save them from the militants at the Embarcadero.

What followed was a triangular drama. The San Francisco stevedores set a strike date for March 23 and elected a committee of twenty-five to direct it—again testifying to their distrust of the ILA leadership. Their fears were not unwarranted. A day before the scheduled walkout, a telegram arrived from President Roosevelt asking that the action be postponed pending an investigation by a fact-finding committee. The delay, charged a communist longshore leader, Sam Darcy, was requested so that "a plentiful supply of student scabs might be obtained" by employers when the college semester ended. Nevertheless William Lewis immediately agreed to Roosevelt's suggestion, and for the time being matters were out of Bridges' hands. Lewis entered into private negotiations of his own with the employers, and after six weeks produced a secret agreement that would have undercut the radicals: it provided for registering the stevedores in such a way that the younger and more militant men would be eliminated from the docks.

Once again the San Francisco local decided to short-circuit Lewis: it unanimously voted a new strike date, May 9. And once again the government and the top ILA brass tried to head off the stoppage. Both the U. S. Department of Labor and Joe Ryan sent wires to the ILA locals urging that the strike be postponed. Ryan's telegram temporarily won converts in Seattle, where 60 per cent of the ILA members voted against walking out. Nonetheless this time the stoppage began on schedule, and by May 11, Seattle and other hesitant locals had reversed their decisions and joined the strike. Except for the port of Los Angeles, a notorious open-shop town, the walkout was complete, the docks empty.

"It is a different strike from any the Coast has ever known," reported Evelyn Seeley in *The Nation*. With Lewis and Ryan discredited by the rank-and-file, the framing of future strategy fell to Bridges, and he introduced three creative tactics to the conduct of affairs. The first was determined picketing in San Francisco. One thousand men stood watch at the Embarcadero in twelve-hour shifts, day and night, weekends and holidays, to guard against strikebreakers. Reporter Seeley saw one man with binoculars scanning the great arc from both sides of the Ferry Building, ready to alert fellow pickets should anyone try to sneak through. Patrol cars, manned by unionists, zigzagged in and around nearby streets seeking out would-be scabs. No sensible person would have tried to cross that picket line without a few squads of police to shepherd him through, and even then he might not have made it. The pickets did not have to resort to violence often, for their mere presence was a discouragement to those who had designs on their jobs. But they were a tough bunch and if the occasion demanded it, they did not hesitate to bloody a scab's nose. In Portland one day, twenty-five strikebreakers were tossed into the Willamette River. In San Pedro, pickets stormed a stockade housing strikebreakers leaving one of their own men dead.

In Seattle they caused too much trouble for both the police and the mayor, who fell back on the usual call for troops.

Management of course did lure a few hundred strikebreakers to the docks with promises of $15 to $25 daily pay, which was two to three times what the strikers were asking. They were holed up on ships in the harbors—derisively called "ship-hotels"—and protected by Pinkertons and police. A prime source of scab labor, as predicted by Darcy, was the university campus. Coach Bill Ingram of the University of California recruited scabs zealously from his football squad, as well as among other athletes—for which his school gained the doubtful accolade of "scab incubator." Ella Winter reported in the *New Republic,* early in June, that there were forty to eighty University of California students scabbing, and other busloads scheduled to arrive. Herbert Fleishacker, Jr., son of a leading California banker who controlled the Dollar Lines, toured Stanford University's fraternity houses seeking strikebreakers. At the University of Washington, according to a committee of students that investigated the matter, students were asked to "cut their classes and participate in a labor difficulty of which they had absolutely no knowledge." Nonetheless the number of university scabs over all was small, not enough to threaten the strike's stability.

Many college "finks" quit after a few days, and on the other side, literally thousands of students came to the aid of the waterfront strikers. The National Student Union publicly protested university scabbing. At San Mateo College a large meeting was held to denounce the practice, and in many nearby schools professors and young people sent clothes and food to the strikers. It is worth noting that in the port of San Francisco only five of the regular complement of longshoremen went back to work. Their mood of bitterness sustained the strikers. They knew that the shipowners received annual subsidies of $70 million a year from the federal government. Yet they had refused to follow public policy on collective bargaining. A high level of worker morale was maintained through daily mass meetings, and soup kitchens which fed 1,600 people daily in San Francisco alone.

The second novel aspect of Bridges' strategy was the expansion of hostilities so as to include marine workers and teamsters. "A strike movement," noted Sam Darcy, "cannot stand still. It must either spread and grow in militancy, or recede." As each ship came into port, its crew was met by longshoremen as well as representatives of the Marine Workers Industrial Union, and urged to declare a sympathy walkout. And since the seamen too had grievances similar to those of the stevedores it was not difficult to enlist them. Aboard ship, as on the docks, there were complaints about low wages, poor food, long hours, favoritism, required membership in company unions, and refusal of employers to enter into a coast-wide agreement with the marine craft unions. On May 12 a sizable conference of ship delegates voted to join with the longshoremen, and though the leaders of the International Seamen's Union were lukewarm to the idea, they were overwhelmed by the sentiments of the rank-and-file. Everyone was conscious of the post World War I fiasco when seamen had walked through longshore picket lines in 1919 and longshoremen had walked through maritime picket lines two years later. Now the cry for unity met eager response. As a result, the sympathy strikes of nine West Coast maritime unions, including seamen, engineers, cooks and stewards, mates, pilots, and others were converted into independent strikes with their own specific objectives. Paul Scharrenberg, of the Sailors Union of the Pacific, wired William Green advising him that the price of restraining his men would have been his own removal as leader of the union. By May 27, according to a New York *Times* estimate, there were 25,000 marine strikers from Vancouver to San Diego—not a large number as strikes go, but clearly, strategically placed.

Bridges' legions were able similarly to win the support of truck drivers who hauled cargo from the piers to warehouses and railroads, and vice versa. Michael Casey, president for forty years of the teamsters in San Francisco, at first refused to help the longshoremen. But rank-and-file truck drivers, approached by pickets on the docks overwhelmed his opposition. Paul Eliel, a staff member of the Industrial Association assigned to break the strike, conceded that "the action of the Teamsters' Union in May and the definite boycotting and final refusal by that organization in June to handle waterfront freight were critical factors in the entire San Francisco strike situation." Teamster unions in other cities followed the lead of San Francisco. Thus the entire western waterfront was immobilized. Whatever cargo the strikebreakers might load or unload was destined to stay on the piers or in the ships' holds, with no means of transportation anywhere else.

The third distinctive feature of Bridges' strategy was the formation of a Joint Strike Committee of fifty members, five each from the ten unions on strike, with Bridges himself as chairman. The committee was pledged not to end the stoppage or return to work until *all* the unions involved had won individual agreements they each considered satisfactory. There would no longer be a dividing of shoreside workers from marine workers, or of one port's from another's. A rank-and-file impulse, activated by a desire for solidarity, thus forged the most formidable labor alliance in West Coast history.

IV

From May 8 to the end of the month the shipowners played a cautious, waiting game. They deluded themselves that the workers' unity would dissolve, and that Assistant Secretary of Labor Edward F. McGrady and ILA president Ryan would help their cause. But McGrady, a government "troubleshooter" who boasted he had "been able to crack other strikes," found this one incredibly resistant. He brought the employers and union officials together on May 19 but was unable to effect an agreement on the issue regarding the hiring hall. Then he had Mayor Angelo Rossi of San Francisco invite "King" Ryan to town to convince the men of the need for moderation. The strutting ILA autocrat breezed into the bay area toward the end of the month with a plan that called for recognition of the union but virtually nothing else. There was to be no closed shop, as demanded by the strikers, and the hiring halls, instead of falling under union control would be jointly administered. Everything else, Ryan had decided to relegate to arbitration. Though he traveled up and down the coast to sell this "peace proposal," it was universally repudiated. The stevedores were in no mood to accept a plan so patently a compromise with their five objectives, and one which in addition would leave their allies, the maritime workers without improvement of their lot. Nonetheless, encouraged by McGrady and Rossi, the ILA president on June 16 signed a "binding" agreement with the Waterfront Employers' Union with only slight modifications of his original "peace" plan.

Employers and the conservative press were jubilant over the coup; the strike, they asserted, was over. The strikers thought differently. The next day mass meetings were held in all ports; the dockworkers unanimously rejected the "sellout." In San Francisco Ryan was hooted off the speakers' platform, never again to play a role in West Coast union affairs, except to make a few headlines by calling the strike a communist plot. The only result of the McGrady-Ryan gambit was that the conduct of negotiations, which for some reason had been left in the hands of ILA officials, was now transferred to Bridges' Joint Strike Committee which was managing all other facets of the strike. The employers at this stage would have been happy to accept the McGrady proposal for arbitration by a National Longshoremen's Board, specially appointed by President Roosevelt, but the Joint Strike Committee would not yield either on the hiring hall issue or the one which called for a coastwide pact. Other issues might be compromised, it said, but not those.

In this stalemate the shipowners decided on sterner measures. The stoppage was now seven weeks old; $40 million in wares lay stacked on the piers and ships at San Francisco Harbor alone, and many local industries were beginning to feel the economic squeeze. Earlier in the month, at the suggestion of the San Francisco Chamber of Commerce, they had applied to the Industrial Association for guidance. The association, formed in 1921 under the similar circumstances of a work stoppage, possessed the staff and knowledge to do exactly what the situation required. It raised a large sum of money, formed a special trucking company, Atlas Trucking, leased a warehouse, and hired strikebreakers and armed guards. The mayor, the governor, and the chief of police, all pledged full support for the company in the confrontation they knew would be coming.

At 1:27 P.M. on July 3, with thousands of pickets massed for the critical moment, the steel doors at Pier 38 opened to permit five loaded trucks, protected by eight radio-equipped police cars to move out. To make an impregnable lane for the vehicles to pass through, Industrial Association agents placed a barricade of freight cars belonging to the Belt Line Railway on both sides of Pier 38. With a revolver in his hand, Police Captain Thomas M. Hoertkorn on the lead car proclaimed "the port is open," while the pickets, with a deafening roar descended upon the enemy. As Mike Quin describes it in *The Big Strike*, "the Embarcadero became a vast tangle of fighting men. Bricks flew and clubs battered skulls. The police opened fire with revolvers and riot guns. Clouds of tear gas swept the picket lines. Mounted police were dragged from their saddles and beaten to the pavement. The cobblestones of the Embarcadero were littered with fallen men, bright puddles of blood colored the gray expanse." For four hours the battle flared, while two planes circled overhead and tens of thousands of San Franciscans watched from nearby hills. One picket was killed, a couple of dozen badly hurt.

July 3 was only a warmup for the fifth. By mutual agreement a truce prevailed on the following day, Independence Day; but everyone knew that the battle would resume. The Industrial Association had fourteen freight cars of the state-owned Belt Line prepared to load cargo of the Matson Navigation Company. Governor Frank Merriam had put the National Guard on alert. Among the stevedores massed that morning on the Embarcadero were considerable numbers of youths and workers from other industries, while thousands of people lined the hillsides waiting for the action. At 8 A.M., without any warning, it began. The entire police force of the city was at the docks, charging the pickets, hurling vomiting gas, shooting off revolvers and riot guns. Nauseated men fell back, nonetheless tossing bricks, spikes, and stones as they fled, and picking up hundreds of their fellow workers who were wounded. After an hour and a half the charge had gained its objective. The picket line was dispersed.

The war was not over, however. Convinced that "if they win this, there'll never be another union in Frisco!" the crowd reformed in the afternoon, augmented meanwhile by large numbers of workers belonging to other unions. From Rincon Hill above the waterfront and the railway, laborers once more hurled rudimentary missiles at the enemy below as they were greeted with tear gas and bullets. "Don't think of this as a riot," read a report in the San Francisco *Chronicle*. "It was a hundred riots big and little. Don't think of it as one battle, but a dozen battles." The cargo did move, and two strikers were killed, Howard Sperry, a longshoreman, and Nick Bordoise, a member of the Cooks' Union and of the Communist Party. Hundreds of pickets, police, and onlookers were injured, at least 115 of them requiring hospitalization. Two strikers died of their wounds subsequently. At the corner of Steuart and Mission Streets, where the killings had occurred, pickets placed a mound of flowers and inscribed in chalk: "Two men killed here, murdered by police." At nightfall that Bloody Thursday—as the event became memorialized in union history—Governor Merriam sent 1,700 National Guardsmen to the waterfront, the first troops dispatched there in thirty-five years. Machine guns were set up, barbed wire strung along the streets, and armored cars made ready to police the area. Surveying the situation, Harry Bridges said simply: "We cannot stand up against police, machine guns, and National Guard bayonets." The strike would have to be expanded or die.

For the next seventy-two hours the city's focus was on the two martyrs of Bloody Thursday. Laid out in coffins at the ILA Hall, a block from the waterfront, the bodies were viewed by thousands who walked silently past them in double file. Just before the funeral procession, on the fourth day, bareheaded sympathizers for five blocks around the ILA office listened to a pledge over union amplifiers: "You have been killed because of your activity in the labor movement. Your death will guide us to our final victory." The procession, at first forbidden by the chief of police, was quiet and impressive as 25,000 San Francisco proletarians walked slowly up Market Street.

The first reaction of the employers to Bloody Thursday had been exhilaration; the strike had been smashed. The management victory, however, was questionable. Merchandise might be delivered from the waterfront to a warehouse, but from there truck drivers refused to haul it inland. So it sat. And from San Diego to Seattle there were still 250 idle ships, sailing nowhere. Bloody Thursday might have been the beginning of the end of the strike if the Industrial Association had been able to build on its partial victory over the teamsters. Instead the initiative fell to the unionists once more.

San Francisco was buzzing. Workers in hundreds of factories and various jobs heatedly discussed how to respond to the police attack. Local 1158 painters and Local 68 of the machinists had suggested a general city-wide strike in support of the waterfront workers, even before Bloody Thursday. After July 5 it became an irrepressible cry, so much so that even the moderate leaders of the Central Labor Council agreed. The communists were heavily involved in the waterfront leadership, but even the "red" issue no longer dissuaded unionists from their cause. President Edward Vandeleur and secretary James A. O'Connell of the Labor Council were so fearful that matters might go beyond them, they agreed to the general strike and accepted its leadership. AFL president William Green warned that they had no such authority, but they insisted that unless they went along, the action would become "totally uncontrolled."

In reality, the general strike was already evolving on its own. On July 11, 4,000 teamsters halted deliveries in San Francisco and Oakland, throwing both cities into semi-paralysis. In the next two days thirteen other unions—butchers, machinists, welders, laundry workers, etc.—joined the walkout, putting the total of workers participating at 32,000. On the 14th, representatives of 115 unions voted by a conclusive 315 to 15 tally to make the general strike official. A few hours later Market Street railwaymen, with grievances of their own, joined the movement. Finally, on Monday, July 16, San Francisco was virtually at a standstill, and other East Bay towns, such as Oakland, Alameda, Berkeley were in about the same condition within the next twenty-four hours. This was only the third time in U.S. history that a metropolitan area had been gripped by a general strike—St. Louis in 1877 and Seattle in 1919 were the focal points on the other two occasions.

The San Francisco stoppage was never total—the ferryboat workers, for instance, did not participate, thus keeping open one of the six main inlets to the city. Yet the fact that all other forms of transport were halted, including private automobiles which were cut off from gasoline sources, slowed the city to a snail's pace. Pickets were placed at the main highways leading into the city and at other strategic points of entry, such as railroad terminals, effectively isolating the area from the outside world. And with deliveries choked off, one retail store after another was forced to close its doors. If the city seethed emotion, its commerce and other normal activity were thoroughly inhibited. Labor had seemingly won a total victory.

The general strike, unlike the waterfront strike, however, was afflicted by timidity within and naked assault from without. The hawk-faced Harry Bridges argued for continued tight restriction of all but the most essential activity. Some gasoline had to be made available to doctors; the powerhouses had to be kept open to supply electricity; nineteen restaurants were permitted to operate the first day; milk, bread, and food trucks were allowed to run. But the conservatively led General Strike Committee loosened the knot labor had tied tightly almost every hour. Carmen were returned to work on the first day because the committee felt their civil service status might be jeopardized. The newspapers had never suspended, typographical workers and reporters continued to work on sheets that spewed forth the vilest red-baiting propaganda. Labor leaders, despite Bridges' opposition, not only issued permits for an increasing number of business activities, including the opening of thirty-two additional restaurants, but went so far as to permit striking sheet-metal workers to return to their jobs in order to repair police cars. By the fourth day the strike was all but emasculated. Sam Darcy was far from grossly inaccurate when he said that Vandeleur's Committee had been "appointed to kill the strike, and not to organize it."

During the four historic days that the general strike lasted, all segments of the establishment joined forces against the "insurrection." The publishers of three newspapers in San Francisco and two in Oakland formed a council to do their part in crushing the strike. None of them bothered to discuss the basic issues at hand, the longshoremen's grievances. Instead, in military unison, they pictured the over-all stoppage as a "revolution against constituted authority." It was not a labor dispute, they said, but an insidious plot by 1,200 communists who had forced tens of thousands of "reluctant" workers to quit their jobs, thereby endangering the lives of more than a million innocent citizens in the community. William Randolph Hearst cabled an editorial from London to his San Francisco *Examiner*, warning that "if the small group of Communists, starting with their control of the longshore and maritime unions, extend their power over the community of the bay area—and thence into the whole, or even part of the State—California would be no more fit to live in than Russia." The purpose of this red-baiting was to drive a wedge between the conservative labor leaders and the radicals; it was called the "split strategy." Bridges was invariably referred to as an "alien," and his associates "communists" or "subversives." On the other hand, conservative union leaders like Vandeleur were complimented, and John F. Neyland, chief of the newspaper council, entered into direct negotiations with conservatives to try to break them away from Bridges.

The split strategy was given an impressive assist by a high federal official, General Hugh Johnson, head of the National Recovery Administration. Speaking to a University of California audience on the second day of the strike, he gave left-handed sanction to the red scare. While defending the principle of collective bargaining and criticizing the shipping industry for failing to "freely accord these rights," he attributed the strife in the bay area to the "subversive element" and urged the labor movement to "run these subversive influences out from its ranks like rats . . ." What was happening was no strike, he said, but a "bloody insurrection" by "one-half of one percent of our population to try to strangle the rest of us into submission . . ."

The red scare, as always, camouflaged official and semi-official violence on the part of the establishment. On July 16 Mayor Rossi declared San Francisco in a state of emergency, blaming the city's woes on "communists," and promptly proceeded to organize forces of repression for a showdown. A "Constitutional Committee of Five Hundred," made up of businessmen and professionals, was formed to devise means for resuming transportation. Five hundred police were added to the force (increasing it to 1,800), and approximately 3,000 more National Guardsmen were brought in. The Crime Prevention Bureau of the police department had its name changed to the "Anti-Radical and Crime Prevention Bureau," indicating its new focus. With the government's assent, vigilante groups sprang to life, such as the Citizens' Committees and the American Legion's Anti-Red Committee.

On the seventeenth the reign of terror began. "The first indication of the concerted drive against radicals," reported the New York Times, "came from Charles Wheeler, vice-president of the McCormick Steamship Line, who said in a talk at the Rotary Club here today [July 17] that the raids would start soon. He intimated government consent had been obtained . . ." The first target of course was the Communist Party headquarters where a band of vigilantes beat up the few people it could find there, and wrecked everything in sight. Next came a combined assault by police and hoodlums on the offices of the Marine Workers Industrial Union, in which sixty seamen were arrested for no other reason than that they were on the premises. All told, more than a dozen places were raided and demolished that day, including the offices of the *Western Worker,* a communist sheet which for a time had served as the official organ of the strike, the Workers Book Store, Workers School, Ex-Servicemen's headquarters on Valencia Street, the headquarters of the International Seamen and Harbor Workers' Industrial Union, as well as a private dwelling in San Francisco and two in Richmond, across the bay, presumably the homes of radicals. Communists charged that this was the work of vigilantes and "Legionnaires reinforced by Bergoff gunmen," but the local press pictured the outburst of violence as an expression by enraged strikers of their disaffection with radical leadership.

Evelyn Seeley, reporting in the *New Republic,* was present at the raid on the *Western Worker* office, which according to her followed the general pattern of illegality. First an automobile pulled up with a few occupants, tossed a few bricks into the building, and drove off. The damage was negligible. Four police cars soon followed, however, and the fifteen or twenty police on hand finished the job, destroying furniture, typewriters, books and other office equipment. One man was dragged out bleeding profusely, pleading with police as they beat him: "I didn't do nothin'." Presumably he was thrown into jail, along with some four hundred other "radicals" who were arrested in those chaotic days. The West Coast region was experiencing "one of the most harrowing records of brutality to be found outside of Hitler's Third Reich." Not a single vigilante was ever arrested for these crimes, nor for the kidnaping of fifteen or twenty people in San Jose, who were forcibly driven 300 miles south and abandoned.

Given this repression and red-baiting, the conservatives in the San Francisco Labor Council were able to re-establish their authority and control. On the seventeenth they carried a resolution by a vote of 207 to 180, calling on the striking unions to accept immediate arbitration by the National Longshoremen's Board—a course which Bridges had repeatedly rejected, especially insofar as the hiring hall issue was at stake. On the eighteenth, restrictions were lifted on all fuel oil, gasoline, and food deliveries, and restaurant openings. General Johnson held a meeting with the General Strike Committee at which he proposed that the stoppage be abandoned. William Green added some cowardice and further confusion to the situation by announcing that the "American Federation of Labor neither ordered the strike nor authorized it." On the nineteenth, at a stormy session in the Labor Temple, the conservative outvoted the more radical delegates by a razor-thin margin of 191 to 174, to call off the walkout. The biggest blow of all was the decision of the teamsters —1,139 to 283—to resume work after Michael Casey, their leader, explained that they could still refuse to haul "scab" cargo. In fact, however, the vote was interpreted as meaning a return to normal activity "without reservation."

The collapse of the general strike in San Francisco was a traumatic blow to organized labor's high gear campaign of the day, particularly since it had not been extended to other cities. Portland unions on the fifteenth had voted for a general strike, but had been talked out of it by the liberal New York senator, Robert F. Wagner, who was sent there by the National Labor Relations Board expressly for that purpose. Violence flared in Seattle, where a policeman and a picket had been killed on July 7 and where a heavy attack against 2,000 strikers on July 20 was directed by Mayor C. L. Smith himself. The maritime and waterfront strike had lost its forward momentum, and Bridges and the Joint Strike Committee were quick to realize it. On the twenty-first they agreed to arbitration, and were upheld by an ILA vote of 6,378 to 1,471. The seamen and other maritime crafts accepted arbitration a week later.

Though forced to retreat from their original thoroughly uncompromising position, the strikers had displayed so much solidarity and power and generated so much public sympathy that they could not be altogether defeated. This kind of moral victory was in fact to be the result in many of the disputes of the turbulent thirties, to be seen most pronouncedly in the automobile sitdown strikes that would come two and a half years later. With the National Longshoremen's Board acting as mediator, the employers agreed to fire all strikebreakers and rehire the strikers without discrimination. In the interim, while arbitration proceedings were under way, the longshore union was to have observers in the hiring halls to assure workers equal opportunity for employment.

The terms of the agreement handed down by the board, composed of McGrady, A. K. Cushing, and Archbishop Edward J. Hanna on October 12, 1934, provided for union recognition, a thirty-hour week (instead of forty-eight), a wage raise of a dime an hour to ninety-five cents, and joint operation with employers of central hiring halls in each of the seventeen West Coast ports. This last term constituted a setback, in theory at least, since it afforded work opportunities for non-union as well as union members. But since the union was to pick the dispatchers in each of the halls, it meant union control in practice and a situation closely akin to a closed shop.

The board's decision on the maritime crafts' demands, made on February 2, 1935 also raised wages and set up a central labor relations committee of three representatives from each side to resolve future disputes. Members of the seafaring unions were to be given

first choice in employment over non-union workers. These gains were
not as decisive as those won by the longshoremen, but the unions
had secured most of their demands, and in succeeding years would
consolidate their gains appreciably.

v

Few of the labor wars of 1934 ended as fruitfully from labor's
standpoint as the one on the West Coast. Though the rate of influx
of workers into unions was often remarkable—the United Textile
Workers of America, for instance, grew from 50,000 in 1933 to 300,000
by mid-1934—most organizations were unable to initiate collective
bargaining, one of the unionist movement's major goals. A flash of
hope, sparked by Section 7(a), swelled union membership rolls, but
the organized workers found before long that the National Recovery
Administration in fact guaranteed them very little. After a while they
were calling it the National Run Around.

Typical was the experience of the textile union, which conducted
the largest strike of the year. The NRA's textile code, the first adopted
under General Johnson, provided for a forty-hour week and minimum wages of $12 in the South, $13 in the North. The rates, however,
were for the most part ignored, as indicated by a U. S. Department
of Labor statistic which showed a national average wage of $10.86
a week for textile workers for June 1934. Adding to the economic
travail of the laborers in some 5,870 mills, was the "stretch-out" by
which the work load was gradually increased by a quarter, a third,
and sometimes as much as 100 per cent. When the operatives flocked
to the United Textile Workers for protection, they found the heralded
guarantees of 7(a) meaningless. Four thousand unionists were summarily fired by their employers. A stream of complaints to the Cotton
Textile Industrial Relations Board about violations of the wage-and-
hour provisions of the code went unheeded. Finally, when worker discontent became unbearable, five hundred rank-and-file delegates convened at New York's Town Hall on August 31, 1934, to vote a national
strike. Their demands called for the thirty-hour week at the established pay scales for forty-eight hours, $12 and $13, the end of the
stretch-out, recognition of the union, and reinstatement of the thousands of workers discharged for union activity.

The chairman of the general strike committee was a stocky, vigorous
man in his forties, Francis J. Gorman. Brought up in Yorkshire County,
England, where his father owned a pub in a mill town, he migrated to
Providence, Rhode Island, at the age of thirteen to find work in a mill
at $4 a week. In 1922 he was appointed union organizer and in 1928
vice-president of the UTW. As his first major task in the new post he

was sent to Marion, North Carolina, in 1929, to manage a strike in which six workers were killed. It was a shattering experience. "We buried them out in the open, under the sky," recalled Gorman. "I'll never forget that." He was a talented and tireless man, but, as events were to prove, myopic in a number of key respects.

The response to the strike call was most gratifying to Gorman and the president of UTW, Thomas F. McMahon. According to an Associated Press tally, 364,795 working men and women had walked out of the mills from New England to the Deep South as of September 6— 60,000 of them in Georgia, 110,000 in Massachusetts. Gorman developed a highly successful technique called the flying squadron, for closing the Southern mills. After shutting down a factory in one town, the members of the squadron would hop into their old jalopies to move to the next. For nearly three weeks inspired strikers in sixteen states challenged tens of thousands of National Guardsmen, police, private guards, sheriffs' deputies, and vigilantes. Governor Eugene Talmadge of Georgia declared martial law and opened a concentration camp for "disorderly" strikers. Thirteen strikers were slain, six in a confrontation between deputies and a flying squadron near Greenville, South Carolina.

Gorman, however, had been in the moderate AFL hierarchy too long to think of broadening the strike or involving other forces. Leftists who offered the union help were rebuffed and even castigated. No effort was made by the UTW to call city or state strikes, or to involve the garment-industry unions, beyond securing financial help from them. The strike was by no means crushed when, on September 22, at the urging of President Roosevelt, Gorman called it off. No effort had been made to poll the hundreds of thousands still on the picket lines. Indeed, according to labor writer Edward Levinson, there was no reason not to believe that the old-line Federation leaders had themselves proposed to the President that he give them a pretext for ending hostilities.

Unlike the union members involved in the West Coast strike, the UTW members gained nothing. FDR appointed the Textile Labor Relations Board, to enforce the labor provisions of the NRA code, and a second one to deal with the work load problem. But they proved in practice as sterile as the previous board. In fact, in the aftermath of what the AFL called a "sweeping" success, troops prevented workers in hundreds of plants in Georgia and the Carolinas from returning to their jobs. In some factories the "victorious" strikers had to sign yellow-dog contracts before being admitted back to their looms. Fifteen thousand of the more militant unionists never got their jobs back at all in what Gorman's opponents called a "dishonorable surrender," and Levinson "the peace of defeat." The stretch-out remained unchanged, wages continued at less than $10 a week, and the union's roster fell to 79,200 members by August 1935.

If the textile rout was the rule, however, there were two other situations, in addition to the West Coast strike of 1934, that were sensational and prophetic exceptions. In both instances the strike leadership was left-wing (Musteite in one, Trotskyist in the other), and in both they refused either to be shackled by abstract "law and order" or place any faith in "liberal" government. One of them, the Toledo Electric Auto-Lite strike was a milestone in the building of a powerful automobile union; and the other, the Minneapolis teamster strikes cleared the roadblocks for the teamster organization nationally to become the largest single union in the country.

VI

In 1934 Toledo, Ohio was an industrial center of 275,000 people, specializing in the manufacture of glass and auto parts. Four of its banks had closed their doors in June 1931—after some of the bigger firms had secretly spirited away their funds—wiping out the savings of thousands of citizens. At the peak of the Depression, one third of the people in town were dependent on relief of one kind or another, and large numbers of them had joined the Lucas County Unemployed League, run by the followers of A. J. Muste. Muste, a lanky, thin clergyman, born in Holland, was one of those unique figures, an independent radical. Having lost his church for opposing World War I, he helped form an independent textile union after the war and was a leader of another strike at Lawrence, Massachusetts. Then, resigning as general secretary of the Amalgamated Textile Workers of America in 1921 he became the educational director and leading figure of the Brookwood Labor College in Katonah, forty-one miles from New York City. Here were trained some of the young men and women who would later excel in the organizing drives of the 1930s.

Throughout the 1920s, A.J., as he was known to his friends, remained a vague socialist, unaffiliated with any of the leftist parties because of what he considered their inadequacies. In May 1929, assisted by Louis Budenz (later to become a communist and still later to return to the Catholic Church as a violent anti-communist) and James Burnham (who after a career in the Trotskyite movement moved into the camp of the right-wing *National Review*), Muste founded the Conference for Progressive Labor Action. The CPLA showed promise of unifying the many radicals who felt the Socialist Party too timid, and the Communist Party too closely controlled by Moscow.

The strikes called by AFL Federal Local 18384 against Auto-Lite and its two affiliated companies, Bingham Stamping and Logan Gear, were entirely independent of Muste or the Lucas County Unemployed League. The in-plant leader of the stoppage was a swarthy young man, George F. Addes, who would eventually become secretary-treasurer of the United Auto Workers. But without the league the job actions would have expired quickly and in glum disorder. The first one began on February 23 and was quickly terminated by AFL leaders. Under AFL rules, a "federal" local was directly attached to the AFL, rather than to a national union. In that status it enjoyed no autonomy and was subject to the full control of William Green, who in this as in many other instances simply called off the strike on his own motion. A month and a half later, after losing faith in another one of Roosevelt's alphabetic wonders, the Auto Labor Board, more than 4,000 Auto-Lite workers took to the streets again. Within a couple of weeks the company prevailed on a friendly judge to issue an injunction limiting the numbers of pickets to twenty-five. This was a familiar ploy to cool down a strike that had worked for management on hundreds of occasions, and since the union officers decided to respect the decree, the company was able to wheedle 1,800 strikebreakers into its shops within three weeks.

The strike thus was on the verge of slowing to a complete halt when a committee of union men visited the Unemployed League headquarters to secure its support. The league, like the federal local, had been enjoined from picketing, but its officers had less respect for the sanctity of the courts. Unity of the jobless with strikers was a cardinal principle, almost a religious dogma, with the revolutionaries of the American Workers Party. Sam Pollock and Ted Selander, two young Musteites, wrote Judge R. R. Stuart on May 5 advising him that "On Monday morning May 7, at the Auto-Lite plant, the Lucas County Unemployed League, in protest of the injunction issued by your court, will deliberately and specifically violate the injunction . . ." True to their word, they mobilized 1,000 unemployed before the Auto-Lite gates on the first day, 4,000 on the next, and 6,000 on the third. The two league leaders were arrested, tried on the charge of violating the injunction and released with a court warning not to do any further picketing. The judge evidently felt that if two of the leaders would agree to sin no more, the pickets would all go home. But the two revolutionaries confounded him by going directly from the courtroom to the picket line. For the next two weeks a tenuous stalemate prevailed; each day thousands massed in front of the plant—while county deputies, on the roof, trained tear-gas guns on them.

A small incident on the twenty-third shattered the uneasy calm. A strikebreaker inside the plant hurled a bolt that hit a woman picket and sent her to the hospital. By the time one hundred police arrived to escort more scabs into the shops, tempers on the line were beyond control. The pickets assembled piles of rocks, stones, and other missiles, as well as a wagonload of bricks. "Suddenly," according to the Associated Press version, "a barrage of tear gas bombs was hurled from upper factory windows. At the same time, company employees armed with iron bars and clubs dragged a fire hose into the street and played water on the crowd. The strike sympathizers replied with bricks, as they choked from gas fumes and fell back." But from behind billboards and from alleyways and roofs, the unemployed continued their barrage. Police, with clubs swinging, themselves choking by now from the tear gas, tried to clear a lane for the strikebreakers, but had to give up. The first round went to the strikers and Muste's Unemployed League. As the police retreated, pickets surged to attack. Reforming their lines they fashioned slingshots out of rubber inner tubes, and flung bricks through the factory's windows until the lights inside the plant were doused and the strikebreakers cowering in confusion. It was not until fifteen hours later that 900 National Guardsmen rescued the men inside. They looked, according to press reports, a "sorry sight."

For the next six days the combat continued, this time directed against the guardsmen. Pickets, particularly women pickets, taunted the soldiers with epithets and "suggestions that they 'go home to mama and their paper dolls.'" In between taunts they tried to convert the guardsmen—a technique the radicals had copied from the Russian and French revolutions. Women and bemedaled World War I veterans engaged them in conversation or explained from soapboxes the issues involved in the strike. The proselytizing had an effect and some of the guard deserted for home. But the confused troops were edgy, and on the twenty-fourth they fired directly into the crowd, killing two and wounding two dozen more. The pickets retaliated. As night fell they attacked small groups of guardsmen in the six-block zone where martial law prevailed and forced them to retreat into the plant.

By the thirty-first, with scores of guardsmen in the hospital and the rest sadly demoralized, the state government ordered the troops removed and the company agreed to close its plants to strikebreaking workers to avoid further bloodshed. In addition to the dead, two hundred strikers and non-strikers had been injured, and about the same number arrested. The next day a giant rally of 40,000 people heard denunciations of the authorities at the Lucas County Courthouse Square by a variety of speakers. That day, too, ninety-eight of the ninety-nine unions in the city voted to call a general strike—a month before the general strike in San Francisco. On June 4, the company surrendered. It signed a six-month contract granting a 5 per cent pay raise and accepted Local 18384 as the "exclusive" bargaining agent. "This was the first contract under the code," wrote Art Preis, a participant in the events, "that did not include 'proportional representation' for company unions. The path was opened for organization of the entire automobile industry. With the Auto-Lite victory under their belts, the Toledo auto workers were to organize nineteen plants before the year was out and, before another twelve months, were to lead the first successful strike in a GM plant, the real beginning of the conquest of General Motors."

VII

The three Minneapolis strikes of 1934 were of the same type as those on the West Coast and in Toledo. They displayed radical leadership's reliance on the rank and file, advance planning as meticulous as that of an army and a defiance of what is commonly called "law and order" when law and order was specifically directed at crushing their union.

In the fall of 1933, emboldened by Section 7(a), Karl Skoglund, a middle-aged Swede, began organizing the drivers of the sixty-seven coal companies in the city. Skoglund, a gentle, red-faced man an inch or two under six feet, had emigrated from the old country at the turn of the century. Before he learned to speak English he laid ties for the Northern Pacific railroad in the Minnesota hinterlands, and after 1914 went to work in lumber camps. Had it not been for an accident he might have continued as a lumberjack indefinitely. But a pine tree crushed one of his feet, and after an operation and a nine-month convalescence in the hospital, the husky immigrant took a job as a mechanic for the Pullman Company in Minneapolis. When the railroad shopmen went on strike in 1922, Skoglund, still single, contributed $1,000 of his savings to the union, and when the strike was lost, refused to go back to work because management insisted he join a company union. Subsequently he became a coal driver, and had been working for the same company for eight years when he began enrolling fellow workers into General Drivers Local Union of the AFL International Brotherhood of Teamsters.

A steady, slow-moving but thorough person, and an effective speaker whose sincerity came forth through a heavy accent, Skoglund had become associated with a small leftist group which had broken away from the Communist Party in late 1928 to follow the precepts of Leon Trotsky. The Minneapolis leaders of that group—variously called the Communist Party (Left Opposition), Communist League of America, then Workers Party—were three brothers, Vincent, Miles, and Grant Dunne, who also worked in the coal industry, though not as drivers. Together with Skoglund and two or three other organizers, they converted the national Teamsters' organization—then with a membership of only 95,000 members—into a formidable movement. To do so they had to engage and defeat the uncommonly powerful Citizens' Alliance, which had made Minneapolis and its twin city, St. Paul, strongholds of the open shop. With eight hundred members from the business community, an efficient staff, and a trained crew of undercover agents, the Alliance had broken every important strike in the city for a generation. Its leaders boasted that they had smashed the trucker stoppage of 1916 at the meager cost of $25,000 and had thereby undercut the threat to Twin City transport for a generation.

By February 1934, Skoglund and a personable driver named Bill Brown, who "for some reason or other" had been appointed an international organizer for the Teamsters, were ready to move against the Alliance. With the Dunne brothers they mapped a detailed plan for a blitzkrieg—the closing of all coal yards by "cruising picket squads." Each picket captain was given specific instructions and a map beforehand, telling him what yard his squadron was to attack. The tactic caught the Citizens' Alliance and the coal companies off guard. Within three hours, sixty-five of the sixty-seven yards were closed tight. Most of the men responded eagerly; a few had to be prodded with a show of force. Taken by surprise the employers signed a union contract fairly quickly and granted the workers a wage increase. Ironically, a letter from Daniel Tobin, national president of the Teamsters, refusing to sanction the strike was received two days after the strike had been won.

The February foray was the prelude to a larger battle. On its heels, the Dunnes, Skoglund, and Brown began organizing not only truck drivers but inside warehousemen—an innovation for the Teamsters—and quickly enlisted 3,000 new members in Local 574. With the Regional Labor Board acting as go-betweeen the union demanded recognition, in accord with Section 7(a), seniority in layoffs and rehiring, and non-discrimination for union membership. It was a modest proposal, not including the closed shop, but the trucking companies would not agree to it—often absenting themselves from meetings with the Board. A. W. Strong, founder of the Citizens' Alliance, later told author Charles Rumford Walker, that while he could "conceive of dealing with a conservative and responsible labor leader," it was out of the question to negotiate with the headstrong men of Local 574. Thus on Tuesday, May 15, 1934, their demands rebuffed, 5,000 drivers and warehousemen left their jobs to gather around a large garage at 1900

Chicago Avenue, which had been rented by the union for strike headquarters.

For the first three days of the stoppage, the city was paralyzed; and, everything was peaceful. Only drivers of ice wagons, and of beer, milk, and coal companies—already unionized—continued working. Flying squadrons roamed everywhere, closing down operations. "With nearly 3,000 pickets blocking every entrance to the city and massed about the gates of every large fleet owner," reported the Minneapolis *Tribune*, "they succeeded in halting most of the ordinary trucking movements . . . In the central market the tie-up was particularly effective. No trucks were allowed to come in with farmers' loads of vegetables. . . . Newspaper deliveries Wednesday were made by police escort." The fleets of automobiles used by the flying squadrons found opposition to the strike only among gas stations, whose owners closed down when they arrived, but then tried to reopen when the squads were gone. After a hundred cars full of pickets demolished a few gas pumps, however, the gas stations too were quiet. Only a few stations for their own use were permitted to operate.

Even more than the San Francisco and Toledo strikes, the Minneapolis stoppage was an amazingly well-organized performance. The garage headquarters, with a great Local 574 banner under its roof top, served as the nerve center of the strike—a refuge where thousands of workers slept and ate, an auditorium for union meetings, a hospital when injured men were brought in. Special worker task forces were assigned to guard against raids, with husky drivers and warehousemen standing watch at every door. Picket captains, dispersed through the city, were instructed to phone in every ten minutes. They sent such messages as the following to headquarters: "Truck attempting to move load of produce from Berman Fruit, under police convoy. Have only ten pickets, send help." Inside headquarters were a few hundred men ready to act in response to a situation such as this one at a moment's notice, on the order of Vincent Dunne or Farrell Dobbs (also a Trotskyite) who acted as dispatchers. When the police began tapping union phones, the pickets were given codes to disguise their messages. And, police short-wave messages were intercepted so that the union officials always knew what their adversaries were planning. A motorcycle squad of five roamed the city day and night, and pickets were always on hand at the forty or fifty roads leading into the city. For the less dramatic tasks, the union called on unemployed groups and a large 574 Women's Auxiliary—to type, mimeograph bulletins, run the kitchen, and occasionally to join the pickets in their battered trucks or jalopies.

Having secured their base among drivers and inside men, the

"574" leaders extended outward to gain support in a widening arc, both from other workers and the public at large. In these arenas too they won a surprisingly strong commitment. On the second day of the strike, cab drivers left their taxis. A few days later 35,000 building trades workers, ordinarily a relatively conservative group, joined the strike. Ten thousand streetcar employees expressed sympathy and threatened to link hands with the truckers. Finally the Central Labor Union, not known for its radicalism, endorsed the stoppage. One of the points repeated over and over again by the Dunnes and Skoglund was a warning not to place any faith regarding settlement in government officials, not even in Governor Floyd B. Olson, elected on a Farmer-Labor Party ticket. The strike, they said, must build its own power and spread into working-class constituencies to attain a strength and unity that could not be broken or compromised.

On the other side, the members of the Citizens' Alliance opened an office at the Radisson Hotel to grind out press releases and copy about the strike for full-page ads, as well as to give advice to harassed businessmen. The alliance expected that as food supplies dwindled the public would be sufficiently outraged to mass for a counterattack. Two thousand businessmen gathered at the Radisson Hotel and selected a Committee of Twenty-five, whose job was to enlist doctors, lawyers, clerks, salesmen, and businessmen, for a "Citizens' Army." Like the strikers, the Citizens' Army opened a headquarters and commissary, in preparation for battle. To give the army official sanction its members were designated by the authorities as special police.

The first step in the spiraling confrontation was a series of guerrilla Actions by the Alliance. A few truckloads of pickets, for instance, were lured to an alley near the Minneapolis *Tribune,* encircled by police and armed guards, and thoroughly beaten. Three of the women suffered broken legs and almost everyone was bloodied by clubs and fists. It later turned out that the man who had dispatched the pickets from strike headquarters was a Burns detective, specially insinuated into the union for such provocations. The full-scale engagement between strikers and the Citizens' Army took place on Monday and Tuesday, May 21 and 22, as police and deputies prepared to move perishable goods from the closed central market. Local 574 was ready. It had secreted 600 men in the Central Labor Union office and held another 900 in reserve at the Chicago Avenue garage. Small squads— without union buttons—were dispatched to key places in the market.

At the appointed hour, the contingent at the Central Labor Union marched toward the market from one side, four abreast, while the force from headquarters attacked from the other side, completely surrounding the police and 1,000 deputies. Pickets swung pipes, clubs, bricks, and in one or two cases wielded knives. At the peak of fighting a driver with twenty-five pickets on his truck drove headlong into the police to prevent them from using their guns. The winner this first day was unquestionably the union; thirty police were hospitalized, while union casualties were by comparison, one broken collarbone, a few broken ribs, and one cracked skull. Most important of all, no trucks moved.

The next day—called the Battle of Deputies Run—there was less planning, but more men on each side. At least 20,000 people left their jobs and homes to assemble at the market. A minor incident— an effort by a small merchant to move a few crates of tomatoes— precipitated a wholesale outbreak which spilled over into scores of attacks by unionists and sympathizers against the more than 2,000 police forces. By nightfall the deputies had been routed. Arthur Lyman, for sixteen years attorney for the Citizens' Alliance, lay dead, along with one other special deputy, and the number of injured on both sides, never tallied, ran into hundreds. At Governor Olson's urging a truce was called, during which no trucks were to be moved and negotiations were to proceed.

Three days later there was a settlement—but not before both parties had prepared for further hostilities. A strategy committee of the employers met and discussed plans for arresting the strike leaders and mobilizing greater police forces. The union, meanwhile, called a massive demonstration, addressed by top officials of the state, city, and building trades' councils, as well as Lieutenant Governor K. K. Solberg. Governor Olson put 3,700 National Guardsmen on the alert, much to the discomfort of the strike committee. A mood of war hung over the negotiations. Union negotiators, arriving at the hotel where the conference was to take place with four picket cars in front of them and four in back, just in case police tried to serve warrants, found 150 officers waiting for them. They refused to take part in meetings until the uniformed men were withdrawn. The settlement itself hinged on such questions as union recognition for *both* the truckers and inside workers—in effect making Local 574 an industrial union—and a written contract. What emerged was a modest victory, in which the employers signed their names to an agreement according full reinstatement to formerly held jobs for the strikers, granting a minimum wage and arbitration for future increases and seniority rights. The recognition issue was clouded in ambiguity which the union took to mean—and Olson seconded—recognition of both groups. But the employers took the terms of the settlement to mean exclusion of inside workers. Nonetheless after only eleven days Local 574 had made a solid beginning.

The ambiguity over recognition led to a third strike, in July, and another fierce encounter on "Bloody Friday," July 20, in which fifty-five pickets were shot and two killed. Governor Olson, roundly castigated by the strike committee, now sent in the National Guard, which in turn raided the strike headquarters and arrested the Dunnes, Bill Brown, and one hundred other union leaders. Nonetheless the stoppage continued under a second leadership especially-prepared for just such a contingency. Unionized cab drivers, ice, beer, and gasoline drivers immediately left their vehicles, and though thousands of strikebreakers were found to man other trucks the flying squadrons continued to harry and stop them—guard or no guard. Forty thousand workers came out to the funeral of one of the victims of Bloody Friday; 40,000 more at another demonstration, after the Dunnes and Brown were arrested. So fierce was the outcry of the workers this time that the jailed men were released in a few days.

After five weeks the employers again conceded defeat, granting recognition of the "inside workers." Despite the use of state militia and a condemnation of the strike leaders by Daniel Tobin as "radicals and Communists," the radicals in fact prevailed. Moreover, they used their victory as a steppingstone to organize over-the-road haulers. Every time an out-of-town truck driver came to a dock or warehouse, he was forced to show a union card, or turn back with his truck unloaded. In this way the union in Minneapolis, and then in other cities, drew to its fold the key intercity drivers, without whom the present Teamsters' union could not have achieved its position as the largest and most powerful union in the country

14

Clearing the Cobwebs

"The country is full of spontaneous strikes," wrote Benjamin Stolberg in December 1933. "Wherever one goes one sees picket lines." From mid-1933 to early 1938 there was an outbreak of class warfare matched only by that which followed World War I. How fierce it was can be measured by the telling statistics of repression. From August through October 1933, fifteen strikers were murdered on picket lines. Another forty were slain in 1934, and forty-eight more in the next two years. In a year and a half, from mid-1933 to the end of 1934, troops were called out to quell strikes in sixteen of the forty-eight states. Eighteen thousand strikers were arrested from 1934 through 1936, and no one knows how many thousands were beaten or wounded.

Almost all of the labor warfare of this period was in fields either previously immune to unionism or where the existing labor organizations were in a comatose state. Where there *was* a base from which to operate, a functioning union machine to co-ordinate efforts, labor fared well, and without being driven to violent extremes.

The outstanding example as noted above was in coal. Immediately after the passage of Section 7(a), John L. Lewis gambled the meager $75,000 treasury of the United Mine Workers on a rapid and successful organizing drive that recaptured miner allegiance in the South, where it had almost vanished, and within a few months lifted national membership from 150,000 to a half million. UMWA staff men flooded the coal patches with leaflets proclaiming that "the law is on our side, the government's with us." President Roosevelt, they told miners, wants you to join the union. Simultaneously Lewis promoted legislative measures to introduce stability to the industry. Under the Guffey Act—the National Coal Conservation Bill—soft-coal operators were permitted to engage in co-operative marketing practices, thereby eliminating cutthroat price wars, and a Coal Labor Board was established to monitor and mediate union-management problems. With this combined offensive, helping the coal industry as well as his miners, John L. reversed the tide of disintegration in his union. He was able to win wage scales for his men of $5.50 for a seven-hour day in the North, and $5.10 in the South. In similar blitzkriegs the Ladies' Garment Workers enrolled 100,000 additional members and the Amalgamated Clothing Workers 50,000. Other established organizations of this kind also filled out and won impressive wage gains with little resistance.

The fledgling groups in the mass production and other industries, however, were less fortunate. There was no leadership as yet to synchronize their efforts, to help them raise funds during strikes, to bring them into contact with those who had similar interests. Auto workers in a General Motors plant at Detroit, for instance, might form a local union on their own, but they had no firm channels for communicating with GM workers, e.g., in Atlanta or Cleveland. Each self-contained local therefore was a clay pigeon for the huge corporations, shot down repeatedly until the CIO finally gave them cohesion.

Where there was no strong union already in existence, the discontented really had little place to turn. They could form independent organizations outside the AFL, but that had many drawbacks, the most important of which was that they would have been starting without necessary resources or contacts. As another alternative, they could join the communist-led Trade Union Unity League, which at one point spiraled to 125,000 adherents. But the TUUL combined economic demands with political ones, such as "Defend the Soviet Union," to the point where it alienated many workers whose only interest was simple unionism. Finally, the new unionists could seek out the main body of labor, the AFL. But the old Federation had become tepid, hesitant and conservative, and in both spirit and ideology, at loggerheads with the "hotheads" banging at its doors. Thus, in addition to their rigorous struggle against capital, the new unionists found themselves in both secret and open combat against the AFL patriarchs. And the two conflicts were interrelated. There could be no success possible in the fight against management unless and until there was a basic refashioning of the house of labor itself. Old cobwebs had to be cleared away before labor could make its next quantum jump.

William Green's first reaction to the upsurge in the number of new unionists was one of jubilation. His AFL at that point was down to 2.1 million members, but he confidently predicted at the Federation's convention in October 1933 that it would soon grow to ten million, and ultimately twenty-five million.

This was for Bill Green the moment of opportunity. He had risen high in the ranks of labor but he was overshadowed in the public mind by his former boss, John L. Lewis, and he needed some successes on his own to enhance his status. Born in Coshocton, Ohio, in 1873, Green had nursed ambitions as a youngster to become a Baptist minister; necessity, however, drove him into the coal pits with his English-born father. It was just as well. The United Mine Workers of America was beginning to assert itself as a force in American life, and young Green, cautious, shy, but serious and competent, was able to get himself elected a sub-district president in 1900. Six years later he became president for the whole Ohio district, a position he held for some years, until he made a detour into politics.

A politically oriented miner those days had an advantage in that he had a solid constituency in the coal patches on which to build. William Green used his position in the union as a jumping-off station for politics, then politics as a means of improving his position in the United Mine Workers. As a regular and loyal Democrat he was selected as a delegate at large to the 1912 Democratic convention and the next year was elected to the Ohio State Senate, where he served for four years, part of the time as floor leader. He distinguished himself by introducing liberal legislation that was not too extreme to offend anyone but was solid enough to win him prestige with progressive-minded people. One of his bills changed the basis of payment for miners so that it was no longer computed on coal *after* it was screened —a technique which permitted of much cheating—but on coal exactly as it came out of the mines, "mine run." It won Green considerable plaudits from his digger comrades. On the other side, however, the future president of the AFL showed he was a "responsible" labor man when, as chairman of the legislative investigating committee during his second two-year term, he denounced the IWW leaders who were heading a rubber workers' strike in Akron, as "outside agitators."

Bill Green's success in state politics propelled him to the office of secretary-treasurer of the UMWA in 1913, while he was still in the Senate of Ohio; and when a vacancy arose in the AFL executive council a year later Senator Green was designated vice-president of the Federation as well. He might have remained an AFL vice-president indefinitely, for John L. Lewis was the odds-on favorite of many in the UMWA to go on to the AFL presidency. But the more colorful

Lewis made many enemies when he ran against Gompers for the presidency of the AFL in 1921, among them Matthew Woll, president of the small Photo-Engravers Union, whom Gompers had been grooming as his heir apparent.

When the founder of the AFL passed on in December 1924, after serving as its president for thirty-seven years, Lewis, the head of the AFL's largest affiliate, repaid Woll for his hostility by executing a coup. With the help of William Hutcheson of the carpenters' union and T. A. Rickert of the United Garment Workers, he arranged a special meeting of the AFL executive council six days after Gompers' death and saw to it that the "dark horse," William Green, was unanimously chosen as Gompers' successor, pending a formal election at the next AFL convention. Though Woll had had his late mentor's nod it was obviously not enough to prevent Lewis from putting in his own man.

Green seemed like a good choice. The man from Coshocton was offensive to no one. Careful and plodding, apple-cheeked, he was a good family man, with a fine wife, four daughters, and one son; he was a model Elk and Odd Fellow, and a fervent dry. "Labor is safe under his leadership," commented a Richmond, Virginia, newspaper, "capital has nothing to fear during his regime and the public is fortunate in having him as the responsible spokesman of a highly important group of citizens." Neither dramatic nor highly imaginative, Green spoke in fine platitudes about the "greatness of our Country" and love of America. Where Gompers had been his own man and an impressive leader, whatever one thought of his policies, Green was little more than a servant of the baronies. In the nearly nine years he had been president of the AFL prior to the October 1933 convention he had no great achievements to his credit; the Federation indeed had languished in stagnation, its only "accomplishment" the purging of "reds" from its ranks. Now in 1933 Green saw the prospect of a major breakthrough that might make his Federation a most important center of economic and political power, and himself a figure of imposing proportions.

With all the enthusiasm he could muster, the AFL president dispatched members of his staff to "organize the unorganized in the mass production industries." For the most part the organizers appointed were old warhorses, out of touch with the new reality—like William Collins and Francis J. Dillon, sent to the auto cities, or Coleman Claherty, assigned to the rubber capital of Akron. But they had little trouble proselytizing. Unionism was an idea whose time had come, workers were clamoring to be enlisted, and all an organizer needed was application cards.

At the San Francisco national convention, in 1934, the AFL executive council reported that "there was a virtual uprising of workers for union membership. Workers held mass meetings and sent word they wanted to be organized." The number of federal unions into which these new recruits were placed skyrocketed from 307 in 1932 to 1,788 in 1934. There were 100,000 converts in the auto industry; 60,000 in Akron's rubber and related industries; 90,000 fighting their way into "Grandmother" Mike Tighe's Amalgamated Association of Iron, Steel and Tin Workers; 40,000 metal miners in the Mine, Mill and Smelter Workers—successor to Bill Haywood's Western Federation of Miners; 90,000 lumber and sawmill workers; 20,000 in cement; and almost 400,000 workers flooding into the textile union before its tragic strike that year.

But with all this success in numbers, President Green's joy was somewhat muted in 1934 as it became evident that the hundreds of thousands of workers filtering into AFL ranks were neither malleable nor what is euphemistically called "responsible." They were resentful at being treated like orphaned wards and were particularly uneasy about being pushed into so-called "federal unions," under which they enjoyed no autonomy. Ordinarily a worker joins a local craft union in his city, which in turn is affiliated with a national union—e.g. the International Association of Machinists. Within certain limits, depending on how democratic the national union happens to be, the local union has a considerable number of rights. It can write its own by-laws, vote on its agreements with management, order a strike, control its funds. The federal union too was a local union directly affiliated with a national organization—the AFL itself. But Green's staff wrote its constitution, and held veto power over everything it did, including especially its right to strike or enter into a collective-bargaining ageement with employers. Worse still, the new members were alarmed by the explicit and implicit threat that at some time in the near future their federal union would be sliced into bits and pieces, and apportioned to the national craft organizations that made the strongest claims for them. Thus in the summer of 1933, when two inspired young men in Akron organized 4,500 rubber workers, Coleman Claherty generously separated them into nineteen craft locals—boxmakers, blacksmiths, masons, carpenters, pipe fitters, printers, sheet-metal workers, etc. Had the new unionists bowed to the sanctity of organization by craft, the lords of labor might have been free from worry. But the new converts were knowledgeable enough about organized labor to insist on being represented by a single industrial union. They also demanded the right to run their affairs free of President Green's veto, and, most disturbing, were ready to strike over wages, the discharge of a militant, or the issue of union recognition at the drop of a hat. Green constantly instructed them to delay a showdown, or told them to return to work after going out. But the fresh generation of unionists, and the unknown radicals who as often as not were their leaders, obviously were of a different type than the old hacks around Green. Dan Tobin, president of the teamsters, called them "rubbish," a sentiment undoubtedly shared by many of his older colleagues.

But whatever the feelings of Tobin, the "rubbish" could neither be sidetracked nor disregarded. They were a whirlwind of motion, always leaving behind them a storm for the AFL to cope with. Auto unionists, for instance, went out on a total of one hundred strikes in 1933, from which emerged scores of federal locals, collectively demanding a national industrial union charter. Equally brash young men in the rubber, aluminum, cement industries were making similar demands, each one, if granted, a menace to the balance of power within the AFL. From inside and outside there were challenges to the old patriarchs that threatened to sweep them aside—young new unionists inside the AFL ready to oust them from leadership posts they had held for decades, and similar young new unionists who were forming independent unions outside the AFL that might eventually become a stronger labor center than the old Federation itself.

Typically, in April 1934, 250 steel unionists—part of the new upstarts—met and designated a committee of ten to prepare a national strike, something that was anathema to the ancient chieftain of the Amalgamated Association, Mike Tighe. Tighe responded to what he viewed as an outrage by denouncing the plan as "illegal," and in the in-fighting that followed eventually expelled three quarters of the membership rather than submit to their militancy. Admittedly, this was like throwing out the baby with the dirty bathwater, but the steel union leaders saw no other recourse.

Another problem for the entrenched AFL bureaucracy was the independent union. In April 1933 a small group of class-conscious tool-and-die makers formed the Mechanics Educational Society of America under the stewardship of Matthew Smith. Nine months later, after a successful eight-week strike in Flint, MESA's membership grew to 25,000, and Smith cast his eyes on organizing production workers. Who could tell at what point such a group would make the grand breakthrough and become predominant in this mass production industry? Another example of the independent union was the Automotive Industrial Workers Association, led by Richard Frankensteen, a forty-nine-cent an hour trim operator in a Dodge plant in Detroit, who tried to bring together all company unions in the Chrysler system. Supported and endorsed by the nationally known, radio broadcasting "priest of the Shrine of the Little Flower," Father Charles E. Coughlin, the AIWA, despite its unusual notions on dues and other matters, had serious potential power outside the AFL. Nor were the communists to be entirely ignored; sectarian or not they were bringing tens of thousands of new men and women into the TUUL, and at any moment, given a single sensational victory, might become a pole of attraction for hundreds of thousands of workers. This was not the 1920s; communism was not acceptable to most people, but as the experience in the movement of unemployed workers had revealed, few among the downtrodden quavered any longer at the mention of this or other forms of leftism. If the AFL, then, showed an influx of a half million new members, most of them were tenuously held. And the independents, which had grown by perhaps half that number, might coalesce at any moment into a new labor center giving the AFL more competition than it had bargained for. Harnessing the new militants within and without the Federation thus became as necessary a precondition for the good health and survival of the old-liners as upsetting the established AFL practices became for the new breed.

At the 1934 AFL convention, held in San Francisco a few months after "Bloody Thursday," Green and his associates grappled with this problem. The only answer they could come up with was to tighten the shackles around the newcomers. John P. Frey, president of the metal trades department, introduced a resolution calling for direct enrollment of skilled and semi-skilled men into established craft unions, leaving only the residue for the federal unions. Such heavy-handed division would, of course, make industrial workers impotent. Another of the fourteen resolutions on this subject, put forth by the boilermakers, went further, urging that the AFL abandon entirely the policy of forming separate federal locals for factory workers.

By now an opposition to AFL leadership had crystallized around John L. Lewis, and Charles P. Howard of the typographical union. These men were not committed leftists by any means, but they had seen the potential of the union newcomers and for a variety of reasons were insistent that they be given national industrial union charters. Whatever the specific motive of each of the middle-of-the-road leaders, one shared by all of them was that if the AFL didn't make a suitable home for the mass-production workers, someone else, far more radical, would. After much debate, some of it not very genteel, a compromise was put together at the 1934 AFL meeting. Written by Howard, it gave priority of control to the craft unions for those who fit their jurisdiction, but authorized the AFL executive council to issue individual industrial charters for the remainder. Thus, for example, rubber workers would have to trim away machinists, construction workers, teamsters, etc. before being permitted to operate their own union.

When Green did finally grant charters to automobile workers and rubber workers—the only two industrial unions formed under his administration—their wings were clipped by the AFL, their ranks subject to constant "raids" by the craft organizations. Edward Levinson, in his book, *Labor on the March*, tells of one auto union in Toledo which "had its members parceled among seven craft organizations, until none but sweepers remained." A Cleveland local seceded and went independent rather than be decimated by craft-union claims. In an Akron rubber plant, 432 workers were chipped away from their united organization and transferred to the machinists' union; only five "chose to continue their membership." The Mechanics Educational Society of America, ready to merge with the United Automobile Workers Union (UAW) changed its mind when the AFL machinists demanded all the skilled MESA workers for itself.

The patchwork peace made at the 1934 convention turned out to be useless and could not last. Adding insult to injury, Green insisted that he personally choose officers for each of the new organizations. In August 1935, when he offered an industrial charter to delegates of eighty-three federal unions in automobile manufacturing, the offer was contingent upon their acceptance of Francis J. Dillon, a fiercely despised member of his staff, as their president. Homer Martin, a former preacher from Kansas City, who had lavished sycophantic praise on Green at a previous meeting, was hand-picked to be vice-president. When the delegates demanded to elect their own leaders, Green told them either to honor his appointees or forfeit the charter. Robert Travis and another delegate from Toledo were so furious that they vainly urged the convention to reject Green's "offer." Twelve days later, when Green tried the same tactic on delegates from twenty-seven rubber locals, the tumult was so loud he was forced to yield. But his clear intention, where possible, was to retain as much control for his office as each situation permitted.

As events were soon to prove, the ingrained AFL hostility to the "rubbish" in the mass-production industries was so pronounced that, short of a minor revolution, little headway could be made under its banner. And with thousands of militants being discharged by auto, steel, rubber, and other corporations, and both the AFL and President Roosevelt constantly counseling against strikes, rank-and-file demoralization was widespread. By February 1935 the federal unions in the auto industry were down from 100,000 members to 20,000. Of the 163,150 workers polled by the Auto Labor Board in April 1935, only

14,057 chose AFL representatives. The 100,000 steelworkers who had signed cards in Grandmother Tighe's Amalgamated Association had deserted or been expelled to the point where only 5,300 remained. The 60,000 union members recruited in rubber and related industries had shrunk by March 1935 to perhaps 3,000, due to AFL interference. Requests for national charters by other industrial groups—workers in radio, cement, aluminum, public utility, gas, oil—were petulantly brushed aside by Green. It was obvious that before the new unionists could rally for an effective fight, they needed shelter in a more sympathetic institution than the AFL, just as earlier unionists had required a base from which to operate other than the Knights of Labor in 1886. The situation came to a head late in 1935.

II

It was off-season on Atlantic City's famous boardwalk when 500 delegates of the American Federation of Labor met at the Chelsea Hotel for what was to be their most critical convention. The mood was not totally dour. Joseph V. Moreschi, whose Hod Carriers Union hadn't held an election since 1911, sat regally at a raised table, sipping wine and savoring Italian delicacies with a host of friends. For those who wanted it, a not inconsequential number, there was plenty of fun and joy to be had both on and off New Jersey's seacoast. On the agenda was that troublesome question of industrial unionism, but this issue was within the province of only a handful of the "lords of labor" in the AFL. Most of the other delegates would present themselves in body, raise their hands when told to, and then be off for their much-deserved pleasures.

Among the AFL monarchs defending lucrative empires were William L. Hutcheson, whose 200,000 members represented a fifth of the organizable carpenters in the nation; Arthur O. Wharton of the machinists (92,500 members in an industry with 774,701 employees); Daniel Tobin of the teamsters (137,000 organized out of 1.6 million); a diadem of representatives from the metal trades unions, including president John P. Frey and Matthew Moll, acting president of the National Civic Federation; Joseph P. Ryan of the longshoremen; a few racketeers such as George J. Scalise, who would be in prison in a few years; and of course Bill Green, Frank Morrison, and other respectable officials of the Federation. In the institutionalized structure of the AFL, these men had the votes, the power to deal with the convention as they wished, and for some reason they felt that these votes were all they needed to settle the issues they faced.

Among the insurgents were Charles P. Howard, of the typographical union, a number of needle trades leaders such as David Dubinsky,

Julius Hochman, and Sidney Hillman, all with socialist backgrounds, chiefs of the bakers' and brewery workers, also with socialist beliefs, a whole array of newcomers such as Wyndham Mortimer and George Addes of the UAW, James B. Carey from Philadelphia, of the radio workers, the rubber union's Sherman Dalrymple, and last but not least, John L. Lewis. The bushy-browed president of the coal miners still held his own union in an ironlike vise and still enjoyed such privileges as being driven about in a chauffeured Cadillac, but he had learned some things in the last few years. He had learned for one thing that his organization to remain healthy needed support from steelworkers, if only because the steel magnates owned so many coal mines. Unchallenged any longer by the assorted socialists, communists, and progressives who had harried him in the 1920s, Lewis had also developed a tolerance for his adversaries and a recognition of their considerable organizational talent and determination. John Brophy and Powers Hapgood, who had been severely beaten up by Lewis' goons a few years before, and who in turn had damned him for "election stealing, convention packing and slugging of delegates," were invited back into his camp. Brophy soon would assume the focal role in the fledgling CIO as executive director.

Regardless of his past behavior Lewis' horizons had been broadened by the experiences of the 1930s. Uppermost in his mind was the realization that if the middle-of-the-roaders did not organize the potpourri of laborers banging at union doors, the radicals eventually would. Howard, speaking on his own and Lewis' behalf, expressed this idea most forcefully at the Atlantic City convention: "Now let me say to you that the workers of this country are going to organize, and if they are not permitted to organize under the banner of the American Federation of Labor they are going to organize under some other leadership or are going to organize without leadership. I submit to you that it would be a far more serious problem for our government, for the people of this country and for the American Federation itself than if our organization should be so molded that we can organize them and bring them under the leadership of this organization."

It is the folly of emperors that they seldom see the cracks in their empires, until the cracks become unmendable. Such was the case with the grand factotums of the AFL. In two weeks of heated rhetoric the issue of industrial unionism was debated endlessly, on the convention floor and in the hotel lobbies. Lewis stayed at a hotel a half mile from the Chelsea, with an array of lieutenants that included the lieutenant governor of Pennsylvania, a UMWA official Thomas J. Kennedy, Philip Murray, Van A. Bittner, John Brophy, and a full contingent of statisticians, writers, and other contributors feeding him material for the debate. The resolutions committee, dominated by Frey, in the meantime discussed twenty-one resolutions favoring industrial forms of organization and invariably brought in proposals to uphold the sanctity of ancient craft jurisdictions carved out when the American economy was much less complex.

The AFL delegates got the chance to vote on the industrial union issue three times, always defeating it by almost a two to one margin. Speaking for the majority of the resolutions committee Frey invoked the hoary argument about the sacredness of "contracts" entered into between the AFL and its craft affiliates dozens of years before. Howard, reporting for the minority, pointed out the obvious, that there were "industries where the work performed . . . is of such a nature that it might fall within the jurisdiction of more than one craft union, or no established craft union . . . Jurisdictional claims over small groups of workers in these industries prevent organization by breeding a fear that, when once organized, the workers in these plants will be separated . . ." He persisted in the demand for "unrestricted" charters in the mass-production industries.

It remained for Lewis, in electrifying prose, to put the matter in the boldest possible perspective. "There has been a change in industry . . . Great combinations of capital . . . have assembled to themselves tremendous power and influence, and they are almost 100 percent effective in opposing organizations of the workers under the policies of the American Federation of Labor. . . . If you go in there with your craft union they will mow you down like the Italian machine guns will mow down the Ethiopians in the war now going on in that country . . ." In a thrust at the pretensions of the craft leaders, the fifty-five-year-old Lewis mocked their illusions. "The strength of a strong man," he said, "is a prideful thing, but the unfortunate thing in life is that strong men do not remain strong. . . . Whereas today the craft unions of this country may be able to stand upon their own feet and like mighty oaks stand before the gale, defy the lightning, yet the day may come when this changed scheme of things—and things are changing rapidly now—the day may come when those organizations will not be able to withstand the lightning and the gale. Now, prepare yourselves by making a contribution to your less fortunate brethren, heed this cry from Macedonia that comes from the hearts of men. Organize the unorganized. . . ."

Lewis concluded; the vote on the minority report was taken—10,993 for, 18,024 against. How strained were the tempers and how important the stakes was indicated by a fist fight between Lewis and Big Bill Hutcheson of the carpenters. When the latter raised a point of order against further discussion of the industrial union question, Lewis needled him about this being "rather small potatoes." A few minutes later as the former Iowa coal miner, still 225 pounds of muscle, passed Hutcheson's table he was called a "bastard," whereupon, with a single blow, he dropped Hutcheson to the floor, splattering his face with blood from chin to eyebrow.

If there were any symbolism to this incident it was that the breach between the AFL and those who were defeated on the industrial union issue would not be healed for twenty years. The day after the convention, Lewis, Hillman, Dubinsky, Howard, Brophy, and four others held a preliminary meeting to lay plans for a "Committee for Industrial Organization," and on November 9, in Washington, proclaimed its formation. Formally, the CIO purported to be solely "educational and advisory," thereby safeguarding a tenuous affiliation with the AFL, but in fact, the CIO was already a dual organization whose purpose was "to encourage and promote" organization of whomever was unorganized, in particular groups of workers in the mass-production fields.

"Dear Sir and Brother," Lewis wrote in a pithy communication to Green on November 23, 1935, "Effective this date I resign as vice-president of the American Federation of Labor." Demands that the CIO "be immediately dissolved" went unheeded; instead the "Committee" continued to add affiliates—the Mine, Mill and Smelter Workers (once the Western Federation of Miners), an oil union, the auto workers, rubber workers, nuclei affiliates in glass and radio. Lewis' greatest coup was to maneuver Tighe's Amalgamated Association of Steel, Iron and Tin Workers into a pact which yielded to the CIO organizing rights in steel. Lewis thereupon established a Steel Workers Organizing Committee (SWOC), under his close lieutenant Phil Murray, and provided it with an initial treasury of a half-million dollars. By the time the CIO unions were officially tossed out of the AFL in August 1936, their independent drive in the steel and auto industries was, if not in high gear, at least substantially advanced, and the prospect of rewedding the disputants, near zero.

III

American labor has always shown surprising resilience. Given a ray of hope it has often climbed from the depths of demoralization to new peaks of sustained activity. The emergence of the CIO in November 1935 seemed to provide organized labor with just such a boost at just such a bad time. Innumerable workers who had given up on the AFL were happy to re-enlist in the CIO, even where the CIO denied autonomy to local unions, as in Phil Murray's SWOC.

There was a luster to the CIO that had worn off the AFL; young men and women who had lost confidence in winning strikes or for that matter achieving any other durable gains as long as they were accountable to Bill Green, felt that with the CIO they had replaced quicksand with bedrock. The first signs of this renaissance in organized labor were evident in the rubber tire factories of Akron, Ohio.

The bestowal of a charter on the rubber workers by the AFL in September 1935 had been an empty gesture. It was not a true industrial charter, and the union was given no treasury and only a handful of members. At the Goodyear plant, for example, which employed 14,000 workers, only two hundred paid dues or allegiance to the United Rubber Workers of America. Sherman H. Dalrymple, the bruising six-foot-two World War I veteran who had been elected president of the URW, officiated over the mere-shell of an organization that had 3,000 members at best.

But three months after he took office, in January 1936, there was a small flare-up at Firestone. One of the company's "pacemakers"—a fellow who speeded up operations, forcing all those behind him to keep pace—was forcibly slowed down by his fellow workers. A fight ensued and one of the union men was fired. Usually such incidents ended at this point; this time the other workers demanded that the discharge be rescinded. When the company refused, the workers stopped work and sat down near their machines—much as the Wobblies had done at the General Electric Schenectady plant three decades before. No one planned the sitdown in advance; it just occurred. But having begun it moved like an electric shock wave. The machines shut off one by one; by 2 A.M. January 29 the whole plant was in absolute silence. "Jesus Christ," yelled out one worker amid the quiet, "it's like the end of the world." The sitdown lasted three days and was a complete success: the union man was reinstated, and the company agreed to reduce speed-up. Four hundred triumphant Firestone workers, who had previously drifted away from the union, rejoined.

The rubber workers of Akron had been long suffering and long frustrated in trying to find a forum in which to air their grievances. In 1920 Akron factories employed 75,000 laborers; in 1936 scarcely half that number, 40,000; but the number of tires produced was now double what it had been in 1920. Technological change and speed-up accounted for the increase. Attempts to unionize the mills dated back to 1902, when the International Association of Allied Metal and Rubber Workers of the AFL tried to organize, but such attempts invariably failed because of spies, strikebreakers, and other anti-union elements. Even the Wobblies failed in 1912 when they took over leadership of a spontaneous strike. The passage of the NRA in the 1930s of course was a new stimulant to organization, and 30,000 workers rushed into AFL federal unions, closely supervised and dominated by Coleman C. Claherty. Once more, however, a promising beginning for unionization in the industry failed to bear fruit. Claherty denied the rubber workers permission to conduct a national strike, all the while his own negotiations with the tire companies were absolutely fruitless. A walkout by 1,100 factory hands at General Tire, the first big strike since 1912, lasted a month and ended in fiasco. By the time the CIO was formed, innumerable rubber workers had torn up their AFL membership cards. The company unions reigned almost unchallenged.

In January 1936, before the Firestone sitdown, John L. Lewis came to Akron and was given a hero's welcome by thousands of tire employees and their families. There was an excitement in the air that at last something was going to happen, an excitement bolstered by two brief sitdowns at Goodyear and Goodrich. Coal miner Adolph Germer, an old socialist who had fought Lewis in the 1920s but was now a member in good standing in the CIO, was assigned to head the rubber union drive. A big, heavy man of exceptional warmth and fluid rhetoric, Germer was the antithesis of Bill Green's emissaries. He was the compleat rank-and-filer, a man who could establish easy rapport with the socialists and Trotskyites who had been at the hub of Akron's unionizing campaigns. With their help he began holding meetings to win back the thousands who had deserted because of the AFL's ineffectiveness, and was beginning to show significant results in recruitment (or re-recruitment) when the Goodyear Tire & Rubber situation reached a crisis in mid-February. This was to be the CIO's first major test.

The immediate cause of the trouble at Goodyear was the discharge of 137 workers on the third shift. Under the NRA code for the rubber industry, the work day had been set at six hours, but Goodyear decided to raise it to eight, thereby reducing the number of workers needed and dooming many of its employees to the "pink slip." Though the NRA bureaucrats rebuked the huge corporation, the company went ahead with its plan anyway and on February 15 began layoffs. For the company's workers, it was the last straw, a new burden added to the two wage cuts instituted in November 1935 and January 1936—all these measures taken by a company which showed a profit of five and a half million, and had been so prosperous through the years that its stock had been split 96 to 1. As the 137 men were given notice of their termination of employment, others on the shift refused to work. "I favor shutting her down!" cried out one man. On the evening of the seventeenth, after a big rally earlier in the day, the shutdown began.

Goodyear was confident it had matters well in hand. Its company union, the Goodyear Industrial Assembly, was among the best organized in the country. Another line of defense was the secretly established Akron Employers Association, committed to a common strikebreaking endeavor, and with adequate funds to hire Pearl Berghoff detective agency thugs. Nonetheless the fury of the rebellion was more than either the company or union president Dalrymple—who at first refused to authorize the strike—had expected.

The night of February 17, 1936, was bitter cold, with temperatures reaching nine below zero, a forty-five-mile wind blowing, and heavy snow falling. It was hardly a good day for a work stoppage, especially in a plant of 14,000 workers where the number of union adherents was a mere two hundred. Yet thousands of men poured out of the largest rubber plant in the world to establish an eleven-mile picket line around the company's fences and gates—the largest such line in labor history. By the second day 10,000 employees had joined the walkout—and rejoined the union. At selected points around the factory complex, they set up sixty-eight shanties of tin, paper, and wood, as picket stations, and settled in for the expected long battle.

The previous year when the rubber companies had flouted orders by the National Labor Relations Board for elections, AFL leaders Green and Claherty had added insult to injury and refused to sanction a strike. The CIO in 1936 plunged in to settle old accounts. Lewis sent both money and some of the most capable organizers in the movement to Akron—Powers Hapgood; Leo Krzycki of the Amalgamated Clothing Workers (both Socialist Party members); Rose Pesota, a firebrand from the Ladies' Garment Workers, and John Schafer of the oil workers. McAlister Coleman, another socialist and the author of a book on the coal industry, was brought in from New York to handle publicity. Heartened by being able to call on an army with much more power than they could muster themselves, the strikers warded off every attempt at strikebreaking, and did so thoroughly without violence.

At the outset of the stoppage, six judges in Summit County signed a joint restraining order against mass picketing. But no one dared to enforce it. The Akron Central Labor Union, though dominated by craft organizations, announced that there would be a general strike in the city if the authorities resorted to force. The governor of Ohio was asked to provide troops to break the strike, but, deterred by the consideration that it was a sensitive election year, refused. When a "Law and Order League" was formed by a city politician, similar to

the well-known Citizens' Alliances, war veterans in the union's ranks
began regular military drills. Everyone was now prepared for a violent confrontation.

On the day when the vigilantes were expected to attack, CIO
officials leased a radio station from 11 P.M. to 8 A.M., with its members
instructed to stand by their sets to await the word for mobilizing.
Through the night, Germer, Coleman, and others broadcasted music,
and delivered pep talks on union solidarity. The attack did not come.
After four weeks, Goodyear entered into negotiations, and a week or
so later, it agreed to recognize the union, reinstate the discharged
workers, grant seniority rights and reduce the work week to thirty-six
hours. It was not a total victory for the workers, since management
continued to deal with its own creature, the Goodyear Industrial
Assembly. But the company union, having failed to head off the
increase in hours or do anything about the discharges, was totally
discredited by its worker members. And, more important, the bona
fide unions' momentum could not be halted. In the next ten months
there were no fewer than 180 sitdown strikes in the rubber plants,
almost every one leading to some gain for the unionists and filling out
the ranks of the United Rubber Workers of America.

The Goodyear strike was the first success in a billowing CIO drive.
From all over the nation other idealistic men were bolstering that
drive in 1936, most of them leading small but potentially powerful
organizations ready for major thrusts on behalf of their member
workers. In the radio and electrical industries, James B. Carey, who in
1933, barely beyond the age of majority, had formed a thriving union
at Philco Radio in Philadelphia, and Julius Emspak, a GE tool maker
with a degree in philosophy, had brought a dozen federal locals and
independents together early in 1936 to establish the United Electrical,
Radio and Machine Workers of America (UE). Operating from a
$27.50-a-month headquarters at Twenty-sixth and Broadway in New
York, UE had a few thousand members at most. But it was soon
embroiled in a strike of 6000 employees of the Radio Corporation of
America in Camden, New Jersey, which after four bloody weeks of
picket-line battles and 175 arrests, wrested bargaining rights from
RCA's David Sarnoff, who previously had refused to negotiate. Then,
from 14,000 members in October 1936, UE burgeoned to 100,000
eight months later, and eventually to a half million. John Green, a
sheet-metal worker in the Camden shipyards, and Philip Van Gelder,
a socialist and a former philosophy instructor at Brown University,
teamed up to establish the Industrial Union of Marine and Ship-
building Workers, which joined the CIO late in 1936. Nascent industrial unions agglomerated among glass workers, newspapermen,

transport workers, office and professional employees, oil workers and packinghouse workers. The CIO was succeeding brilliantly.

John L. Lewis and organization director, John Brophy, unlike Green, encouraged all of these efforts with aid in the form of both money and organizers. The CIO leadership didn't have to initiate these drives because most of them got under way independently, usually under the aegis of virtually infinite varieties of left-wingers.

The CIO's own concentration, even to the exclusion of the auto industry was in the steel industry. On June 13, 1936, a week and a half after the agreement with Tighe that gave the CIO the organizing privilege and responsibility in this fortress of the American economy, the drive was officially launched under the guiding hand of Phil Murray. This time there was no shortage of funds or organizers as there had been in William Z. Foster's attempt in 1919. Murray hired a staff of 433 full-time and part-time organizers, (not a few of whom were communists, Trotskyists, and socialists), opened thirty-five regional offices, and began publishing a newspaper—*Steel Labor*. By November he was able to report that scores of company union officials had converted to the SWOC and that 82,315 steelworkers had signed application cards. A few months later the figure was 125,000. As in Foster's day there was no problem in enrolling steelworkers in a union, assuming the drive was serious. When the American Iron and Steel Institute delivered its usual anti-red bombast and placed ads in 375 newspapers denouncing the SWOC operation, John L. Lewis bought national radio time to challenge the corporate "declaration of war." Instead of getting bogged down with the "red" issue, he countered with statistics showing that the steel companies were paying fifteen cents an hour less than coal and construction companies. He accused them of violating the Wagner Act, exploiting consumers, using spies, and robbing employees of their freedom by imposing company unions on them. He proved, with carefully compiled figures, that of twenty-one top industries, steel ranked twentieth in pay scales. His counterthrust emboldened steelworkers and gave them an even greater sense of purpose and determination.

Presumably, then, the showdown between labor and capital in 1936–37 should have taken place in the steel industry. That was certainly where Lewis planned it to be. But as happens so often in the calculations of men and institutions, the pivotal struggle of that year came in an unforeseen crisis situation, in the automobile industry. It was at General Motors in Flint, Michigan, where the CIO was "made," and where American labor finally came of age.

15

Sitdown! Sitdown!

The "horseless carriage" was in many respects like the "iron horse." Evolving from inauspicious beginnings, it was becoming, after four decades, both a sub-culture and *the* crucial center of American manufacturing. A four-billion-dollar industry by 1936, producing cars, trucks, taxicabs, hearses, buses, and tractors, it traced its origins to the steam carriage and gasoline engine displayed in Europe before the American Civil War. No one paid much attention to these toys until the 1880s, when Gottlieb Daimler of Germany built a single-cylinder combustion machine, using the principle of carburetion developed by Siegfried Marcus. A decade later this joyous novelty spread to America, where dozens of self-made mechanics and promoters, the most noteworthy Henry Ford and William C. Durant, engaged in a mad race to put their models on the street first. As of 1900 there were 8,000 motor driven vehicles registered; in 1913, one million. By that time there were five dozen companies turning out a host of models, the best known being the Olds, Ford, Maxwell, Reo, Cadillac, Studebaker, and Packard. In 1914, Ford alone sold 248,000 cars—as against 10,607 five years before—on which he earned a neat profit of $30.3 million.

Henry Ford's contribution to the automobile mania was a rugged box on wheels, the Model T, that sold for $950 when originally introduced, and on the mechanical side, the mass-production techniques that were designed by Walter E. Flanders. Automan Ford, native of Dearborn, Michigan, born in 1863, was a bigoted and semi-literate man. (He had never heard of Benedict Arnold, couldn't define the word "commenced" during a 1919 libel suit, confused "ballyhoo" for "blackguard," and was an anti-Semite who later accepted an Iron Cross from Hitler). But he knew automobiles, and he appreciated the value of a mass market. The "tin Lizzie" brought him wealth and power, and the five-dollar-a day wage he paid, put into effect in 1914 when labor turnover was at almost 900 per cent a year, gave him the aura of a benefactor.

William C. Durant's contribution on the other hand was that of a promoter. He invented no cars, but he had an unfailing knack for exchanging stocks and agglomerating individual companies into empires. As a twenty-four-year-old Flint insurance salesman in 1885, Durant and another salesman formed the Durant-Dort Carriage Company. The two-wheeled carts they sold—the manufacturing was done by others—were peddled through farm-implement firms and were immensely popular. A millionaire at forty, Durant next turned to the horseless carriage. He picked up the small, all but bankrupt Buick Manufacturing Company, and with the help of technical geniuses such as Charles Mott, an axle-maker, and Albert Champion one of the great names in spark plugs, converted it to one of the leading corporations in the auto industry. Then, using the Buick organization as a base, he turned to a wild and woolly promotion of mergers, in an undisguised effort to corner the market. By exchanging stock with various firms he was able in 1908–9 to amalgamate Buick, Cadillac, Oldsmobile, Oakland, ten parts makers, three truck companies, and five smaller auto manufacturers into the General Motors Company. He would have liked to have included Ford and Reo, two of the big four, but neither J. P. Morgan or other Wall Street titans were interested in committing funds to the expansion of the upstart company as yet.

A year later, during an economic slump, Durant turned to Wall Street for a $15 million loan to salvage his operations. He not only paid the bankers $2.5 million, as well as $6 million in GM stock, but had to step aside as head of the company in favor of Walter P. Chrysler and Charles Nash. Undaunted nonetheless, Durant secured the services in 1911 of a Swiss mechanic, Louis Chevrolet, and began producing the immensely successful, low-cost model named after the mechanic. Before long the Chevrolet company, with the aid of Pierre du Pont and John J. Raskob, bought out the General Motors Company, rechristening it the General Motors Corporation. A decade later, founder Durant was again eased out—this time by du Pont and the House of Morgan—but he left behind a formidable empire which in the meantime had absorbed, among many companies, United Motors, Delco, Hyatt Roller Bearing, Frigidaire, Fisher Body, and Warner Gears. As a duchy of the du Pont family, which owned ten million shares, and the Morgans, GM eventually replaced Ford as the auto industry's leader.

The trend toward empire building indicated in the GM saga paralleled an amazing advance in the industry's mechanization. Ford had already proven that the method of fabricating interchangeable parts and assembling them in large quantities was vastly superior to former methods in which each skilled mechanic did many operations. The linking of electricity with machinery and the power-driven conveyor belt made mass production even more efficient; with the same human hands twice as much could be manufactured in 1929 as in 1919. The result was a growth of massive factories, oblong structures of brick, stone and glass, with thousands of workers under a single roof. Another result was the stop-watch, time-study work culture, whereby fractions of a second became religiously important to production, and laborers were reduced to adjuncts of the machine.

Frederick W. Taylor, scion of the stop watch and father of scientific management, had predicted that mass production, with its enormously expanded yield, would not only ease industrial discord, but bring a measure of harmony between capital and labor as well. For presumably, with larger profits capital could afford to pacify its workers. Taylor was wrong. Mass production led, instead, to a "speed-up" by which the employer increased the speed of the machine and forced the worker to keep pace with it. Workers subjected to these additional physical demands became old before their time and were discarded like so much industrial waste. "Men near 40," reported economist Leon Henderson in 1935, "find great difficulty in securing jobs with the industry or being rehired after layoffs." Only the young were capable of standing the pace.

"You should see [my husband] come home at night, him and the rest of the men in the buses," an autoworker's wife told an interviewer in Flint. "So tired like they were dead, and irritable. . . . And then at night in bed, he shakes, his whole body, he shakes." In the words of another wife: "They're not men any more if you know what I mean. They're not men. My husband he's only thirty but to look at him you'd think he was fifty and all played out." The work pace in the auto industry was so furious that during a heat wave in July 1936, with the temperature at 100 plus degrees for a full week, scores of workers died, hundreds were hospitalized, and the ambulance siren could be heard uninterruptedly in Michigan's motor cities. The plants drained the best years of a man's life and left him an empty shell with a dubious future. While he worked he might be paid better than most workers in other industries, but he worked furiously in the busy season only to be laid off in the slow season. And if he were too old or too tired, he was not called back.

In the light of such conditions and the worker grievances that arose from them, unionism should have swept the motor plants early in their existence. It didn't. Though there were already 127,000 men and women employed in automobile, parts, and body factories as of 1907 and 377,000 a decade later, no appreciable number was covered by a union contract. A combination of tenacious employer resistance and AFL ineptitude had impeded the process of unionization. In 1901 the AFL granted jurisdiction over organization in the new field to the Carriage and Wagon Workers' Union, but claims of craft organizations were so insistent that at the 1913 AFL convention, the Carriage and Wagon Workers were ordered to surrender carpenters, electricians, pattern makers, and a host of other kinds of auto workers to their respective craft unions. When it refused it was expelled from the AFL in 1917. The Wobblies tried their hand at unionizing the Ford Highland Park plant, but were undercut when the Model T manufacturer himself introduced the five-dollar-a-day wage. With 10,000 job seekers waiting in line to reap what was then inordinately high pay, the IWW was unable to plant its seed. Another feeble effort at worker organization, as already related, was made by the AFL in 1926, but was suspended when General Motors and Ford refused to sanction the union drive.

The Depression of course made auto workers' situations even worse than before. By 1933 the total number of employees in the plants had slumped to 244,000—down from 435,000 in 1928—and average pay checks had been trimmed from a peak of $33 a week in 1928 to $20.10. During those four years auto workers, like others, had remained quiescent. With the New Deal and Section 7 (a) of the NRA however, the tide turned. It was no problem at all for the young radicals in the vanguard of the unionist drive to organize their factories, and organize them they did. The problem was to win recognition. The auto moguls, instead of bargaining with the new, dynamic and crusading unions, some AFL-affiliated, some independent, undercut them by forming company unions or strengthening existing, less forceful ones. After the outbreak of 100 auto strikes in 1933, for instance, the first wave, General Motors held a series of company-union elections and proclaimed that it was now duty-bound to bargain with its own creations.

Another obstacle in the auto industry for the bona fide labor groups' attempts to organize was the company-hired spies and provocateurs. Henry Ford, ever the individualist, spurned outside agents, entrusting the job instead to an ex-boxer, Harry Bennett, who headed a special "Service Department." The Service Department was composed of a core of a few hundred hoodlums who on more than one occasion committed physical violence against suspected unionists. It had on its staff as well, thousands of simple workers who were seduced with a few extra pennies an hour to inform on their fellows. Chrysler and General Motors preferred to have the corporate espionage and provocation handled by outside professionals. According to the LaFollette Civil Liberties Committee of the U. S. Senate, in a report made public late in 1937, Chrysler paid one firm, Corporations Auxiliary, $72,000 for espionage agents in 1935 alone. General Motors spent an astounding total of $994,855 from January 1, 1934, to July 31, 1936, for the same purposes. The spies not only gathered information that resulted in the firing of literally thousands of militants, but caused whatever havoc they could to disrupt and destroy the budding unions. A Pinkerton spokesman boasted to LaFollette that his detectives had burrowed so deeply into the union structure that one had risen to vice-president of a national union, fourteen had become presidents of local unions, and thirty-eight, local secretaries. Another Pinkerton agent, Lawrence Barker, replying to a question by Senator LaFollette about how effective agents had been, said "very effective, especially in the local to which I belonged. . . . One time at Lansing-Fisher they were almost 100 percent organized. And finally it went down to where, as I said, there were only five officers left."

II

These circumstances of tension were approximately the situation in Flint, Michigan, early in June 1936, when Wyndham Mortimer, first vice-president of the UAW, parked his Dodge at the less-than-lavish Dresden Hotel, and rented a twelve-dollar-a-week room. At one time 26,000 of Flint's 45,000 GM workers had belonged to the union; now there were exactly 122 local members, and many of these were spies. One UAW local had a paltry treasury of $24.41—and debts of $700. The national union itself, the UAW, had freed itself from William Green's bondage in April when it tossed out his subaltern, Francis Dillon, and elected its own officers. But it was anything but robust, even nationally. Its membership was a slim 20,000, only half of whom paid dues, and its bank account about a dollar per member, $20,000. Of 250,000 auto workers in Detroit a mere 1,000 were in the UAW. Even worse, the union had few footholds in the factories of the Big Three, Ford, Chrysler, and General Motors.

Despite the mismatch, Mortimer had come to match wits and determination with General Motors, the strongest of the automobile baronies, and do so in its own citadel, Flint. He had hardly gotten settled in his room when a voice over the phone advised him to "get the hell back where you came from if you don't want to be carried out in a wooden box." He was not surprised; this was the kind of thing he had expected in General Motors country.

At fifty-two, Mort—as his friends called him—was one of the "old men" in a union whose leaders were mostly in their twenties or thirties. UAW President Homer Martin was a boyish thirty-four, executive board member Walter Reuther was twenty-eight, secretary-treasurer George F. Addes, twenty-nine. But Mortimer, though he would later be squeezed out of the leadership in bitter internecine struggles, was then the most influential figure in the UAW. At the South Bend convention in April 1936, he had had enough support to win the presidency, but rather than risk a debilitating fight with Martin for the position, he chose to back off. He was, however, the prime mover and strategist behind the campaign against General Motors, and he was happy to take the assignment in Flint himself, rather than pass it on to a younger man.

Mortimer was a controversial person, repeatedly accused of being a communist or a communist sympathizer. But he fitted no stereotype, was friendly, likable, and inspired confidence. Neat, bright-looking, with deep-blue eyes, glasses, a receding forehead, and carefully combed hair, he could have passed for a good-humored professor. Unlike Martin, whose work experience in the auto factories was limited to a few weeks, Mort had unionism virtually in his genes. His mother was a Welsh farm girl who had pitched hay like a man; his father a devout Englishman who had worked in the Welsh coal mines before coming to Philadelphia in 1881, the day President Garfield died.

At the age of twelve Mortimer had gone to work in the coal fields of Clearfield County, Pennsylvania, at the generous wage of seven cents per hour. Like his father he was a devout union man. After a half-dozen years in the pits he shifted to a United States Steel plant in Lorain, Ohio, then worked as a teamster, a railroad brakeman, and finally, in 1917, began running a drill press with the White Motor Company in Cleveland, which manufactured trucks and buses. Taking this position turned out to be a piece of good luck, for while White Motor was no paradise, its working conditions, according to Mortimer himself, were a few degrees better than those of other firms, and its wages about ten cents an hour higher. Thomas White, founder of the company (which first produced roller skates) and his son Walter were open-minded men of good will and followed what could be called a "paternal" policy regarding their employees. One day in 1920 during a philosophical discussion with the production manager, Mor-

timer was asked "Are you a Socialist?" and replied quite frankly that
he was. Almost anywhere else that reply would have led to discharge,
but not at White Motor. In spite of such benevolence, there was no
true, independent union at White, only a company union, but Mortimer
had never worked anywhere without becoming involved. He was soon
a member of the "shop committee," representing the transmission
machine department.

For a decade Mortimer did his job, for the most part quietly, and
raised a family. He did needle the company at shop committee meetings, but saw no opportunity to form a legitimate union. The Depression changed matters. And, the company meanwhile had undergone
some changes in management. Conditions had deteriorated to the point
where most people were chafing at the bit over the short work weeks.
In the summer of 1932, with the help of a few trusted friends,
Mortimer enrolled half the shop in a bona fide union, which he at first
affiliated with communist-led Trade Union Unity League, then
transferred it to the AFL Federal Local 18463. It soon showed itself
to be one of the most effective of the new organizations, winning a
fifty cent per hour minimum wage for its members at a time when the
national scale set by the NRA was forty-three cents. Mortimer was
elected its president in mid-1934.

With Local 18463 as a base, he federated the other auto unions in
Cleveland into a Cleveland Auto Council (against the wishes of the
AFL, needless to say) and began publishing a regular newspaper
The United Auto Worker. It was on his initiative that three national
conferences were called in 1934–35 to exert pressures that ultimately caused Bill Green to issue to auto workers a limited national
charter. After this, Mortimer was chosen chairman of a protest committee of five to demand from the AFL executive council the additional right to elect the UAW's officers. Though his mission failed, he
worked closely with his inner-union rivals, Martin and Ed Hall to remove Dillon at the 1936 convention. And it was this triumph that
finally liberated the auto militants from AFL shackles. It was at this
same convention, incidentally, that the brash, twenty-eight-year-old
socialist, Walter Reuther, representing a local of only thirteen members, was inducted onto the UAW's executive board. He and his
brothers, Victor and Roy—especially the latter—were to play an important role in the forthcoming battle of Flint.

Mortimer's strategy for bringing General Motors to reasonable terms
for his UAW workers was as simple as it was audacious. The battle was
to be quick and decisive, concluded victoriously within a half year. In
that short period, of course, it would be impossible to enroll all the
auto workers in General Motors' shops. But Mortimer planned to con-

centrate on two key plants, Fisher Body number one in Flint, and Fisher Body in Cleveland, which between them stamped out all the bodies for Buicks, Oldsmobiles, Pontiacs, and Chevrolets. Once these two factories were closed down it would become impossible for GM to assemble automobiles, and most of the other plants would grind to a halt. The date for a national strike was set for January 1, 1937, the day a liberal Democrat, Frank Murphy, was expected to replace the reactionary Republican, Frank Fitzgerald, as governor of Michigan. January 1 would also be two weeks after the GM workers pocketed their fifty-dollar Christmas bonuses.

No realist would have expected this neat little plan to work. Fisher One in Flint had 8,000 employees, all of whom were required to belong to the company union, the International Motors Association, and many hundreds of whom were members of a viciously anti-union organization, the Black Legion, which did not hesitate to beat or shoot union organizers, radicals, blacks, Jews, and Catholics. Hundreds of leftists and active unionists had been fingered and fired by the company in previous union organization efforts. The city fathers had passed ordinances making it illegal to distribute leaflets, or to use sound trucks. Mortimer himself after being told in Flint that he would "be carried out in a wooden box," was followed persistently by company detectives. Moreover, the leadership of Flint's UAW Local 156 was generally distrusted by the workers because it was known to be filled with stool pigeons.

Nonetheless, Mortimer overcame all these obstacles. He established what in effect was a guerrilla movement. Bypassing the suspect local union leaders, he compiled a list from the Flint city directory and from old membership files of 5,000 General Motors auto workers, and began sending them weekly letters, each one arguing a specific UAW issue, of obvious concern to any auto worker. Recipients were asked to fill out UAW membership applications to be mailed back to the office of UAW secretary-treasurer George Addes, so that no one but Mortimer and Addes would see them. Those workers who wanted to talk with Mortimer personally were asked to indicate this in a box at the end of the letter and were then visited at their homes. Where Mortimer felt he had trustworthy contacts, he organized small meetings in private homes. On one occasion he met a group of eighteen black workers from the Buick foundry in a tiny church at midnight and with only a small candle burning, so that no one on the outside would be aware of the gathering. Slowly, then, he built clandestine UAW organization nuclei in each of the plants, waiting for the proper moment to act on his instructions.

Mortimer was fortunate that there were a sizable number of communists in the UAW he could rely on, as well as Trotskyists and socialists, none of whom needed any prodding to become active in the union. The leftist movements in the country were then on the upswing. The Communist Party, for example, had grown from 7,500 members in 1930 to 41,000 in 1936, with perhaps a million additional sympathizers and friends. There were, then, many leftists constantly in and out of the plants, just waiting to be called on to express their sentiments, and Mortimer, with his own radical ties, was able to engage their services. When he couldn't find anyone, for instance, to distribute the UAW newspaper at factory gates, he enlisted an unemployed communist, who had been fired by GM, and his militant wife. Within the Fisher One plant he formed a union nucleus of three friends, Bud Simons, Walter Moore, and Joe Devitt, all close to the communists. In Flint's Chevrolet No. Four plant there was a Trotskyite named Kermit Johnson who would play a major role in the Chevy Four sitdown. In addition, on call were young radicals who could be summoned in from other cities, each of whom had his own contacts in Flint. One of them was Roy Reuther, a member of the left-wing in the Socialist Party. Another, of general leftist persuasion, was Robert Travis of Toledo. The presence of such men aggravated the tensions with conservative elements in the union, who castigated Mort for building a "Red empire." But they were brilliant strategists, and above all dedicated to the union cause.

III

Mortimer left Flint in October 1936, after planting the seeds for an uprising, primarily to avoid continued conflict with Homer Martin, a narrow-minded colleague who constantly feared rivalry. But he was in and out of Flint thereafter, and would play a key role with John L. Lewis, John Brophy, and Martin in eventually negotiating a labor-management settlement. Before agreeing to shift locale, Mortimer insisted that his close associate, Bob Travis, replace him as director of the drive, and in winning approval for his designee assured a continuation of his own strategy and tactics.

Bob Travis, thirty years old, just under six feet tall, a handsome man with blue eyes and brownish hair, was universally liked, even by those who had reservations about his politics. Quick to make decisions, an extrovert by nature, he was neither imperious nor volatile—he could discuss issues calmly even with his worst enemies. Born in Toledo in February 1906, Travis like Mortimer and the Reuther brothers became saturated in radicalism early, at the family table. His father, a shoe salesman, was a devotee of Eugene Debs, socialism and especially racial equality. Bob, the third of seven children, attended two years of high school in Toledo and then went to work as a bullard operator at Chevrolet, a local plant with about 1,800 workers. He was on the picket line during the 1934 Auto-Lite strike, and a year later was one of the leaders of the indecisive nine-week walkout in his own Chevy plant, which gained a four-cents per hour raise and partial union recognition. Though this strike and its results fell short of the union's goals, it laid the basis for one of the few stable organizations in the GM chain. And this was a noteworthy achievement in light of the previous failure of 5,000 Fisher One strikers at Flint to win the reinstatement of twenty-five discharged activists, and the fizzling out of stoppages by 30,000 other GM workers. As president of the Toledo UAW union, Travis ranged far and wide to unionize the whole city. In addition to auto workers his local brought into the fold women in a dress shop, cafeteria workers, laborers in a rubber factory, even employees of the Harbauer Ketchup plant, all of whom were later turned over to other unions. At the 1935 AFL convention Travis moved to reject Bill Green's restricted charter, a sin for which the AFL president punished him—and Mortimer—by refusing to allow them any leadership position in the national UAW.

A week or two after Travis was put in charge of the UAW campaign at Flint, Mortimer's earlier seeding on behalf of the union paid its first dividend. The UAW was still underground, hiding its membership lists, recruiting by ones and twos, waiting for the propitious moment to come out into the open. There are two ways to organize a union: one is to bring in members one at a time until by a process of accretion a majority among the local workers is secured; the other is to keep a small cadre functioning secretly until a particularly strongly felt grievance thrusts hundreds or thousands of workers toward the union in one grand sweep.

Such a major grievance arose in November when Fisher One supervisors cut a three-man crew to two. The three men, including two brothers named Perkins sat sullenly through their shift refusing to work. The next day, upon entering the plant, they were called into the employment office and fired. This was just the kind of situation and moment Bud Simons had prepared for. He and his committee ran through various departments shouting that the "Perkins boys were fired! Nobody starts working." A sitdown by seven hundred men began and continued while a group of eighteen—now openly identified as representing the UAW—negotiated the immediate reinstatement of the discharged men. One of the Perkins brothers, out on a date, had to be tracked down that night by the Flint police and brought back to the plant before his fellow workers would resume working. By the following afternoon word of the situation had spread throughout the city, and hundreds of men flocked to the cause. Travis himself signed up fifty workers from Fisher Two in a nearby beer hall. That evening Mortimer came back from Detroit to address an overflow meeting of workers, the first public gathering since the campaign began.

Another incident that sparked workers' confidence in the union and overcame their fears of involvement with it was the exposure in late December of two Corporations Auxiliary spies, one of whom had been responsible for the recent discharge of some active unionists at Chevrolet. At the first open meeting of the Chevrolet division of Local 156, attended by 150 workers, Roy Reuther dramatically called out the names of the two spies, and had one of them escorted home, under guard, to relinquish the union records in his possession. The names of these agents had been passed to Travis and Reuther by the LaFollette Committee staff. The fact that the UAW could lay its hands on such information gave the membership a feeling of power and reassurance.

Other sources of encouragement were UAW victories elsewhere. Wherever one turned, it seemed, the union was conducting a sitdown strike—and not faring badly at all. There was the seven-day sitdown by 1,500 workers at the Bendix Products plant in South Bend in November, which gained the strikers a number of major concessions. There was the fourteen-day sitdown of 2,000 at Midland Steel Products in Detroit, a plant which supplied frames for Ford, Plymouth, and other automobile manufacturers. The main provisions agreed to in negotiations with Mortimer, Dick Frankensteen, and Adolph Germer were not put into writing because the employer was afraid of reprisals by the major auto and steel firms. But the UAW won every single one of its demands—recognition, seniority, raises.

There was also the sitdown at the Kelsey-Hayes plant in Detroit, organized by Walter Reuther, with his brother Victor acting as the main agitator inside the factory. When word came down to the union leadership after nine or ten days that Ford, for whom Kelsey-Hayes produced wheels, was going to remove its dies from the plant, Frankensteen sent in "Flying Squadrons" from his own Dodge local, and at Reuther's request, a tough young teamster, Jimmy Hoffa, sent a detachment of truck drivers to guard the gates. Inside the factory an associate of Reuther's, George Edwards, had the sitdowners build three-foot walls of steel containers loaded with castings. Placed at the main gates, they effectively prevented Ford from getting his dies.

Kelsey-Hayes settled with the union for a seventy-five-cents-an-hour minimum wage, recognition of UAW stewards and other concessions. Even at that, however, the offer was almost rejected. The sitdowners were so "fired up," said a UAW publicist, Frank Winn, that Reuther was able to sell the proposal to his own demanding members only on the grounds that it was "just an armed truce, because we had to clear the decks for General Motors."

IV

The time was now at hand for the finale—or at least one finale. Mortimer, Travis, and Roy Reuther, it will be recalled, had planned a pincer movement by the union to begin with the New Year and to center on the two Fisher body plants in Flint and Cleveland, the "mother plants" which produced three fourths of the body stampings for the empire, and whose closing would immobilize GM. Travis and Roy Reuther held to this strategy even in the face of disheartening losses, such as multiple discharges at one of the Chevrolet plants. They would not be goaded or provoked to alter their planned course.

But in Atlanta, Fred Pieper, one of Homer Martin's supporters and therefore hostile to the Mortimer-Travis-Reuther leadership axis, jumped the gun by calling a strike at the southern plant early in November. There was certainly good reason for the stoppage—a 20 per cent cut in wage rates, as well as the firing of men for wearing union buttons—but it was like one platoon falling out of ranks with a division. Then, another strike broke out a few weeks later at a GM plant in Kansas City, where a worker named Roy Davis was fired for hurdling over a conveyor line to save himself a roundabout walk of 300 yards to the toilet. Pieper was adamant in calling for an immediate national strike, and Mortimer and his allies on the International Union's executive board had their hands full fighting it. The board's vote to keep to the original strike target date, New Year's Day 1937, was a bare seven to six.

Even after this vote, the all-out clash against GM began three days early. On December 28, Travis, Mortimer, and the editor of the union paper, Henry Kraus, were sitting in Travis' room at the Hotel Dresden in Flint, when a call came through from Cleveland with the message that an unexpected sitdown had started at Fisher, the other pivotal plant in Mortimer's blueprint. It had begun over a relatively trivial matter, the postponement by the company of a meeting with the union to discuss wage-slashing grievances, scheduled for the afternoon. But it was the last straw for 7,000 men and women disgusted with cuts in piecework rates and a plethora of other grievances. "To hell with this stalling," someone shouted, and in a few moments the power in the plant was shut off and the whole place gripped with silence. Most of the workers simply went home. But a thousand men and women remained for the sitdown that ensued.

Just as the UAW considered a shutdown at Cleveland-Fisher absolutely necessary to its over-all strategy, GM was equally as anxious to keep the plant working. Plant Manager Lincoln Scafe and Cleveland Mayor Harold Burton (later a Supreme Court Justice) asserted that the dispute was "local" and tried to effect immediate negotiations for a settlement. Mortimer, Travis and the UAW leadership, however, realized they were the heirs of a bonanza. Three days early or not, one of the two plants they were banking on in their strategy had been closed. Hastening to Cleveland on the first train available, Mortimer told the assembled local reporters that there would be "no settlement without a national agreement." The long awaited battle had begun.

Two days later, on the thirtieth, it spread to Flint. That evening Travis received a call from John ("Chink") Ananich of Fisher One telling him that the company was moving dies out of the plant. Four or five freight cars had been stationed at the loading dock to haul the equipment elsewhere. This transferring of equipment and operations to places where labor relations were less turbulent was standard practice for General Motors in the 1930s, in its attempts to cauterize "trouble spots." It had been done in Travis' own plant in Toledo, as well as elsewhere, costing thousands of workers long-held jobs. The removal of dies from Fisher One clearly constituted an emergency that might upset the whole strategy that Travis and his friends were trying to implement. Production of bodies would continue from other plants to which the dies were to be transferred and where the union was weaker. Across from Fisher One, at the union hall, an office girl turned on the "flicker"—a 200-watt bulb which advised key unionists of a crisis and was a signal to them to come to a special meeting. At lunchtime, 8 P.M., Travis proposed to the packed hall that they seize the plant, a proposal that needed little seconding. Shortly thereafter while Travis, Roy Reuther, and Kraus waited outside the plant for a few tense moments, a majority of the 3,000 workers at Fisher One completed the operation. "Chink" Ananich yelled out from a third-floor window: "Hooray, Bob! She's ours." There had been no problems; neither the plant police nor anyone else had dared interfere. A few hours later, a grievance over the transfer of two employees at Fisher Two led to the occupation of a smaller shop two miles across town.

Before long, as in so many other labor wars, someone composed a bit of doggerel, this one to the tune of "The Martins and the Coys," that memorialized the great events:

> Now this strike it started one bright Wednesday evening
>> When they loaded up a box car full of dies.
> When the union boys they stopped them,
>> And the railroad workers backed them,
> The officials in the office were surprised.
>
> These four-thousand union boys,
>> Oh, they sure made lots of noise,
> They decided then and there to shut down tight.
>> In the office they got snooty,
> So we started picket duty,
>> Now the Fisher Body shop is on a strike.

Lyrics for a more widely known song were later written by the UAW's lawyer, Maurice Sugar, epitomizing the union's feeling of power. Its chorus went:

> When they tie the can to a union man,
>> Sit down! Sit down!
> When they give him the sack they'll take him back,
>> Sit down! Sit down!
> When the speed-up comes, just twiddle your thumbs,
>> Sit down! Sit down!
> When the boss won't talk don't take a walk,
>> Sit down! Sit down!

Strictly speaking a sitdown—the occupation of corporate private property—was illegal, but legal or not it was contagious. The Wobblies had tried the tactic briefly in 1906 at General Electric in Schenectady. Workers in Italy had used the sit-in as a revolutionary weapon in 1919. Prior to Flint, coal miners in Pecs, Hungary, Terbovlye, Yugoslavia and Katowice, Poland, copper miners in Huelva, Spain, and a million French workers had adopted the sit-in technique, as well as laborers at the Hormel packinghouse plant in Austin, Minnesota, at Bendix, Kelsey-Hayes, Midland Steel, Hercules Motor in Canton, Ohio, and innumerable rubber factories. From 1935 to 1937 there were nine hundred such sitdowns, few of them of such duration as the Flint sitdown, but the vast majority of them were similarly successful. There was no specific person who could claim exclusive invention of the tactic; it was an action which flowed naturally from circumstance. Outside pickets, during the 1933–35 strike waves, had been beaten and arrested, maimed, and killed in large numbers. It was no wonder, then, that after many brushes with the law in which police, troops, and common thugs attacked pickets with everything from brickbats and tear gas to machine guns, the thought occurred to many unionists that it would be infinitely easier on their skulls and their nostrils to stay inside. There on a familiar and sheltered terrain they were not so vulnerable, and they knew where they could hide if necessary. Moreover the corporations would think twice before subjecting their expensive machinery to the inevitable damage of warfare with the workers. The sitdown clearly was invented in self-defense against physical assault, and while it lasted—before Lewis put a stop to it—it gave American industry's management its worst headache. As a refinement of the strike technique, it was the most effective weapon American labor had ever used.

v

Organizing the forty-four-day stay-in at Flint was a complicated matter. The 500 to 1,000 men holed up at Fisher One (women were sent home) had to be molded from anarchy into a disciplined force, had to be fed and be offered opportunities for relaxation. As his first act, Bud Simons enlarged his plant committee to include representatives from each department. This committee had over-all command of the strike, subject to review at the membership meetings which convened each night. The workers themselves were divided into "families" of fifteen, each headed by a "captain," each finding its own nook to set up house. Sleeping facilities were either car-cushion wadding placed on the floor, or the insides of unfinished auto bodies, which were lovingly referred to as "Mills Hotel" or "Hotel Astor." Food was prepared by a group of women outside the factory and brought in; three warm meals were served daily and coffee and sandwiches made available around the clock. Every man was required to shower each day and to put in six hours of work—in the kitchen, on patrol duty at the gates, sweeping up, etc. For relaxation there was ping-pong in the basement cafeteria, cards, checkers, books and magazines, and even some football and boxing. Two UAW educators taught classes on labor history, how to conduct a meeting and other relevant union subjects. Each evening before the daily meeting, there was an hour of singing and of entertainment, most of it provided by sympathetic artists outside. Thus what had begun as an unformed mass was converted into a community.

The sitdowners recognized the urgency of protecting General Motors' property, for if the machinery were abused or the plant made into a pig sty, intervention by the military and police would be inevitable. Not even Governor Murphy or President Roosevelt could have resisted management pressures. A special patrol was organized therefore to keep "law and order." Every hour it made a half-hour tour of the plant to see that no one was drinking or smuggling in liquor, that there were no fights and that no false rumors were being spread. The plant and rest rooms were kept meticulously clean and machines and equipment serviced when necessary. There was so little disorder and disharmony that at first after the plant was shut down, the union permitted foremen and company police to remain in the factory. But on New Year's Eve, the corporation people brought in liquor which they passed around clandestinely, as well as two prostitutes, also "passed around" clandestinely. In addition, so many strikers asked permission to leave the plant to continue celebrations that night that the company could have retaken Fisher One had it so stirred itself. After that the foremen and company police were expelled, and discipline among the strikers was severely tightened.

As Mortimer had anticipated, the simultaneous strikes at the Fisher plants in Flint and Cleveland had a progressively paralyzing effect on all GM operations. In the first week, the corporation itself suspended production at Delco-Remy, AC Sparkplug, Pontiac, Oldsmobile, and assembly lines at Buick and Chevrolet. And the sitdown continued to hedgehop to other sections of the GM domain as a mood of contagion and increasing worker excitement took hold. Many of these plants would have been forced by the shortages of parts to close anyway, but there was a restive spirit at work which drove the unionists to act first. It seemingly became a matter of honor to beat the company to the punch and sit in. Atlanta and Kansas City were already striking. On December 31, the Guide Lamp Plant in Anderson, Indiana, where Vic Reuther had readied unionist support, was caught in the swirl of stay-ins, to be followed the same day by a stoppage at Norwood, Ohio (near Cincinnati), and in the following few days by similar sitdowns at Toledo-Chevrolet, Ternstedt in Detroit, Janesville-Fisher, Fleetwood, and Cadillac in Detroit. As of January 11, three quarters of all of General Motors' blue-collar employees were idle, by their own or through the firm's actions.

Stunned, the colossus of the auto industry, which had earned profits of $228 million in 1936, struck back early and with time-tested methods, but a sitdown was not as easy to contend with as a traditional strike. Three days after it began, GM's attorneys appeared before Judge Edward D. Black of the Circuit Court of Genesee County and quickly secured an injunction ordering the sitdowners not only to leave the plant but to refrain from picketing once outside. Sheriff Thomas Wolcott, a former butcher with a heavy paunch, deputized one hundred men and together with sixty company police tried to serve his papers. But it was not so simply accomplished. The men at Fisher One refused to find Bud Simons or Walter Moore for him, and playfully heckled the sheriff off the speaker's platform. He gave them a half hour "to clear out of here," but he knew, as he left to the strains of "Solidarity Forever," that this could not be accomplished with the small force he had at hand. The deputies would have been lured into a dozen traps in the plant and would also have been attacked from the street by thousands of men the UAW was now capable of mobilizing from Detroit, Toledo, Saginaw, and Flint itself.

Sheriff Wolcott had no better luck trying to serve papers on the national officers of the UAW who were in Flint that late December day for a conference. While Adolph Germer engaged the sheriff in conversation, the officers sneaked down a fire escape. No gains were made by management from the injunction anyway. Lee Pressman, the CIO's national counsel, made public the fact that Judge Black owned 3,365 shares of GM stock, worth $219,000, and was therefore in clear violation of section 13888 of the Michigan legal code which prohibited a judge from participating in "any case or proceeding in which he is a party or in which he is interested." The GM lawyers had to transfer their case to another court, where it languished for three critical weeks.

Normally at such a juncture a prestigious corporation like General Motors would appeal to the governor or President for troops, as happened so frequently in earlier strikes. But in the climate of the 1930s it was impolitic for a liberal politician to respond by resorting to the strikebreaking techniques of 1894 or 1919. Governor Frank Murphy, carried into office by the Roosevelt landslide, after strong endorsement by the UAW, denied GM requests for calling out the state militia, trying instead to bring the parties together for negotiations, as did President Roosevelt and Secretary of Labor Frances Perkins.

Nor could GM depend on John L. Lewis to help bail them out, as William Green had done—advertently or inadvertently—for corporations in the past. Lewis was a moderate and what is euphemistically called "responsible." He was philosophically opposed to the seizure of capitalist property, and eventually did put an end to the sitdown wave. But he was realistic enough to know that the whole future of the CIO depended on the success of this pivotal strike. "The CIO," he stated on December 31, "stands squarely behind these sitdowns," and when GM vice-president William S. Knudsen demanded the plants be evacuated before negotiations began, Lewis thundered back that the only way to end the sitdown was to grant a national contract. It came with ill grace for a corporation which was itself violating the Wagner Act, said Lewis, to talk about the illegal acts of others. He wired the UAW a pledge from the CIO of whatever funds it needed, and then came through with considerable sums from the UMWA, the Amalgamated Clothing Workers and other CIO union treasuries.

Though disappointed by Lewis' attitude and by the procrastination of Murphy and Roosevelt, the General Motors executives did not lose their aplomb. It did not seem possible to them that six hundred sit-downers in two Flint body plants could capture so many world head-lines and cause so much mischief. (Those at Cleveland-Fisher had left their factory because they were confident it could not be re-opened.) The company proceeded along the customary path toward breaking a strike, confident it would succeed. The first task was a back-to-work movement. (It was deemed too risky to bring in outside strikebreakers.) The second task was to manufacture an act of vio-lence that would pressure Governor Murphy to change his decision not to use force.

Early in the strike, GM president Alfred P. Sloan dispatched a paternalistic letter to all company employees, assuring them of his concern for their welfare and promising to protect them from the "labor union dictators" who were trying to exact "tribute" for the right to work. Following the sending of the letter, Flint's city manager, James Barringer, a claque for GM, brought together those company union representatives classified as "reliable," and formed them into the "Flint Alliance," dedicated to "the security of our jobs, our homes, and our community." George Boysen, a friend of Barringer's, a former mayor of Flint and an ex-paymaster at Buick, was engaged to "smother" the strike movement, "restore peace in Flint and men and women to their jobs." Though currently the manager of a small manu-facturing company, Boysen posed as the spokesman for the aggrieved auto employees. Within twenty-four hours after opening offices in the center of town he claimed that 15,000 of Flint's proletariat had signed applications to join the alliance, as well as petitions pledging loyalty to management. Whether or not this impressive figure was an exag-geration, the signatures they did have had of course been solicited in a blitzkrieg directed by GM's superintendents and foremen, and with not a few threats of discharge to the workers approached. Boysen hired a public relations expert from New York and began making the now-familiar charges that the strike was begun by "communists" and "outside agitators" who were attempting to impose the will of a "radi-cal" minority on an "American" majority. This refrain was as usual echoed by the newspapers, also by a Catholic bishop in Detroit who saw "Soviet planning" behind the sitdowns, and by John P. Frey, chief of the AFL metal trades' department, who assured GM he had "no quarrel" with the corporation and was sending craftsmen in Cleveland under his jurisdiction back to work. For the time being the Flint Alliance contented itself with enrolling GM workers and spawning a few relatively minor acts of intimidation and violence. But it was preparing the way for a major double-cross which, had it worked, might have cheated the UAW of its victory.

The next gambit against the strike was more direct, an amazingly maladroit effort by GM and the police to evict the sitdowners in the small Fisher Two shop, resulting in the most famous skirmish in CIO history—the Battle of Bulls' Run, or the Battle of the Running Bulls. There was no need to eject the Fisher Two men because this factory had no strategic significance—its particular work was duplicated in a dozen other plants throughout the country. But GM needed to hammer home an object lesson for its employees, and Fisher Two was far more vulnerable and conquerable than the much more important Fisher One. For one thing, it was held by strikers only tenuously, since company guards were still present on the ground floor and still controlled the entrances. As a matter of fact it was only by the sufferance of these guards that union messengers were permitted to bring food to the sitdowners, clustered on the second floor under the leadership of William (Red) Mundale. Moreover, at this juncture, as a Pinkerton spy advised the company, there were only 100 men in the small plant.

The eviction plan was simple: first to deny heat and food to the strikers, second to find and use a pretext for the physical siege. GM had continued heating the factory from the time the strike began, not out of concern for the sitdowners so much as to prevent the freezing of its water pipes and damage to delicate equipment. Now in sixteen-degree weather on January 11, 1937, and with temperatures due to fall further, it shut off the heat. A few hours later, union supporters carrying the evening dinner to sitdowners were denied entry to the plant—for the first time. Anxious to avoid a fight the pickets outside raised a twenty-four-foot ladder to the second-floor windows, and tried to haul the food in that way. The guards, however, formed a phalanx and captured the ladder.

On hearing of the developments at Fisher Two, Bob Travis, Roy Reuther, Victor Reuther (in a sound car with a loud-speaker) and hundreds of experienced men, from Travis' local in Toledo and a few from Norwood, Ohio, hurried to the scene for the next engagement. Inside the factory, meanwhile, a squad of twenty tough young men, armed with billy clubs the strikers themselves had manufactured for just such an emergency, descended the stairs to demand from the captain of the guards the key to the front gate. When they were refused they broke down the locks on the gate.

This was a minor skirmish, but it buoyed strikers' spirits. It also gave the corporation the pretext to act that it had been waiting for. The handful of company guards on the ground floor had retreated sheepishly into the women's washroom during the struggle for the gate, and their captain had telephoned police headquarters to say that they had been "kidnaped." It was now up to the deputies and police—some of whose commanders had been specially primed for this confrontation and were eagerly awaiting it—to rescue the "kidnaped" guards, and in the process retake the factory. Police squad cars screeched down Chevrolet Avenue and the sheriff, with a dozen deputies dressed in riot gear, all converged on Fisher Two. For the next five hours there, there was a state of bedlam.

Over the Fisher Two sound system Victor Reuther cried out: "Pickets, back to your posts! Men in the plant, get your fire hoses going!" As members of the charge-up police force began releasing tear gas into the plant and at the pickets, women with children first rushed to a nearby restaurant, then returned to stand with their men. Serious as events became, there were elements of comedy in the situation. The tear gas, for instance, was blown back at the cops by a favorable wind—for the strikers—blowing from the north. Mundale's men dragged one fire hose to the main door and another to an upstairs window, and began hosing the cops away while other strikers inside and out, threw two-pound automobile-door hinges at them. The skirmish ended in a few minutes when the police officers, their uniforms freezing on their bodies, retreated. Unionists cried out in wild joy—and prepared themselves for the next battle, dumping hinges, empty soda-pop, and milk bottles on the sidewalk for the use of the pickets outside.

About 9 P.M. half of Flint's police force, about fifty men, arrived for the second assault. Vic Reuther shouted: "We want peace. General Motors chose war. Give it to them." And the strikers did just that. Sheriff Wolcott's car was rocked back and forth—with the corpulent official and some of his deputies still in it—and overturned. Wolcott had all he could do to crawl out of it, and upon emerging finally was hit on the temple by a hinge, though he was not seriously hurt. Three other police cars were seized by the pickets. From the roof, sit-downers with home-made slingshots heaved hinges at the beleaguered police, and the outside pickets, after forming a barricade of automobiles between themselves and the police, hurled nuts, bolts, empty bottles, and an assortment of other missiles at them. The police never made it to the plant; they were pushed back to a bridge about 150 feet away.

Enraged by their setback, however, the police, who had used no rifles or pistols until then, reached for their weapons—against Wolcott's orders—and the engagement took a more serious turn. A sitdowner on the roof shouted "I've been hit," and then there was another and another similar cry, as some bullets and buckshot came from the Chevrolet plant across the street. Bob Travis was carried off to Hurley Hospital with gas burns from a tear gas grenade. Fourteen union men were wounded, and thirty-six police were sent to the hospital for treatment. At midnight, five hours after the fighting had started, the police made another attempt to rush the plant and were again driven off by the strikers' high-pressure water hoses and a rain of missiles. The Battle of Bulls' Run was over—the Bulls had run. It was certainly not the fiercest engagement in the history of labor wars—not as violent as Pittsburgh in 1877 or Homestead in 1892—but it presaged, though it did not assure, labor's pivotal victory in Flint. In fact, GM made no further effort to retake any of its factories by force. Vice-president Knudsen explained to all who would listen that "We are not going to attempt to shut off heat, light, and water. We never intended to."

VI

The sitdowners had won a major physical battle, but the strike was not over. An hour after the skirmish ended, Governor Murphy arrived at the Durant Hotel to talk to local authorities who had petitioned him to send the National Guard, and to Adolph Germer and Bob Travis. "Fourteen workers were carried away from the plant on stretchers," Travis told Murphy. "One will be dead before morning the doctors say. If one more worker is hurt there will be warfare on the streets of Flint." In spite of this prophecy, the Governor decided to bring in 1,500 Guardsmen to the city, but he still refused to accept the counsel of the Flint Alliance and the mayor, to dislodge the sitdowners.

At the union office next morning there was a double line of workers from all the GM plants waiting to sign UAW application cards and pay their initial dues. Many had sat glued to their radio the previous night, and had been thrilled vicariously by reports of workers like themselves giving the most prominent manufacturing company in the nation a bloody nose. At the base of the two hills in Flint where the fighting had taken place, 10,000 people gathered, many hundreds from Detroit, Lansing, Toledo, Cleveland, and South Bend, who had come to view the hallowed ground. From time to time someone would start up a chorus of "Solidarity Forever" and the words would ring thunderously through the crowd. No one expected trouble at this point from the militia (now housed in a schoolhouse in the center of town, rather than present at the plants), but no one would have run away from it either.

At Governor Murphy's invitation, representatives of both the strikers and GM met in his Lansing offices on January 14—Homer Martin, Wyndham Mortimer, and John Brophy for the union; Knudsen, John Thomas, GM's top corporate lawyer, and Donaldson Brown, a du Pont son-in-law, for the company. Eleven days before, (which seemed like a generation ago now), a national conference at Flint of GM unionists had designated a Board of Strategy composed of many of their leaders and had formulated eight demands. These included a national conference with the company, seniority rights in layoff and recall, reinstatement of those "unjustly discharged," an end to the speed-up, a six-hour day, a thirty-hour week, abolition of the piece work system, higher wages, and above all, recognition of the UAW as the "sole bargaining agent" for all GM factory workers. In Governor Murphy's office, however, the UAW negotiators did not press any of these demands; at this point they were only seeking conditions under which to begin negotiating for them. After sixteen hours of talks, a wan-looking governor emerged from the meeting and announced an agreement. The union would evacuate the struck GM plants all over the nation not later than the following Sunday, January 17; the company pledged not to resume operations or remove dies or equipment for at least fifteen days. For many, including Bob Travis and his staff, the "truce" was a letdown—they had expected substantive concessions, especially on the issue of "sole" bargaining rights for the UAW. Top union officials, however, were not sure they could squeeze such gains from the company at this point.

What the results of the strike might have been if it had ended at this point, is difficult to say, but it soon became clear that GM officials had not yet given up their offensive. The UAW and the CIO went ahead with plans to vacate all the GM plants. But the company and local authorities responded with provocation and repression. The Guide Lamp shop in Anderson, Indiana, was the first GM plant emptied. Its new picket lines outside the factory, however, were immediately attacked by police and deputized foremen, who scattered the union forces. After leaving company factories in Detroit, some workers received telegrams to return to work the following Monday, in patent disregard by management of the truce agreement not to operate. Great tension prevailed in Flint, where Travis, Roy and Vic Reuther, Herb Kraus, and three rubber unionists (who fled the state) were arraigned for inciting to riot. Though charges originally leveled against the fourteen wounded strikers from the Battle of The

Running Bulls were dropped, prosecutor Joseph Joseph secured 300 "John Doe warrants" to be served *carte blanche* on other strikers.

There was enough seriousness to all of these incidents to cause worry on the part of the workers, but the UAW enthusiasts, still reveling in the victory of Bulls' Run, were confident in their belief that further victories lay ahead. On Saturday the sixteenth, the sitdowners in both Fisher plants in Flint, along with hundreds of freeloading guests, enjoyed a roast chicken dinner. Sunday, they were scheduled to leave the premises, with bands playing and flags flying, and hold a massive demonstration. Sunday morning, however, a United Press reporter gave Bob Travis a copy of a press release he had stolen from the Flint Alliance offices, the content of which was supposed to have been kept secret until after the evacuation. The release proclaimed that George Boysen of the alliance had asked GM's Knudsen to enter into collective bargaining talks for "the great majority of your employees," and that Knudsen had agreed.

The import of this cordial exchange between GM and its hireling was obvious. The central demand of the UAW auto workers had been "sole" collective bargaining rights. Insistence on the word "sole" was predicated on the firm belief that unless the UAW were to be the exclusive bargaining agent, the corporation would divide the workers by bargaining with company-dominated unions such as the Flint Alliance, with AFL craft organizations and with other, more controllable union groups. GM might in that case, for instance, grant the alliance a seven-cents-per-hour raise while giving UAW only five cents; or it might settle a few grievances favorably with its own "union" creation, while being resistant to UAW grievances. In the resulting chaos, the power of the UAW, the legitimate organization, would be shredded to ribbons. The word "sole," therefore was more than a rhetorical expression, it was the very essence of the UAW-GM conflict. In the truce settlement the corporation had pledged to negotiate with the UAW on this issue of "sole" collective bargaining rights. But Knudsen's secret assurances to Boysen that he was ready to talk with "your group or any group of employees" were a rejection in advance of negotiations of the UAW's primary objective. One could be sure that in the near future Knudsen would sign agreements with the Flint Alliance and "alliances" in other cities that would leave the bona fide union virtually impotent.

Travis was outraged by the broken promise. Sunday morning, Wyndham Mortimer was standing by at Fisher One to lead the parade of workers coming out, with Vic Reuther at Fisher Two ready to do the same. But after consulting with Lewis' representative, John Brophy, Travis sent them messages to rescind plans for evacuation of the plants. The sitdowners, cynical about the truce to begin with, were not unhappy when Mortimer announced a resumption of the stay-in to 5,000 people inside and outside Fisher One. He was given a tumultuous ovation.

Everything, then, was now back to the former strike-peak conditions, except that both sides dug in with more determination than ever. In Washington, John L. Lewis denounced General Motors for "a barefaced violation of the armistice," and called on President Roosevelt, much to the President's discomfiture "to help the workers in every reasonable way."

But in the dozens of motor cities, GM launched a vigorous counterthrust. Even though the shortage of workers made it impossible to assemble complete cars (weekly output by GM had slumped from 31,830 autos to 6,100), the company reopened some plants, where there were no sit-ins, and simply stockpiled parts and motors. This time, however, the number of company guards at these plants were increased and hundreds of "loyal workers" were armed for defense against possible sitdowns. Some of the loyalists even slept overnight in the factories. The Flint Alliance distributed leaflets and held meetings urging workers to "direct and forceful action to keep GM in operation." At a Cadillac plant in Detroit, police attacked former sitdowners, now doing their picketing outside, and literally cracked a number of skulls. In Anderson, Indiana, a mob led by the GM plant manager himself dispersed the picket line outside the factory and went so far as to invade the local UAW union headquarters. A half-dozen UAW organizers at Bay City, Michigan, were followed by vigilantes to Saginaw and severely beaten in the lobby of the Bancroft Hotel, while police stood by without interceding at all. To escape their tormentors, the union men finally jumped into a Yellow cab, and with police cars ahead and behind them, raced out of town at sixty miles an hour. When the cab got to Flint, however, a sedan driven by vigilantes insinuated itself into the procession and forced the taxi off the road into a telephone pole. Three of the UAW organizers were so badly injured that they were hospitalized for several months. In addition to these incidents, and perhaps more serious, was the multiplication of discharges of UAW members for such offenses as wearing union buttons. At the end of the month, too, the GM lawyers went back to court, the court of Justice Paul V. Gadola, to renew their request for an injunction against the UAW.

With union morale skidding and the strike evidently past its peak of strength, the strategists at the Pengally Building union headquarters realized that something new and dramatic was needed to revitalize the sitdown. Planning their moves as quietly and carefully as generals organizing a coup d'état, the UAW leaders decided to capture another equally vital shop in the GM chain, Chevy Four. The Chevrolet complex in Flint comprised nine factories and a power station, covering eighty acres. Three of the plants, Chevy Four, Six and Nine, were arranged in a triangle, each a few hundred yards from the other. Chevy Nine produced ball bearings and was not particularly important to the over-all manufacturing scheme. Chevy Six was similarly peripheral in importance except for a strong union contingent. But it was Chevy Four that produced the motors without which a single Chevrolet could not be assembled. The UAW tactical plan for attacking the complex, devised by Travis, was to create a diversion action at Chevy Nine so that the company would draw its guards away from other plants to the besieged ball-bearing shop. In the meantime three hundred men from Chevy Six would be assembled to help the relatively weak UAW force at Chevy Four seize that plant, the main object of all these maneuvers.

Taking only three young unionists into his confidence, besides Roy Reuther and a few other trustworthy leaders, Travis let the word seep out through known stool pigeons that there would be a sitdown at Chevy Nine the next day, in protest against the firing of three men for various union activities. On Monday afternoon February 1, thousands of UAW men and a sizable group from its Women's Auxiliary proceeded to the ball-bearing plant just before the day shift was going home and the second shift coming on. As Travis had expected, GM did concentrate its guards at Chevy Nine. At 3:20 P.M., unionists inside gathered at the cafeteria and from there fanned out into the shop shouting, "Strike, strike." In the next half hour there were dozens of fights in the center of the factory, and though the UAW men were badly outnumbered, they held out with grim determination. Two were knocked unconscious. Guards filled the shop with tear gas, while women on the sidewalk smashed windows to let air in for their besieged men. Promptly, after forty minutes, as planned, the UAW members took their injured comrades and marched out of Chevy Nine. They had done their job.

But as so often happens even in the best-laid plans, the forty-minute diversion to accomplish the main objective was not long enough. Ed Cronk, a big, husky young man in his early twenties, and one of the three UAW men sworn to secrecy on the strategy the night before, ran through Chevy Six carrying a small American flag and a metal pipe, shutting down one assembly line after another. But he prepared to move on to Chevy Four without waiting to mobilize the full contingent of three hundred men needed for action at the latter, where Kermit Johnson, a socialist, was waiting for them.

Cronk had arrived first with a mere twenty men, and though they were rough and ferocious-looking, they were not enough to take Chevy Four, and he had to go back to Chevy Six to recruit a couple of hundred more.

The delay, unfortunately for Cronk and Johnson, gave Chevy Four supervisors some precious moments to organize for the UAW assault. For the next hour, there was a seesaw battle for the allegiance of the Chevy Four workers. As fast as Cronk and Johnson's forces shut down one assembly line, foremen prevailed on hesitant employees to return to work. Gradually, however, the lines of striking union men parading through the plant grew larger, and the company loyalist workers began to seek shelter away from the factory floor. Except in a few instances, Cronk's fierce looking followers, some armed with claw-hammers, did not have to resort to violence; the mere sight of them was enough to scare off the workers undecided about their loyalties. After two hours, while UAW leaders in the Pengally Building head-quarters were biting their fingernails, Chevy Four fell to the sit-downers, like a fortress after a long siege. Many hundreds of its workers signed immediately with the UAW; those who didn't, were asked to leave the plant. Supervisors were herded out; factory guards returning from Chevy Nine, seeking to re-enter Chevy Four through the northeast gate, were driven away with water hoses and a barrage of pistons, connecting rods, and other metal weapons. To seal the plant off to potential GM invading forces, great barricades were placed against doors—so firmly it took days to remove them after the strike was over. And outside, large numbers of pickets, many from Walter Reuther's west-side local in Detroit, paraded up and down to prevent a counterattack by the outmaneuvered guards. The shop simply could not be retaken. From the union's point of view, the complicated plan, despite a few uneasy moments, had achieved its goals. Two thousand workers were ensconced inside Chevrolet's indispensable motor plant.

The events of February 1, of course, created a furor among GM's top management, in the press and elsewhere. Governor Murphy, too, was furious. He had, as an interim act, obtained welfare payments for the strikers and had been trying to arrange for renewed GM-UAW negotiations. The Travis-Reuther gambit, he felt, had violated his good faith. In response, the governor placed twelve hundred militia around Chevy Four, and it appeared for a while that the troops would try to evict the sitdowners. On Murphy's orders, no food was permitted inside, heat and light were cut off, and union leaders and other union supporters were driven off the property.

Except for the telephones they had inside, the sitdowners were completely cut off from the outside world.

As so often has happened in the major labor wars, however, at the bleakest moment, the situation was turned around. With Walter Reuther threatening GM that his men might build bonfires inside the plant to keep warm—posing the obvious potential danger of burning the plant down—and with Brophy using his persuasiveness on the governor in a long phone conversation, Murphy relented. Heat was turned on temporarily. No militia attack on the workers inside was launched. Nor, for the time being, was any thrust made by police or troops against Fisher One, where 5,000 pickets armed with pipes, clubs and crowbars were gathered to ward off an expected attack following the UAW's ignoring of an injunction issued by Judge Gadola to halt the strike on February 2 (and the threat to levy a $15 million fine).

In these tense circumstances General Motors suddenly agreed to negotiate directly with John L. Lewis. On February 3, after hastening to Flint, Lewis, with Mortimer and Martin at his side, began the crucial talks with Knudsen. GM was definitely on the defensive at this point. On February 7, its directors reduced dividends by 50 per cent. Weekly production of GM automobiles was reported to have fallen to a mere 1,500 (as against 28,825 at Ford, and 25,350 at Chrysler). Nonetheless it took a week of fierce bargaining before an eight-paragraph pact was put in writing on February 11. The corporation agreed to recognize the UAW in the seventeen plants that had been struck, to drop pending lawsuits, to take no reprisals against strikers, even those who had engaged in violence, or to interfere with the right of its employees to join the UAW. The agreement was to run for six months, and though its language on union recognition did not include the words "sole," or "corporation-wide," it did contain a paragraph by which the company promised not to deal with any other organization after the six months without "gaining from you [the UAW] the sanction of any such contemplated procedure." As the forty-four day strike ended, GM announced a five cents per hour wage increase.

"Another milestone on labor's march," exulted John L. Lewis. It was indeed that, and more: the beginning of a *qualitative* change in the status of American labor.

VII

"It is inevitable," Nobel-prize-winning novelist Sinclair Lewis once said, "that the Committee for Industrial Organization will do to the American Federation of Labor what the Federation did to the Knights of Labor." He was wrong. The AFL not only survived after their seeming defeats of 1936–37 but prospered. Yet after the General Motors strike the letters of C-I-O gained an especially magical luster that attracted millions of workers to the union fold in just one year. John Brophy could report to the CIO conference in Atlantic City on October 4, 1937, that "When the Committee was formed two years ago its members did not total one million. Now there are four million. And the demand for organization in the CIO continues so strong that a membership of four million is merely a passing marker . . ." There were thirty-two national unions in the new federation by that time, including sizable organized labor forces in rubber (75,000), textiles (400,000), oil (100,000), transport (80,000) in fur, municipal workers, (including office and professional people) longshore, aluminum, and of course in the two pivotal industries of auto and steel.

The UAW victory over General Motors was not total by any means. The contract fought for so hard was only binding for six months, and, as mentioned above, only seventeen of the sixty-nine GM plants were covered under it. But the success of sitdowns in Flint had given the UAW movement irrepressible momentum. Just after the GM settlement there were eighteen additional sitdowns in GM plants within twenty days. A few months later a larger stay-in occurred among the 59,000 Chrysler workers in Detroit. There was a considerably less tense atmosphere to the Chrysler strike than there had been in the GM action, as thousands of workers simply sat peaceably inside a number of Chrysler shops. At one point, when a rumor spread that the National Guard might make an effort to eject the strikers, 50,000 people congregated in front of the Dodge Main plant in Hamtramck (a small, independent community within Detroit). No confrontation came, however; even the most headstrong employer and political leader recognized by now that the third strike wave during the New Deal could not be set back. On the lips of innumerable workers in countless industries was the mystical word "sitdown." A month after the conclusion of the GM war there were 247 stay-ins involving 193,000 workers, from the Chrysler workers to dime-store employees, Western Union messengers, glass blowers, hotel workers, and even garbage collectors. Only two dozen sitdowns were smashed by police in 1936–37, an amazingly low figure given the tradition of heavy police participation in U.S. labor strikes. The number of work stoppages in 1937, including stay-ins, was double what it had been in 1936—4,470 as against 2,172—and embraced almost two million unionists. The reign of the open shop had been halted, and the morale of the American working class never had been higher.

On March 2, 1937, less than two months after the Battle of Bulls' Run, the nation heard the electrifying news that U. S. Steel had accorded bargaining rights to the Steel Workers Organizing Committee for its major plants, had raised wages 10 per cent, reduced the work week to forty hours, and granted time and a half for overtime. Without any public labor-management war whatsoever, the world's largest steel company had come to terms with John L. Lewis after three months of quiet, behind-the-scenes negotiations with Big Steel's chief, Myron C. Taylor. According to "two financiers closely identified with Morgan interests," said the New York *World-Telegram* of March 4, the House of Morgan had recognized "that complete industrial organization was inevitable . . ." Rather than face the prospect of long and possibly violent sitdowns and radical "hothead" labor leaders like the young men in the automobile industry, the Morgans accepted bargaining with Lewis and his subaltern, Phil Murray, as the lesser evil. Hundreds of other steel firms followed suit. By the time of the Little Steel strike of May 1937, 140 firms with 300,000 workers had appended their names to an SWOC contract. As of September the figure had risen to 415 firms and a half-million workers.

But the full fury of employers accustomed to having their way so long, was not yet consumed. Even though unionism had turned the corner, there were still other labor wars to come. Of these the most savage by far was the Little Steel strike that began two months after Lewis' settlement with Big Steel. The five corporations that comprised "Little Steel"—Bethlehem, Republic, Youngstown Sheet & Tube, Inland, and National Steel—continued their campaign against the SWOC with undiminished vigor. In late May and June, 70,000 workers in the first four of these companies hit the bricks in the traditional kind of walkout rather than via a sit-in, and were badly mauled. It was the bloodiest labor war of the decade. Eighteen workers were killed, ten of them in the famous Memorial Day Massacre outside Tom Girdler's Republic plant on the South Side of Chicago. One hundred and sixty people were wounded, hundreds sickened by tear gas, and hundreds more arrested—two hundred in Youngstown alone. The National Guard fanned out in Ohio to disperse picket lines in Niles, Canton, Massillon, Cleveland, Warren, and Youngstown. Back-to-work movements were led by the usual citizen groups, by "independent," i.e., company unions, and by government officials such as Mayor Daniel J. Shields of Johnstown, who, according to testimony before the National Labor Relations Board, was rewarded with $31,456 from the Bethlehem Steel coffers for his efforts during the walkout.

But no incident that labor had seen in all the labor wars of the previous six decades contained as much outright, unadulterated viciousness as the massacre on May 30, in Chicago. A Paramount News photographer captured the scene on film, but it was so gruesome, his company refused to exhibit it publicly for fear of "inciting riots." Later the LaFollette Committee in the Senate was shown the movie privately. The St. Louis *Post-Dispatch*, which also got a view of the massacre on film, described the unfolding scene in these dramatic paragraphs: "A vivid close-up shows the head of the parade being halted at the police line. The flag-bearers are in front. . . . Behind the flag-bearers is the marchers' spokesman, a muscular young man in shirt sleeves, with a CIO button on the band of his felt hat. . . .

"Then suddenly, without apparent warning, there is a terrific roar of pistol shots, and men in the front ranks of the marchers go down like grass before a scythe. The camera catches approximately a dozen falling simultaneously in a heap. The massive, sustained roar of the pistol shots lasts perhaps two or three seconds.

"Instantly the police charge on the marchers with riot sticks flying. At the same time tear gas grenades are seen sailing into the mass of demonstrators, and clouds of gas rise over them. Most of the crowd is now in flight. . . .

"In a manner which is appallingly businesslike, groups of policemen close in on these isolated individuals, and go to work on them with their clubs. In several instances, from two to four policemen are seen beating one man. One strikes him horizontally across the face, using his club as he would a baseball bat. Another crashes it down on top of his head and still another is whipping him across the back . . .

"A man shot through the back is paralyzed from the waist. Two policemen try to make him stand up, to get him into a patrol wagon, but when they let go of him his legs crumble, and he falls with his face in the dirt, almost under the rear step of the wagon. He moves his head and arms, but his legs are limp. He raises his head like a turtle, and claws the ground . . .

"There is continuous talking, but . . . out of the babble there rises this clear and distinct ejaculation:

"'God Almighty!'

"A policeman, somewhat disheveled, his coat wide open, a scowl on his face, approaches another who is standing in front of the camera. He is sweaty and tired. He says something indistinguishable. Then his face breaks out into a sudden grin, he makes a motion of dusting off his hands, and strides away. The film ends."

In due course Little Steel too would be tamed by the CIO, and Henry Ford, last of the anti-union holdouts in the automobile industry would be brought into line. The labor movement would quadruple and sextuple in size. But the cost, in human lives alone in retrospect, had been titanic; the martyrs, legion.

In criticizing Franklin Roosevelt for failing to come to the aid of the Little Steel strikers, John L. Lewis on Labor Day 1937, told a nation-wide radio audience: "Those who chant their praises of democracy but who lost no chance to drive their knives into labor's defenseless back must feel the weight of labor's woes even as its open adversaries must ever feel the thrust of labor's power.

"Labor, like Israel, has many sorrows. Its women weep for their fallen and they lament for the future of the children of the race."

Toward the end of an era finally crowned by a sweeping success, this was a fitting epitaph for the stupendous tragedies that had been suffered along the way.

16

The Ides of Yesterday
and Tomorrow

I

Are labor wars now a thing of the past? Has capitalism become sufficiently humanized that they will never be renewed? Certainly no one in the labor movement, or friendly to it, looks back on the six troubled decades discussed above with nostalgia. The only aspect of the period that can be recalled with pride is the incredible idealism and self-sacrifice of common working men seeking both their just economic rewards and their dignity. But for the most part, it was a blood-soaked era which left an indelible blot on American history.

The question to be asked today is whether the year 1937 marked the terminal point of those savage class outbreaks. Are there new features built into the American system which now make their recurrence impossible or unlikely, or is the United States in the midst now of an economic and political transition that will make their reappearance all but inevitable? Short of clairvoyance, of course, no one can be certain. But history since 1937 explains why each strike wave after that year has been a little more muted, a little less violent than the previous one, and gives us one or two clues as to what circumstances can reverse this process, so as to bring forth a new type of labor wars.

There were in fact several years after 1937 in which the number of work stoppages was greater than in that peak "war" year (the years 1944–46, 1952–53, 1968–69, 1971, for instance), and the number of workers on picket lines larger. In no country on earth, in fact, have there been so many walkouts as in the United States. But the boundary lines of the labor-capital conflict, after 1937, have become progressively narrower. The general policy of both business and government on labor seems to have changed from full-scale assault to containment, from frontal attack to flank attack, from total hostility to partial, if arm's-length, accommodation.

One still read in the newspapers items such as this one from the New York *Times* of September 8, 1953: "Hyden, Ky., Sept. 7—In the capital of this non-union coal producing country here, John L. Lewis' United Mine Workers Union has been waging a campaign for more than two years to bring the operators under contract. Eight organizers have been shot, one of them died, another is completely paralyzed. Cars have been dynamited and union meeting places, members' homes and friendly merchants' stores have been blasted or fired upon. The union and its local leaders have been sued, indicted, enjoined and even jailed." Another item: the dispatch of January 25, 1972 reporting the death of an eighteen-year-old college volunteer, Nan Freeman, who was run down by a scab-driven truck while on picket duty in front of the Talisman Sugar Company in Dade County, Florida. On a lesser scale of violence, there have been hundreds of news stories over the years such as this one: "Edison, N.J., Feb. 29/1972/ —Police assaulted strikers yesterday who were trying to prevent strikebreakers from entering the Fedders Air Conditioning Co. Women strikers were pushed to the ground by police . . . Judge Furman of the Superior Court of New Jersey yesterday issued an injunction limiting picketing to 25 at the main gate, eight feet apart and to 10 at the truck gate . . ." Thus, old strike-breaking and union-busting methods have not yet become entirely extinct. Even Franklin Roosevelt tried his hand at them in June 1941 when he sent 3,500 troops to seize the plant of the North American Aviation Company at Inglewood, California. By this action, the strike there of 12,000 United Auto Workers was effectively smashed.

Furthermore, despite the sextupling of organized labor's membership in the last three and a half decades, there still have been innumerable instances in which labor has shown itself to be next to impotent. A case in point is the Kohler stoppage. The strike of Local 833 UAW against the Kohler Company of Kohler, Wisconsin, began on April 5, 1954, and continued for eight harrowing years. The UAW was a strong union, part of what the press called "Big Labor." Yet it could not subdue this anti-labor employer—and not a few others— for a long time. And weaker organizations were repeatedly frustrated and made only little progress. The experience of the United Textile Workers at Darlington, South Carolina, in the 1950s was not atypical of recent labor history. After winning a Labor Board election to represent 600 operatives employed by one of the largest textile chains (Deering, Milliken), the union stood by helplessly while the company closed its doors rather than negotiate a written agreement. In Fredericksburg, Virginia, where in September 1957 the same union won another election for 300 workers, the company discharged forty-two members of its leadership committee and forced the union into a vain strike that ended fruitlessly.

There has been a clear discrepancy between the unionizing campaigns of organizations which had "primary" economic power (those that could shut down a plant or an operation through their own efforts), and those whose members were unskilled or small in number, so that they were easily replaced in case of a strike and therefore were forced to rely on outside help from truck drivers, railroad workers and others to achieve victory. "Little Labor" by contrast with "Big Labor" has been repeatedly frustrated and has made only meager headway in achieving organizational strength. Agricultural workers, for instance, were beaten back in one drive and one strike after another, until Cesar Chavez's organization won a few victories in the late 1960s and early 1970s. And even with these victories, his organization numbered a mere 30,000 members as late as 1972, in an industry which employs more people than basic auto, steel, and trucking combined. Despite the great success in enrolling blue-collar workers (two thirds have been organized), there have been enormous pockets of industry where labor's hold has been tenuous—in agriculture, textiles, engineering, department stores, chemicals, government, the services and among white collar workers of all kinds.

Nor has the labor movement, with all its alleged strength, been able to ward off legislative attacks such as the Taft-Hartley Act, the Landrum-Griffin bill, and the twenty state "right-to-work" laws. In many places, where the power of the unions has been negligible, the attitude of local or state administrations has remained savagely feudal. In Henry Ford's bailiwick, Dearborn, Michigan, as late as 1940, organizers were prevented from distributing leaflets under a special "traffic" law prohibiting such activity. The South Carolina General Assembly, seeking to prevent unionization of textile mills, approved six ordinances in August 1957, requiring "a permit in writing" before any labor official could solicit members. In Baxley, Georgia, an annual license fee was imposed on unions costing $2,000, plus $500 for "each member signed up." In nearby Carrollton, organizers were required to pay $100 a day for the privilege of "doing business," and in Osceola, Arkansas, $1,000 a day.

Yet, despite innumerable such examples to the contrary, it is undeniable that from September 1937 onward there has been a *qualitative* change in the nature of industrial relations. In the single year 1935, the National Guard had been called out against strikes and strikers on seventy-three occasions in twenty states; no such wide-scale use of troops occurred after 1938. There were no major sit-down strikes, no more Homesteads, no "Debs Rebellions." Indeed, there has been a progressive tapering off of violence. At Ford, for instance, Harry Bennett's thugs had beaten up hundreds of union members and thwarted every effort at unionization prior to 1941. But during the 1941 strike there was only one major skirmish, in which thirty-six pickets were hurt, and in postwar stoppages at Ford there were no disorders at all. For the most part, strikes have become contests of endurance, in which each side has relied for ultimate victory on economic attrition, rather than physical upheaval. When Harry Bridges' West Coast longshoremen struck the docks in 1971–72 for a total of almost twenty weeks, there was not a single bloody nose to mar the "peace," or a single attempt to bring in scabs or open any of the ports.

This modification of class relationships has been the result of four interrelated phenomena: the fashioning of a number of mechanisms, such as the National Labor Relations Board, to impose "order" on the class struggle, (coincident with the shift from *laissez-faire* to controlled capitalism); the nation's enduring prosperity; the willingness of large numbers of employers to enter into arrangements with AFL "moderates" to avoid the fury of the CIO "radicals"; and the slow institutionalization of the CIO after its great initial victories.

II

There were approximately thirty-five million "organizable" workers in the United States as of 1933, of whom less than 8 per cent, or 2.8 million, were union members. Four years later the number of union-card holders had grown to 7.7 million, about 22 per cent of the organizable work force. The CIO, whose eight unions comprised approximately one million members at birth in 1935, had thirty-four national organizations with 3,727,350 adherents in 1937. It seemed to be sweeping the union field, overwhelming the AFL just as the AFL had overwhelmed the Knights of Labor in the 1890s.

The evangelical fervor of the CIO, however, cooled with surprising suddenness. After 1937, John L. Lewis opposed further sitdown strikes more firmly than ever, and they virtually disappeared. One union after another established machinery to discipline workers engaged in strikes not specifically authorized by the union leadership. Even the UAW, the most dynamic of the CIO organizations, voted at its board meeting of September 1937 to permit General Motors to fire any worker participating in an "unauthorized" stoppage. In the Steel Workers Organizing Committee, Phil Murray yielded a heavy hand, banning not only wildcat strikes but the formation of opposition factions.

In the 1930s, Lewis did not hound the radicals as Bill Green had or as the CIO itself was to do in the late 1940s. The CIO national executive board, elected in November 1938, was said to have included fifteen men who were either close to the communists or in the party. Communists were also a major or dominating force in the auto, rubber, steel, electrical, longshore, maritime, transport, and a half-dozen other unions, as well as in many city and state CIO councils. Many of the leftists personally, however, had become more subdued. Some—Walter Reuther, for example—had already quit the Socialist Party, the Trotskyists, or other radical groups and were drifting toward the political center. And Communist Party adherents in the CIO establishment no longer were so flamboyant after Roosevelt granted diplomatic recognition to the Soviet Union. Thus, movement militancy tapered off, and, as a result, the CIO lost some of its flair and appeal. It added less than a half-million members to its ranks in the two years after September 1937.

But if the CIO found itself in suspended animation, the AFL was in the process of recuperation and growth. When the CIO walked out of the old Federation in 1935 its ranks had been depleted to about two million members. By 1939 that membership figure was up to four million and five years later almost seven million. Far from being eclipsed by the CIO, the AFL eventually grew larger than its adversary. AFL affiliates, in particular the machinists and teamsters, quietly adapted to industrial unionism and organized whole factories or warehouses on the same principles as the CIO. The AFL also benefited from a host of other circumstances: the fact that many employers chose to deal with it as the "lesser evil" than the CIO militants, the fact that some company unions sought shelter under its umbrella, and the fact that vast war construction added a million and a quarter new constituents to AFL building trades unions.

After the sitdowns, capitalists in increasing number made peace with the AFL. Gone was management's haughty attitude of the 1920s and early 1930s when Green's proffered hand had been disdained by the captains of industry. Now their choice was no longer between having or not having to deal with a union, but between having to deal with a moderate one or a militant one. In instance after instance, during and after the mid-1930s, employers entered into "back door" contracts with an AFL union to undercut a drive by the CIO. At Consolidated Edison in New York, for example, where the United Electrical and Radio Workers, CIO, had thoroughly taken over an AFL local, management hastily signed a contract with the AFL to freeze out the UE. In another electrical firm, where UE had collected application cards from 1,000 of the 1,600 employees, the AFL and the employer entered into a closed-shop contract—even though the Federation had no local on the scene and very few members, if any. This obviously ran counter to the spirit and letter of the Wagner Act, but it occurred nonetheless.

In Chicago, during a six-month strike by six hundred CIO-affiliated employees of a large grocery chain warehouse, the company signed a contract with an old company union, which in the meantime had recruited scabs and acquired an AFL charter. This same chain, plus others, granted a union-shop agreement to a hoodlum named Max Caldwell who held a charter in the AFL's Retail Clerks International Protective Association, even though he had not a single member at the time from among grocery workers. Henry Kaiser signed pacts with AFL affiliates for plants which had only skeleton crews—before a full complement could be organized by the CIO. Thus, one such local in Portland, No. 72 of the AFL boilermakers, had only five hundred members when the agreement was reached, but grew to 65,000 when the plant was in full operation. In Kansas, Oklahoma, and Missouri, where the CIO Mine, Mill and Smelter Workers had unionized thousands of miners who had formerly been forced to join the Blue Card Union, a corporation-run organization, the AFL chartered the company union under the name Tri-State Metal, Mine and Smelter Workers.

"Organizing the employer" rather than the employee became a widespread phenomenon in the late 1930s and 1940s. There are no statistics on this matter but hundreds of thousands of workers were dragooned into the AFL; many, if not most, without being consulted and against their will. Not a few AFL leaders, indeed, considered this kind of back door arrangement one of their major activities. Here for instance, is a letter from A. O. Wharton, president of the machinists, to vice-presidents, grand lodge representatives, business agents, and general chairmen of his organization, dated April 20, 1937, which shows how much stock was put in "organizing the employer":

"Since the Supreme Court decision upholding the Wagner Labor Act," it read, "many employers now realize that it is the Law of our Country and they are prepared to deal with labor organizations.

These employers have expressed a preference to deal with AFL organizations rather than Lewis, Hillman, Dubinsky, Howard and that gang of sluggers, communists, radicals and soap box artists, professional bums, expelled members of labor unions, outright scabs and the Jewish organizations with all their red affiliates.

"We have conferred with several such employers and arranged for conference later when we get the plants organized. The purpose of this is to direct all officers and all representatives to contact employers in your locality as a preliminary to organizing the shops and factories."

Although the letter urged officials to arrange conferences "when we get the plants organized," it must be obvious that entrepreneurs, fearful of the CIO "hotheads," were not too squeamish about whether the AFL did or did not represent a majority of the workers covered in the contracts. There were also other ways that employers "friendly" to the AFL could give the AFL a boost over the CIO, by having foremen, for example, actively or secretly proselytize for the AFL. Thus, by legitimate organizing methods and by "organizing the employer" or at least securing his help, the machinists of the AFL more than tripled their membership in six years.

Another circumstance favorable to AFL fortunes was the enormous expansion in building construction coincident with the Second World War. From 1939 to 1942, new construction, even apart from residential, tripled, from an index number of 81 (based on 1923–24 production averages) to 235. Both the federal government and private industry were building factories, roads, tunnels, buildings, and airfields—and on virtually all of those projects, applicants for jobs were automatically required to join the AFL. Thus, for instance, when the labor forces on a project grew from 500 to 2,000 the unions grew apace, without any additional organizing efforts needed. Had there been another recognized union in the construction field, workers would have had a choice. But John L. Lewis' attempt to form an industrial union, amalgamating all the crafts in the building trades was poorly handled, and too late by at least two or three years. Lewis' brother, A. D. Lewis, was put in charge of this campaign in 1939, but was too inept to wean away from the AFL any considerable number of craftsmen. And when issues concerned their own interests, the AFL construction groups showed they were able to defend themselves against such vices as scale slashing and wage differentials with astonishing vigor. Hundreds of small strikes that they conducted ended victoriously almost overnight, thereby stealing the potential thunder away from A. D. Lewis' fledgling organization.

Moreover, when CIO vice-president Sidney Hillman, a close associate of President Roosevelt, became associate director of the U. S.

Office of Production Management in 1941, he gave a spectacular gift to the AFL by granting it exclusive bargaining rights on all the contracts covering war-affiliated construction. In Detroit, for example, a corporation which submitted the lowest bid for a military housing project but which recognized the CIO, was rejected in favor of a company whose bid was higher but which had an agreement with the AFL. The only *quid pro quos* demanded by Hillman, who by now was at severe odds with John L. Lewis, were the waiving of certain premium pay for overtime and a ban against jurisdictional strikes, by which one craft union tried to get work assigned to its members at the expense of other unions. Offered such rich benefits, it is no wonder that the building trades groups under the AFL banner added approximately one and a quarter million new members by 1944. The boilermakers grew from 28,000 in 1938 to 336,900 in 1944; the hodcarriers from 147,700 to 333,100; the plumbers from 37,700 to 130,000; the electrical workers from 175,000 to 312,900; the carpenters from 300,000 to 600,000.

Thus though it had universally opposed the major strikes of 1934–37, the AFL capitalized on the momentum they generated to again establish its pre-eminent position in the house of labor.

III

Parallel to the subjective developments on the labor-management front were objective ones more grandiose; America remodeled many of its political and economic institutions and fabricated a long-term prosperity based on Keynesian theory and military spending.

The year 1938 was one of severe if brief depression, in which national production slipped by more than 20 per cent in just a few months. This marked a sharper turndown than even that suffered during the first months of the Great Depression. But the economy revived quickly. Production soon jumped from an index figure of 88 (based on 1935–39 averages being equal to 100) to 108 in 1939, 122 in 1940, and 247 in October-November 1943. Corporate profits, before taxes, doubled from 1938 to 1939, and by 1940 were already higher than the 1929 boom levels. By the time America entered the war even those grandiose figures were far eclipsed; profits in 1943 were three times as large as in 1929 and nine times as great as in 1938. From 1939 through 1972 there was never a year when the economy skidded more than a few percentage points; and from 1942 onward no twelve-month period when unemployment reached as high as 7 per cent (as against 24.9 per cent in 1933 and 14.6 per cent as late as 1940). The gross national product, that statistical religion of Keynesian economists, skyrocketed from $90.5 billion in 1939 to $1,050 billion in 1971—eleven times as much as thirty-two years before. Even allowing for inflation, the GNP was four times as large as in 1939 and despite the considerable growth in population, the actual *real* income available to each American was more than twice as great.

True, this largesse was the result in large part of military spending—$288 billion for World War II, followed by a trillion and a quarter dollars in the next quarter of a century. But synthetic or not, it was still prosperity; and its long duration had the effect of easing the sense of desperation in working-class ranks, as well as dulling the attitude of resistance toward unionism of many employers. There is little question, for instance, that the 123-million-dollar federal contract for aviation engines given Ford in November 1940 was a vital consideration in the company's decision to come to terms quickly after the short April 1941 strike, and its granting of a union shop contract to the UAW—the first of its kind in the automobile industry. The strike at Ford was the kind of situation which in the past had been thoroughly conducive to violence and warfare; the forming of large mass picket lines as the union policed an area ten square miles around the River Rouge plant, Harry Bennett's "service" men flexing for action, the company calling for troops. But the strike had only one important physical confrontation, on the morning of April 3, and by the sixth day of the strike Ford was proposing a truce. With the plant totally inoperative, and facing the prospect of a drawn-out struggle which might jeopardize lucrative war orders, the corporation yielded. At other times and in less affluent circumstances, Henry Ford might have fought longer and harder.

A similar situation occurred at Bethlehem Steel about the same time. With its bins full of approximately one billion dollars in military contracts, the company, which had resisted efforts at unionizing for half a century, was ambivalent about provoking full-scale industrial war. Thirty-eight hours after 13,000 workers at Bethlehem's mill in Lackawanna, New York, went on strike to win the reinstatement of 1,000 fellow workers discharged as a means of intimidating organizing efforts, the company beat a full and hasty retreat. Here, too, there was one big all-day battle, as management evidently probed for union weakness. But after less than two days it decided to lift the "indefinite suspensions" without carrying the "probe" very far. A month later, a slightly longer strike by 20,000 employees at the company's main complex in Bethlehem, Pennsylvania—called to protest a planned company union election—ended with similar success for the union. Eugene Grace, Bethlehem's president, granted "sole" collective bargaining rights to the Steel Workers Organizing Committee. Again, here, were all the makings of a labor war, as there were in 1937 or 1919, especially after the state's mounted police and the coal and iron police attacked picket lines and forbade further picketing. But the common working men and women defied the ban and the company called off hostilities before the public reaction to unrestrained strikebreaking might have caused it to lose some of its lucrative war contracts.

In the period of unwavering prosperity that began in 1939, it has been relatively easy for the larger companies in the U.S. to pass the cost of wage boosts onto the consumer. That obviously has been true of military procurement, where there has been little competitive bidding, and where many contracts have been on a "cost-plus" basis. The greater the "cost," in such instances, the more the "plus"—making a wage increase not only painless but profitable. This situation has held true, however, in much of industry geared to the private consumer. Collusion between large entrepreneurs—more properly "conspiracies" —to fix prices has been a long-standing practice in the United States. Franklin B. Gowen, it will be remembered, organized "pooling" arrangements with other railroads to set rates for coal. The New Deal, under the National Industrial Recovery Act, made such collusion legal for a time, as Frances Perkins noted in her book on Roosevelt, by "suspending the effect of the anti-trust laws in return for voluntary agreement by industries for fair competition, minimum wage levels, and maximum hours."

But during and after World War II, the more potent corporations freed themselves from the vicissitudes of the competitive market to an extraordinary extent. One means of getting around the "problem" was "target pricing." Companies in industries where three or four corporations dominated more than half the market, set themselves a profit "target," e.g., 15 per cent on their original investment. Then, after estimating potential demand, they announced a price which would assure that profit level. If the demand turned out to be greater, so much the better, and if lower, they raised prices to meet the target, knowing full well they had nothing to fear from competitors. The latter almost invariably raised prices in concert, instead of trying to corner the market by lowering them.

Henry Ford II once testified before a congressional committee that he was *forced to increase* the charge for his cars because General Motors had boosted theirs. This is a novel revision of standard economics, but it has been the operative one, according to Ralph Nader, in "such major industries as autos, steel, copper, aluminum, containers, chemicals, detergents, canned soups, cereals." Prices in these and other industrial sectors of the economy were "administered"—set by secret agreements and thousands of *sub rosa* "arrangements," rather than by the free operation of the market. As Morton Mintz and Jerry S. Cohen have observed in their *America, Inc.,* "one company sets the price and the rest follow in lockstep fashion. Smaller companies either go along or face destruction by the giants." According to the Federal Trade Commission, if the giants were broken up so as to foster true competition, prices in those industries would fall by one quarter or more. The giants, however, have not been broken up, and their administered and target-pricing policies have made it simple for them to shift the burden of wage increases to the consumer rather than absorbing it themselves.

This opportunity of management's to convert pay boosts to product price boosts has made it less overwrought about strikes than in the past. Thus the strike wave of 1946, which brought four and a half million workers to the picket line and caused 116 million man-days of idleness (four times as much as in 1937), provoked little more than a bellowing of rhetoric from industrial barons. There were nationwide stoppages in auto, steel, coal, electric, petroleum, maritime, railroad, and packinghouse industries, as well as general strikes in seven cities. But everyone knew in advance that there would be no trouble. Why should there have been? Under a favorable tax law pushed through Congress to cushion conversion by business to peacetime production, the corporations could keep their plants closed and earn large tax rebates. According to Phil Murray, even if the steel industry had been out of operation from the time the strike began in late January to the end of the year, it would have received $149 million in tax refunds— 29 per cent more than its normal profits before the war.

Relieved of economic pressure, the captains of industry therefore concentrated their efforts relating to labor on negotiating with government officials on the size of price increases to be wrung from the Office of Price Administration (OPA) rather than on breaking strikes. In no labor-management dispute was management particularly excited. No attempt was ever made to run in scabs or reopen struck plants. The Truman administration sent no troops to any factories and sought no injunctions—none of the titans asked for them. And when OPA finally agreed to the desired raise in prices the major strikes were settled, most of them for an 18½ cents an hour raise.

The only jarring aspect of this idyllic situation (for management) in 1946 was Walter Reuther's insistence during the 113-day strike at General Motors that the company not only grant a pay hike but agree to maintain its old price levels. This "socialistic" scheme, however, was effectively throttled with the help of Phil Murray, who in his public utterances made it abundantly clear that his union was not concerned with prices. William H. Davis, chairman of the War Labor Board, intimated that wages could be hiked 40 to 50 per cent in the following five years without any need for boosting prices. Secretary of Commerce Henry Wallace released a study to show that auto wages could rise 25 per cent in 1946 without undue effect on normal profits. But the pressures of management, abetted by Murray, a man of moderate outlook, were irrepressible. Truman finally agreed that prices and wages would go up together, and the strikes were settled. The price of steel was raised $5 a ton, a raise which the Chicago *Sun* estimated would net the companies $435 million more in annual income; the cost of the wage increase, employers said, was $185 million—less than half as much.

It has been one of the noteworthy features of subsequent contract negotiations in the larger industries, that nearly every time a wage agreement has been concluded, management has announced a price increase, always blaming it on "higher costs due to pay boosts." In the state-managed war and postwar economy, the nation has sustained the longest period of prosperity in its history, and no one has seemed to care about the artificial manipulation of prices. Fifteen to twenty million unionists have won annual pay hikes— uninterrupted even by the five recessions that followed World War II. In turn, businessmen raised their prices accordingly to the consumer, and in many cases have even raised it a little more. And both major segments of the economy could get bigger slices of the pie because the pie itself—the GNP—has been growing steadily from year to year. Not that employers have been any more happy about granting wage increases than in the past—for, after all, even if competition has been restricted in a particular industry, there still has been the competition for the consumer's dollar *between* industry and industry—between gas and coal, railroads and trucking, steel and aluminum, etc. Nonetheless in the climate of prosperity the entrepreneurial seismograph has showed smaller shock waves when one of the 70,000 local unions has gained more pay for its members.

IV

Perhaps the most interesting factor in the decline of labor wars has been the institutionalization of labor-capital relationships. Over the years, the government has tried to set limits on the class struggle through such institutions as the National Labor Relations Board, the War Labor Board, and, under President Richard M. Nixon, the Pay Board. These mechanisms have been in direct opposition to Adam Smith's *laissez-faire* doctrines, under which the price for labor like the price for every commodity is to be determined on the free market, without government interference. But these measures have been vitally necessary for the very survival of the social order.

By the time Franklin Roosevelt took office in March 1933 it was clear to almost everyone in the nation but those people on the far right that only government action could prevent the U.S. from collapsing. What remained of *free* enterprise was in a shambles, and if the danger of revolution was not as imminent as the radicals contended, it was not entirely negligible either. Banks were going bankrupt, the wheels of industry were refusing to turn, foreign trade was at a near standstill. The ruling capitalist class itself was mired in economic quicksand, incapable of creating motion and order without a centralized directing agency to enforce its will, by police measures if necessary.

Unless price levels could be raised, more corporations and more banks would go bankrupt. The lack of consumer purchasing power combined with uncontrolled competition had forced prices so low—despite the still lower wages—that marginal producers were being driven out of business. Among scores of measures taken by the New Deal, Roosevelt remedied the lag in purchasing power through "pump priming," direct relief and work relief. He raised farm prices by the simple expedient of giving farmers subsidies to *curtail* production, thereby bringing supply closer to demand. And most of all, he openly encouraged, through the NRA, concerted monopolistic action by business. In essence, what his program amounted to was a pledge by government that if industry raised wages and reduced hours, it would be allowed to set prices for its products without anti-trust prosecution. All told, NRA head "Ironpants" Johnson, and Donald Richberg, his successor after September 1934, supervised the elaboration of 576 basic and 189 supplementary codes of "fair competition" for various segments of industry.

As a corollary to this program, the New Deal realized it had to appease organized labor, for political reasons, and did so. It could have abolished unions, and made strikes, unemployed workers' demonstrations, veterans' marches, farmers' holidays, and all other forms of mass action illegal, as was done in Germany, Italy, Austria, and Spain. But there was the danger that if such measures were introduced, the unco-ordinated struggles on the streets might flare into actual revolution. This was certainly not outside the realm of possibility. Roosevelt, in any case, was not favorably disposed toward fascism. Instead he tried to mute the class conflict by including the aforementioned Section 7(a) in the National Industrial Recovery Act. His intent in using it was made evident in an appeal to the nation on July 24, 1933, in which he said: "The workers of this country have rights under this law which cannot be taken from them, and no one will be permitted to whittle them away but, on the other hand, no *aggression* is necessary now to attain these rights [emphasis added]." In return for "7(a)," in other words, FDR expected labor to curb its "aggression"—strikes.

Section 7(a), labor's so-called "Magna Charta," however, was inadequate to still the grievances among its rank and file. So too was the National Labor Board, the National Labor Relations Board (not to be confused with the NLRB designated under the Wagner Act), and the special boards Roosevelt appointed for specific industries—to mediate, conciliate, and if called upon, to arbitrate disputes between labor and management. For since they had been given no means of enforcing their decisions they were constantly defied by employers. The result of this federal ineffectiveness was that, contrary to FDR's wishes, labor's "aggression," far from subsiding, mounted greatly.

Finally Senator Robert F. Wagner introduced his famous National Labor Relations Act and it became the law of the land in July 1935. This date marked in a sense a continental divide in the history of labor legislation. In a nutshell, the act forbade company unions, recognized the right of workers to bargain collectively, and created a three-man board, the National Labor Relations Board, to hold elections for a particular unit, e.g., a factory or a warehouse, and if the union won a majority of the votes cast, to certify it as the "sole" collective-bargaining agency. That certification generally could not be upset in court. The board was given the additional authority to rule on "unfair" employer practices that might impede a worker or a labor organization in exercising their rights, e.g., such as the discharge of an active unionist or the refusal to bargain.

The Wagner Act contained provisions far different from any labor bill or administrative decree of the past. In 1918, Woodrow Wilson had established a War Labor Board, composed of five members each from business and the AFL, plus two "public" members who acted as co-chairmen, William Howard Taft and Frank P. Walsh. The WLB mediated and helped settle more than a thousand labor-management disputes, and held elections for shop committees in 125 factories. But the WLB was, from labor's standpoint, ineffectual as evidenced in the steel industry, in that it lacked the power or the will to confer recognition on bona fide unions in non-union shops. The WLB moreover was primarily designed to meet emergency situations when uninterrupted production was absolutely essential to the war effort. Though the WLB ceased functioning after World War I, regulation of industrial relations in the railroad industry continued through a Railway Labor Board and, in 1926, through a Board of Mediation which was authorized not only to mediate but to appoint "emergency boards" to hear the facts at issue in rail disputes and make definitive recommendations. Under the 1926 law, modified by the Emergency Transportation Act of June 1933, rail strikes were forbidden during mediation and emergency proceedings. What this meant in practice was that carriers procrastinated for long periods of time while strikes were forbidden, and it was not unusual for a settlement to be delayed two years or more from the time bargaining began.

But the Wagner Act, unlike railway legislation, was not confined to a single industry, nor did it limit the right to strike. It established machinery that was permanent rather than temporary, machinery that provided an orderly means by which unions could gain bargaining rights, without resorting to strikes. Whether intended or not, it was in effect a trade of union recognition for a toning down of labor militancy. Though Roosevelt was averse to introduction of the bill at first, and though it took the Supreme Court two years to uphold its constitutionality (on April 12, 1937, just two months after the Flint sitdowns), the Wagner Act played a major role in transforming labor-capital relations. By 1945 the NLRB had processed 36,000 cases concerned of "unfair labor practices" and 38,000 concerned with employee representation. It conducted 24,000 elections among six million workers to determine bona fide bargaining agents, and it reinstated 300,000 workers unfairly dismissed, including the Little Steel strikers of 1937, awarding many millions of dollars in back pay. The board did become increasingly less liberal in ensuing years, offering labor far less protection against illegal discharges and other unfair practices. The Taft-Hartley law of 1947 placed further restrictions on union activity, most notably the eighty-day cooling-off period the President may invoke against strikes in major industries. The Landrum-Griffin Act of 1959 hobbled labor still more, especially with its provision against "secondary boycotts" which also weakened the effectiveness of some strikes. Nonetheless the National Labor Relations Board has now functioned for more than a quarter of a century, and, for good or ill, has prevented thousands of strikes for recognition that otherwise would have brought on further industrial bloodbaths.

During World War II government intervention in the labor-management area took the form of a tripartite War Labor Board, similar in purpose to that of World War I, except that it had the power to issue binding decisions in labor disputes, including on all grievances, and to establish wage scales and most other work provisions. The formation of this board was coupled with a no-strike pledge by the labor hierarchy (except for John L. Lewis) more precise than the implicit one given by Sam Gompers during the First World War. For all practical purposes, the WLB became the ultimate arbiter between all labor-management adversaries. Against the wishes of the unions for a closed shop and of the employers for an open shop, it granted the unions a "maintenance of membership" where no other form of security existed. A worker was free, under this decision, to join or not to join a union; but once he had joined he was required to maintain his membership.

On the issue of wages, the War Labor Board proclaimed a "Little Steel formula," restricting pay raises to a total of 15 per cent, corresponding to the rise in the cost of living from January 1941 to May 1942. The WLB, of course, ceased its operations after the war, but the pattern of government intervention into labor-management disputes was now firmly set. Henceforth, especially after passage of the Taft-Hartley Act, the government had available to it a number of levers to mitigate and moderate class strife. Through the NLRB it could prevent strikes for recognition, since the board had the authority to send strikers back to their jobs pending a Labor Board election. It could enjoin a strike in a key industry and impose an eighty-day cooling-off period. It enjoyed strong controls over collective bargaining in the railway industry, which in the last quarter of the nineteenth century had been a focal point of labor wars. And it could proceed legally against strikers in any industry where the union was engaged in "unfair labor practices" or "secondary boycotts."

On the other side of the ledger, union leaders in a number of industries felt it necessary to seek federal intervention on labor's behalf, not only through the normal Federal Mediation and Conciliation Service but up to and including the White House itself. The enormous growth in steel production, for example, placed steel union officials in a quandary. Normally, prior to a strike, the corporations invariably were able to produce enough steel to meet the demand of their customers for three to five months. That meant that when the strike took place the unionists would have to walk the picket line for ninety to 150 days before they even began to hurt the industry's economic position.

In these circumstances, it was not at all unusual for steel union officials to quietly call on the White House to ease the parties into a settlement. Since government was now a major purchaser of steel and since it also set quotas for imports of steel, it obviously held enough power to exert influence on the corporations. The same was true in virtually every key industry. Under controlled capitalism, the federal government has had overpowering means of pressuring both sides, and while it has been more favorably disposed to business than labor, even under Democratic administrations, it has had no desire to upset the delicate balance. In the meantime, union leadership, having grown somewhat fat and complacent as its forces climbed to fourteen million at the end of the war and nineteen million by 1970, has been a force for moderation that the government could not carelessly alienate. Thus, while all three leaderships in the continuing conflict—those of labor, government, and management—have been theoretically free to act with abandon, in practice they have felt the urge for accommodation.

In any case, to summarize in a single sentence, the labor wars have tapered off in cadence with the fashioning of an enduring prosperity and the evolution from *laissez-faire* to controlled capitalism.

v

The great unknown at this point is the stability of this situation. Is it so stable and permanent that there will never be any labor wars again? Or, assuming that it is unstable, will impending class struggles take the same form as those of 1875, 1877, 1886, 1892, 1894, 1903-4, 1912, 1919, and 1934-37. It is highly unlikely that they would. And it is unlikely not because the United States has suddenly unshackled itself from social tumult, but because that tumult is destined to take another form, at least as political in nature as economic.

The conflict between the privileged and underprivileged has been a central feature of American life ever since Captain John Smith and a band of 120 men settled in Jamestown in 1607. The American heritage is full of rebellion, revolts, uprisings and violent confrontations, between slaves and masters, tenants and landlords, hawks and doves, workers and bosses. There seems to have been, for instance, at least forty conspiracies and armed revolts by black slaves in colonial times and by a number of white slaves (indentured servants). There were uprisings by backwoodsmen, such as that led by Nathaniel Bacon in 1676, that rocked colonial regimes to their foundations, or the rebellion under Captain Jacob Leisler against landlord-merchant domination in New York which lasted for more than a year. There were tenants' strikes and anti-British boycotts and the resistance of individual Quakers to tyranny of all sorts. But all these social clashes fit the milieu in which they took place. There were no strikes such as we know them today because there was no working class or capitalist class as we know them today.

From the Revolution to the Civil War the oppressed again fought oppression in a variety of ways—through political action, Workingmen's Parties, producer and consumer co-operatives, phalanxes, unemployed demonstrations, agrarianism, but only to a limited extent through unionism and strikes—and then, usually, only for short periods. Capitalism was still infantile, production primarily agrarian, the working class embryonic. Neither labor nor capital had reached what may euphemistically be called the age of maturity.

It was with the maturation of industrial capitalism, and the concurrent growth of a sizable proletariat that the labor wars became a frequent and necessary response to unbridled capitalist greed. There existed, on the one hand, an ambitious entrepreneurial class infused with the robber-baron philosophy, which brooked no interference with its expansion, and respected neither the human rights of the lower classes nor their juridical ones. And, on the other hand, there was a new proletariat, self-exiled from Europe or torn from small, rural U.S. villages, which had no place to go for support, neither the courts, the government, nor the major political parties. In other words, there simply was no mechanism for easing the class struggle, and consequently, on innumerable occasions, it turned naked and violent.

The labor wars ended, for the most part, when capitalism entered a new phase in its development during and after the 1930s. Though there were 65,000 strikes from 1940 through 1955, the social climate was relatively mild. The opposition to World War II, mainly by the Trotskyists and pacifists, was negligible. Even the repression that followed the war, conducted under the Smith Act, by the House Committee on Un-American Activities (HUAC), and through the aegis of Joe McCarthyism, was tame compared to the Palmer Raids, prosecutions, and deportations that followed World War I. America— except for tens of millions of poor—was wallowing in prosperity, while the American government and American business were establishing a world-wide Pax Americana. When a new social insurgency came to the fore in the 1950s and 1960s it was not based upon economic problems, as previous ones had been, but upon humanistic grounds. Martin Luther King, Jr., led a bus boycott in Montgomery, Alabama, and soon there was a massive movement by black people and their friends for black liberation. Young people protested the transgressions against democracy by the anti-communists in HUAC, the Eastland Committee, and others. The dissent of the youth escalated beyond the beatnik, who had "resigned" from his father's alienated and materialistic society, to the Students for a Democratic Society, which resolved to build a new social system. The revolt of the New Left, as C. Wright Mills called it, then coalesced with the existing anti-militarist and anti-war movements to conduct the heated and bitter campaign against the imperialistic adventure in Vietnam. Thus, the focus of domestic internecine strife shifted from labor to the young, the blacks, the Chicanos, the pacifists, and the disenfranchised.

This recent history too, it now seems, was only a transition, for coincident with the war in Indochina, America seems to be headed again for another face-lifting. In the second half of 1971 President Richard M. Nixon took two steps which represented back-handed admissions that Pax Americana on the international scene and the synthetic prosperity at home might be in serious trouble. For a quarter of a century Washington had been talking about "containing," and then "rolling back" communism. Early in that period some stalwarts even suggested a preventative war against the Soviet Union and the other communist states. But President Nixon's decision in 1971 to partially recognize China and his historic visit there in February 1972 was a partial admission that the U.S. could no longer win the cold war. It was seeking a *modus vivendi*—peaceful co-existence with the "enemy," because it could not defeat him.

The New Economic Policy, proclaimed at approximately the same time as the announcements regarding China, reflected an international trade and money crisis, and probably forecast the end of the international Pax Americana, at least in its most ambitious forms. The inflation and the 6 per cent unemployment rate that tore at American economic stability were symptoms of a deeper crisis, which became patently visible in the third quarter of 1971 when the unfavorable balance of payments rose from an annual rate of $5.7 billion to $12.1 billion. America was spending so much on its "defense" machine, on its war in Indochina, on its thousands of foreign military bases, and was exporting so much of its surplus capital overseas, that its accounts with foreign nations were seriously unbalanced, and its gold supply only slightly more than a third of what it had been after World War II. For the first time since the 1890s, Uncle Sam's balance of trade, as well as his balance of payments, was unfavorable—imports exceeded exports by billions of dollars. The dollar was declining in value more rapidly than the yen, the mark, the Swiss franc and other currencies, presenting the United States with its most serious economic emergency in three decades.

Against this background President Nixon elaborated a much tighter control of business and labor than Washington had exercised since the Second World War. It was not, as many believed, a carbon copy of what happened during World War II. It began, first of all, with a *freeze* of all wages and almost all prices. For ninety days all raises were prohibited, even those provided for in previously negotiated union contracts, the first time any practice of this sort has ever occurred. In effect, collective bargaining agreements were abrogated. And though the period of the freeze was short, it was a major extension of presidential power. Future Presidents doubtless will use it as a precedent for executive reversal of labor-management relations on a broader front.

The wage and price *controls* that followed the freeze also differed from previous policies of this type, because they were introduced in a different context. World War II controls were instituted solely to check the rise in purchasing power at a time when consumer production was cut to the bone. With so many dollars jingling in proletarian pockets as a result of full employment, prices would have gone sky high if purchasing power had not been curtailed by the War Labor Board and by draining off potential spending through the sale of billions of dollars in war bonds. The war economy, however, did flourish, and after the war it was scheduled to—and did—expand massively. The wartime economic regimentation therefore was temporary.

Richard Nixon's economic nostrums, however, were introduced in the context of a sluggish economy, when the national plant was operating at only seventy-three per cent of capacity and when the nation was in its first war-time recession. If, over the years, then, the trade and balance of payments crisis should persist, and if the economy should fail to expand adequately or should slide backward, the regimentation of American life will not only continue but become permanent—providing of course that the government can overwhelm opposition. Moreover, economic regimentation would inevitably be followed by political regimentation. You cannot whittle away at collective bargaining for any length of time without restricting the right to strike, and you cannot restrict the right to strike without restricting the right to dissent.

Should America suffer such a mishap (evident in its initial stages in 1971–72), the character of the struggle between the privileged and underprivileged would change again. The labor movement, shorn of much of its idealism as the unions became institutionalized, would inevitably seek a new beginning. The "hotheads," visible so far primarily among the college youth, would certainly surface within the unions again, as well as within black and minority organizations, and fashion new weapons for righting injustice. And if the organs of the establishment should resist this new hypothetical upsurge as fiercely as they resisted labor's quest for industrial democracy in the six decades described in this book, there would certainly be an outburst of new labor wars—but of a different and more political character.

None of this of course is predestined, nor does it befit a book on labor wars to roam too far along the byways of high economics and politics. But the possibility of executive capitalism or forms of a corporate state in which the government regiments the economy and the people to an extent unknown before, cannot be ruled out. Should that occur we will doubtless see another spurt of very sharp labor resistance.

To every action, as the physicists say, there is a reaction. The old type of labor wars were a reaction to one form of tyranny. The new ones, if they come, will be a reaction to another form. Only the balm of prosperity, equality, and justice can prevent them.

Bibliography

There are few general histories of the labor movement based primarily on original sources. The two that I have relied on most are:

Perlman, Selig, and Taft, Philip. *History of Labor in the United States, 1896–1932.* (Part of four-volume work by John R. Commons and others.) Macmillan. 1935.

Foner, Philip S. *History of the Labor Movement in the United States.* Vols. 1 to 4. International Publishers. 1947, 1955, 1964, and 1965.

Another history, covering the period of 1877 to 1934, and the most useful and well-documented source for anyone who wants to probe deeper into the study of the labor wars is:

Yellen, Samuel. *American Labor Struggles.* S. A. Russell. 1936.

In addition, the following histories, particularly those with asterisks, are excellent sources:

*Boyer, Richard O., and Morais, Herbert M. *Labor's Untold Story.* Cameron Associates. 1955.
Dulles, Foster R. *Labor in America.* Thomas Y. Crowell. 1949.
Bimba, Anthony. *The History of the American Working Class.* International Publishers. 1927.
Adamic, Louis. *Dynamite: The Story of Class Violence in America.* Viking. 1934.
Lens, Sidney. *Left, Right and Center.* Regnery. 1949.
——. *Radicalism in America.* Thomas Y. Crowell. 1966.
*Harris, Herbert. *American Labor.* Yale. 1941.
*Rayback, Joseph G. *A History of American Labor.* Macmillan. 1959.
Faulkner, Harold U., and Starr, Mark. *Labor in America.* Oxford. 1955.

Beyond these general works there are specialized studies on most of the labor wars dealt with in this book, as well as material in various autobiographies. I have not listed newspaper sources (they are usually identified in the text), and only occasionally books on economic and related subjects, where they are especially significant. Because some magazine articles and books, in addition to the general ones by Yellen, Foner, and Perlman-Taft are pertinent to more than one subject, I have listed them under two or more chapter headings. I indicate by an asterisk which books I consider the best one or two single sources on each subject.

1 The Six-Decade War

No single volume is of particular significance for this introductory chapter, though the following have been consulted:

The American Socialist. July 26, 1877.

Butterfield, Roger. *The American Past.* Simon and Schuster. 1957.

Faulkner, Harold U. *American Economic History.* Harper. 1949.

Holbrook, Stewart H. *The Age of the Moguls.* Doubleday. 1953.

Lens, Sidney. *Poverty, America's Enduring Paradox.* Thomas Y. Crowell. 1969.

Seligman, Ben B. *The Potentates, Business and Businessmen in American History.* Dial. 1971.

2 The Molly Maguires

American Historical Review. Vol. 15. Rhodes, James F. "The Molly Maguires in the Anthracite Region of Pennsylvania."

*Bimba, Anthony. *The Molly Maguires.* International Publishers, 1932.

Bining, Arthur Cecil. *The Rise of American Economic Life.* Scribner's. 1943.

*Broehl, Wayne G., Jr. *The Molly Maguires.* Harvard. 1965.

Coleman, James W. *The Molly Maguire Riots: Industrial Conflict in the Pennsylvania Coal Region.* Garrett (Richmond, Virginia). 1937.

Coleman, McAlister. *Men and Coal.* Farrar & Rinehart. 1943.

Dewees, Francis P. *The Molly Maguires.* Lippincott. 1877.

Friedman, Morris. *The Pinkerton Labor Spy.* Wilshire Book Co. 1907.

Lucy, Ernest W. *The Molly Maguires of Pennsylvania.* George Bill and Sons (London). 1882.

Pinkerton, Allan. *The Molly Maguires and the Detectives.* G. W. Dillingham. 1905.

Roy, Andrew. *A History of the Coal Miners of the United States.* J. L. Travger (Columbus, Ohio). 1907.

3 Two Weeks of Insurrection

*Bruce, Robert V. *1877: Year of Violence.* Quadrangle. 1970.

Dacus, Joseph A. *Annals of the Great Strikes.* L. T. Palmer (Philadelphia). 1877.

Faulkner, Harold U. *American Economic History.* Harper. 1949.

Holbrook, Stewart. *The Age of the Moguls.* Doubleday. 1953.

Josephson, Matthew. *The Robber Barons: The Great American Capitalists, 1861–1901.* Harcourt, Brace. 1934.

Lewis, Lloyd, and Smith, Henry Justin. *Chicago: The History of Its Reputation.* Harcourt, Brace. 1929.

Martin, Edward Winslow. *The History of the Great Riots*. National Publishing Co. 1877.

The Nation. "Railroad Wages." August 16, 1877.

North American Review. September 1877. Scott, Thomas A. "Letter to Editor."

Parsons, Lucy E. *Life of Albert R. Parsons with a Brief History of the Labor History of the Labor Movement in America*. L. E. Parsons (Chicago). 1889.

Pinkerton, Allan. *Strikers, Communists, Tramps and Detectives*. G. W. Carleton & Co. 1878.

Seligman, Ben B. *The Potentates, Business and Businessmen in American History*. Dial. 1971.

Ware, Norman J. *The Labor Movement in the United States 1860–1890*. D. Appleton. 1929.

Williamson, Harold F., editor. *The Growth of the American Economy*. Prentice-Hall. 1957.

4 The Bomb at Haymarket

Altgeld, John P. *Reasons for Pardoning Fielden, Neebe, and Schwab* (Pamphlet). 1893.

Barnard, Harry. *Eagle Forgotten*. Duell, Sloan & Pearce. 1938.

Century Magazine. April 1893. Gary, J. E. "The Chicago Anarchists of 1886: The Crime, the Trial, and the Punishment."

*Davis, Henry. *The History of the Haymarket Affair, A Study in the American Social-Revolutionary and Labor Movements*. Collier Books. 1963.

Lewis, Lloyd, and Smith, Henry Justin. *Chicago: The History of Its Reputation*. Harcourt, Brace. 1929.

Parsons, Lucy E. *Life of Albert R. Parsons with a Brief History of the Labor Movement in America*. L. E. Parsons (Chicago). 1889.

Powderly, Terence V. *Thirty Years of Labor 1859–1889*. Excelsior Publishing House (Columbus, Ohio). 1889.

Taft, Philip. *The AFL in the Time of Gompers*. Harper. 1957.

5 Naval War at Homestead

Burgoyne, E. G. *Homestead: A Complete History of the Struggle of July, 1892, between the Carnegie Steel Company, Limited, and the Amalgamated Association of Iron and Steel Workers*. Pittsburgh, 1893.

The Forum. April 1886. Carnegie, Andrew. "An Employer's View of the Labor Question."

Goldman, Emma. *Living My Life*. Knopf. 1931.

The Nation. August 11, 1892. "Congressman Oates's Report."

North American Review. September 1892. Oates, W. C. "The Homestead Strike. A Congressional View." Curtis, G. T. "The Homestead Strike. A Constitutional View." Powderly, T. V. "The Homestead Strike. A Knights of Labor View."

Seligman, Ben B. *The Potentates*. Dial. 1971.

U. S. House of Representatives. *Employment of Pinkerton Detectives.* 52nd Congress, 2nd Session, Report 2447.

Wolff, Leon. *Lockout, the Story of the Homestead Strike of 1892.* Harper & Row. 1965.

6 The Debs Rebellion

*Buder, Stanley. *Pullman.* Oxford. 1967.

Burns, W. F. *The Pullman Boycott: A Complete History of the Great R. R. Strike.* McGill Printing Co. (St. Paul, Minnesota). 1894.

Carwardine, William H. *The Pullman Strike.* Chas. H. Kerr. 1894.

Coleman, McAlister. *Pioneers of Freedom.* Vanguard. 1929.

——. *Eugene V. Debs.* Greenburg (New York). 1930..

Frankfurter, Felix, and Greene, Nathan. *The Labor Injunction.* Macmillan. 1930.

Ginger, Ray. *The Bending Cross, A Biography of Eugene Victor Debs.* Rutgers. 1949.

Gregory, Charles O. *Labor and the Law.* Norton. 1946.

Holbrook, Stewart H. *Age of the Moguls.* Doubleday. 1953.

Lewis, Lloyd, and Smith, Henry Justin. *Chicago: The History of Its Reputation.* Harcourt, Brace. 1929.

Lieberman, Elias. *Unions Before the Bar.* Harper. 1950

*Lindsey, Almont. *The Pullman Strike.* University of Chicago Press. 1942.

Madison, Charles A. *Crusaders and Critics.* Holt. 1947–48.

McClure's Magazine. July 1904. Cleveland, Grover. "The Government in the Chicago Strike of 1894."

Meyers, Gustavus. *History of the Great American Fortunes.* Modern Library. 1937.

Morais, Herbert M., and Cahn, William. *Gene Debs, The Story of a Fighting American* (Pamphlet). International Publishers. 1948.

Russell, Charles Edward. *Railroad Melons, Rates and Wages.* Charles H. Kerr. 1922.

U. S. Senate. Report on the Chicago Strike of June-July 1894 by the United States Strike Commission. 53rd Congress, 3rd Session, Ex. Doc. no. 7.

Weinberg, Arthur, editor. *Attorney for the Damned.* Simon and Schuster. 1957.

7 War in the Rockies

Dubofsky, Melvyn. *We Shall Be All.* Quadrangle. 1969.

Groat, George Gorham. *An Introduction to the Study of Organized Labor in America.* Macmillan. 1916.

Haywood, William D. *The Autobiography of Big Bill Haywood.* International Publishers. 1929.

Holbrook, Stewart H. *The Rocky Mountain Revolution.* Henry Holt. 1956.

Jensen, Vernon H. *Heritage of Conflict; Labor Relations in the Non-Ferrous Metal Industry Up to 1930*. Cornell. 1930.

Langdon, Emma F. *The Cripple Creek Strike*. Denver. 1904–5.

Mississippi Valley Historical Review. Vol. 21. Fuller, Leon W. "Colorado's Revolution Against Capitalism."

Overland Monthly. Vol. 26. The Coeur d'Alene Riots 1892.

*Rastall, Benjamin McKie. *The Labor History of the Cripple Creek District*. Bulletin of the University of Wisconsin, No. 198, February 1908.

U. S. Senate. A Report on Labor Disturbances in the State of Colorado. From 1880 to 1904 Inclusive. 58th Congress, 1st session, document 122. 1905.

Williamson, Harold F., editor. *The Growth of the American Economy*. Prentice-Hall. 1957.

8 Halfway House

Christie, Robert A. *Empire in Wood*. Cornell. 1956.

*Coleman, McAlister. *Men and Coal*. Farrar & Rinehart. 1943.

Derber, Milton. *The American Idea of Industrial Democracy, 1865-1965*. University of Illinois Press. 1970.

Lens, Sidney. *Poverty, America's Enduring Paradox*. Thomas Y. Crowell. 1969.

Lundberg, Ferdinand. *America's Sixty Families*. Vanguard. 1937.

Mitchell, John. *Organized Labor*. American Book and Bible House (Philadelphia). 1903.

The Outlook. August 30, 1902. Warne, F. J. "The Real Cause of the Miners' Strike."

Report to the President on the Anthracite Coal Strike of May–October 1902, by the Anthracite Coal Strike Commission. Government Printing Office.

Roosevelt, Theodore. *An Autobiography*. Macmillan. 1913.

Yale Review. November 1902. Roberts, P. "The Anthracite Conflict."

9 The Wobblies

Brissenden, Paul F. *The I.W.W.: A Study of American Syndicalism*. Columbia. 1920.

*Dubofsky, Melvyn. *We Shall Be All*. Quadrangle. 1969.

Flynn, Elizabeth Gurley. *I Speak My Own Piece*. Masses & Mainstream (New York). 1955.

Ginger, Ray. *The Bending Cross, A Biography of Eugene Victor Debs*. Rutgers. 1949.

Haywood, William D. *The Autobiography of Big Bill Haywood*. International Publishers. 1929.

International Socialist Review. August 1905. Simons, Algie. "IWW."

*Kornbluh, Joyce L. *Rebel Voices, An I.W.W. Anthology*. University of Michigan Press. 1964.

Labor History. Fall 1960. McKee, Don K. "Daniel DeLeon: A Reappraisal."

Labor History. Winter 1962. Doherty, Robert E. "Thomas Hagerty, the Church, and Socialism."

Pacific Historical Review. November 1950. Elliott, Russel R. "Labor Troubles in the Mining Camp at Goldfield, Nevada, 1906–1908."

Renshaw, Patrick. *The Wobblies, The Story of Syndicalism in the United States.* Doubleday. 1967.

Solidarity. August 14, 1915. Ettor, J. J. "A Retrospect of Ten Years of the IWW."

Survey. May 4, 1912. Hill, Mary A. "The Free Speech Fight at San Diego.

Thompson, Fred. *The I.W.W.: Its First Fifty Years.* IWW. 1955.

10   Bread and Roses

American Magazine. May 1912. Baker, Ray Stannard. "Revolutionary Strike."

Cole, Donald B. *Immigrant City: Lawrence, Massachusetts, 1845–1921.* University of North Carolina. 1963.

*Dubofsky, Melvyn. *We Shall Be All.* Quadrangle. 1969.

Ebert, Justus. *The Trial of a New Society.* I.W.W. Publishing Bureau (Cleveland). 1913.

Harper's Weekly. March 16, 1912. Vorse, Mary H. "The Trouble at Lawrence."

Haywood, William D. *The Autobiography of Big Bill Haywood.* International Publishers. 1929

House of Representatives. 62nd Congress. 2nd Session. The Strike at Lawrence, Massachusetts. Hearing before the Committee on Rules. House Doc. 671

International Socialist Review. April 1912. Marcy, Leslie H., and Boyd, Frederick S. "One Big Union Wins."

Kornbluh, Joyce L. *Rebel Voices, An I.W.W. Anthology.* University of Michigan Press. 1964.

Outlook. January 15, 1912. Fosdick, Harry E. "After the Strike—in Lawrence."

Outlook. February 10, 1912. Weyl, Walter E. "The Strikers at Lawrence."

Survey. February 3, 1912. Palmer, Lewis E. "A Strike for Four Loaves of Bread."

Survey. April 6, 1912. Carstens, C. C. "The Children's Exodus from Lawrence."

Survey. July 6, 1912. Heaton, James P. "The Legal Aftermath of the Lawrence Strike."

Survey. November 2, 1912. Summer, Mary B. "Arturo Giovannitti."

*U. S. Senate. 62nd Cong. 2nd Session. Report on Strike of Textile Workers in Lawrence, Mass. in 1912. Senate Document 870.

11 First Round in Mass Production

*Brody, David. *Labor in Crisis. The Steel Strike of 1919*. Lippincott. 1965.

Brooks, Thomas B. *Toil and Trouble*. Delacorte. 1964.

Draper, Theodore H. *The Roots of American Communism*. Viking. 1957.

Dubofsky, Melvyn. *We Shall Be All*. Quadrangle. 1969.

Foster, William Z. *American Trade Unionism*. International Publishers. 1947.

——. *The Great Steel Strike and Its Lessons*. Huebsch. 1920.

——. *Pages from a Workers' Life*. International Publishers. 1939.

Hanna, Hilton E., and Belsky, Joseph. *Picket and the Pen*. American Institute of Social Science (Yonkers, New York). 1960.

Keiser, John Howard. Unpublished dissertation. "John Fitzpatrick and Progressive Unionism." Northwestern University. 1965.

The Nation. November 15, 1919. Vorse, Mary H. "Civil Liberty in the Steel Strike."

Report on the Steel Strike of 1919 by the Commission of Inquiry, the Interchurch World Movement. Harcourt, Brace and Howe. 1920.

Seligman, Ben B. *The Potentates*. Dial. 1971.

Staley, Eugene. *History of the Illinois State Federation of Labor*. University of Chicago Press. 1930.

Survey. December 4, 1920. Vorse, Mary H. "Derelicts of the Steel Strike."

Taft, Philip. *The AFL in the Time of Gompers*. Harper. 1957.

Thompson, Fred. *The I.W.W.: Its First Fifty Years*. I.W.W. (Chicago). 1955.

Tuttle, William M., Jr. *Race Riot*. Atheneum. 1970.

U. S. Senate. Report Investigating Strike in Steel Industries. 66th Cong. 1st Session. Senate Reports. Vol. A, No. 289.

Warne, Colston E., editor. *The Steel Strike of 1919*. D. C. Heath. 1963.

12 The Lean Years

Beard, Mary R. *American Labor Movement*. Macmillan. 1928.

Carnes, Cecil. *John L. Lewis, Leader of Labor*. Robert Speller (New York). 1936.

Coleman, McAlister. *Men and Coal*. Farrar & Rinehart. 1943.

Draper, Theodore H. *The Roots of American Communism*. Viking. 1957.

Faulkner, Harold U. *American Economic History*. Harper. 1949.

Foster, William Z. *American Trade Unionism*. International Publishers. 1947.

——. *Misleaders of Labor*. Trade Union Educational League (New York). 1927.

Haas, Eric. *John L. Lewis Exposed* (Pamphlet). Socialist Labor Party. 1938.

Lens, Sidney. *Poverty, America's Enduring Paradox*. Thomas Y. Crowell. 1969.

Levinson, Edward. *Labor on the March.* Harper. 1938.

Minton, Bruce, and Stuart, John. *Men Who Lead Labor.* Modern Age Books. 1937.

Saposs, David J. *Left Wing Unionism.* International Publishers. 1926.

Taft, Philip. *Organized Labor in American History.* Harper. 1964.

Walsh, Raymond J. *C.I.O.* Norton. 1937.

Wechsler, James A. *Labor Baron, A Portrait of John L. Lewis.* Morrow. 1944.

13 Impending Victory

Bernstein, Irving. *Turbulent Years. A History of the American Worker 1933–1941.* Houghton Mifflin. 1970.

The Communist. July 1934. Darcy, Sam. "The Great West Coast Maritime Strike."

———. October 1934. Darcy, Sam. "The San Francisco Bay Area General Strike."

Dunne, William F. *The Great San Francisco General Strike* (Pamphlet). Workers Library Publishers.

Editor and Publisher. July 28, 1934. Burke, E. "Dailies Helped Break General Strike."

Hentoff, Nat. *Peace Agitator, The Story of A. J. Muste.* Macmillan. 1963.

Levinson, Edward. *Labor on the March.* Harper. 1938.

Minton, Bruce, and Stuart, John. *Men Who Lead Labor.* Modern Age Books. 1937.

The Nation. June 13, 1934. Seeley, Evelyn. "San Francisco's Labor War."

New Masses. July 31, 1934. Dunne, William F. "Fascism in the Pacific Coast Strike."

New Republic. June 13, 1934. Winter, Ella. "Stevedores on Strike."

———. August 1, 1934. Seeley, Evelyn. "War on West Coast."

Preis, Art. *Labor's Giant Step.* Pioneer Publishers (New York). 1964.

Taft, Philip. *Organized Labor in American History.* Harper. 1964.

Vorse, Mary Heaton. *Labor's New Millions.* Modern Age Books. 1938.

Walker, Charles R. *American City, A Rank-and-File History.* Farrar & Rinehart. 1937.

14 Clearing the Cobwebs

Alinsky, Saul. *John L. Lewis. An Unauthorized Biography.* G. P. Putnam's. 1949.

CIO Menace or Promise? Industrial Union Party (Pamphlet).

Cormier, Frank, and Eaton, William J. *Reuther.* Prentice-Hall. 1970.

Goodelman, Leon. *Look at Labor.* Modern Age Books. 1940.

Harris, Herbert. *Labor's Civil War.* Knopf. 1940.

How the Rubber Workers Won (Pamphlet). Committee for Industrial Organization. 1936.

Huberman, Leo. *Labor Spy Racket.* Modern Age Books. 1937.

Josephson, Matthew. *Sidney Hillman, Statesman of American Labor.* Doubleday. 1952.

Levinson, Edward. *Labor on the March.* Harper. 1938.

Minton, Bruce, and Stuart, John. *Men Who Lead Labor.* Modern Age Books. 1937.

The Nation. August 8 and 15, 1936. Stolberg, Ben. "The Education of John L. Lewis."

The Nation. January 2, 1937. Levinson, Edward. "Bill Hutcheson's Convention."

Perkins, Frances. *The Roosevelt I Knew.* Viking. 1946.

Review of Reviews. November 1933. Clapper, Raymond. "Labor's Chief: William Green."

Seligman, Ben B. *The Potentates.* Dial. 1971.

Vorse, Mary Heaton. *Labor's New Millions.* Modern Age Books. 1938.

15 Sitdown! Sitdown!

Bernstein, Irving. *Turbulent Years. A History of the American Worker 1933–1941.* Houghton Mifflin. 1970.

Cochran, Thomas C., and Miller, William. *Age of Enterprise.* Macmillan. 1942.

Cormier, Frank, and Eaton, William J. *Reuther.* Prentice-Hall. 1970.

De Caux, Len. *Labor Radical.* Beacon. 1970.

Fine, Sidney. *Sit-Down, The General Motors Strike of 1936–1937.* University of Michigan Press. 1969.

Foster, William Z. *History of the Communist Party.* International Publishers. 1952.

Goodelman, Leon. *Look at Labor.* Modern Age Books. 1940.

Howe, Irving, and Widick, B. J. *The UAW and Walter Reuther.* Random House. 1949.

*Kraus, Henry. *The Many and the Few.* Plantin Press (Los Angeles). 1947.

Levinson, Edward. *Rise of the Auto Workers* (Pamphlet).

———. *Labor on the March.* Harper. 1938.

Minton, Bruce, and Stuart, John. *Men Who Lead Labor.* Modern Age Books. 1937.

Mortimer, Wyndham. *Organize, My Life as a Union Man.* Beacon. 1971.

Preis, Art. *Labor's Giant Step.* Pioneer Publishers (New York). 1964.

Seidman, Joel. *Sit Down.* League for Industrial Democracy. 1937.

Seligman, Ben B. *The Potentates.* Dial. 1971.

Vorse, Mary Heaton. *Labor's New Millions.* Modern Age Books. 1938.

16 The Ides of Yesterday and Tomorrow

Cochran, Bert, editor. *American Labor in Midpassage.* Monthly Review Press (New York). 1959.

Harris, Herbert. *Labor's Civil War.* Knopf. 1940.

Lens, Sidney. *The Crisis of American Labor.* A. S. Barnes. 1961.

——. *Radicalism in America.* Thomas Y. Crowell. 1966.

Preis, Art. *Labor's Giant Step.* Pioneer Publishers (New York). 1964.

Seidman, Joel. *American Labor from Defense to Reconversion.* University of Chicago Press. 1953.

Uphoff, Walter. *Kohler on Strike, Thirty Years of Conflict.* Beacon. 1966.

Vorse, Mary Heaton. *Labor's New Millions.* Modern Age Books. 1938.

Index